Derek Wilson is one of  with more than sixty books to h e he graduated from Cambridge ain passion has been the Refor

A BRIEF HISTORY OF

The English Reformation

DEREK WILSON

ROBINSON

RUNNING PRESS
PHILADELPHIA · LONDON

Constable & Robinson Ltd
55–56 Russell Square
London WC1B 4HP
www.constablerobinson.com

First published in the UK by Robinson,
an imprint of Constable & Robinson Ltd, 2012

A copy of the British Library Cataloguing in
Publication data is available from the British Library

ISBN: 978-1-84529-646-9

Printed and bound in the UK

1 3 5 7 9 10 8 6 4 2

First published in the United States in 2012 by Running Press Book Publishers,
A Member of the Perseus Books Group

US ISBN: 978-0-7624-4626-1
US Library of Congress Control Number: 2011942355

9   8   7   6   5   4   3   2   1
Digit on the right indicates the number of this printing

Running Press Book Publishers
2300 Chestnut Street
Philadelphia, PA 19103-4371

Visit us on the web!
www.runningpress.com

Printed and bound in the UK

Contents

Prologue

Four hundred and eighty years ago, a movement began which transformed every aspect of English life. It changed the social order. It changed the way the nation was governed. It changed intellectual assumptions. It changed educational aspirations. It changed the seasonal rituals which defined reality for every man, woman and child. It changed the very landscape of England. More importantly, it changed what people thought and believed about the 'big' questions of life, death, eternity and God. For, whatever its political, social and cultural consequences, the English Reformation was, essentially, a *religious* movement. By that I do not just mean that it was the process by which the official religion of the country changed from Catholicism to Protestantism. Though it may seem a strange claim to make, I believe that change was almost a by-product. To understand this remarkable revolution we have to see it as the supreme example in our history of what later ages would call 'revivalism'. Like all revivals, the Reformation 'worked' because the conditions in society were right for it, because 'Gospel propaganda' in the form of sermons, printed works and person-to-person evangelism was remarkably effective, and primarily because of the explosive impact of the vernacular Bible. This revival was a religious high tide which beat upon the cultural coastline and permanently altered its configuration. Then, as revivals always do, it retreated, leaving the people to adjust themselves to their new environment.

And that presents a problem to anyone setting out to tell the story of those momentous years for a twenty-first-century audience. A society which is or, at least, which constantly tells itself that it is 'secular' or 'post-Christian', will find it difficult to understand what all the fuss was about. Why on earth should it matter if, in the central ritual of the Christian church, Christ is 'really' or 'symbolically' present in bread and wine? The argument of whether man's relationship with God rests on faith or good works must appear arcane in the extreme to anyone who considers himself 'not religious'. That believers were prepared to be burned alive or hanged, drawn and quartered rather than deny the truth as they understood it must look like deluded fanaticism to modern people free from such inconvenient convictions. And that rulers in church and state should actually inflict those punishments on citizens can only appear from the standpoint of a more 'enlightened' age as proof of the barbarism and bigotry of our ancestors.

The modern historian might almost wish that he could set aside the religious 'aspect' of the Reformation and concentrate exclusively on its momentous political, social and intellectual consequences. These are easier to explain to today's readers. Some commentators have actually adopted an analytical method that marginalises the spiritual dynamic. They have focused on the emergence of the nation state or the loss of great medieval artistic treasures or the tussle between Crown and Parliament or the development of capitalism or the emergence of rational individualism. These are all important elements in the Reformation story, but they are the branches and leaves of the tree and not its trunk. As Diarmaid MacCulloch observes, 'Social or political history cannot do without theology in understanding the sixteenth century.'[1] But we must not fall into the opposite error of discussing the Reformation as merely a revolution in the world of ideas, a shift in the intellectual balance of theological and philosophical debate. Religion, after all, claims to offer an explanation of what the totality of life is about and the means of coping with it. So in our survey we must try to keep our eyes fixed on what the momentous changes of the sixteenth century actually meant to real people – at every social level.

Another fact of modern life is the virtual absence of sectarian conflict. Relations between the mainstream Christian churches are more cordial than they have ever been. This, in turn, makes the arguments between Catholics, Protestants, Lutherans, Calvinists, Zwinglians and Anabaptists seem not only irrelevant but regrettable. Given this background, fresh approaches to the subject tend to downplay the deeply felt animosities between the various faith groups which confronted each other in the sixteenth century. This can be as distorting as the blatantly partisan historiography which has dominated scholarly debate for most of the last four hundred years. Foxe, Strype, Burnet, Constant, Dodd, Froude, Dixon, Gairdner, Dickens, Hughes and Duffy are just some of the honoured names in the annals of Reformation scholarship, but all of them either did not seek or experienced difficulty in finding objectivity.

The inescapable fact is that if you are a student of the Reformation, as I have been for five decades, you are either on the inside or the outside. To be on the inside, that is to say, with a personal conviction concerning the religious issues at stake which goes beyond the mere intellectual, is to run the risk of getting too close to them; to have sympathies which influence judgement. One finds some of the characters in the story appealing or repulsive, some of the happenings desirable or reprehensible. One is more disposed to find particular arguments convincing and to give little weight to opposing viewpoints. To be on the outside, that is to say with a limited concern for the rival theologies involved, is, as it were, to look through the misted window of history and miss the finer nuances of the decor and furnishings within.

The chronicler of the Reformation, therefore, faces two inter-related challenges – to construct a balanced narrative as devoid of prejudice as possible and to convince his readers that it matters. Whether I have succeeded in the first of these endeavours I must leave you to decide. On the second I should perhaps try to explain at the outset why I believe an understanding of the English Reformation has relevance in the twenty-first century.

If we think about it at all, we probably consider that there is a large degree of inevitability about the way our society has evolved. It is, we suppose, shaped by developments over which we have no control. The growth of democracy, the advance of technological innovation, the displacement of religion by science, the triumph of consumerism are juggernauts which the individual and even governments cannot stop. But this isn't necessarily the case. From time to time, individuals emerge who *do* change history. New and challenging patterns of thought *do* emerge. Catastrophes and other stirring events happen which *do* alter the direction in which communities and nations move. Such individuals, patterns and events challenge the assumptions of contemporaries and oblige them to re-examine their values. This is uncomfortable but ultimately beneficial. There is a sense in which humankind actually *needs* wars, natural calamities, financial meltdowns and cultural renaissances. They concentrate the mind. They make us ask again the basic questions of existence.

A decade or so ago, Francis Fukuyama sparked off a debate by proposing that history had come to an end. A long period of peace, the collapse of communism, the development of weapons which are too terrifying ever to be used, and the emergence of a superpower capable of acting as an international policeman, had produced a situation of stasis. There could be no further significant developments, no exciting, fresh chapters of the human story to be written. Such a proposition has already been rendered questionable by subsequent events. But, if we want to reject fatalism and take hold of our future, where should we look for clues as to possible new beginnings? Where might we seek inspiration or discern dire warnings about the redirection of our stumbling national footsteps? Where else but the past? It is part of the historian's responsibility to hold up for examination patterns of social interaction that have pertained in other ages. Life in earlier times was not a primitive existence from which we have 'progressed' to better ways of organising our communal life, any more than it was a 'golden age' since when everything has gone to the dogs. It was, simply, different. That very difference may have things to teach us.

The Reformation, as I have already suggested, was an event of seismic power, which changed – it is no exaggeration to say – everything. It was also an era whose social 'machine' was activated by power sources very different from ours. Autocratic monarchy, a hierarchical social system, a church which was an important partner in government, pulpit oratory which took the place occupied in later centuries by the press in informing and inflaming public opinion, a kaleidoscope of beliefs about time and eternity promoted by astrologers, necromancers and fortune-tellers, as well as ministers of religion – these were the influences which pushed, nudged and guided all English men and women along the twisting path of life. This is the world we must enter in the following pages. It is a world in which religion bred division and intolerance, but which also gave England a new and enhanced sense of identity. It was a world in which ordinary people were tightly controlled by their superiors but one in which individual conviction refused to be suppressed. It was a world whose inhabitants saw beyond the limits of time and space and found in the heavenlies comfort and courage which emboldened many to suffer ostracism, imprisonment and death. It was a very different world from ours.

Yet its people were not. They shared our basic concerns. They were worried about making ends meet in an era of economic uncertainty. They were indignant about the behaviour of those who controlled their lives and set the national agenda. They wanted to see, in their own lifetime, the emergence of a better world where poverty was reduced and crime effectively dealt with. Their basic concerns were with the here and now. But they knew that there is another realm, above and beyond the material, which every one of them would have to encounter after death. It was the big question, 'What next', that propelled them along religious paths that diverged alarmingly before their gaze. However much modern man may try to ignore that question or to insist that it is not real, there remains for many a nagging doubt about man's ultimate destiny. To consider how our fore-bears of a pre-enlightenment, pre-scientific, pre-secularised age dealt with doubt, certainty and all the shades of belief between, and the effects the resulting spiritual and intellectual tumult had on our developing culture might be informative.

So, if you are ready, if you have the stomach for it, if you are prepared to come without your twenty-first-century baggage, and if you are open to the possibility of having some of your preconceptions challenged, let us go together into the England of half a millennium ago.

Chapter 1

Circumference and Centre

The lands inherited by the 17-year-old Henry VIII in 1509 were no nation. England was a conglomeration of semi-isolated local and regional communities over which royal control diminished with every muddy or dusty mile of the highways and byways leading from London. The peoples who lived south of Hadrian's Wall still spoke no common language; travellers from London arriving in Cornwall or Northumberland might as well have found themselves in France or Hungary for all they were able to understand local dialects. There was no administrative unity. Wales and the North were governed by councils appointed by the king but were, in reality, self-regulating. They and various regional 'liberties' were under the sway of powerful local families. Those families were preoccupied with their own concerns (which often involved bitter, generation-spanning feuds with their neighbours), in relation to which the maintenance of even-handed justice, peace and good order were low priorities.

The vast majority of country men and women were dependent on their local landlords. Patronage was the glue that held society together. It was also the measure of a lord's wealth and influence. In 1471 the Duke of Suffolk had disdained to come to court because 'his servants were from him', several having been allowed home for Christmas. For the duke and his peers, display was vital to their prestige and he could not appear in public with a depleted retinue. In his household a great lord employed for a wage or 'livery' a wide variety of servants – men-at-arms, chaplains, stewards, farriers, musicians, cooks and scores of 'attendants' who were there to do his bidding and boost his image. Outside the household were families who had for generations held their land from him, sold their produce to his kitchen and provided foot soldiers when he raised a contingent for the royal army or had some private war to fight. Naturally the first loyalty of such people was to the leaders of regional society. The old baronial dynasties were strongest in the areas furthest from London – the far North, the South West and Norfolk. To most people, especially in these areas, the king was a distant figure they had never seen and were never likely to see.

The king's father, Henry VII, had begun the process of centralization. He had put an end to the rivalry of Lancaster and York, the years of anarchy during which the Crown had been the tennis ball of competing magnates. He had inhibited the independence of the nobility by clamping his bony fingers on their purses and, through statutes limiting livery and maintenance, had prevented them keeping large bodies of retainers. He had chastened the heirs of Yorkist barons by grasping their hereditary lands. He had dispensed with the advice of the great lords and raised men of humbler origin to his Council. He had reduced the number of temporal peers in Parliament from around fifty-five to forty or so. The new Tudor dynasty had undoubtedly brought peace to the realm but, in so doing, it had paradoxically imposed a measure of insecurity on the nation. In the localities the time-honoured order of things had been disrupted and resentment and anxiety seeped down through the strata of society. When the great men of a locality were brought down their dependants felt the effects.

On the other hand, it mattered little to a cottager facing dispossession or the loss of livelihood if the ultimate cause of his misery was a king exceeding his God-given authority or a semi-independent nobleman taking advantage of the weakness of central government. The Wars of the Roses might be over but old animosities remained. Throughout the early 1500s life was made very unpleasant for the people of west Kent by the mutual animosity of the Guildford and Neville clans. About 1505 George Neville sent a mob to break up a Guildford seigneurial court meeting at Aylesford. In retaliation the offended magnate closed Tenterden market. Affrays and disturbances of the peace continued year in and year out. A decade later we find Sir Edward Guildford complaining that Neville gangs were touring his estates intimidating his tenantry. When one of Sir Edward Neville's thugs, appropriately known as Black John, was apprehended by the king's officers, his patron simply summoned the sheriff before him and ordered him to set the culprit free.[1]

Throughout the country such unruly behaviour was the norm rather than the exception.

> where your said beseechers were in God's peace and yours, one Robert Warcoppe the elder ... Robert Warcoppe the younger and other riotous and misruled people, to the number of 53 persons and more, the 14th day of the month of October last past, with force and arms, that is to say with bows, arrows, bills, swords and bucklers ... made assault upon your said beseechers and there beat, wounded and put in jeopardy of their lives, without occasion on their part giving, to the great peril of your said beseechers and to the worst example of others like offending unless due punishment be had.[2]

So complained some of the king's Westmorland subjects in 1500.

The England of 1509, then (a full decade before the Reformation can be said to have 'started'), was a nation conscious of going through a period of change and change is something which most people resent. The most eloquent spokesman for English traditionalists was Thomas More, a young London lawyer, hoping to ingratiate himself with the new regime. He knew that relations between the new king and his father had been far from cordial and this undoubtedly coloured the tone of the congratulatory ode he wrote for the coronation of Henry VIII. However, More certainly gave expression to his own conviction that Henry VII had been a tyrant and his hope that there would now be a return to the 'good old days'.

> The nobility, long since at the mercy of the dregs of the population ... whose title has too long been without meaning, now lifts its head, now rejoices in such a king, and has proper reason for rejoicing. The merchant, heretofore deterred by numerous taxes, now once again ploughs seas grown unfamiliar. Laws, heretofore powerless – yes, even laws put to unjust ends – now happily have regained their proper authority. All are equally happy. All weigh their earlier losses against the advantages to come.[3]

In *A Lawde and Prayse Made for Our Sovereigne Lord the Kyng*, the poet John Skelton, a former tutor of Prince Henry, prophesied that Henry VII's evil counsellors were about to get their comeuppance:

> Of this our noble king
> The law they shall not break;
> They shall come to reckoning,
> No man for them will speak.[4]

Widespread euphoria greeted the accession of England's new king. Educated men close to the centre of power, like More, looked to Henry to bring the vigour of youth to the business of government while relying on a Council drawn from the 'quality', the great lords temporal and spiritual. They accepted that centralized power did not necessarily imply tyranny. There was a plus side to the establishment of the Tudor state. England was at peace. Relations with neighbouring nations were on a sound basis. For the first time since anyone could remember, Englishmen had a king who ruled by hereditary right and not by usurpation and a throne which did not rest on the shaky foundation of deals and alliances. There was no reason to suppose that Henry's comely Spanish bride would fail to produce a bevy of princes. The new dynasty offered the nation security and stability and if the regime could be shorn of abuses the roseate vision presented in the coronation ode just might bear some relation to reality.

'Anything for a quiet life' was probably the motto of most English men and women. As they struggled to make a livelihood from peasant holding, farm, market stall or high street shop they clung to the old certainties and conventions that held their communities together. Most but not all. Few towns and villages in the realm were without their advocates of change. Edmund Dudley, a councillor to the old king and now a prisoner in the Tower of London, wrote a little treatise to explain how a well-ordered state should be run. One of the evils he found it necessary to warn against in his *Tree of Commonwealth* was the anarchic, social-levelling rabble-rouser:

He will show you that you be made of the same mould and metal that the [nobility and gentry] be made of. Why, then, should they sport and play and you labour and till? He will tell you also that at your births and at your deaths your riches is indifferent. Why should they have so much of the prosperity and treasure of this world and you so little? Besides that, he will tell you that ye be the children and right inheritors of Adam, as well as they. Why should they have this great honour, royal castles and manors with so much lands and possessions, and you but poor tenements and cottages? He will show you also why that Christ bought as dearly you as them, and with one manner of price, which was his precious blood. Why, then, should you be of so poor estate and they of so high degree . . . Why should they have [over] you so great authority and power to commit to prison, to punish and to judge you?[5]

Popular insurrection was an ever-present fear among the ruling classes. Only a dozen years before, Cornishmen, protesting at taxation, had marched unchecked to within a mile of the royal palace at Greenwich. A thousand rebels had paid with their lives for their audacity on that occasion. Such major demonstrations were rare. We have to go back another 47 years to 1450 for Jack Cade's revolt and a further 69 years for the great Peasants' Revolt of 1381. However, localised outbreaks were much more common. Spontaneous violence was always a possibility when the lower orders had no other means of airing their grievances. In York, for example, mayoral elections were frequently marked by protests from the artisan community who resented the oligarchic 'closed shop' which controlled their city. In 1517 Thomas More was involved in suppressing an apprentices' uprising on 'Evil May Day', after which sixty rioters were hanged (see below pp. 17f).

On first inspection it may appear that there was nothing new about subcutaneous violence in the English body politic. Closer examination, however, reveals a subtler reality. It was not just the underprivileged in Tudor society who were conscious of injustice and the need for reform of abuses. There was a new critical spirit abroad among the intellectual elite. Edmund Dudley's *Tree of Commonwealth* was a very minor contribution to a debate which was gathering momentum about what consti- tuted a well-ordered 'commonwealth'. The idea that a realm should be governed for the 'common weal', the general wellbe- ing of all the people, was novel but, once enunciated, its attraction was obvious to scholars. Just how such a happy state of affairs might be realized became the subject of books, sermons and university debates for several decades.

All this might have remained erudite, academic disputation among Europe's dreaming spires had it not been for an inven- tion which revolutionised media communication and education. Johann Gutenberg of Strasbourg completed a reproduction of the Bible using movable type about 1455. By 1509 there was not a town of any importance in Europe which did not have at least one printing press. In that same year one of the books to come from a London print shop was an English translation of

Sebastian Brant's *Ship of Fools*. In the fourteen years since its first publication in Germany, Brant's verse satire had taken Europe by storm and been translated into most of the continent's principal languages. The *Ship of Fools* held its place in the 'bestseller lists' because it said what most people thought but did not dare say. It poked fun at all sorts and conditions of men.

> He that office hath and high authority
> To rule a realm, as judge or councillor,
> Which, seeing justice, plain right and equity,
> Them falsely blindeth by favour or harshness,
> Condemning wretches guiltless while
> To a transgressor he showeth favour for cash,
> Such is as wise a man
> As he that would cook a live pig in a pan.

Brant established a fashion which was quickly taken up by other members of the intelligentsia. The convention of using the jester or fool as a mouthpiece enabled authors to expose the evils of society without falling foul of the authorities. This was important because, as we have already seen, establishments were sensitive to criticism. Most regimes exercised a measure of censorship and offending authors would face worse punishment than having their books banned. The runaway success in the satirical literature genre was another treatise written in that same year, 1509, and published two years later. *The Praise of Folly* came from the pen of the man acknowledged as the greatest scholar of the day, Desiderius Erasmus. In elegant Latin and wickedly biting wit Erasmus poked fun at the leaders of church and state and the official beliefs which undergirded their power. Good satire always provokes both approbation and outrage. Erasmus professed himself shocked by the attacks of those who were offended by his book. Urbane scholars, on the other hand, applauded it and angry young men regarded it as a call to reform contemporary evils.

Erasmus had been staying with his friend Thomas More

when he completed his manuscript and seven years later More added his own contribution to the genre. The 'hook' he used to catch the attention of readers was not the outrageous jesting of the fool but the intriguing 'discoveries' of a voyager in distant lands. *Utopia* caught the spirit of the age because people were fascinated by travellers' tales. Thanks to the exciting exploits of Columbus, Dias, Da Gama, Ojeda, Vespucci, Cabral and Cabot, the planet was suddenly getting bigger and smaller. Bigger in the sense that cartographers were adding new lands to their maps. Smaller because mariners had reached those lands and it seemed that there could not be much more of the earth's surface still to be discovered. English sailors were not yet ready to compete for a share of the Indies trade but this did not stop them returning from their voyages with wondrous tales of sea monsters and strange savage creatures who populated the heathen continents and islands beyond the pale of Christendom. Attempts by Spanish and Portuguese governments to build walls of secrecy around the travels of their captains and merchants only fuelled curiosity. It was this curiosity that Thomas More cashed in on when, in 1516 (three years before Magellan set out on the first circumnavigation), he published a political and social treatise and chose to set it in the 'newly discovered' land of Utopia.

More's treatise was not a manifesto for reform. One might almost say it was a counsel of despair. His Utopians had achieved a society of liberty, equality and fraternity by somehow conquering the natural vices that flesh is heir to. Those vices – avarice, cruelty, exploitation, perversion of justice – lay at the root of all that was wrong in England and there was little hope, More concluded, of eradicating them. 'So must I needs confess and grant,' he wrote, 'that many things be in the Utopian weal public, which in our cities I may rather wish for than hope after.'[6] Covered by this disclaimer, More exposed self-interested royal councillors, turbulent magnates, engrossing landlords, harsh laws and other contemporary evils.

At the very beginning of Henry VIII's reign, therefore, we can detect a restlessness, a quivering in the air, a sense that the times were changing. This made some people anxious. For others reform could not come soon enough. There was, of course, a wide gap between spontaneous violence on the 'mean streets' and polite debate among the dreaming spires. But that gap was beginning to narrow. Literacy was confined to a small minority of the population but it was encouraged by the growing number of vernacular books. There is a point in any society when profound change becomes inevitable. It is the point at which a significant literate class emerges. Anyone with a little disposable income could now actually *own* books and could, therefore, enter a world previously only open to monks, scholars and lawyers. It was a heady experience. England was now approaching that point.

A man did not need to be able to read to participate in the exchange of ideas. He might listen to his more erudite neighbours, appropriate their ideas for himself and pass them on at next market day. Years of peace were slowly increasing the mobility of the king's subjects. This meant that local grievances might take on a wider significance. When a landowner in Leicestershire turned tenants out of their holdings because he had decided to enclose his estate and make it over to sheep pasture, it took the dispossessed little time to realise that this was part of a trend and that families as far afield as Somerset and Suffolk were suffering in the same way. Enclosure was just one of many changes that were coming over the agricultural and commercial life of the country and causing great hardship. A popular ballad complained

> The places that we right holy call,
> Ordained for Christian burial,
> [Remove] them to make an ox stall.
> These men be wondrous wise
> Commons to close and keep,
> Poor folk for bread cry and weep.
> Towns pulled down to pasture sheep.
> This is the new [fashion].[7]

But now it was not only members of the underclass who were raising their voices against injustice and poor justice. Thomas More drew attention to several social evils, including enclosures. 'The sheep that were wont to be meek and tame and no small eaters,' he wrote, 'now become so great devourers and wild that they eat up and swallow down the very men themselves. They consume, destroy and devour whole fields, houses and cities.' He exaggerated the importance of this particular change in the rural economy of some counties but he touched on a grievance that was keenly felt by its victims and resented by a wider constituency. Here is the same author on the subject of crime and punishment:

> this punishment of thieves passes the limits of Justice, and is also very hurtful to the weal public. For it is too extreme and cruel a punishment for theft, and yet not sufficient to refrain and withhold men from theft. For simple theft is not so great an offence, that it ought to be punished with death. Neither there is any punishment so horrible, that it can keep them from stealing, which have no other craft, whereby to get their living. Therefore in this point, not you only, but also the most part of the world, be like evil schoolmasters, which be readier to beat, than to teach, their scholars. For great and horrible punishments be appointed for thieves, whereas much rather provision should have been made, that there were some means, whereby they might get their living, so that no man should be driven to this extreme necessity, first to steal, and then to die.[8]

If words were now being used to urge reform, so were pictures. The uneducated masses had been accustomed for generations to having their imaginations stirred by 'sermons in stone' – or in paint or stained glass. Now, in addition to the visual stimuli approved by church authorities, they could buy cheap woodcuts, take them home and pin them to their walls where they could laugh at the drollery of England's first caricaturists or take inspiration from devotional images.

It would be wrong to conclude from all this that there was a rising tide of liberated thinkers longing for a brave new world. If anything, the reverse was true. Most people at most times are conservative in their attitudes and beliefs and if we speak of Henry's subjects as conscious of standing on the brink of a new age it might be truer to say that what they really hoped for was to return to a previous, supposedly golden age, an age which their forefathers had known and which had worked better than the one which had superseded it in recent times. Thomas More was certainly nostalgic for an ordered, earlier epoch. In his unfinished and unpublished *Life of Richard III* he confidently stated that England had enjoyed a measure of felicity during the reign of Edward IV (1461–70, 1471–83). More's ideal England would have been one in which the ancient conventional, uncomplicated, paternalistic structures would operate to the benefit of all. Noblemen, merchants, artisans, lawyers – all sorts and conditions of men – would be allowed to occupy their places in the divinely ordained pattern of human existence and royal government would oversee and guarantee the benign working of society. The reality, in More's view, was a land in which feudalism based on mutual responsibility had given way to a price/wage economy which inevitably led to exploitation. Landowners engrossed their properties for maximum profit and merchants colluded to drive down the prices they paid for goods. In a stratified society in which it was commonly said that 'justice is a fat fee', those who could not afford such fees relied on the patronage of powerful lords and gentlemen. Men and women who lacked such support and who, by misfortune or accident of birth, could not sustain a viable lifestyle slipped into poverty and, eventually, vagrancy. It was a situation about which More, unlike his friend Erasmus, found it impossible to be flippant.

But was More's Cassandra-like appraisal justified? Were things really that bad? It would be misleading to generalize about the state of the nation, divided as it was into regions with which their inhabitants identified more readily than with

England as a whole. By far the most important part of the kingdom – culturally, politically and economically – was the capital.

> The streets be appointed and set forth very commodious and handsome, both for carriage, and also against the winds. The houses be of fair and gorgeous building and on the street side they stand joined together in a long row through the whole street without any partition or separation. The streets be twenty foot broad. On the backside of the houses through the whole length of the street lie large gardens enclosed roundabout with the back part of the streets . . . They set great store by their gardens. In them they have vineyards, all manner of fruit, herbs and flowers . . . the houses be curiously builded after a gorgeous and gallant sort, with three storeys one over another . . . They keep the wind out of their windows with glass.[9]

This was Thomas More's description, not of London, but of Amaurote, the principal city of Utopia. His readers would have identified, point for point, the contrast with their own capital.

In 1509 London was overcrowded and was steadily becoming more so. This is well illustrated by the story of some of its more imposing buildings. In 1491, the year that Henry VIII was born, the Mayor of London was Sir Hugh Clopton, a wealthy mercer. The house he occupied in Old Jewry, at the commercial heart of the City, was a substantial residence called Fitzwalter House. Before the expulsion of the Jews by Edward I in 1291 it had been a synagogue. Thereafter, only the name of the street survived to testify to the fact that it had been the centre of the Jewish merchant community. Subsequently, the building was the headquarters of the Friars of the Purse, a minor mendicant order. After their suppression the house came into the hands of the mighty Robert Fitzwalter, the leader of the barons who forced Magna Carta upon a reluctant King John. Within a couple of centuries changing social patterns were reflected in changes of property ownership. Aristocratic residences like

Fitzwalter House were being taken over by leaders of the merchant community who could now aspire to live in such impressive 'des reses', conveniently near their business premises in Cheapside and the neighbouring streets. It was here that Hugh Clopton held court during the years of his greatness. Many were the important burgesses and, perhaps, courtiers entertained here in early Tudor times. But further humbling changes were in store for Fitzwalter House. John Stow, writing his *Survey of London* in 1603, reflected that this imposing building had, since Clopton's day, descended the social scale still further; it had become a wine tavern, the Windmill.

The fate of this fine city mansion was typical of the inexorable transformation that was happening in London during the reign of the first two Tudors. Many substantial properties were being downgraded or divided into tenements. Others were being pulled down to make room for rows of smaller dwellings. The few gardens and open spaces were disappearing under the unrestricted spread of timber and brick buildings. The City was smelly, airless, vermin-ridden and, at the height of summer, everyone who could escaped from its fever-laden alleys and rutted lanes. London was bulging at the seams. Its centre, bounded by the ancient wall with its ten gates, extended from the Tower in the east to St Paul's Cathedral in the west, symbolic of the power of church and state. But London was already pushing outwards. It was linked by its river bridge to Southwark, London's 'Latin quarter', and by the Strand to Westminster. To the east the process of slum development had already begun which was later lamented by Stow. The sprawl behind the waterfront with its docks and warehouses and wretched dwellings, he wrote, formed 'a continual street, or filthy, straight passage, with alleys of small tenements or cottages builded . . . along by the river of Thames, almost to Ratcliff'.[10]

Fastidious citizens voted with their feet. They moved out of the cramped and heaving city as soon as they could afford to do so. This explains the row of riverside villas built between Temple Bar and Westminster (the beginnings of the 'West

End') by courtiers, councillors and noblemen whose lifestyle and ambition obliged them to spend part of the year in close proximity to the royal court. Some VIPs preferred to become 'suburbanites', living in leafy villages close to the capital. As soon as he could, Thomas More acquired a house upriver at Chelsea. And as for the king, he was very rarely to be seen within the most important city of his realm. When he travelled from Greenwich to Richmond or Westminster to Greenwich he chose to go by water or to ride along the south bank. Yet vibrant, rich, progressive London was vital for the prosperity of the nation and the Crown – and the Tudors knew it. The centralization of economic activity went hand in hand with the centralization of political power.

So what drew people to this cramped, overcrowded, unsanitary wen? Why was its 60,000-strong population increasing so inexorably? The short answer is that London was a 'capital' in a sense that was probably true of no other major European city. Together with neighbouring Westminster, it was the focus of the nation's governmental, commercial and judicial life. By 1500 it had long been customary for the king to make Edward the Confessor's old palace at Westminster his headquarters and to reside there for half of each year. When Parliament was summoned its two houses met separately in different parts of the palace or abbey complex. Close by was Westminster Hall, which was the location of major national events such as Henry VIII's coronation banquet but, on a regular basis, it was also where the law courts met and where subjects came seeking justice at the hands of the king's judges. These experts received their basic legal training at the inns of court, situated around Chancery Lane, halfway between Westminster and the City. During the reigns of the first two Tudors the inns of court grew in number and importance. It was not only young men destined for a career in the common law who attended these schools. The sons of noblemen and gentlemen were sent there to complete their education and to acquire a smattering of legal knowledge to help them in the running of their estates. The inns thus became highly fashionable places where those who were or aspired to become members of the establishment kept three or more terms, making the right contacts and doing what we now call 'networking'.

The court and the lawyers' 'village' were powerful magnets attracting hundreds of new residents and visitors every year to London and its environs, but it was trade which brought most newcomers from the provinces and from abroad to what William Dunbar, the flattering Scottish poet/diplomat, called 'the flower of cities all'. There was a geographical inevitability about the growth of London's economy. Upriver, the navigable Thames reached deep into the Midlands, while its tidal estuary brought shipping from the continent and facilitated regular coastal trade with ports from Newcastle to Southampton. The sure foundation for England's commercial wealth was the trade in woollen cloth, derived principally from the sheep farms of Somerset, the Cotswolds, Yorkshire and East Anglia. Buyers from Antwerp, Bruges, Hamburg and other continental entrepôts could scarcely get enough of it. There was a boom market and London had the lion's share of it. The quantity of cloth passing through the capital increased from 50 per cent in 1400 to around 83 per cent by 1540. Money makes money. Wealthy merchants and their wives enjoyed considerable disposable income. Clopton and his friends entertained lavishly, setting their tables with gleaming plate. They adorned their bodies with incredibly expensive imported silks and furs. They decorated their homes with paintings and tapestries to impress visitors with their cultivated taste. They were, of course, following the fashions set by their aristocratic 'betters' in their town houses. And the aristocrats were adopting the style and tone set by the king.

Thus, it was the proximity of the royal court that provided the *real* stimulus for conspicuous consumption. The fifteenth-century jurist Sir John Fortescue had coined the splendid word 'dispendiousness' to indicate the lavish expenditure he considered to be essential for the proper exercise of monarchy. Kings had to impress all who saw them and who visited their palaces.

It ought to be obvious that the sovereign was richer and, therefore, more powerful than any of his nobles. Henry VII used very permanent splendours to indicate that the Tudors had come to stay. He made additions to Windsor Castle's living quarters and rebuilt Richmond Palace to a wholly new design. When the first Tudor conceived the magnificent Henry VII Chapel at Westminster – the soaring, breathtaking apogee of High Gothic – it was not only as a personal mausoleum and a dynastic shrine, but as a deliberate rival to Edward IV's Chapel at Windsor, a triumphalist statement that whatever the Yorkists could do the Tudors could do better. Armies of masons, glaziers, wood-carvers, gilders, painters and sculptors were brought together to create and adorn these new royal edifices. But they are only the more obvious symbols of Tudor greatness, and are among the few objects we still have by which to measure their self-projection. Thousands upon thousands of other artefacts were constantly being commissioned – dazzlingly illuminated books, intricate tapestries, meticulous jewellery, sumptuous gold plate, paintings and sculptures from the best artists who could be lured to England. What Henry VII achieved in the way of patronage of the arts his son was determined to outdo. No other buyer, including the church, came remotely close to rivalling royal expenditure on luxuries. Most of it was channelled through the shops and ateliers of the capital. And not only luxuries. Even the most sophisticated household had need for humbler objects. London, therefore, became the centre where an enormous number of trades proliferated – goldsmiths, pewterers, leatherworkers, cutlers, textile workers, sculptors, armourers, painters, bell founders and the makers of memorial brasses so immensely popular at this time.

Boom economies inevitably attract immigrant labour – and the problems which go with it. 'Whoreson Lombards! You rejoice and laugh! By the mass, we will one day have a day at you, come when it will!'[11] The angry speaker who flung those words at a group of Italian merchants in the spring of 1517 was not a young hothead but a respected member of the Mercers'

Company. The fact that a substantial citizen whom one might have expected to have better manners should give vent to his emotions in this way indicates just how high feelings ran on the 'immigration question'. Craft masters and apprentices bitterly resented the presence of foreign workers whom they accused of stealing their markets. 'Strangers compass the City round about in Southwark, in Westminster, Temple Bar, Holborn, St. Martins, Saint John's Gate, Aldgate, Tower Hill, Saint Katherine's and forestall the market . . . which is the cause that Englishmen want and starve while they live abundantly in great pleasure',[12] claimed another disgruntled tradesman and his words succinctly explain the problem. London artisans had to undergo apprenticeship in the appropriate trade guild and then become members before they could offer their wares to the public. By settling outside the City boundary foreign workers, mostly from the Netherlands or France, avoided such restrictions. Wealthy patrons often made the situation worse by preferring the work of the aliens because it was better or more fashionable and (since they had no guild to protect them) often cheaper. It was a perennial problem which not infrequently gave rise to nasty incidents on the streets and in the taverns of the capital. But, in 1517, it came to a head.

May Day was a holiday, a day of relaxed merrymaking by apprentices and students of the inns of court and a day of anxiety for the shopkeepers of Cheapside, who habitually shuttered their windows and bolted their doors against boisterous gangs of youngsters rollicking their way from alehouse to alehouse. As the day of traditional exuberance approached, the City fathers sensed that the mood in the streets was particularly ugly. On 30 April the lord mayor summoned a group of leading citizens to the Guildhall to discuss tactics. Thomas More, now a prosperous lawyer with important court connections, was of their number. The London establishment debated the worrying situation for several hours. Their dithering proved disastrous. It was only as darkness fell that a delegation was sent to the royal court to seek permission to impose a curfew and ask for military back-up to enforce it. Around eleven o'clock More was touring the streets with a small escort when, not far from Newgate, he encountered a belligerent crowd in no mood to disperse. He rode in among them, seeking out the ringleaders and warning them of the consequences of continued defiance. It was one of those moments when anything could happen. Authority and mob rule hung in the balance. Then someone threw a stone. More and his companions wavered. The troublemakers grasped the initiative. They surged forward and moments later the lawyer was spurring his horse away from the scene, missiles clattering on the roadway behind him. Chaos reigned throughout the hours of darkness. It was left to the king's soldiers to restore order at first light. Amid the shambles of staved-in doorways, looted shops and burning wagons they arrested 300 curfew-breakers. More was appointed to the subsequent commission of enquiry which condemned a handful of young protesters to be hanged and scores more to be jailed or pilloried. And, inevitably, very few of the householders who suffered at the hands of the screaming, cudgel-brandishing mob were foreigners.

We might feel inclined to sympathise with honest English tradesmen trying to protect their livelihood, even if we deplore their methods. However, the boot could be, and often was, on the other foot. 'The rich men, the clothiers, be concluded and agreed among themselves to hold and pay one price for weaving, which price is too little to sustain households upon, working night and day, holiday and weekday, and many weavers are therefore reduced to the position of servants.'[13] Just as today's supermarkets impose their own conditions on suppliers of meat and vegetables, so London merchants in the sixteenth century maintained a stranglehold on all aspects of the cloth trade. The clothiers were regional proto-capitalists who had the whip hand in the complex chain of production outside London. Their agents controlled the cottage industries which turned wool into various grades of cloth: shearers, transporters, carders, spinners, weavers, fullers and dyers. It was a cost-intensive business and the clothiers were determined to keep their overheads to a minimum. They, in their turn, were at the mercy of the London dealers. Once the packhorses were unloaded at Bakewell Hall in Basinghall Street (just around the corner from Hugh Clopton's house) the bales of finished cloth were bought by members of the Merchant Adventurers' Company. There could be little or no bargaining since the Merchant Adventurers held the monopoly of cloth exports. Exploitation was, thus, built into the system and it was almost impossible for the rural craftsmen to maintain their independence and bargaining power. By the middle years of Henry VIII's reign some of the London 'millionaires' had bought their own sheep runs and could, therefore, control the whole process. Most ironical of all, in the light of the complaints about immigrant tradesmen, is the fact that, in order to increase pressure on the native weavers, the London men were bringing in craftsmen from Flanders.

London sat like a great commercial spider at the centre of a web that drew wealth from an area of southern and midland England south of a line from Bristol to Hull. Those areas closest to the capital shared its prosperity. Those further away suffered varying degrees of economic depression (a fact we need to bear in mind when we consider the political disturbances which occurred in the second half of the reign). There were complex reasons for the decline of urban and rural communities. Patterns of production and trade changed and London's entrepreneurs were best placed to take advantage of them. Fundamental was the replacement of wool by cloth as England's primary export, a change which had been in train for more than a century. English woollens were the finest in Europe and much in demand. The capitalists in London had the foreign contacts which best enabled them to take advantage of the situation. By 1509 70 per cent of England's overseas trade was handled in the City.

Economic dislocation was felt more acutely in the towns, several of which lost their traditional internal and external markets. York and its outport of Hull had grown rich on wool exports. They were powerless to stop clothiers dealing directly with London. When they looked to foreign trade they found that both the German Hanse merchants and those of Antwerp preferred to ship their goods in and out of the Thames. Once the capital of the North, York had, by 1520, declined to the status of a market town. It was the same story for many metropolises which fell outside the charmed circle of the London network. In Lincoln and Plymouth, Leicester and Southampton visitors reported streets of empty, decaying houses.

Of course, that was only one side of the coin. Centres of cloth production in East Anglia, the Cotswolds and the South West blossomed into proud, modern towns boasting substantial houses of timber and brick. Civic pride was proclaimed in spacious guildhalls and soaring Perpendicular churches. By 1520 the tiny Suffolk village of Lavenham had become the thirteenth wealthiest town in the realm.

Early Tudor England, thus, presents us with the picture of a divided society, and one not fully at ease with itself. The country experienced internal peace but this only freed many people to concentrate more on other problems. The economic and social changes working through the economy were long term but not so much so that Henry's subjects were entirely aware of them. Unemployment, inflation, trade dislocation, disparities of wealth from region to region – all these made for a feeling of insecurity.

Yet one senses beneath this an even deeper unease. It may be partially explained by 'millennium fever'. The *fin de siècle* years leading up to 1500 seemed, to those who read the signs of the times, to be doom-laden and the mood was sustained as the new century got into its stride. In the 1490s the church worldwide was on the march. The Muslims had been thrown out of Europe. Columbus and those who followed him were carrying the Cross to all parts of the known world. The triumph of the faith had long been prophesied as a sign of the 'end of the age'. Yet, at the same time, writers and artists perceived a rottenness at the heart of Christian Europe which invited a visitation of divine wrath.

> The whole world lives in darksome night,
> In blinded sinfulness persisting,
> While every street sees fools existing.[14]

So complained Sebastian Brant. Hieronymus Bosch's lurid *Ship of Fools* portrayed a boatload of doomed merrymakers. Albrecht Dürer's *Four Horsemen of the Apocalypse* was printed off in Nüremburg and widely circulated. It was in 1525–6 that Hans Holbein the Younger produced his masterly series of Dance of Death engravings. But these were only the leading exponents of the new technique of cheap print. Other artists provided the market with numerous apocalyptic visions involving scenes of violence and destruction. None of this was new, as the thousands of medieval church 'doom' paintings and sculptures prove, but it was more intense. What would have made a greater immediate impact was the preaching of itinerant friars. Dominicans, Augustinians (or Austins) and Franciscans were masters of the art of colourful oratory and did not hesitate to flay their audiences with verbal scourges.

> O prostitute Church, thou has displayed thy foulness to the whole world, and stinkest unto Heaven. Thou hast multiplied thy fornications in Italy, in France, in Spain, and all other parts. Behold, I will put forth my hand, saith the Lord, I will smite thee, thou infamous wretch; my sword shall fall on thy children, on thy house of shame, on thy harlots, on thy palaces, and my justice shall be made known. Earth and heaven, the angels, the good and the wicked, all shall accuse thee, and no man shall be with thee; I will give thee into thy enemy's hand . . . O priests and friars, ye, whose evil example hath entombed this people in the sepulchre of ceremonial, I tell ye this sepulchre shall be burst asunder, for Christ will revive His Church in His spirit.[15]

Few preachers rose to the rhetorical, crowd-pulling heights of the Florentine Dominican, Girolamo Savonarola, but many were capable of creating the sort of atmosphere we now associate with horror films.

If the uneducated looked to men of learning for guidance they discovered that all intellectuals no longer stood four-square behind Catholic orthodoxy. We will consider in a later chapter the impact of Renaissance thought. All I suggest at this point is that the fashionable freethinking now evident in the universities and carried thence by the ex-students who went on to serve in churches and royal and noble courts was making common cause with the doubts and ribaldries of alehouse sceptics. Within days of the end of the fifteenth century Erasmus wrote to a friend to express his delight at the intellectual climate he had discovered in England and the friends he had made among the advanced thinkers of the realm. They had abandoned the 'out worn, commonplace' sort of learning which had dominated the curricula for generations for purer and more wholesome classical studies:

> When I listen to my friend Colet, I seem to hear Plato himself. Who would not marvel at the perfection of encyclopaedic learning in Grocyn? What could be keener or nobler or nicer than Linacre's judgement? . . . It is marvellous how thick upon the ground the harvest of ancient literature is here everywhere flowering forth.[16]

All this was happening within the expanding culture of print. It is perhaps easy for us who have lived through the IT revolution to appreciate the impact of the new technology upon the early sixteenth century. We buy a laptop and have immediate access to a world-spanning, culture-spanning internet which enables us to tap into an ever-pouring cornucopia of information. Our Tudor ancestors had to go to the trouble of learning to read but this opened up for them a seemingly inexhaustible world of exhilarating, challenging, inspiring and troubling knowledge.

But let us away from these generalities and focus our attentions upon a town in the centre of England. Stratford-upon-Avon was one of those places enjoying a period of prosperity. It was also the birthplace of Sir Hugh Clopton. In the years after his mayoralty he spent more and more of his time (and money) there. In 1496 he made his will and this document provides us with a useful entry point for the world of traditional religion.

Chapter 2

Earth, Purgatory, Heaven and Hell

... one Clopton, a great rich merchant and mayor of London, as I remember, born about Stratford, having never wife nor children, converted a great piece of his substance in good works in Stratford, first making a sumptuous new bridge and large of stone, where in the middle be vi great arches for the main stream of Avon and at each end certain small arches to bear the causeway, and so to pass commodiously at such times as the river riseth. The same Clopton made in the middle of the town a right fair and large chapel, endowing it with £50 land, as I heard say, by the year whereas v priests do sing. And to this chapel belongeth a solemn fraternity. And at such time as needeth, the goods of this fraternity helpeth the common charges of the town in time of necessity.[1]

This was not the total extent of the ex-mayor's charitable benefaction. By the terms of his will he not only provided Stratford with a fine, new bridge; he left money to complete refurbishment of the parish church and for substantial extensions to the chapel of the Guild of the Holy Cross. This guild (referred to above) was a fraternity of most of the town's leading citizens, a sort of combination of freemasons' lodge, Round Table branch and chamber of commerce. If not the heart of the community, it was certainly its head and controlled everything from market regulations and local festivities to the maintenance of roads and bridges and the disbursement of charitable funds. Clopton left a hundred marks per annum for dowering twenty-four maidens and four pounds to provide exhibitions at Oxford and Cambridge. Further sums went to charities administered by the Mercers' Company and other mercantile bodies.

Private and corporate charity was a vital part of community life in the country where poverty was an increasing problem and where there was no mechanism for relief by central government. Every parish was expected to take care of its own destitute inhabitants but such support was haphazard and, in some cases, non-existent. This was because fear overcame compassion. Many of the unemployed and unemployable became vagrants and professional beggars. They easily slipped into a life of crime and constituted a threat to honest citizens, especially when they formed themselves into wandering gangs. The government were tougher on crime than they were on the causes of crime. The growing nervousness of the legislators can be sensed by comparing parliamentary enactments of 1495 and 1531. Henry VII's statute ordained that vagabonds were to be set in the stocks for three days without sustenance, and for six days on second offence. Upon pain of further punishment they were to return to their own native town or village and refrain from troubling other communities. A generation later the government deemed that much harsher deterrents were necessary. Any 'able-bodied vagabond or idle person' was to be

> tied to the end of a cart naked and be beaten with whips throughout the same market town or other place till his body be bloody by reason of much whipping; and after such punishment and whipping had, the person so punished . . . shall be enjoined upon his oath to return forthwith without delay in the next and straight way to the place where he was born, or where he last dwelled before the same punishment by the space of three years, and there put himself to labour like as a true man oweth to do.[2]

Considerations of public order, therefore, went hand in hand with those of Christian compassion in stirring men like Hugh Clopton to generosity. But there was another, more compelling motive for his good works. As Leland noted, the retired mercer handsomely endowed the Holy Cross chapel in order to support no fewer than five chantry priests. They taught some of the local children and performed other acts of public service. But prayer was their priority. The principal purpose of Clopton's religious foundation was the saying of masses for the repose of his own soul. He was typical of many good sons of the church whose devotion in this world was driven by their concerns about the next. They built and adorned churches, decked altars and paid for practical improvements to their neighbourhoods. Yet, however heartfelt was their love of their fellow men (which of course we can never know), their charitable actions were performed with the motive of winning heavenly reward. Thus, for example, every traveller crossing Clopton's bridge was enjoined to offer up a prayer for his soul's repose. In such ways were the worlds of here and hereafter held together. Christian men and women were urged to perform good works *and* to ensure that the religious professionals maintained constant or at least regular intercession for the repose of their souls. For Thomas More, as for the majority of his countrymen, the obligation of lay Christians was obvious:

All the whole church from the beginning to this XV C hath believed that good works wrought in faith, hope and charity, shall be rewarded in heaven, and that it is well done to go on pilgrimages, and to pray to saints, and to pray for all Christian souls, and that the prayer and [charitable] deeds of good Christian folk here, doth help to relieve the souls in the pains of purgatory, that the very blessed body and blood of Christ is in the sacrament of the altar, and that therefore it is there to be honoured, and that no person professing and vowing chastity, may for his pleasure lawfully break his vow and wed.[3]

All religions are, basically, about death – what lies beyond it and how our behaviour in this world may affect our eternal destiny in the next. The parish church was the portal between the two realms and in frescoes, stained glass and sumptuously decked altars it offered glimpses of the spiritual realm. They were far from reassuring. The lavishly decorated interiors of most churches were sure to include in their schema a 'doom', a lurid representation of Christ the judge seated in the heavens and dividing the sons and daughters of men between those destined for eternal bliss and those consigned to the fiery maw of hell. The problem for those who gazed on these awe-inspiring images was that none of them could be sure whether he or she would eventually be found on the side of the angels or the demons. All the devout could be sure of was that between death and their ultimate destination there stretched aeons of time in purgatory. All they could do was remain aboard the good ship Church, follow the orders of the crew (the clergy) and hope for the best.

Their imaginations were constantly fed and their devotion encouraged by the familiar round of rituals and the reassuring ministrations of the clergy.

The procession with the Blessed Sacrament now approached the parochial procession gathered at the 'churchyard' Cross, and, according to the ritual, three clerks wearing surplices and plain choir copes sang an anthem, 'Behold, O Sion, thy king cometh', after which clergy and choir venerated the Sacrament by kneeling and kissing the ground before it . . . The two processions then merged, and a series of invocations to the Host were sung . . . During the singing the procession moved round the east end of the church to the south side, where a high scaffold had been erected. Seven boys stood on this scaffold and greeted the Host with the hymn 'Gloria laus et honor' ('All glory, laud and honour to Thee, Redeemer King'). In a further elaboration of the prescribed ritual, flowers and unconsecrated Masswafers ('obols' or 'singing-cakes') were usually strewn before the Sacrament from this scaffolding, to be scrambled for by the children . . . The procession then moved to the west door, where the clerks carrying the Sacrament in its shrine stood on either side of the door and raised the poles above their heads . . . The clergy and people entered the church, passing under the shrine with the Sacrament, and then the whole procession moved to its culminating point before the Rood-screen. All through Lent a great painted veil had been suspended in front of the Crucifix on the Rood-screen. This veil was now drawn up on pulleys, the whole parish knelt, and the anthem 'Ave Rex Noster' was sung, while the clergy venerated the cross by kissing the ground.[4]

Such was the Palm Sunday ritual performed in the great 'wool' church of Long Melford in Suffolk and similar rites took place in hundreds of centres throughout the country. If we were to judge the vibrancy of church life by externals we would have to give pre-Reformation England a high score. Between 1500 and 1530 more money was lavished on the refurbishment of churches and the maintenance of religious 'theatre' in all its forms that in any earlier period for which we have reliable records. In the virtually closed communities of fifteenth-century England the annual repetition of feast, fast and festival was a comforting element in the cycle of life. Familiarity bred reassurance. Every family, every craft guild, every generation had its own role, learned by heart and passed down from age to age. Henry's subjects were, by and large, attached to their ceremonies, as they were to more infrequent religious happenings such as pilgrimages to distant shrines and the performance of miracle plays. These activities were invested with emotional power.

Whether or not those caught up in such holy rites had a clear understanding of the Christian Gospel is problematic. Preaching was rare and most parish clergy were not up to providing instruction in the basic elements of the faith. Reforming bishops and doctors of divinity frequently identified the low educational standards of parish priests, most of whom seemingly could do little more than mumble their way through the Latin mass, as a serious crisis which needed to be urgently addressed. 'Sermons' in stone and paint and stained glass and printed image provided a hotch-potch of Bible stories, legends of the saints and apocryphal tales (mostly centred on the Virgin Mary). Every church interior made a powerful emotional impact on worshippers with its candle- and lamp light playing on carved saints festooned with votive offerings, its polychromed frescoes and intricate patterns in stained glass. These were the manifestations of the pop culture of the age. People were as addicted to these as their twenty-first-century descendants are to TV soap operas.

And, just as many modern highbrows are dismissive of the TV entertainment which appeals to the masses, so sixteenth-century intellectuals made fun of ill-informed reliance on religious externals. Erasmus, in his *Praise of Folly*, satirised the naivety of ignorant folk who prayed to images and Thomas More rather more cautiously took up the same theme. He pointed out the absurdity of loyalty to particular images and shrines. In an imaginary conversation between two devotees he depicted their argument about whether Our Lady of Walsingham was more efficacious than Our Lady of Ipswich. In his concern for a more intelligent and intelligible Christianity Erasmus went further than his friend:

> No veneration of Mary is more beautiful than the imitation of her humility. No devotion to the saints is more acceptable to God than the imitation of their virtues . . . it has long been my cherished wish to cleanse the Lord's temple of barbarous ignorance and to . . . kindle in generous hearts a warm love for the Scriptures.[5]

Such an intellectually and morally demanding faith was not yet to the taste of many people outside the rarefied atmosphere of the European intelligentsia. They were accustomed to spiritual truth being mediated to them via their physical senses. It was the sight of polychromed statues and gilded reliquaries, the sound of plainsong chant, the smell of incense and candle wax that stimulated their imaginations. Just how painted images could change and even distort history is illustrated by the legend of St Nicholas. Very little was known about this fourth-century Middle Eastern bishop but he was credited with converting several peoples to Christianity. In early iconography he was often represented as baptising three pagan kings in a pool. In accordance with current artistic convention the kings were depicted smaller than the saint. Over the centuries the baptism candidates became children and the pool a cauldron. Thus grew the miraculous legend of how three children were boiled to death but subsequently restored to life and drawn forth from the steaming water by Nicholas.

These tall stories were the very stuff of such preaching as did take place.

There was a man that had borrowed of a Jew a sum of money, and sware upon the altar of S. Nicholas that he would render and pay it again as soon as he might, and gave none other pledge. And this man held this money so long, that the Jew demanded and asked his money, and he said that he had paid him. Then the Jew made him to come before the law in judgment, and the oath was given to the debtor. And he brought with him an hollow staff, in which he had put the money in gold, and he leant upon the staff. And when he should make his oath and swear, he delivered his staff to the Jew to keep and hold whilst he should swear, and then sware that he had delivered to him more than he ought to him. And when he had made the oath, he demanded his staff again of the Jew, and he nothing knowing of his malice delivered it to him. Then this deceiver went his way, and anon after, him list sore to sleep, and laid him in the way, and a cart with four wheels came with great force and slew him, and brake the staff with gold that it spread abroad. And when the Jew heard this, he came thither sore moved, and saw the fraud, and many said to him that he should take to him the gold; and he refused it, saying, [that] and if he [the dead man] came again to life, he [the Jew] would receive baptism and become Christian. Then he that was dead arose, and the Jew was christened.[6]

In this time it happed that there was at Rome a dragon in a pit, which every day slew with his breath more than three hundred men. Then came the bishops of the idols unto the emperor and said unto him: O thou most holy emperor, sith the time that thou hast received Christian faith the dragon which is in yonder fosse or pit slayeth every day with his breath more than three hundred men. Then sent the emperor for S. Silvester and asked counsel of him of this matter. S. Silvester answered that by the might of God he promised to make him cease of his hurt and blessure of this people. Then S. Silvester put himself to prayer, and S. Peter appeared to him and said: 'Go surely to the dragon and the two priests that be with thee take in thy company, and when thou shalt come to him thou shalt say to him in this manner: Our Lord Jesu Christ which was born of the Virgin Mary, crucified, buried and arose, and now sitteth on the right side of the Father, this is he that shall come to deem and judge the living and the dead, I commend thee Sathanas that thou abide him in this place till he come. Then thou shalt bind his mouth with a thread, and seal it with thy seal, wherein is the imprint of the cross. Then thou and the two priests shall come to me whole and safe, and such bread as I shall make ready for you ye shall eat.'

Thus as S. Peter has said, S. Silvester did. And when he came to the pit, he descended down one hundred and fifty steps, bearing with him two lanterns, and found the dragon, and said the words that S. Peter had said to him, and bound his mouth with the thread, and sealed it, and after returned, and as he came upward again he met with two enchanters which followed him for to see if he descended, which were almost dead of the stench of the dragon, whom he brought with him whole and sound, which anon were baptized, with a great multitude of people with him. Thus was the city of Rome delivered from double death, that was from the culture and worshipping of false idols, and from the venom of the dragon.[7]

A poor widow possessed nothing but a single pig, and a wolf had violently made off with the pig. The woman implored S. Blaise to get the pig back and the saint smiled and said, 'Good woman, don't be sad; your pig will be returned to you.' Within minutes the wolf came up and gave the pig back to the widow . . . [She] killed the pig and delivered its head and the feet, a candle and a loaf to S. Blaise. He thanked her, ate and told her, 'Every year offer a candle in the church named for me and all will be well with you and with all who do the same.' The widow did as he told her and enjoyed great prosperity.[8]

These are some of the hundreds of stories recorded in the medieval bestseller the *Legenda Aurea* (or *Legenda Sanctorum*) of Jacobus de Varagine. It was written in the thirteenth century as a compendium of sermon illustrations. It was immensely popular with parish clergy and wandering friars and was one of the first books to be printed by William Caxton. It gives us a good idea of the kind of religious fare on which ordinary people were fed. The saints were the celebrities of late-medieval England. Their wondrous adventures were avidly listened to. Their shrines became centres of pilgrimage and did a roaring trade among men and women who travelled many miles to gaze in awe on fragments of bone or clothing reputed to have come from the saints.

It would not become us to be scornful of such credulousness. We live in a society many of whose members desire vicarious excitement from the exploits (usually exaggerated) of celebrities from the small or large screen. They flock in their multitudes to gaze on the stars of film and reality TV shows, eager to see them, touch them and win autographs. Millions slavishly follow soap operas and some fans identify so closely with the characters that they might be real rather than fictional. In the bizarre lengths to which fan clubs of *Coronation Street* or *Dr Who* go we can see something of the fanatical devotion with which medieval religious guilds celebrated their favourite saints.

Henry VIII's subjects were fascinated by the miraculous, but wondrous interferences with the natural order were not restricted in popular belief to God and his earthly and heavenly representatives. Indeed, it is impossible to discern a clear dividing line between religion and magic. If people consulted their priests, they also resorted to a motley crew of magicians, necromancers, alchemists, cunning men, sorcerers, conjurors, astrologers, fortune-tellers and witches. Some time in the late 1530s five sinister-looking men came together in a Sussex village for a nocturnal gathering. They inscribed a magic circle on the floor and proceeded to engage in a complex ritual involving holy water, and a sword and a ring, both of which had been blessed. They were attempting to summon an aerial spirit called Baro. The objective was probably to persuade the otherworldly visitant to reveal the location of a buried treasure. Sadly, he did not show up! What is revealing about this incident is that two of the participants were priests. If that strikes us as odd, or even shocking, it is because we have come to assume that there are clear lines to be drawn between religion, superstition and empirical science. In the early sixteenth century no such divisions existed. Knowledge (*scientia*) was a multi-coloured landscape bordered by mountain peaks obscured in mist. Human exploration of the unknown regions beyond the horizon might follow any of several narrow passes – theology, mathematics, physic, astrology, alchemy – all of which had the same ultimate destination: God, the *fons et origo* of all *scientia* and *sapientia* (wisdom). However, because knowledge is power, there were those whose thirst for it took them beyond the limits of permitted Christian enquiry. Marlowe's *Dr Faustus* opens with the central character, bored with all the conventional fields of study, conjuring up the devil. It was a fiction and it was not written for another half-century but it took its inspiration from a real character who lived in Germany during the years when a youthful Henry VIII occupied the English throne. Those who claimed arcane knowledge were held in awe by ordinary mortals at all social levels. Henry himself was known to consult astrologers and other kinds of diviners at crisis points in his reign. He did so when Anne Boleyn was about to give birth to their first child. Of course, all the 'experts' dutifully prophesied the safe delivery of a male heir. Since specialist *scientia* of all kinds set a person apart from his/her fellows and conveyed considerable kudos it is not surprising that members of the clergy should have been among those tempted to cross the boundary into the forbidden world of ethereal spirits.

There was a sense in which priests were, in any case, the ultimate magicians. Every time they celebrated mass they 'made God' on the altar. According to the doctrine of transubstantiation, the consecrated elements of bread and wine were actually changed into the flesh and blood of Christ. There could scarcely be a more striking miracle than that nor one which responded more closely to the materiality of the popular psyche. People were told that they did not need to receive communion regularly or to be present for the whole mass. It was sufficient for them to gaze upon the host (the consecrated bread) to receive blessing. Some confessors even urged their clients to spend the time of divine service reading their own devotional manuals. Small wonder that the rite was commonly regarded as a piece of ritual magic or that people sometimes took consecrated bread out of the church to use as a charm for easing childbirth or healing sick animals or even as an aphrodisiac.

The ingenuity of uneducated folk overlaid regular church rituals with a plethora of beliefs which bore no relation to their true intention. Thus, for example, performing a requiem mass for someone still alive was widely considered a powerful curse capable of shortening the life of the victim. Such abuse of the system obviously involved the complicity of clergy, as did the practice of baptising animals to ensure their healthy growth. Officially the church rejected the superstitious accretions which had attached themselves to the sacraments but in practice many a blind eye was turned, either because the priests benefited financially from the ignorance of their flocks or because encouraging (or not discouraging) ignorance kept parishioners firmly under the sway of their spiritual superiors. Many theologians would have agreed with the cynical Inquisitor in Shaw's *St Joan*: 'A miracle is an event which creates faith. That is the purpose and nature of miracles. They may seem very wonderful to the people who witness them, and very simple to those who perform them. That does not matter: if they confirm or create faith they are true miracles.'

The hierarchy were far from immune to a mechanistic view. For example, while they frowned on the use of requiem masses for maledictory purposes, they accepted that trentals were particularly efficacious for departed souls. A trental was the recitation in a single day of thirty requiem masses. The celebrant's stamina presumably contributed to the efficacy of the sacrament. Such mathematical packages were far from rare. Nor were the spiritual 'deals' offered in connection with various observances. Pilgrimage to shrines held out quite specific quid-pro-quo benefits. A devout Norfolk churchman carried around with him three facsimile nails from the true cross purchased in the souvenir shop of such a shrine and recited prayers to them daily in the belief that the pope had ordained very precise contingent blessings for such devotion. He would be protected from sudden death; he need have no fear of meeting his end at swordpoint; he would be defended from the attacks of his enemies; he would be immune to poison and fever; he would be defended from malign spirits; he would prosper in this world and be assured of the last rites of the church when he departed it. It was a comfortingly comprehensive list and, in the event of one or more of its items failing to be realised, the obvious response was that the bearer of the nails had failed to keep his side of the bargain. Somewhere along the line he must have lapsed in his daily devotions. This was precisely the same get-out clause as that used by magicians and charlatans when their prescribed rituals failed. Their spells usually involved the participants preparing themselves by fasting or abstaining from sexual intercourse, timing their rites with absolute precision to ensure the propitious alignment of heavenly bodies, using considerable paraphernalia, such as candles, holy water, swords and magic circles, and reciting with absolute precision specific incantations. Failure of any one ingredient would render the whole proceeding void.

It was but a short step from claiming spiritual power on behalf of the clergy to offering eternal rewards for payment. The concept of the 'treasury of merit' asserted that Christ and the saints held a limitless heavenly bank balance of virtue which could be made available to penitent souls on earth. The only human 'teller' empowered to draw on this fund and issue payments was the pope. These payments took the form of 'indulgences', remission of specified terms spent in purgatory. The payee was expected to show that he/she deserved this bounty by performing acts of penance *and* by contributing to church funds. With the passage of time the latter obligation became the more prominent and a very useful means of supplementary income for the pope or whoever received from him a permit to issue indulgence certificates. At the end of the fifteenth century Rome pushed this spiritual 'insurance scheme' to the ultimate. A papal bull announced that indulgences could also be issued for the benefit of departed loved ones currently, it was supposed, on their journey through purgatory. The emotional pressure brought to bear on people who believed in the system can easily be imagined. Who would be so cold-hearted as to deny a measly cash payment which would ease the punishment of a departed parent or child?

Given the importance placed by church authorities on pilgrimage, the identifying of holiness with material objects and significant sites and the spiritual benefits supposedly derived from relics, it was inevitable that rivalry would develop between the keepers of various shrines. Monks who guarded – and profited from – the holy places used a variety of methods to attract devout visitors. They entered wholeheartedly into the relic market. They sought ever more generous papal or episcopal backing in the form of indulgences they might offer. A few even descended to deliberate fraud (see below, pp. 209f). Such cynical jiggery-pokery was rare and was dealt with firmly whenever it came to the attention of the bishops. What is significant is that it highlights two facts. The first is that most lay people craved the certainty offered by the church's means of grace. The second is that there existed, at least in some sections of the clergy, a patronizing attitude with regard to simple layfolk. Those outside the religious establishment were to be kept in their place by whatever means came to hand. The clerical control mechanism worked because those on both sides had, or believed they had, a vested interest in making it work.

The system briefly described above was the ground bass of England's religious life when Henry VIII inherited his father's throne in 1509. But there were innumerable melodies and rhythms overlaying it. Not only did people have their own favourite saints and shrines, and not only did they have recourse to the peddlers of superstitious potions and nostrums, they also adhered to individual – not to say quirky – doctrinal beliefs. It cannot be stated too strongly that pre-Reformation religion was not a seamless robe of orthodox belief. It was a melange of official teaching, folk religion, magic, fashionable scepticism and ribald satire. Church courts had to deal on a fairly regular basis with a variety of eccentric opinions. For example, John Crayer believed that abstention from the use of holy bread and water would bring a man riches. Henry Potter declared that he would not believe in the resurrection of the dead unless he saw it. An unnamed free-thinker was condemned for asserting that 'a man hath no soul but a breath'.[9] There is nothing remotely unusual about this. At any time and in any nation which possesses an officially approved religion there always exists a wide spectrum of public reaction to conventional teaching. It ranges from fanaticism via earnest devotion, worship of externals, apathy, scepticism and cynicism to outright atheism. It is only the numbers of people who fall into each category which change.

Attempting to calculate the strength or weakness of officially sanctioned religion in this period has become the battleground of generations of historians. Everyone who has ever written about the Reformation has had to contend with the marshy ground of early-sixteenth-century religious sensibilities – and most have got bogged down in it. Some have concluded that the English church was in fine fettle (and, therefore, must have had change foisted upon it by the king). Others claim to have discovered a people panting for reform who eagerly associated themselves with the wave of radicalism which swept across from the continent. In reality we can do little more than try to identify something of the range of religious opinion and expression that existed in the years 1500–1530.

In the early sixteenth century very few English men and women would have owned up to disbelief. The majority, as I have already suggested, went along with the traditional local customs well hallowed by the ages. But there was a dissenting minority of people who not only admitted to offbeat personal beliefs but also declared their dissatisfaction with the clergy or what they had to offer.

The existence of a privileged caste, enjoying power over the souls of those in the next world as well as the bodies and goods of those in this world, inevitably provoked a measure of resentment. Ever since Henry II had done penance for the murder of Thomas Becket in 1172 and made large concessions to the pope, men in holy orders had enjoyed considerable exemption from common law. Thus, if a priest found himself arrested by the king's officers, he could claim 'benefit of clergy', which meant that he would be tried in the bishop's court and, as like as not, get off with performing some penance that would fall far short of the imprisonment, branding or execution which would have been the lot of a layman found guilty of the same offence. This evasion of royal justice rankled at all levels from the king downwards and frequently led to breaches of the peace. In the 1430s the people of Kingswinford, near Dudley, 'enjoyed' the ministrations of their rector, John Bredhill. He seems to have been the worst kind of arrogant, rapacious incumbent, more assiduous in collecting his tithes than in ministering to the needs of his flock. On various occasions he had escaped punishment for a variety of crimes ranging from poaching and theft to arson and rape by claiming benefit of clergy. The lord of the manor, John Dudley, was angered by the complaints of his tenantry but was powerless to intervene within the bounds of the law. Dudley was not a man to be trifled with and, at last, he took matters into his own hands. He led a posse to the priest's house and vented his rage in a well-orchestrated orgy of destruction. They broke down fences, filled ditches, lopped trees, trampled crops and removed from the rectory everything that was portable. Bredhill reckoned his losses at around £150,000 (in modern terms). Whether he ever gained recompense through the courts the records do not say but he certainly responded in kind, carrying out his own raids on the property of his enemies. Such violence was, of course, not common but scarcely a decade went by without some face-offs between laity and clergy. In 1527, for example, the people of Newark staged a demonstration against the bishop in a dispute over demesne land.

Much more common were low-key disagreements over issues such as the non-payment of tithes, the demanding of allegedly exorbitant mortuary fees, the failure of clergy to carry out their allotted tasks and objections to priests' moral shortcomings. The sort of issue that led to confrontations was the practice of some clergy of taking to market grain or stock that had come to them by way of tithes and selling it alongside the parishioners who had been obliged to contribute it. And we may feel some sympathy for William Bull, a shearman, who found himself in trouble in Yorkshire for refusing to go to confession. 'Why should I confess to the priest an affair with a pretty woman when I know that, given half a chance, he will use her the same way himself?' he demanded.[10] It was the ramshackle system of providing pastoral oversight in England's parishes which was at root responsible for any lack of empathy between chancel and nave. Benefices were regarded by their patrons as economic units which might be bestowed on trusted servants as a means of providing income or rewarding faithful service. This led to absenteeism and pluralism. The career ladder climbed by a certain John Jamys, who entered royal service around 1460, is an interesting object to consider:

> In January 1484 he was presented to Mundesley parish in Norwich diocese, in February to Balighem in the Marches of Calais, and in November to a third portion of Crewkerne in the diocese of Bath and Wells. The following year he was presented to Little Cressingham in Norwich diocese, two years later to Berkswell in Coventry and Lichfield diocese and to Coston in Lincoln diocese . . . in May 1492 he was presented to Old Romney in Canterbury diocese . . . It is doubtful if he ever set foot in his benefices.[11]

Jamys was employed as a clerk in Chancery where work for his royal masters kept him well occupied. Out of the income from his portfolio of ecclesiastical sinecures he appointed curates to perform his parish duties, probably for very modest stipends. He was far from being a rare phenomenon.

Episcopal visitations indicated that hundreds of English benefices were held by absentee incumbents. For example, in 1518 25 per cent of parishes in Lincoln diocese fell into this category. The system had been in existence from time out of mind. It was more than a century earlier that Chaucer had contrasted his 'poor parson of a town' with his clerical brethren:

> For loath was he to threaten for his tithes,
> But rather would he give, without doubt,
> Unto his poor parishioners about
> Of his offering and also of his substance . . .
> He did not put his benefice out to hire,
> And leave his sheep wallowing in the mire,
> And run to London unto Saint Paul's,
> To seek out a chantry for souls

Or to be employed by a brotherhood;
But dwelt at home and kept well his fold.
But Christ's lore and his apostles twelve
He taught, and first he followed it himself.[12]

Official (or approved) treatises were no less insistent on the need for priests to be committed to the service of their parishioners and to personal holiness. John Mirk, a cleric whose life overlapped with Chaucer's, wrote a verse treatise, *Instructions for Parish Priests*. Before going into detail on the technicalities of celebrating the sacraments, teaching, and hearing confession, the author outlines the qualities of Christian living expected of a spiritual shepherd:

From nice japes [i.e. shady practices] and ribaldry
Thou must turn away thine eye . . .
Thus this world thou must despise
And holy virtues have in use.[13]

Ordinary parishioners were, of course, fully aware of any clerical shortcomings that might be evident. They were perfectly capable of identifying lack of learning, rapacity, ambition and failure to live up to the high moral standards the clergy urged upon their flocks. And there must have been many down-to-earth countrymen like Richard Gavell of Westerham, Kent, who sat in the local alehouse while most of his neighbours were at mass and entertained any who cared to listen with his bar-room rhetoric: 'Now the priest standeth in the pulpit and . . . doth nothing but chide and brawl (revile) [but] I look more on his deeds than on his words, whatsoever he saith there.'[14] Some church leaders certainly cast critical eyes over the situation. Archbishop Lee of York acknowledged in 1536,

Many benefices be so poor, £4, £5, £6, that no learned man will take them, and therefore we be forced to take such as be presented, as long as they be honest of conversation and can

competently understand what they read and minister sacraments and sacramentals, observing the due form and right . . .
And in all my diocese I do not know priests that can preach,
any number necessary for such a diocese, truly not twelve,
and they that have the best benefices be not here resident.[15]

One of the fashionable new thinkers who troubled colleagues
set in their ways was John Colet, Dean of St Paul's. In 1512, he
addressed the convocation of the province of Canterbury about
the need for reform. Church leaders *had* recently been bestir-
ring themselves to stamp out Wycliffite heresy (see below, pp.
55ff). That was all very well, Colet said,

We are . . . nowadays grieved of heretics, men mad with
marvellous foolishness. But the heresies of them are not so
pestilent and pernicious unto us and the people as the evil
and wicked life of priests, the which, if we believe Saint
Bernard, is a certain kind of heresy and chief of all and
most perilous.[16]

If those within the government of the church were aware of
growing hostility towards members of their brotherhood, Colet
insisted, they had only themselves to blame. He told them to
clean up their act. If they wanted to go on enjoying their privileged position in society, they must show that they deserved it.
Those were strong words, even for a pep talk, and they were
necessary because, although many senior members of the ecclesiastical hierarchy were aware of discontent in the pews, no one
seemed to be doing anything about it. This was borne out by
what happened at the Fifth Lateran Council, which was conven-
ing in Rome even as Colet spoke. Delegates attended meeting
after meeting for five years and agreed on the need for widespread reform, but 'no-one was prepared to offend vested
interests by enacting concrete proposals which would significantly change anything.'[17]

But the picture of the late-medieval church that we can paint from all the available sources was not uniformly black. There *were* bishops who carried out effective reform. There *were* clergy who took seriously their responsibility to teach the faith and deepen the spiritual experience of their parishioners. There *were* layfolk who were not content with a passive religious role.

The printing press and the pulpit were both pressed into service on behalf of the pastoral and educational needs of the local church. From the mid-fifteenth century bishops were commissioning books in considerable numbers to help clergy (or, at least, literate clergy) to carry out their duties. Such manuals, originally in Latin but increasingly appearing in the vernacular, covered the ritual basics – the proper administration of the sacraments and the hearing of confession. But they also offered guidance on the instruction of the faithful through teaching of the catechism and preaching. The doctrinal basics to be imparted were the Creed, the sacraments, the seven sins, the seven works of mercy, the seven virtues, the ten commandments and the dominical summary of those commandments (Love the Lord your God with all your heart, soul and mind and your neighbour as yourself). But some books, such as the *Manipulus Curatorum* (1498), went so far as to urge that clergy should know and be able to expound the Bible and that they should preach regularly on Sundays and festival days. This was a counsel of perfection given the limited education of most parish priests and curates but it indicates that some church leaders understood well what was lacking in the routine religious life of the nation.

It is not surprising that many lay people who were serious about their faith should have expressed their devotion by paying for and maintaining religious externals. The rebuilding, extension and ornamentation of parish churches in the half-century before the Reformation far exceeded in quantity and (some would argue) quality any previous comparable period. The large, graceful examples of the Perpendicular style still to be seen in East Anglia, Somerset and the Cotswolds are testimony both to the wealth of these cloth-producing regions and the commitment of their inhabitants to traditional religion. How were they conceived, paid for and built and by whom?

Pilgrimage was an important source of revenue and not only at major national shrines. St Day, near Redruth, Cornwall, was a small hamlet gathered round its tiny Holy Trinity chapel, but to it 'men and women came in times past from far in pilgrimage. The resort was so great as it made the people of the country bring all kind of provision to that place, and so long it continued with increase that it grew to a kind of market to this day.' So wrote John Norden in the reign of Elizabeth I. The poor inhabitants of St Day doubtless relied on pilgrim gifts. Their celebrated painting of the Holy Trinity certainly seems to have done the trick for them. It was a similar story at St George's Island, off Looe, in the same county. 'In the feast of . . . St George there is a great resort of all the country thereabout for their pilgrimage to an image in the said chapel of St George.'[18]

All enterprising church officers strove to attract pilgrims but the main burden of the upkeep of churches was carried locally. In the 1530s the parishioners of Chittlehampton, Devon, erected an impressive new tower. Much of it was financed by offerings to the local saint, Hierithra, which brought in about £50 per annum. Some of this came from the offerings of pious visitors but the bulk of the money took the form of regular donations by the local people. The townsfolk of Louth in Lincolnshire had, at about the same time, seen their own fund-raising efforts come to fruition in the topping of their tower with a soaring spire. Raising money for the church was a community affair. Congregations were accustomed to putting their hands in their purses for the maintenance of their buildings; it is not only modern churchgoers who shoulder the burdens of maintaining and beautifying medieval edifices.

> Against a Christmas, Easter, Whitsunday or some other time, the churchwardens . . . provide half a score or twenty quarters of malt . . . which malt being made into very strong ale or beer, it is set to sale, either in the church or some other place

assigned to that purpose . . . They repair their churches and chapels with it.[19]

Church ales formed a regular and enjoyable part of parish life. Of St Michael's, Thorpe-le-Soken, Essex, all that remains of the fifteenth-century church is the tower, but an inscription still informs visitors that it was erected by local 'bachelors' from the sale of ale. At St Agnes, Cawston, Norfolk, evidence of a permanent brewhouse can still be seen on the exterior west wall. An inscription in the tower gallery at South Tawton, Devon, quotes a popular late-medieval song:

> God speed the plough
> And send us corn enow . . .

This is a reminder of the celebration of Plough Sunday every January, which marked the end of the festive season and the return to work. It consisted of a procession round the village collecting alms, organized by the plough guilds, the agricultural equivalents of urban merchant guilds. The revellers ended up in the church for the blessing of the plough. The funds gathered were put to various uses but the South Tawton inscription concludes,

> Be merry and glad,
> With good ale was this work made.

Major building works inevitably involved prolonged campaigns led by town guilds and clergy. Wealthy citizens, such as Sir Hugh Clopton, left substantial legacies. Not infrequently this action ensured them a prominent burial place within the church. In 1485, John de Vere, Earl of Oxford, proposed to the burghers of his manor of Lavenham that only a new church would provide an adequate thank offering for the Tudor triumph at the Battle of Bosworth. Between them the nobleman and the guildsmen raised funds for and supervised the building of one of the most impressive of the 'wool churches'. Some would say that it is the best of them all. Certainly it was the last of the great Perpendicular parish churches, having been completed in 1530, by which time the Reformation was already under way. Permanent reminders of the principal benefactors featured in the fabric of the church. The earl's heraldic device of the boar and molet is to be seen carved many times on interior and exterior walls. The wealthiest merchant of the town, Thomas Spryng, achieved pride of place for his remains in a parclose tomb within the nave. Not all parishioners could be so lavish when it came to contributing to major construction works but all were expected to throw in their mites. Inducements were offered. If a householder could not 'buy' a prominent memorial he might have his name carved at some point within the church.

Whatever pious sentiments may or may not have inspired the boom in church building and decoration, there is no doubt that civic pride played its part. North Somerset boasts a 'forest' of stately Gothic towers. They display very similar architectural features and were constructed by a small coterie of masons. The appearance of so many similar structures within such a limited area is evidence of inter-town competition. Piety, pride, rivalry, a sense of belonging to a community with its feet in history and its head in heaven – all played their part in the lavish demonstration of religious commitment which is a strong feature of the early Tudor years. In tight-knit rural and urban communities the local church played a central part. The people were emotionally attached to the largest and most ornate building in their neighbourhood. Their corporate identity was bound up in it. (Even in our own day we are familiar with the outcry which is often provoked by the threat to close a church. Local people who seldom if ever darken its doors rise to its defence – usually for reasons they find difficult to articulate.) But we must never overlook the motive of spiritual self-interest. Today, any business wanting to attract new customers is almost obliged to offer 'free gifts' or entry to a prize draw. Our ancestors of five hundred years ago were little different from us; they were not a breed of super-pious men and women. When they parted with their cash they wanted to know what was in it for them. And what was in it was heavenly reward: the assurance that, as they made their weary way through purgatory they would be borne along by the prayers of chantry priests, guildsmen, poor recipients of their bounty and their erstwhile neighbours who read their names on the roll of local benefactors.

What has just been described was a way of life – and death – which, we must assume, satisfied most people. But within the Christian church there have always been those who could not content themselves with a ritualistic, priest-dominated, quid-pro-quo kind of religion. They needed more assurance of forgiveness; could not be convinced by the indulgence 'deals' offered at shrines and pilgrimage centres; wanted to see within their own lives evidence of the working of divine grace. Generations of dire warnings about heaven and hell had done their work too well. Unless those with tender consciences could feel *now* the workings of an interiorised, affective religion their souls could know no peace. The traditional route to their required haven lay through the cloister. The houses of monks, nuns and friars were, theoretically at least, centres of holy living. Their inmates were dedicated to a life of prayer and meditation, free from the distractions of the world. So sacred was the religious life reputed to be that some people believed that to be buried in a monastic graveyard or even in a monastic habit would secure them a good passage to the afterlife.

Unfortunately, this traditional image had lost some of its gilding by 1500. Surviving episcopal visitation records give a mixed impression of the health of English monasticism in the pre-Reformation period. The largest problem was recruitment. The religious life had taken an extremely severe hit in the mid-four-teenth century. The Black Death had killed off more than half of all the inmates of communities. This presented the remaining houses with a problem: should they struggle to maintain, with their lower numbers, a rigorous devotion to their vocation or lower their standards in order to attract more members? Different orders solved the problem in different ways but recovery was, of necessity, slow. In 1348 there were probably about 17,500 religious in England. By 1500 there were fewer than 12,000. Before the great pestilence there were perhaps 1,000 monasteries. At the start of the Tudor age there were about 900. This numerical decline inevitably weakened common perceptions of the importance of the religious vocation. That in its turn made it easier for convents to be closed from time to time and their assets appropriated for other purposes. Henry VII's mother, Lady Margaret Beaufort, was a woman of awesome piety but when she decided to found colleges at Cambridge University she did not hesitate to obtain from the pope dispensations to dissolve certain small religious houses to fund her new creations. Thirty years later, when Cardinal Wolsey was planning to build colleges at Oxford and Ipswich, he made much more sweeping confiscations.

David Knowles, the great twentieth-century historian of English monasticism, compared its declining status to that of the leading aristocratic families in the years between the two world wars.

> In both cases a class of great wealth and social influence lost much of its power and prestige not precisely through any degeneration on its own part, but by reason of revolutionary social and economic changes in the world around it, and through the consequent changes of sentiment in its regard.

In Edwardian England large swathes of territory were under the sway of a small upper class who dominated not only their own tenantry but also a wider circle of neighbours, tradesmen and artisans. Much the same, Knowles argued, was true of the monasteries.

> historians have often assumed that while all else remained steady the monks fell into moral and pecuniary bankruptcy. It would be a truer view to see the world changing around them while they, for their part, were unable either to

accompany that change or to adapt themselves to the demands and necessities of a different world.[20]

This was a Europe-wide phenomenon and one which, by and large, had not, before 1500, affected England as much as its continental neighbours. For example, the commendatory system never took root on this side of the Channel as it did in France. This was the arrangement whereby a powerful layman assumed control of a monastery as commendatory abbot, disposing of and enjoying all its temporal assets. Theoretically, this freed up the inmates to concentrate on their spiritual duties. In practice it subjugated their priorities to those of the wealthy landed class. An overall assessment would suggest that English monks, nuns and friars were faithful in maintaining their rule of life insofar as falling numbers permitted. But there was one fact that stared contemporary non-religious in the face: these diminished communities of other-worldly men and women were sitting on enormous reserves of landed wealth and precious artefacts. Centuries of generous donations had made many of the monasteries extremely wealthy and the process had continued even while the number of vocations to the religious life had declined. Westminster Abbey, which was, admittedly, at the top of the monastic premier league, enjoyed an annual income of £3,470. But the community seldom numbered more than forty monks. When monasteries were 'awash' with money harmful results could follow, internally and externally. The austerity of life could be relaxed with a corresponding decline of spirituality while observers might be critical of all that wealth being 'locked up' in establishments that were unproductive. There were landholders who looked with envious eyes on the monastic estates, especially if they perceived those estates to be poorly managed, and there were reformers who believed that part of such vast resources should be diverted to educational and other social uses.

Relations between the laity and the monastic orders were complex and by careful selection of the evidence it would be possible to make a case for affectionate trust or latent hostility.

Most people knew the abbeys as landlords and employers. They were dependent on them for their livelihood. They paid them their tithes. In many cases monks served as their parish clergy. Dependence provided a comforting security. It could also lead to resentments. Occasional conflicts did arise and could be violent. Today the abbey church in Sherborne, Dorset, is rightly admired for its intricate fan vaulting and we might suppose that this provides impressive evidence of the dedication of the parishioners who paid for the fifteenth-century rebuild and their good relations with the monks who shared the building. John Leland, in his *Itinerary* (1540), dispels such an assumption.

> This was the cause of the abolition of the parish church there. The monks and the townsmen fell at variance, because the townsmen took privilege to use the sacrament of baptism in the chapel of All Hallows. Whereupon one Walter Gallor, a stout butcher dwelling in Sherborne, defaced clean the font stone and after the variance growing to a plain sedition and the townsmen [with the aid] of an Earl of Huntingdon, lying in those quarters taking the townsmen's part and the Bishop of Salisbury the monks' part, a priest of All Hallows shot a shaft with fire into the top of that part of St Mary's church that divided the east part that the monks used from [the nave] the townsmen used, and this partition, chancing at that time to be thatched in, the roof was set afire, and consequently all the whole church, the lead and the bells melted, was defaced. Then Bradford, Abbot of Sherborne, prosecuted [the perpetrators of] this injury and the townsmen were forced to contribute to the re-edifying of this church. But after this time All Hallows church and not St Mary's was used for the parish church.[21]

Such disputes were rare but they had a long history and they continued right up to the eve of the Reformation. Thus, we find a gang of three hundred parishioners, in 1527, destroying a weir belonging to Tavistock Abbey because it interfered with the fishing rights of the local people. The background to such events was the continuity of prayer offered by the religious for their neighbours and the continuance of offerings made to the convents by lay donors. The fact that extreme crises were rare unfortunately does not allow us to make any generalizations. Among the generality of men and women monastic life had long been the butt of ribald humour and many fashionable scholars, including Erasmus, were sceptical about its overall validity. As Knowles suggested, the cloistered life was no longer a self-evidently essential part of the religious scene. Relations between cloister and guildhall varied enormously from place to place depending on history and local personalities. Not until the monasteries came under threat in the 1530s do we have clear evidence which helps us to assess the reactions of the people.

What is obvious is that few lay people were attracted to the monastic way of life. If they wanted to deepen their spiritual experience they had to find other ways to do it. The well-to-do commissioned their own devotional aids. Several beautiful books of hours have survived from the late-medieval period. These were collections of psalms, hymns and prayers in Latin and based on the seven offices of the daily monastic routine. The earliest and most elaborate examples had been produced by monks patiently and lovingly working at their desks in the scriptoria of great abbeys, but by the early fifteenth century demand had well exceeded supply and workshops had been set up in many parts of Europe by enterprising entrepreneurs. It was inevitable that the printing trade would from a very early date muscle into this market. The pictures in these books personalised the decorative ornament to be seen in church interiors – illustrations of the sacraments mingled with those of Bible stories and the lives of the saints. By this time the rosary had come into fashion as an aide-memoire, each bead on the string representing a prayer or invocation to be used in private devotion.

The church, as well as producing manuals for clergy, oversaw the manufacture of catechisms, primers and other educational aids for the laity. They were intended for private meditation and also to be used during the mass. If the uninitiated could not follow the sacred mysteries being performed at the altar, he/she could profitably spend the time in other holy thoughts prompted by the printed text and illustrations. A good example of this kind of literature is *The Craft to LiveWell And to DieWell* (1505), a manual stressing the essential nature for the individual believer of all the church's rites. What the authorities did *not* provide for the questing soul was vernacular Bibles.The Fourth Lateran Council of 1215 had laid it down that 'The secret mysteries of the faith ought not to be explained to all men in all places . . . For such is the depth of divine Scripture that, not only the simple and illiterate, but even the prudent and learned are not fully sufficient to try to understand it.' In the rigidly two-tier medieval church it was the role of the laity to do what they were told and believe what they were instructed to believe. As a result they were never given the opportunity to explore the outworking of the divine plan of salvation as revealed in Scripture. Bible passages and stories were certainly provided for them but they could only be viewed through layers of doctrinal and liturgical lenses.

Those who found the 'approved' literary fare restricting might turn to the writings of men and women on the fringes of traditional religion. These were the 'awkward squad' – zealous souls, like Francis and Catherine of Siena, who had blazed their own spiritual paths, been eventually accorded sainthood status, but who had been thorns in the flesh of the religious establishment in their own day. Devout seekers even read the sermons and meditations of Girolamo Savonarola, who, in 1498, was burned as a heretic in Florence's Piazza della Signoria for condemning the papal regime of Alexander III (Rodrigo Borgia). England had its own mystic tradition. Richard Rolle (d. 1349) and Walter Hilton (d. 1396) wrote movingly about experiencing the love of Jesus. The anonymous fourteenth-century author of *The Cloud of Unknowing* offered a meditative path to union with the divine. Julian of Norwich (d. 1443) described her glowing visions of the Saviour. Such anchorites and conventuals saw, or claimed to have seen, beyond the outward show of medieval religion. That was why they were viewed with suspicion by their superiors. Perhaps more significant was Margery Kempe (d. *c.* 1440). Margery was a married woman and the mother of fourteen children but her piety led her to adopt a pseudo-monastic regimen. It included arduous pilgrimages, ascetic practices, and a vow of mutual chastity with her husband. Her charismatic lifestyle involved visions, groanings, swoonings and other ecstatic states.

Margery Kempe became a pattern and exemplar for those who wanted to live a disciplined devotional life *outside* the cloister, who aspired to be in the world but not of it. One of the ladies who took up this challenge was none other than Lady Margaret Beaufort, the mother of Henry VII. She, too, lived a life of strict devotion and abstained from all sexual contact with her husband. Margaret was accepted as a member of no fewer than five religious houses, but did not actually join any of them. Instead, she observed the daily offices in her own home. She became the patroness of new devotions, such as that to the name of Jesus and the *Scala Coeli* (the Heavenly Ladder, a devotion drawing its inspiration from St Bernard's vision of angels assisting human souls to ascend to God), and she became the greatest founder of colleges in the history of Cambridge University. The queen mother realised the potential of the printing press for raising the spiritual life of her son's kingdom. Among the devotional aids she caused to be printed was one which had taken Europe by storm since its first publication in 1486. This was Thomas à Kempis's *Imitation of Christ*. Margaret caused an English version to be published in 1503–4 and she translated part of the book herself. This Christian classic made – and still makes – its appeal because it is, in the words of George Eliot, 'a lasting record of human needs and human consolations; the voice of a brother who . . . felt and suffered and renounced . . . the same passionate desires, the same strivings, the same failures, the same weariness'. The *Imitation* was a manual for men and women inside and outside the cloister. It illumined a way of life in which meditation on Christ could be turned into imitation of him. It spoke directly to the condition of those people we have been considering who were seeking sure and certain ways to find a faith that *worked*.

> What have we to do with . . . the dry notions of logicians? He to whom the eternal Word speaketh, is delivered from a world of unnecessary conceptions. From that one Word are all things, and all speak that One . . . No man without that Word understandeth or judgeth rightly. He to whom all things are one, he who reduceth all things to one, and seeth all things in one, may enjoy a quiet mind, and remain peaceable in God. O God, who art the truth, make me one with Thee in everlasting charity.[22]

With Thomas à Kempis we arrive at the spiritual movement which, throughout the fifteenth century, spread steadily throughout north-west Europe, the *devotio moderna*. This was a schema of prayer, meditation and study which focused on the life of Christ and, particularly, on the Passion. It formed the rule of life for over a hundred houses of Brothers and Sisters of the Common Life, communities which were not 'monastic' in the full sense of that word. Members were very much engaged in the life of their localities, especially in the running of schools. Thomas was the most outstanding exponent of the *devotio moderna* but there were several other authors who proclaimed the principles of the movement in their treatises. What they proposed was a way of life which could be lived within or without their own communities. It touched a common chord with many who 'hungered and thirsted after righteousness' for various reasons. By concentrating on the central features of the Gospel it deflected attention away from the cult of saints. It offered a programme leading to *direct* access to God. The writers (like the contemporary humanist scholars) were sceptical of scholastic theology, the dry-as-dust, speculative study of traditional texts. They made much use of biblical references, thus directing attention to the source of all Christian theology. And we should not overlook the obvious fact that the brothers were spreading their ideas in vernacular writings. This encouraged lay people to learn to develop the habit of nourishing their faith through reading.

But what they could *not* read in their own language was, as already mentioned, the Bible. England was the only part of western Christendom where study of the vernacular Scriptures was actually forbidden by church law. Article VII of the Constitutions of Oxford (1408) had ordained

> that no-one henceforth on his own authority translate any text of Holy Scripture into the English or any other language by way of a book, pamphlet or tract, and that no book, pamphlet or tract of this kind . . . be read in part or in whole, publicly or privately, under pain of the great excommunication, until the translation shall have been approved by the diocesan of the place, or if need be by a provincial council.[23]

Since no diocesan or council ever had approved a vernacular translation, this amounted to a total proscription. What had brought about this draconian piece of legislation was the establishment's fear of the 'English heresy', unleashed by the arch-heretic John Wycliffe.

Wycliffe was a fourteenth-century Oxford scholar of whom, a hundred and fifty years later, Henry VIII would have heartily approved. He had been a supporter of the regency government headed by John of Gaunt during the minority of Richard II. The politicians had found the brilliant academic very useful during their conflict with Rome over the authority wielded by the English church. In his key book, *De Officio Regis*, Wycliffe had argued that the pope had no power over secular affairs within the realm of England. This was part of a long-running argument but what made Wycliffe's case different was that it was based wholly on Scripture. He was, in effect, pitting the authority of the Bible against that of the church. As his thinking developed further he became convinced of the absolute primacy of Scripture. It was only a small step from that to the assertion that every Christian should be as familiar as possible with its message. That meant translating the Latin Vulgate into English. Wycliffe and a band of scholars who followed him in the closing years of the fourteenth century undertook the task, laboriously copying out parts of the sacred text by hand and necessarily working in secret.

The first striking fact to notice is that these manuscript Bibles and part-Bibles found a ready market. Distribution began among Oxford students who, as always, were eager for new ideas – particularly anti-authoritarian ideas. But within a short space of time the books were circulating in towns, villages and even monasteries across much of southern and central England. There was, as I have suggested, a prevailing atmosphere, among many literate and semi-literate English people, of eagerly seeking religious truth. Just as some gave themselves to the study of the mystics, so others pored over the scraps of vernacular Bibles – even though this was frowned on by the religious authorities. Strong opposition was shown as early as 1382, when the Chancellor of Oxford University organized a purge of town and gown, seeking out the unapproved writings and those who owned them. But persecution did not stop (and, perhaps, actually encouraged) the spread of the new translations. In 1401 the bishops persuaded Parliament to give sharper teeth to anti-heresy legislation with the statute *De Heretico Comburendo*. Seven years later, as we have seen, they proclaimed more forcefully against Wycliffe's disciples in the Constitutions of Oxford. By this time the burning of obdurate Bible-readers had begun and, in 1428, the persecutors carried out an act of symbolic vengeance, designed *pour encourager les autres*. They dug up Wycliffe's body from where it had rested for forty-four years, burned it and scattered the ashes in a nearby stream.

Such a violent reaction could be more easily explained if Wycliffites were seriously troubling the English church by preaching against its doctrines, separating themselves from their local worshipping communities or carrying out energetic proselytising campaigns. With few exceptions, they did none of these things. It was Henry Crump, a Cistercian monk, who first gave these Bible people the name 'Lollards'. Preaching against them in 1382, he likened them to the peripatetic heretics in the Low Countries who 'lolled' or mumbled their pernicious teachings to any who would hear. According to their detractors, these erring children of Mother Church 'learn the gospels by heart in the vernacular and mumble the one to the other'.[24] Lollardy seems to have got under the skin of the authorities, at least in part, because of its quicksilver quality. It was an underground movement with no widespread organisation, no national or regional leaders and no body of doctrine. Its adherents attended their parish churches. When they were apprehended, they usually cheerfully recanted, before proceeding – more cautiously – along their unorthodox way. The Lollards were unlike continental heretical groups, such as Cathars, Waldensians and Joachimites, who almost invited opposition and with whom the Inquisition was used to dealing.

> Lollardy was a religion of the book, and it had the resilience of a movement based on an underground literature, no longer growing, but copied, concealed, read out, and passed from hand to hand, still well able to stir the imagination, to console in adversity and to open simultaneously a world of literacy and of novel religious ideas.[25]

Lollardy tended to be an artisan movement of yeoman farmers, small traders and craftsmen of England's southern and more prosperous counties. There is a marked geographical similarity between the area where heresy took root and the economically more secure part of the country closely linked to the capital. The Lollards were more open to sophisticated ideas spreading outwards from the universities and London. They were respectable members of their communities and not the sort of people who could be subjected to a prolonged campaign of repression. They lived peaceably with their neighbours, who had little reason to denounce them. If their clergy were aware of their opinions, they were probably reluctant to take action against them as long as they came regularly to mass. Lollardy normally ran in families and was spread by intermarriage. Fairly typical must have been the incident recorded of one Robert Durdant, a well-to-do Buckinghamshire farmer, who, in 1521, invited guests from as far afield as London, Windsor and Amersham to attend his daughter's wedding. When they were assembled they met together in a barn to listen to Bible readings, 'which they liked well'.[26] One frustrated bishop complained Lollards 'give a name proper to themselves and call themselves *known men*'.[27] We might, perhaps, draw a parallel with freemasonry, a secret society whose rituals and beliefs are imperfectly understood by outsiders but who do nothing to excite the hostility of non-members. Lollards usually met together in 'night schools' for the reading and discussion of the Bible. They operated an efficient colportage system for the dissemination of their literature. Some of their tracts were certainly critical, even denunciatory, of the religious establishment but they were not manifestos challenging or organizing opposition to that establishment. The prevailing view among them seems to have been that the open Bible would, of itself, act like a solvent on generations of false teaching.

It is easy to draw too clear lines between 'Lollardy', 'Orthodoxy' and the scepticism which shaded into complete disbelief. Religious conviction in late-medieval England was, as I have tried to show, a rag-bag of differing devotions, ideas and superstitions. Against this background the 'known men' did not always stand out clearly; they were just another group of devout men and women seeking a personal, meaningful faith which they did not find in the ministrations of conventional Catholicism. 'Lollard' seems to have been a catch-all term and ecclesiastical records sometimes labelled as Lollards eccentrics whose opinions owed nothing to Scripture and much to angry anticlericalism.

A Hertfordshire butcher, as well as rejecting baptism and the veneration of images, asserted that there was no god but the sun and the moon. A Derbyshire widow in 1481 stoutly rejected the virgin birth of Jesus. When a Berkshire man insisted under interrogation that the Lord's Prayer should be recited backwards, one suspects necromancy rather than biblical devotion. John Florence, a Norfolk wood-turner, must have struck a common chord with his denunciation of tithes. And it is worth recording that the mystic Margery Kempe was on more than one occasion investigated on suspicion of Lollard leanings.

What seems to have distinguished the spiritual heirs of Wycliffe in the eyes of the authorities was an independence which threatened the age-hallowed authority of the clergy. Lollards were not separatists but they *did* make a distinction in their own minds between the Catholic church and their own fellowship. A woman in distant Cornwall, asked for her definition of the church, told her judges that it was 'not your popish church, full of idols and abominations, but where three or four are gathered together in the name of God'.[28] Lollardy was a *lay* movement. Its members believed they could live – and die – without the need of the sacraments or the ministrations of priests. Other 'holiness groups' were tied into the observances of the church. Mystics and followers of the *devotio moderna* modelled themselves on the monastic routine. Lollards, by contrast, took their inspiration from a banned book which they believed they were free to interpret for themselves without guidance from the 'experts'. Indeed, as some of their critics confessed, many of these heretics knew the Bible better than their parish clergy did. Their claim to a superior revelation might also be considered potentially seditious. One of their tracts described how a peasant converted a gentleman. After long debate, the latter was obliged to acknowledge,

> Now I promise thee after my judgement
> I have not heard of such an old fragment
> Better grounded on reason with Scripture

> If such ancient things might come to light
> That noble men had once of them a sight
> The world yet would change peradventure.[29]

'Reason with Scripture', this was the basis of Lollard religion. It declared that nothing was necessary for salvation but the open Bible, understood simply, without the need for guidance by the professionals and certainly without the arcane, allegorical glosses that were the stock in trade of scholasticism.

The fifteenth-century church could find no answer to the Lollard problem. The movement had traditional strongholds, such as the Chilterns and central Kent, but there were cells in London and as far afield as North Wales and Norfolk. There is even some evidence of its appearance in Scotland – perhaps carried thither by English heretics fleeing justice. Persecution of the known men was sporadic, but none the less fierce for that. Incomplete diocesan records list about 400 abjurations and 70 burnings between 1414 and 1522. The real numbers must have been much higher. But Lollardy survived.

If we want to understand the hardiness of the 'English heresy' we have to look deeper than doctrinal disputes and anticlericalism. Lollardy did not constitute an aberration of late-medieval society. It sprang from it and was part of it. In June 1440 a venerable Essex priest, Richard Wyche, was burned on Tower Hill. He was a popular figure, so much so that many people who flocked to his execution scrabbled among his ashes to discover fragments of bone that they could keep as holy relics. Others came by night to erect a cairn and a cross on the site of his martyrdom. This was swiftly removed by the mayor and corporation but that did not stop people turning the place into a pilgrimage centre and claiming that miracles were performed there by the 'saint'. So serious were the subsequent disturbances that a royal edict was issued to the effect that

No person from henceforth presume to resort to the place where the said Richard was executed, under colour of a

pilgrim, or for any other cause of devotion whatsoever; nor
send any offering thither, nor worship him hereafter openly
or secretly, or adjudge, esteem, repute, name or talk of him as
otherwise justified or innocent.[30]

The irony of a Lollard martyr becoming the focus of idolatrous
worship – something abhorrent to his fellow believers – indicates
that Wyche's fate touched something in the common psyche.

Sixty years later the celebrated misadventures of a prominent
London citizen showed that when it came to clashes between
Lollards and the ecclesiastical authorities, popular reaction was
still by no means all on the side of orthodoxy. The classic case of
Richard Hunne bears retelling because it illustrates concisely
the potential points of conflict which existed between clergy
and laity and which, when the right circumstances and personalities were involved, could come to the surface. Richard Hunne
was a prominent London merchant who, in 1511, found himself
at odds with his local rector over dues connected with the
funeral of his baby son. The rector, Thomas Dryffeld, took the
matter to the ecclesiastical court and won his case. Hunne
responded by proceeding in King's Bench against Dryffeld and
his curate for slander and damaging his position in the business
community. Legal proceedings dragged on month after month
and, had the combatants been more even-tempered, the conflict
might have run into the sand. Hunne, it seems, was determined
to make his confrontation into a test case. He and his adversaries believed that points of principle were at stake. The merchant
was probably a known man and he certainly had a smattering of
legal knowledge. His next move was to invoke the ancient law of
praemunire, and claim that the clergy, by citing him into an
ecclesiastical court, had trespassed on the territory of royal
justice. This touched one of the well-gnawed bones of contention between canon and common lawyers. By 1514 the Hunne
case had become a long-running *cause célèbre*. Interested parties
on both sides were egging their champions on. Hunne had
brought the church establishment to the bar of public opinion

and provoked a situation in which it was impossible for either side to back down. Bishop Fitzjames of London now stepped in to defend his clergy. He trumped the *praemunire* ace with an accusation of heresy. From that point the whole affair turned seriously nasty. Hunne was locked up in the bishop's prison and there one morning he was found hanging by the neck. A jury brought in a verdict of murder against the bishop's chancellor. But Fitzjames was not going to allow mere laymen to dictate the fate of his staff. Not only did he prevent the homicide case coming to court; he pronounced Hunne a condemned heretic and had his body publicly burned. This extreme case, whatever its rights and wrongs, raised strong feelings in the capital which raged for months.

That heterogeneous body of people we call 'Lollards' were drawn from a much larger constituency of men and women who were critical of the religious establishment. If we can find a shared factor unique to the known men it will lie not in the realm of doctrine but, as Professor Collinson has suggested, in something deeper, 'a newly-discovered New Testament "feeling" of what it was to be a Christian, even the experience of being born again'.[31] For this transforming experience they were prepared to go out on a limb, to guard the truth in secret, to risk the hostility of neighbours and, in a very few cases, to embrace imprisonment, interrogation or death. No less than those who sought personal holiness and assurance through contemplation and mystical exercises, the Lollards found in Scripture what the liturgical routines of the church could not give them. To that extent we should regard them less as 'forerunners of the Reformation' and more as exponents of one type of late-medieval and early-modern spirituality.

Chapter 3

Keeping an Eye on the Neighbours

England's ties with the movers and shakers of the continent were threefold – diplomatic, ecclesiastical and intellectual. These worlds overlapped. The ambassadors who represented kings were often senior ecclesiastics. The princes of the international church were usually men of considerable scholarship. Members of the European intelligentsia, whether independent thinkers or university academics, were closely in contact with the courts of enlightened princes. Theirs were strong ties in the opening years of the new century. Members of the avant-garde exchanged letters, sent their books and pamphlets to each other (thanks to the revolution of print) and even had their portraits painted for their confrères. They, of course, were united by common languages – Latin for scholars and French for diplomats. The excitement generated by the exchange of ideas and news surmounted the difficulties of maintaining contact. Travel was slow. Even in the warmer months of the northern summer when roads were not deep in mud and the Alpine passes not blocked with snow, it took a fast courier a couple of weeks to reach Rome from London.

But what connected Europe's leading thinkers was more than a love of learning or a self-conscious sense of intellectual superiority. They were not so much bound by cords as connected by electrical wires thrumming with challenging abstractions and world-changing notions. And these men really did believe that the world needed to be changed and that they could lead the way in that transformation. In 1516 Thomas More was offered a place on the royal Council. It was in that same year that he published *Utopia* and, in Book 1, he rehearsed the arguments which we may assume had been going through his own mind as he weighed the pros and cons of involvement in power politics. How might philosophers, he questioned, best affect the course of public life? Should they, as his friend Erasmus urged, jealously guard their independence and avoid high office? It was blatantly obvious to any intelligent observer that corruption and dissimulation were comfortably lodged in royal palaces and that men of principle risked compromising their convictions once they had accepted paid employment. As a free agent the scholar could criticise the actions and pronouncements of national leaders. He could labour for the establishment of a truly Christian commonwealth. But, on the other hand, he lacked the access to power which might make it possible to implement his ideas. So, should one preserve the purity of one's ideals in splendid isolation or, by entering government, accept a measure of compromise in the hope of achieving at least modest reform? More salved his conscience by proposing that the philosopher had a civic duty to deploy his gifts within the councils of the mighty.

> You must not abandon the ship in a storm because you cannot control the winds. On the other hand, you must not force upon people new and strange ideas which you realise will carry no weight with persons of opposite conviction. On the contrary, by the indirect approach you must seek and strive to the best of your power to handle matters tactfully. What you cannot turn to good you must make as little bad as you can.[1]

What were the perceived deficiencies of sixteenth-century society that, in the opinions of the intellectual elite, needed reform? That is a complex question and any attempt to answer it briefly faces the danger of superficiality. Let us try to avoid that trap by taking a step-by-step approach.

The new way of thinking that we call the Renaissance had its origins in Italy: 'by the side of the Church which had hitherto held the countries of the West together . . . there arose a new spiritual influence which, spreading itself abroad from Italy, became the breath of life for all the more instructed minds in Europe.'[2] So wrote Jacob Burckhardt a century and a half ago and his assertion remains essentially true, at least until the impact of Luther and the Swiss reformers exploded into the religious and cultural life of Europe. What we need to consider is why the intellectual impetus should have come from the Italian peninsula and, more particularly, from the northern half of that peninsula.

Northern Italy had three things that uniquely equipped it for intellectual leadership – an almost miraculously vibrant culture, the inheritance of the splendours of ancient Rome and the papacy. The landscape we see today, with its hilltop communes of huddled, terracotta-tiled houses, its castles, girdling walls, terraced vineyards and olive groves, is the direct result of the ebbing away of the western empire in the fifth century. Each dukedom, merchant oligarchy and republic that survived the collapse of the ancient civilisation was fiercely independent and each developed its own polity.

> All states, all powers, that have held and hold rule over men have been and are either republics or principalities. Principalities are either hereditary, in which the family has been long established; or they are new. The new are either entirely new, as was Milan to Francesco Sforza, or they are . . . members annexed to the hereditary state of the prince who has acquired them, as was the Kingdom of Naples to that of the King of Spain. Such dominions thus acquired are either accustomed to live under a prince, or to live in freedom.[3]

This was how Niccolò Machiavelli began his analysis of the political life of the Italian city states. His treatise, *The Prince*, reveals two important facts: it tells us something of how the

leading participant entities in Italian political life had developed
and it demonstrates that Italians reflected on political theory.
The citizens of each *città* knew not only who they were but why
they were who they were. These proud, independent communities collaborated and clashed over the centuries. Some extended
their authority over the surrounding country and brought other
urban centres within their ambit. They prospered through
conquest and trade. Within their walls there grew up rich and
powerful dynasties, such as the Medici, the Gonzagas and the
Sforzas. Some had leisure to indulge their taste for the finer
things in life – to read, to debate, to collect and to patronise men
of talent. Cardinals, aristocrats, condottieri, bankers – all were
eager to demonstrate their cultivated taste by commissioning
palazzos, churches, sculptures, paintings, music and books.
They competed with each other to discover and exploit new
talent. In time, they created a hothouse climate for the growth of
the most luxuriant crop of artistic genius the western world has
ever seen. This flowering of art and philosophy is what we know
as the Renaissance.

It was what the word implies, a *rebirth*, a rediscovery and a
reapplication of all that was considered best of ancient civilisation. Italians were surrounded by the vestiges of classical
grandeur. Ruined temples, broken aqueducts, the statuary occasionally dug up which depicted the gods, goddesses and
emperors of old Rome presented late-medieval man with a challenge and a reproach. They constituted the evidence of a glorious
past which had disappeared beneath the accretions of a millennium of Christian culture which, by comparison, appeared drab
and uncreative. It was not a sudden, unheralded phenomenon.
As far back as the thirteenth century, artists, and particularly
architects, had been drawing on the material remains of the past
which were all around them as they built and decorated churches
and palaces. But the movement accelerated through the fifteenth
century and it was the invention of the printing press which gave
it its greatest boost. The writings of Greek and Roman poets and
philosophers, hitherto only available in manuscripts preserved in

monastic and princely libraries, were published and became the subject of excited debate among scholars. They reflected on and discussed the ideal forms of republican and monarchical government and the principles that determined how people should be ruled. Plato, Cicero and other classical commentators had based their ideas on the assumption that man could calculate the forms of polity which would best serve the good of the state. The concept of *res publica*, which transmogrified in the sixteenth century into that of 'commonwealth', inevitably implied a challenge to the current political correctness of an immutable society with God at its pyramidal apex and men in their designated degrees forming the various hierarchic layers of the structure. The new thinking in art and philosophy redefined the place of man in the created order and, if it did not dethrone God, it at least opened up his position to debate. This is why a later age named this new thinking 'humanism'.

It was not the product of a peaceful age, one which provided creative minds with the atmosphere for calm reflection. Not only were the city states locked in their own rivalries; their wealth, their commercial supremacy in the Mediterranean world and their geographical position provoked the interest of major European nations. France, Spain and the Holy Roman Empire all sought to increase their influence in the peninsula by alliances and conquest. They had expensive nations and empires to run, and salivated greedily as they looked towards Italy, the commercial hub of Europe. Its Croesus-like merchant princes monopolised trade with the Levant, presided over resplendent courts, set the intellectual tone of Europe and, from their bounty, lent money to the hard-pressed kings of the West. Italy drew the Habsburg and Valois monarchs like a magnet and for the first half of the sixteenth century became the cockpit of their conflicting ambitions. The Italian states were, thus, locked in political, diplomatic and military competition, while their rulers and thinkers were grappling with new ideas which defined their identity. In the midst of all this – part of it and yet distanced from it – was the papacy.

The inheritors of the fisherman's shoes had long since ceased to be simply the spiritual rulers of western Christendom. They were territorial princes up to their necks in the political intrigue, diplomatic chicanery and military enterprise necessary for survival in a murderously competitive world. Their authority rested on the twin foundations of their territorial strength in Italy and the spiritual sway they held over the Catholic faithful of Europe (valuably expressed in the taxes paid to Rome from every nation). There were occasionally pious popes, elected for their holiness of living, but they were few and far between and they tended to make little impact because the maintenance of the kind of Roman primacy that had emerged by the late Middle Ages called for leaders who displayed subtlety and ruthlessness rather than piety and humility. Yet, even by the standards of papal worldliness which had come to be expected, the popes who held office at the time of the Renaissance plumbed new depths. The principal achievement of Sixtus IV (1471–84) was the establishment of the Spanish Inquisition under the leadership of Tomás de Torquemada. He raised simony to an art form and, though he spent money on worthy causes such as patronage of Botticelli and the refounding of the Vatican library, he provoked numerous opprobriums, such as that of the later Anglican controversialist who claimed that 'he lowered the moral tone of Europe'. The name of Rodrigo Borgia, Alexander VI (1492–1503), has come down the centuries as a byword in debauchery. Edward Gibbon called him 'the Tiberius of Christian Rome'. Even if only half the stories of his numerous mistresses, bastard children and murders were true they would disgrace any secular ruler, let alone the head of the western church. Julius II (1503–13) drew from the contemporary chronicler Francesco Guicciardini the wry comment that he was 'worthy of great glory if he had been a secular prince'. Julius is chiefly remembered now as the pope who commissioned Michelangelo to paint the Sistine Chapel but in his day he was more famous as a warrior pope who was never happier than when leading his army and who added significantly to the territory of the Papal States. Leo X (1513–21) was, first and foremost, a member of the Florentine ruling house of Medici and concentrated much of his effort into channelling church money and offices to his relatives.

North Italy was, then, the cultural and religious hub of Europe. However, the traffic was very far from being in one direction only. Nations beyond the Alps were asserting their own influences, developing their own identities and contributing to the development of western Christendom. While the popes were, above all, preoccupied with maintaining their own power and authority, they did not go unchallenged. The two major problems they faced were conciliarism and nationalism. Conciliarism was an intermittent campaign involving several heads of government and reform-minded ecclesiastics that aimed at cleaning up the church. There had been long-mounting criticism of the moral and educational inadequacy of the clergy and corruption at the centre. For much of the early fifteenth century, leadership of the church had been contested by rival popes, a state of affairs which had further undermined the authority of Rome. Many believed that the only way to purify the church and keep it pure would be to place ultimate authority in a general council which would meet regularly and oversee the activities of popes, cardinals and bishops. Inevitably, the instinct of succeeding popes had been to resist any diminution of their authority. The conciliarist principle was sound enough but its implementation ran into numerous difficulties, quite apart from papal opposition. There was no agreement about who should be appointed to a general council or precisely what its remit would be. The movement was also vitiated by national rivalries. All this played into the hands of the papacy and applied an effective brake to reform.

For the rulers of France, Spain and the Empire any reform movement was bound up with their determination to strengthen their own power base. They were moving in the direction of establishing centralised nation states and, in this process, extending control over the churches in their own territories was an important strategy. In 1482 Ferdinand and Isabella of Spain reached an agreement with Sixtus IV that gave them the right to appoint to all senior church offices and to endorse or nullify the issuing of papal bulls in their territory. In 1516 Francis I of France obtained a similar concession. Such developments gave the rulers concerned the power to carry out necessary reforms, and ecclesiastical discipline was certainly tightened up, particularly in Spain. But the main advantages were political. The bishops and abbots constituted an influential body of opinion. Through them popes had always brought pressure to bear on kings. Now the kings could ensure that their own supporters held the top jobs. More importantly from the point of view of day-to-day administration was the considerable financial power these agreements transferred to secular hands. Ecclesiastical taxes and payments for institution to office made a very welcome contribution to royal coffers.

Yet, as I have insisted before, any temptation to diminish the Reformation impulse by regarding it only in political terms must be resisted. This was an age alive with all manner of spiritual vitalities, no less in Italy than anywhere else. The fact that corruption and decadence had taken up lodgement in the Vatican does not mean that Christianity was moribund throughout the peninsula. There was a widespread yearning for an interiorised faith, particularly within the mendicant orders. The fifteenth century witnessed the spread of the observant movement, which called the friars to *observe* rigorously the rules laid down by the founders and particularly to espouse poverty and give themselves to preaching. In one sense there was nothing original in this impetus to holiness. Asceticism had always battled with worldly compromise in the life of the cloister but the intensity of this latest manifestation had deep and long-lasting consequences. The movement associated with the names of influential preachers such as Bernardino of Siena and John of Capistrano led to a clear division among the mendicant orders between the Observants and the less rigorous Conventuals. In their devotion to the person of Christ, their simplicity, their insistence on ethical purity and their commitment to charitable works the reformers followed a regime similar to that which would mark the evangelical pioneers of the 1520s and 1530s.

The explosion of piety set off several chain reactions. For example, St Catherine of Genoa became a byword for charity because of her care for the sick and poor in the hospital at Pammatone. Among her disciples was a layman, Ettore Vernazza, who, in 1497, founded the Oratory of Divine Love, a community dedicated to rigid devotion and practical benevolence. Many communities of Divine Love were founded by 1517, including one in Rome which operated a hospice for incurables and became a living reproach to members of the papal court. The Roman oratory attracted an official of the Curia, Gaetano of Thiene, and a papal diplomat, Gian Pietro Carafa (later Pope Paul IV). These two men, in their turn, set up the Theatine Order to unite serving priests who followed an austere rule of personal religious exercises.

When piety and corruption came into contact the results were unpredictable. Sometimes the effect was purgative. At others it was explosive. In 1482, Girolamo Savonarola was sent as a lecturer to the Dominican convent of St Mark in Florence. He rapidly became a religious celebrity because of his harsh asceticism and apocalyptic preaching. Thousands flocked to hear his sermons and to repent of their sins. Like John of Capistrano before him, Savonarola called upon his followers to renounce worldliness by publicly burning their fripperies, works of 'decadent' art, playing cards and other accoutrements of vice – the celebrated 'bonfires of the vanities'. It was not long before the sharp-voiced preacher ventured into the political arena, denouncing the Medicean regime in Florence and, when Alexander VI ordered him to silence, turning his holy wrath on Rome. He insisted that the pope 'was not a Christian and has no faith of any kind' and he called for a general council that would depose the debauched leader of the Church Catholic. As we saw, he paid for his temerity by being burned at the stake as a heretic in the Piazza della Signoria in 1498.

Whatever stance Europe's leaders took on the moral and spiritual issues of their day, they were by definition *political* figures, able to effect change only through political means. Most of them were genuinely committed to some measure of reform and appointed senior advisers (like More) able to develop and implement policies designed to purge and resuscitate church life. Nowhere was this more true than in Iberia. In Spain Catholicism was on a roll. After the union of the kingdoms of Castile and Aragon by the marriage of Ferdinand and Isabella (1469) the Christian North redoubled its efforts against Islamic Granada. The *reconquista*, which was completed by 1492, took on the nature of a crusade – against Jews as well as Muslims. The Inquisition was a politico-religious tool wielded by the hands of a regime determined to concentrate all power in its own hands. It was fortuitous that the emergence of Spain as a monolithic continental power coincided with the European discovery of the Americas, of which Spain was well placed to take full advantage. With papal blessing colonising expeditions were despatched from Seville armed with the Cross and the sword. Their instructions were to bring all the 'inferior' peoples they encountered under the sway of Holy Church. What Spain accomplished in the West, Portugal emulated in the East and Pope Alexander III obligingly divided between the two kingdoms all newly conquered heathen lands (Treaty of Tordesillas, 1494). And at home the monarchs took seriously their responsibility to purge their national churches of error and dubious practices.

This did not just mean consigning hundreds of heretics to the flames or even setting up draconian 're-education' programmes. In Spain authority was invested in a remarkable churchman passionately committed to reform. The career of Francisco Jiménez de Cisneros (1436–1517) bears some similarities to that of Thomas Wolsey in England. Jiménez was a scholar who began royal service as confessor to Queen Isabella and rose to be first minister of Spain, wielding considerable power in church and state. As Archbishop of Toledo (1495) and cardinal (1507) he set about ridding the Spanish church of abuses. His determined rooting out of moral transgressions among the monastic orders and the parish clergy provoked a clerical revolt and four hundred priests actually fled the country. He welcomed all that was 'safe' in humanism and realised the importance of raising educational standards among the clergy. With his own money he founded the University of Alcalá and made provision for the teaching of Greek and Hebrew. He sponsored one of the major scholarly accomplishments of the age, the Complutensian Polyglot, a version of the Vulgate Bible published with the Greek and Hebrew texts and a new Latin translation in parallel columns. He composed a catechism for use at parish level and instructed his clergy to preach and teach the Holy Scriptures. These reforms did not silence all traditionalist and radical critics but they did demonstrate that a national church was capable of revival from within.

But only with strong political support. The difficulty faced by eager reformers is well illustrated by the fate of those in France who took on the forces of entrenched traditionalism. Here, too, there were senior clergy committed to bringing the church into the sixteenth century. Foremost among them was Guillaume Briçonnet, Bishop of Meaux (1472–1534). He was born to power and acquired piety. His father had been an influential member of the royal council and this ensured his own rapid rise through the ecclesiastical ranks. As a young man he embraced both intellectual humanism and devotional practices emanating from the Netherlands and Italy. At Meaux he gathered a group of reform-minded activists and, like Jiménez, he set about tightening up clerical discipline. He demanded regular, good-quality, Bible-based preaching from his priests and a high standard of personal morality. In this work he involved France's leading humanist scholar, Jacques Lefèvre d'Étaples (1455–1536), one of the most formative figures in European thought on the eve of the Reformation, and frequently hailed as a Protestant *avant le temps*.

He gained his reputation as a brilliant and independent thinker when teaching philosophy in Paris around the turn of the century and he influenced a whole generation of French scholars. His studies of the epistles of St Paul led him to question certain traditional doctrines and to assert that salvation is dependent on faith and not church rituals or good works. Such daring innovations brought down a storm about his head and he was obliged to leave Paris. The religious climate in Europe had become decidedly hotter and more tempestuous by 1523 when he joined Briçonnet at Meaux. There he published a French translation of the New Testament. (The Old Testament followed in 1530.) It was only thanks to the support of Francis I and, particularly, of his sister, Margaret of Angoulême, Queen of Navarre, that the reformers were safe. By this time the alarming influence of the radical monk Martin Luther was making itself felt in France and the traditionalists were on the warpath. When confronted by restrictions that were uncongenial or ideas that were unfamiliar they did not hesitate to cry 'heresy'. They took advantage of the king's absence on campaign in 1525 to issue a ban against Lefèvre's books and to charge Briçonnet with championing unorthodoxy. Although any action was quashed on Francis's return and Lefèvre was appointed royal librarian at the royal chateau of Blois, the Meaux group had to be disbanded. The king's Italian ambitions required him to remain on good terms with the pope. He and his arch-rival, Charles of Spain, both wanted to be seen as champions of the church, as symbolised in their royal titles. French kings had long enjoyed the style 'Most Christian King' and Ferdinand of Spain had obtained from Alexander III the right to the hereditary title 'His Catholic Majesty'. The kind of reform Ferdinand had promoted in the 1490s was not possible a generation later without seeming to undermine the church. Francis's support for humanism was, therefore, henceforth muted. The reform in France petered out with Briçonnet mournfully contemplating the state of the national church and Lefèvre spending his last years in the remote Pyrenean kingdom of Navarre, far from the centre of power and influence.

In Germany the situation was more complex because 'Germany' itself was more complex. It was not, of course, a political entity at this time. It was a agglomeration of over a hundred kingdoms, dukedoms, archdioceses and free cities under the umbrella of the Holy Roman Empire. It is not surprising that the peoples of these little states had long been – and would long continue to be – engaged in a search for identity. When humanism made its appearance among them it almost inevitably became mingled with patriotism. The first eloquent spokesman of 'Germanism' was Conrad Celtis (1459–1508). This philosopher-poet studied the classics at Cologne and Heidelberg and spent time in Italy before becoming professor of poetry and rhetoric at Ingolstadt. He immersed himself in German history and culture and was appointed by Maximilian I as the empire's first poet laureate. Celtis looked back to a past, part historical, part mythical, in which German people had triumphed over Roman invaders and others who had assailed their borders from east or west:

Resume, O men of Germany, that spirit of olden times wherewith you so often confounded and terrified the Romans. Behold the frontiers of Germany: gather together her torn and shattered lands! Let us feel shame, yes shame I say, to have let our nation assume the yoke of slavery and pay tribute to foreign barbarian kings.[4]

He looked back with pride to Charlemagne, who, as the Byzantine Empire declined, had created a new Christian empire in the West, centred not on Rome but Aachen. Since then there had been frequent conflicts between popes and emperors over the leadership of Christian society north of the Alps. German princes complained at having bishops foisted on them by the papacy, of paying ecclesiastical taxes, of having important legal cases summoned to Rome. Beneath such political arguments lay racial prejudice. Germans held in contempt 'effete' Italians, while they were regarded by some beyond the mountains as boorish semi-savages.

A close contemporary of Celtis who also taught at Ingolstadt was Johannes Reuchlin (1455–1522). He was destined to suffer a long, debilitating conflict with the forces of reaction. Reuchlin, a leading member of the European humanist fraternity and friend of Erasmus, was the father of Hebrew studies in Germany. His work involved him in close contact with Jewish scholars and their writings. This got up the noses of the anti-Semitic lobby who were intent on destroying all Jewish texts. Inevitably, Reuchlin was denounced as a heretic and the imperial inquisitor, Jacob von Hochstraten, tried to put him on trial in 1513. The scholar was protected by his friends in high places but, terrier-like, Hochstraten persisted and took his case to Rome. Six wearying years later the persecutor secured a ban on Reuchlin's writings, which defended Hebraic studies. Only then was the great Hebraist allowed to spend his remaining months in untroubled obscurity.

If anyone had attempted to prophesy where the Reformation launchpad was likely to be they might well have identified Strasbourg. This fine free city, with its imposing cathedral, standing astride the trade routes between Germany, France, Italy and the Low Countries was a place where religion and religious debate flourished. As in England (and the pattern was the same throughout much of northern Europe) lay involvement in church life, organised by guilds, was enthusiastic and effective. It displayed itself both in support for traditional devotion and in dissatisfaction with the behaviour and privileges of the clergy. Here a German Bible was printed in the 1480s and the presses were kept busy meeting the demand for primers and tracts. When the church authorities tried to silence the cathedral priest, Matthias Zell, by denying him the use of the pulpit, the carpenters' guild made a new pulpit so that he could continue to teach the evangelical doctrine which was attracting crowds of more than 3,000. That was in the 1520s but the foundations of the challenging new preaching had been laid by humanist scholars in the preceding decades. It was here that Sebastian Brant had written his *Ship of Fools*, and a local Franciscan, Thomas Murner, poured forth a series of tracts verbally flaying the clergy between 1509 and 1515. But, by then, Johann Geiler von Keysersberg, the 'German Savonarola', had been entertaining cathedral congregations with his trenchant demands for reform, accompanied by homely illustrations. Geiler was one of those early reformers who (like Colet and More) held back from the logical consequences of the new preaching. He denied, for example, that the laity should have access to vernacular Scriptures. But he was unremitting in his denunciation of clerical abuses and even delivered a series of sermons based on Brant's *Ship of Fools*.

Reading the extant works of prominent scholars and ecclesiastics concerned about the state of the church it is obvious that several of them were very conscious of walking on eggshells. The corruption emanating from Rome had reached such proportions that it could not be ignored, but how could it be attacked without undermining the very fabric of western Christendom? When the Emperor Maximilian sought support from the humanist scholar Jakob Wimpfeling in his quarrel with Julius II, Wimpfeling responded by denouncing the pope's interference in German church and state affairs, including the trafficking in indulgences. But he also expressed his concern at the rising tide of popular discontent and warned, 'It would not take much for the Bohemian poison to penetrate our German lands'.[5] He was referring to the century-old schism caused by the reformer Jan Hus, whose teaching had permanently divided the church in Czech lands and resulted in sporadic outbreaks of bloody violence.

As in England, so in Europe we can observe the existence of several strains of spiritual intensity. They seem to have been particularly prominent in the Low Countries and the Rhineland. It was at Windesheim, near the great Hanseatic trading centre of Zwolle, that Thomas à Kempis wrote his reflections on the holy life, *The Imitation of Christ*. It was one of those rare books which struck such a common chord that it became and remained a bestseller. As we have seen, it was one of the first devotional manuals to be printed in the mid-fifteenth century and it was still being read avidly throughout northern Europe, in various translations, eighty years later. It advocated an interiorised, cross-centred faith which valued but was not dependent upon rituals. Indeed, Brother Thomas warned against a pseudo-religion which set great store by pilgrimage, veneration of saints and other conventional practices. The true believer should rather meditate on the life of Christ and seek to follow his example. Thomas was one of the advocates of the New Devotional System, the *devotio moderna*, which originated from the teaching of Geert Groote at Deventer in the 1380s. In some respects the *devotio* was a conventional reformist agenda; but it insisted that monastic vows were not necessary for those seeking the path of holiness. Lay people, gathered in open communities or even pursuing worldly avocations, could follow a spiritual regime. As we have seen, Henry VII's mother was one of the many lay people who took up this individualistic form of piety.

More, Cisneros and Wimpfeling were among a minority of discerning observers who sensed anxiously the potentially dangerous spiritual and intellectual 'gases' which were seeping into the atmosphere. Most church leaders were either less sensitive to the changing mood of the times or complacent about their ability to control dangerous elements. Heresy was nothing new and they had always been able to rely on the support of secular rulers in bringing subversive elements to heel. All members of the ruling class were as one in their fear of anarchy and it was easy to convince princes that men who rejected the teaching of the church would also turn on their divinely appointed masters if their unorthodoxy was not nipped in the bud. To prove their point they could instance such lamentable sagas as that of the 'Drummer of Niklashausen'.

In 1476 the Bishop of Würzburg had to deal with an outburst of charismania in Saxony. At the centre of it was Hans Beheim, known to his devoted followers as the Drummer of Niklashausen because of the way he attracted attention to his field preaching. With the backing of some renegade Dominicans, Beheim proclaimed a vision of the ideal society. Central to his muddled message was the eradication of all social and religious distinctions. Since God regarded all men equally, everyone from the pope and emperor downwards was to be brought to the same level of wealth and status. This gospel, appealing as it did to popular resentments and jealousies, attracted a huge following. When the bishop had Beheim arrested, a crowd estimated at twelve thousand marched on his palace to demand their leader's release. The authorities made short shrift of the Drummer, who was rapidly condemned and burned. Just another ignorant rabble-rouser suitably disposed of? An unpleasant case swiftly done and dusted? Not quite. What the bishop and his minions were faced with – and what they should have taken more notice of – was the aftermath of the Drummer's execution. He was hailed as a popular martyr and the church where he had done much of his preaching became a shrine. The only way unauthorised pilgrimage was eventually stopped was by rasing the building to the ground.

It was in another Saxon town that the spark was eventually struck which ignited the combined gases of popular discontent, bold intellectual enquiry and spiritual fervour. Wittenberg was a rather dreary town on the middle Elbe, trying to create for itself a new, more glamorous identity. Archduke Frederick the Wise, ruler of this part of Saxony, had a good grasp of PR. His castle overlooking the town housed an enormous and growing collection of holy relics. Curiosity and the availability of indulgences to pilgrims brought thousands of paying tourists to Wittenberg every year. This was a valuable stimulus to trade and urban expansion but it did little for Wittenberg's kudos. What Frederick needed was something that would make a cultural statement. In 1502 he founded a university there. Not just any university. The archduke was not interested in creating a pale imitation of the old – and old-fashioned – schools of Heidelberg, Leipzig or Erfurt. His would be a centre of progressive learning, the first German university fully to embrace humanism. This, he reasoned, would attract avant-garde teachers and students eager to explore the latest intellectual fashions. Among those recruited to the staff in 1511 was a young Augustinian monk from Erfurt who had recently gained his doctorate and who had already earned himself a reputation for being forthright and unconventional. His name was Martin Luther.

Luther's superiors at Erfurt were glad to see the back of him. His stoutly held views and uncompromising delivery had created bitter divisions in the cloister and his removal to the Wittenberg backwater was probably meant to 'cut him down to size'. What it actually did was transfer a brilliant researcher and teacher from the big pool of Erfurt University, where Luther had to swim with other academics some of whom were his intellectual equals, to the little pool of Wittenberg University, where he soon became 'king pike'. Luther was a magnetic and engaging personality with a fine brain and an excellent grasp of language (both Latin, employed in his lectures, and the vernacular, which he used for preaching). In a short space of time students were flocking to Wittenberg to enrol in the classes taken by this celebrity. All of this, naturally, delighted Frederick the Wise.

What the elector could not know was that this talented theology lecturer would put his university on the map in a quite unprecedented way. Luther would make little Wittenberg the epicentre of an ideological earthquake which would devastate the whole of western Christendom. Beneath his boisterous bonhomie Brother Martin was a disturbed soul wrestling with spiritual questions which would give him no peace until he had found answers. What he was searching for was certainty – the conviction that on that awesome day of judgement when the souls of men were to be segregated into those worthy of eternal bliss and those destined for the fiery maw of hell he would find himself among the former. Years of monastic seclusion, self-examination, regular confession and ascetic rigour did not bring him the assurance he sought, as he later wrote:

> I used to be contrite, to confess and number off my sins, and often repeated my confession ... but I always doubted and said, 'You did not perform that correctly. You were not

contrite enough. You left that out of your confession.' The more I tried to remedy an uncertain, weak and afflicted conscience with the traditions of men, the more each day found it more uncertain, weaker, more troubled.[6]

Luther had been sent to Wittenberg to lecture on the Bible and he came to the task with that fresh approach, unencumbered with centuries of politically correct interpretation, which Renaissance scholarship fostered. It was while studying Paul's Epistle to the Romans that he experienced a classical evangelical conversion. By a flash of insight he realised that what the apostle was saying was that no one could ever justify himself to God by good works and self-abnegation.

I began to understand the justice of God as that by which the just lives by the gift of God, namely by faith, and this sentence, 'The justice of God is revealed in the Gospel' [Romans 1: 17], to be that passive justice, with which the merciful God justifies us by faith . . . This straightway made me feel as though reborn, and as though I had entered through open gates into paradise itself.[7]

It is difficult for most of us to understand the emotional release which enabled the introspective, depressed, perfectionist monk to leap off the treadmill which had enslaved him for much of his adolescent and adult life. From henceforth *sola fidei* (faith alone) would be the rock he clung to and the banner beneath which he marched against the forces massed against him.

His life-transforming experience probably came to him in 1512 and he spent the next five years grappling with its implications. If the startlingly simple truth of justification by faith was God's chosen vehicle for universal salvation why was the church not proclaiming it from the rooftops? His research coincided with a fresh initiative by Pope Leo X who was raising funds ostensibly for the rebuilding of St Peter's. He launched a vigorous indulgence campaign, sent out agents to hawk indulgence certificates and made commercial deals with local and national rulers who sponsored the campaign in return for a cut of the profits. To many in Germany this seemed to be just another example of Vatican money-grubbing, so when a challenge was offered to the indulgence scam there were ears willing to listen to it. It was Martin Luther who issued that challenge in October 1517 by inviting a public debate on the indulgence traffic. It took the form of 95 theses or propositions for discussion by theologians and Luther posted it on the castle church door in Wittenberg. By then he was already a celebrity whose fame was extending throughout Germany and beyond. His Ninety-Five Theses were no sooner propounded than they were being copied and sent home in students' letters. It was but a short step to their being published by printers ever on the lookout for sensational copy.

What Brother Martin was doing, he claimed, was protecting the leadership of the church from individuals and activities that were undermining it. By inviting Pope Leo to distance himself from the unsavoury indulgence traffic he was providing the opportunity for the authorities to rebut the scandalous criticisms that traffic was provoking. For example, people were, not unreasonably, demanding, 'If the pope has the power to free souls from purgatory, why doesn't he just do it out of love, rather than for cash?' But Luther's persistent, scholarly mind went beyond such arguments. He probed deeper into the theology on which the indulgence system was based. He concluded that it was unscriptural. A person's eternal destiny was determined by the response of repentance and faith to God's love, *in this life*, and not by what the pope claimed to be able to do for him/her post mortem. But there was another important aspect of Luther's protest: it was couched in language ordinary people could understand. Exposure of abuses of the penitential system had been around for decades but much of it had been within the confines of the international intelligentsia. When Erasmus had made fun of corrupt popes and lazy, luxury-loving shepherds of the Christian flock this had been for the delectation of fellow scholars, who smiled knowingly and did nothing. When the Ninety-Five Theses were translated into vernacular languages – as they soon were – unsophisticated groundlings tended to respond differently. They felt that they had been conned by spiritual superiors more interested in their purses than their souls. Many of them had long suspected this. Now, a clever Christian scholar had come forward offering chapter and verse for rejection of what was being done in the pope's name.

Over the next three or four years the Luther affair became the leading *cause célèbre* throughout Europe. Basically three things happened: 1. As opposition increased, Luther became more stubborn and more extreme. The religious establishment scorned his request for a debate; the demand from Rome was that Brother Martin must recant his heresies and submit to the pope. As the ecclesiastical juggernaut bore down on him Luther became a prophetic 'brick wall'. Convinced now that he had been called to summon the church back to allegiance to the Bible, the certainty grew in him that the pope was not part of the solution; he was the major part of the problem. In a word, he was Antichrist. In an amazing outpouring of books and pamphlets Luther drew logical conclusions from his understanding of Holy Scripture that threw sand into the complex theological mechanism of western Catholicism. There was, he insisted, no sacerdotal priesthood, no miracle of the mass, no purgatory, no array of seven sacraments administered by priests. (He reduced the number to three and, later, to two – baptism and Holy Communion.) 2. Luther's ideas spread; his books and pamphlets were widely read in universities, religious houses and even royal courts; his more contentious observations became the subject of alehouse gossip; those with grievances against the clergy began to look to him as a champion; and the new heresy began to feature in sermons preached by its friends, including many priests, monks and friars.

They were furious because they felt they had been cheated by a papal plot to pervert their own ministry, and that in their

turn, their own blindness had led them to cheat their flocks.
They wanted to convey their anger to ordinary people so that
they might be saved from Hell, and the centre of their message
was to expose the complicated mechanism of the confidence
trick: the Mass and the industry of intercession for the dead.[8]

3. Church authorities, rudely awakened to the danger, deployed
all their forces to silence this latest heretic. In 1521, when other
attempts to extract a recantation from him had failed, Luther
was summoned to appear before the Emperor Charles V at
Worms. This confrontation was supposed to be a showdown at
which the troublesome monk would be either cowed into
submission or handed over to the church courts for trial and,
inevitably, death by burning. The plans of his enemies were
dashed for two reasons. First, Luther refused to budge. 'Unless
I am convicted by Scripture and by plain reason,' he told the
assembled dignitaries, 'I cannot and I will not recant anything,
for to go against conscience is neither right nor safe.'[9]

In those few words we have the nub of what the Reformation
was all about: 1. The Bible is the supreme authority for all
Christians, including the pope; 2. They may read it for themselves, bringing their own reason to bear upon it, without relying
solely on what their priests and bishops tell them about it; 3.
Individual conscience is to be their guide, even if it leads them
to go against church teaching. For the full Lutheran mini-mani-
festo we should add what he had already established, that
salvation depends on faith rather than good works.

The second reason why Luther was not silenced for such
stubborn and monumental heresy was that he was defended by
his prince. Frederick had his pet lecturer 'kidnapped' and
hidden away in a secret location to protect him from the baying
wolves of Rome. While he was a guest in an electoral castle
Luther embarked upon what would be his major contribution to
the Reformation – the translation of the Bible into vigorous
modern German. This was meant to enable the ordinary
Christian to base his/her faith on the sacred text. It was the

liberty Erasmus had called for. But Luther had another motive: he wanted to vindicate his own controversial position on doctrinal issues. In effect, he was saying, 'If you think I'm a heretic, check out my writings for yourself against the word of God.' Bible translation was the most powerful weapon in the armoury of Luther and all the radicals who would follow him; it laid down a challenge everyone could understand: 'Do you believe the pope or the sacred Scriptures – you can't believe both.' Luther's was a very rational religion. Starting from the premise that people should only be required to believe what is clearly stated in the Bible, he followed a logical path through all contemporary doctrine and practice and rejected everything which did not pass the scriptural litmus test. In later years, when he was confronted with the storm he had whipped up, he would respond, with some justification, 'It wasn't me; it was the word of God.'

The impact of the open Bible was staggering. Western Christendom was coterminous with Europe; the church, with its headquarters in Rome, gave it its structure. It seemed inconceivable that this basic fact of life could be denied. Over the centuries heretics had come and gone, making little impact. But now the very *raison d'être* of the pope and his minions had been challenged with reference to an authority that was older and more fundamental than the papacy itself. Not only that; thanks to the invention of the printing press, people could check for themselves the bona fides of the Vatican regime and the activities of their own parish priests. If such fundamentals were open to doubt, what might not be? Protestors now had 'holy' sanction for demanding redress of grievances that, hitherto, they had had to grin and bear. With the support of the Bible, society could be changed – violently if necessary. The mid-1520s were years of social upheaval on an unprecedented scale. Even Luther was alarmed by the furore that his rebellion unleashed. When he returned to Wittenberg in March 1522, he found the town in confusion with bands of image-breakers going round the churches and monasteries pulling down the symbols of the old religion. He managed to put a stop to the destruction there but was powerless to restrain hotheads in other towns. From the Baltic coast to the Alps iconoclastic acts were carried out either by undisciplined mobs or by workmen acting on the instructions of the municipal authorities. In the autumn of 1524 two churches in Riga were burned to the ground. In Braunsberg, near Danzig, the mayor led a band of citizens into the church to smash all the statues and deface the altars. In Zurich the council organised a public debate on the reformation of the churches, as a result of which it was decided to remove all the images in an orderly fashion and to whitewash all the walls.

With everything in turmoil it could only be a matter of time before political agitators began stirring up the people to throw off their shackles and challenge all forms of authority. The outbreak known to history (inaccurately) as the Peasants' War convulsed much of central Europe from the autumn of 1524 to the spring of 1526. It involved more than just the lowest stratum of rural society and it consisted of several unlinked outbreaks and so cannot be called a 'war'. It fell upon a land not unused to revolt caused by economic exploitation. The demands of the rebels varied from place to place and in some areas were couched in religious terms. Like violent malcontents of all epochs the rabble-rousers covered murder and pillage with the camouflage of high moral intent. Some bands marched under banners bearing such slogans as 'The Word of the Lord Abides Forever' and included among their demands the right to choose pastors who would faithfully preach the Gospel to them. The background to the risings was a fervid apocalypticism which gripped the populace in these years. Astrologers read calamity in the stars and fiery preachers prophesied the imminent *Dies Irae*. But this cannot be called a religious uprising. It was much too complex for that and it was uniformly denounced by Luther and other evangelical leaders. The end results were predictable. While some of the rebels were persuaded to lay down their arms and a few even gained some minor concessions, the majority were slaughtered in their thousands, fighting futilely against the pikes, muskets and artillery mustered by their social superiors. With hindsight we can discern this tragedy as a bloody side-show to the Reformation but contemporaries could not make this distinction. Catholic spokesmen pointed out that murder and mayhem inevitably resulted when traditional religious truth was rejected and Luther acknowledged that the Peasants' War had seriously set back the cause of the Gospel. Foreign rulers, like Henry VIII, whose thrones had not been shaken by the uprisings were not slow to draw the moral that those who sought to topple mitres and papal tiaras would not baulk at trampling crowns in the mud.

Another problem faced by the leaders of reform and eagerly exploited by their enemies was the fragmentation of the radical movement. Luther was not the only advocate of 'back to the Bible' reform. One member of the Wittenberg team who parted company with Luther was Andreas Karlstadt, a headstrong and violent revolutionary. He was not content to follow Brother Martin's advice to preach the word of God and let it do its own work. He spent years as a travelling preacher proclaiming a gospel of social levelling and urging individual churches to go their own way. In Zurich, Ulrich Zwingli, a priest in the Grossmünster, was preaching a message similar to Luther's – similar but not identical. The two men disagreed on issues such as the destruction of images and the nature of Christ's presence in the Holy Communion. In Strasbourg, with its long tradition of religious questioning, the irenic Martin Bucer emerged as the leader and devoted much time and effort to consulting with Luther and Zwingli, attempting in vain to heal the breach between them. Suddenly there were evangelical preachers, teachers and pastors everywhere. Once the unsayable had been said – about the pope, the sacramental system, the indulgence racket, idolatrous worship, the sacrifice of the mass and other vital aspects of medieval religion – hundreds of scholars, monks and priests who had long entertained secret doubts on such matters came out of the closet and used their influence to spread the evangelical message – or, rather, variants of the evangelical message.

But it was not only men with some degree of theological training who took it upon themselves to proclaim the new doctrines. Zealous laymen also felt the call to educate their neighbours. Their reasoning was simple: if the Bible was now freely available and if it was no longer necessary to undergo years of university study in order to understand it, why should men who had been liberated by it not proclaim its truths to those still stumbling around in spiritual darkness? But matters did not end there. Women – and for traditionalists this must have been the clinching proof that the reform movement had run well off the rails – were now to be found among the ranks of preachers and teachers. One of the bestsellers of 1523–4 was a compilation of letters by a Bavarian lady written to a variety of aristocratic and municipal authorities, urging them to sponsor evangelical truth and put an end to clerical abuses. She demanded that ecclesiastical 'fat cats' should be called before secular courts, 'to see how much they really earn and ensure that the money is put to some communal use, so that the poor man is not quite so overburdened. Stop absentee priests with benefices that they never visit, filling them with foolish vicars who know nothing!'[10]

As diplomats, scholars, merchants and ecclesiastics returned across the Channel from visits to various European centres they brought back stories of conflict and confusion; of Habsburg and Valois armies battling for territorial gain; of civil unrest; of cities and principalities adopting evangelical reform; of monks and nuns abandoning their vocations; of men and women burned for heresy; and churches despoiled of their ancient 'idolatrous' treasures. It only remained to be seen whether England could remain aloof from all this mayhem.

Chapter 4

Divorce and Divorce

Henry VIII, the king who inherited the English crown at the age of seventeen in 1509, was monumentally self-confident. Seldom, if ever, did he doubt that he was destined for greatness. We can discern three robust streams which fed into his egotism. He had been spoiled and indulged throughout his childhood. Brought up by his mother with his two sisters, he had become accustomed to taking a lead role in day-to-day affairs. The earliest glimpse we have of him is as an eight-year-old receiving a visit from Thomas More and his friend Desiderius Erasmus and engaging these members of the international intelligentsia in debate. He was not the slightest bit overawed. He showed off his command of Latin and then discomfited the Dutch celebrity by demanding a gift of some original composition. He may have been only a child with, as yet, a mere smattering of book-learning but he was also a prince and he was not going to allow his visitors to forget it.

The second influence on the young Henry was his favourite reading matter. He delighted in histories and romances such as Froissart's *Chronicles* and Thomas Malory's *Le Morte Darthur*. These told thrilling tales of knightly derring-do and exalted the code of chivalry. Henry VII had encouraged such studies and deliberately fostered the fiction that the House of Tudor was lineally descended from the Once and Future King. This was why he named his first son Arthur and ensured that he was born at Winchester, the ancient British capital. With the death of his elder brother in 1502 young Henry became convinced that the historic mantle had fallen across his own shoulders. It was his destiny to emulate the deeds of the Round Table knights and lead England once more in the foreign adventures which had brought glory to the nation in the days of Henry V. He delighted in the martial arts of the tiltyard with their prancing horses, gaudily blazoned heraldic trappings and adoring women watching from the gallery (activities restricted by his over-protective father). He yearned for the day when he would resume the Hundred Years War and win his own Agincourt-style victories.

Thirdly, Henry's heroic predilections were buttressed by religious conviction. He firmly believed that he had been singled out for divine favour. This, too, was impressed upon him by his upbringing. The court routine presided over by Henry VII and his awesomely pious mother, Lady Margaret Beaufort, was a devout one. The old king and his parent never ceased to thank God for what, to their thinking, could only be described as miraculous deliverance. Over and again, throughout several years of perilous exile, Henry Tudor had avoided capture by Yorkist agents and survived the diplomatic intrigues that had sought to have him returned to England. God had granted him victory at Bosworth in 1485 and, subsequently, foiled the repeated attempts of rebellious subjects to remove him in favour of one or other Yorkist candidate. The House of Tudor had been God's chosen instrument to bring peace and prosperity to a land sundered by decades of civil war. There was no reason to suppose that, after 1509, he would abandon his new champion, Henry VIII. On the contrary, still greater blessings lay in store for Tudor England.

Early military setbacks had done little to dent this conviction. The brash young king had shouldered his way into the continental rivalries of the Habsburg and Valois monarchs – with distinctly inglorious results. Land and sea campaigns between 1512 and 1514 had cost the treasury a great deal of money for which there was little to show. Henry had made common cause with wily fellow monarchs – Ferdinand of Spain and the

Emperor Maximilian – who had used him for their own purposes and then, when his usefulness was at an end, had ditched him and left him out of their treaty negotiations. In 1520 Henry attempted to dazzle Europe with a spectacular diplomatic production, a summit meeting with Francis I of France at the Field of Cloth of Gold. This eighteen-day extravaganza of banquets, tourneys, masques and exchanges of costly gifts on the most elaborate 'stage set' Europe had ever seen was an attempt to keep England at the high table of diplomacy and impress Henry's fellow monarchs with his splendour, wealth and culture. But, if he was going to profit in any significant way from the rivalry between Francis and the new emperor, Charles V, he had to commit himself militarily to whichever side seemed most likely to come out on top. In 1523, another English army was shipped across the Channel and marched bravely towards Paris, only to limp back to the coast weeks later, its tail between its legs. When, in 1525, the government tried to raise more money from a war-weary populace there was firm resistance in several areas and a distinct threat of civil unrest. This, occurring at the same time as the Peasants' War in Germany, was enough to persuade Henry to back down. In order to avoid losing face, he blamed the debacle on his minister, Cardinal Wolsey, declaring that it had never been his intention to burden his people with more taxes.

War and diplomacy were not the only vehicles Henry used to stamp his personality on the continental scene. Rivalry with his brother monarchs extended to matters cultural. Francis I possessed a library which was the envy of other courts and Henry strove, unsuccessfully, to compete. But his books were not just for show. He liked to think of himself as keeping well abreast of the latest developments in the intellectual world. He was a genuine fan of Erasmus and when the Luther debate began he took a keen interest in it. Initially the German monk seemed to be just another scholar calling for reform, something with which Henry was, broadly, sympathetic. He had always regarded himself as a bit of a theologian. The devotional life of his father's court had been quite intense and had certainly rubbed off on the young prince. Wherever he was staying – whether in his main palaces of Greenwich or Richmond, or in the growing number of houses he acquired to accommodate himself and his entourage during his summer progresses – he attended mass daily, sometimes more than once. Such devotion did not, of course, involve any participation: Henry simply heard the duty priest recite his office. Often the king used this respite from his more energetic pursuits in the hunting field or tiltyard to dictate letters or attend to other business in his closet (a room overlooking or adjacent to the altar). But in the privacy of his chamber or in company with his religious advisers he read theological books and his close attention to their argument is proved by the annotations in his own hand which can still be seen in surviving volumes from the royal library. So it was inevitable that he should follow the controversy stirred up by Luther.

It soon became obvious that Luther had gone much further than the sophisticated scepticism of Erasmus. Possibly the royal secretary, Thomas More, pointed this out to the king. However the truth dawned on him, Henry was genuinely shocked by the radical theology coming out of Saxony. He was determined to demonstrate his own orthodoxy. In 1521, Thomas Wolsey, Henry's principal minister, organised a spectacular bonfire of heretical books in St Paul's churchyard and similar events were staged in the university cities. But the king decided that he should personally enter the literary fray with Luther. The German reformer had attracted considerable response from prominent theologians but Henry's *Assertio Septem Sacramentorum* (*Defence of the Seven Sacraments*) was by no means a lightweight contribution to the debate. He had help from Thomas More but there is no doubt that the main thrust of the argument was the king's own. He quoted effectively from the Fathers to support the official doctrine of transubstantiation (the theory that bread and wine were literally changed into the body and blood of Christ by virtue of the priest's words of consecration). He asserted that masses for the dead were effective and he rejected Luther's central tenet that only faith was necessary for salvation. The king was not entirely driven by defence of the truth; he had a secondary motive for publishing the *Assertio* and for sending copies to all the royal courts of Europe. It was, in part, a PR exercise. Henry was promoting his image as a defender of orthodoxy. His book was particularly intended to impress the pope. The *Assertio* was dedicated to Leo X and a sumptuously bound copy was carried to Rome for presentation to his holiness. Henry's agents were specific in their request for what the king would consider a suitable reward. He wanted the pope to confer a title upon him. If the King of Spain enjoyed the honour of being addressed as 'His Catholic Majesty' and the King of France was entitled to call himself 'His Most Christian King', Henry saw no reason why he should not be similarly honoured. His strategy worked: Leo bestowed upon Henry VIII the title 'Defender of the Faith'.

At the dawn of the 1520s there were, therefore, no obvious signs of any cracks in the fabric of the English church and state. We have to look deeper – quite a lot deeper – to discern the points of stress that were actually there. The fact that Wolsey was able to stage an impressive bonfire of Lutheran books as early as May 1521 is evidence of the large number of such recently published books that must have been already circulating in the capital. They had been sniffed out by the bishops' heresy hounds and we may be sure that many undesirable volumes had gone undetected. Clearly, there were enough customers for this explosive literature to make it worthwhile for merchants to bring it into the country despite the opposition of the bishops and their henchmen. So who was reading these books and how far inland had they penetrated from their ports of entry?

In general terms the answer to those questions must be 'members of the intellectual elite'. The works of Luther and other continental reformers which had created such a stir on the other side of the Channel were of obvious interest to those who wanted to keep up with the latest theological thinking. This category embraced students at Oxford and Cambridge and the inns of court, university teachers, graduates among the secular priesthood and in the religious orders, as well as laymen with a grasp of Latin and a penchant for sensational reading matter. Any educated person with an enquiring mind would want to know what all the fuss was about. The exciting, challenging ideas of Erasmus had found many English admirers and it is not difficult to understand that these new books would be eagerly snapped up by the same clientele. (Critics of the reform later claimed 'Erasmus laid the egg that Luther hatched.') It is significant that the reformist teaching – which we must begin to label 'evangelical' – was soon being contemptuously dismissed by traditionalists as 'new learning', a description equivalent to the modern term 'trendy'. Lutheran ideas appealed to those who liked to think of themselves as au fait with the latest intellectual fashion and particularly to young readers who enjoyed cocking a snook at the establishment. Cardinal Wolsey tended to adopt a lenient attitude towards them, in the conviction that they would soon grow out of their fascination with Dr Luther.

But many of them did not grow out of it. Quite the contrary. As with Luther, several earnest students passed from diligent enquiry to intellectual conviction and thence to spiritual transformation. One such was Thomas Bilney, a diminutive but intense Cambridge scholar. His enlightenment resulted from reading words of St Paul; not, as was the case with Luther, from the Epistle to the Romans, but from I Timothy, 1: 15 in the Greek of Erasmus's version: 'This is a faithful saying and well worthy to be received, that Christ Jesus came into the world to save sinners, of whom I am chief.' The result was a classic evangelical conversion experience. Bilney 'felt a marvellous comfort and quietness, insomuch as my bruised bones leapt for joy'. The convert could not keep his newfound faith to himself; he shared it with a circle of fellow students who met, according to one tradition, at the White Horse Inn, close by King's College. The similarity of Bilney's discovery and the doctrine set forth in Lutheran books studied in secret by members of the group was obvious and its truth seemed borne out by the change which had come over Bilney. So great was his earnestness that he ventured to cross swords with one of his arch-conservative teachers, Hugh Latimer, and completely won him over. The two became firm friends and would go together to the foul-smelling lazar house to minister to the incurables, and to Cambridge jail to preach to the prisoners and urge them to amend their lives in conformity with the Gospel. That gives some indication of the impact made by the new learning and it is not surprising to discover that the Cambridge circle widened steadily as more and more people were infected by justifying faith. Several men whose names were to figure prominently in the story of the Reformation emerged from the Cambridge of the 1520s. We shall meet in later pages the likes of Robert Barnes, Stephen Gardiner and Miles Coverdale. In Oxford the emergence of heretical cells was accelerated by Dr Thomas Garret who, by 1526, was vigorously distributing banned books among the students. According to Dr John London, Warden of New College, Garret's underhand technique was simple but effective: 'he sought out all such that were given to Greek, Hebrew and the polite Latin tongue, and pretended he would learn Hebrew and Greek and bought books of new things to allure them . . . and secretly did distribute them among his acquaintance in sundry colleges and halls.'[1] These early evangelicals were not student revolutionaries, out to tear down the walls of English Catholicism. They were in many respects conventional churchmen. Wolsey was initially disposed to be lenient towards them. As an Oxford scholar himself, he was sympathetic towards academics who explored new ideas. However, many of them inevitably drew radical, logical conclusions from their reading.

'Nests' of evangelicals were not only to be found within the London–Oxford–Cambridge triangle. In 1521, Bishop John Longland of Lincoln undertook a purge of heretics throughout his extensive diocese and their connections further afield. The persecution netted fifty unorthodox believers from Buckinghamshire and Berkshire to London and even as far as

Norfolk. The victims were sentenced to do public penance and were then incarcerated in various religious houses where they were subjected to 'correction'. Six lapsed and were burned. The hodge-podge of heretical opinions these people were charged with embraced such old Lollard shibboleths as rejection of prayers to saints, condemnation of religious images and denial of the priestly miracle in the mass.

As the Reformation unfolded there was to be considerable overlap between this religious viewpoint and that gained from exposure to the teaching of continental reformers, but was there any close connection between Lollardy and Lutheranism in the 1520s? Was the ideological ground ploughed and harrowed by the spiritual heirs of John Wycliffe in readiness for the seed sown by the radical theologians of Wittenberg, Zurich and Strasbourg or were the sophisticated intellectuals of Oxford, Cambridge and London unaware of or uninterested in the conventicles of the humble 'known men'? These questions have been the subject of much debate among historians and will reappear later (see P. 125). For the moment we must simply note that these two types of challenging scepticism and unorthodoxy were to be found throughout a wide area of southern and eastern England.

One fact about which there is no dispute is the momentous impact of a new English translation of the Bible. This was the work of William Tyndale, an extremely gifted graduate. (He was or became fluent in Spanish, French and Italian and had also mastered the ancient Greek, Hebrew and Latin tongues.) He had studied at both universities and by 1522 was working as a tutor in the employ of a Gloucestershire gentleman. This brilliant scholar seems to have been something of an intellectual snob. He certainly upset several of the local clergy whom he dismissed as obscurantist dolts clinging unthinkingly to their old-fashioned ideas and totally ignorant of the new theological understanding of the humanists. Tyndale was particularly convinced by Erasmus's suggestion that every literate Englishman, irrespective of rank, should be able to read the Bible in his mother tongue. He felt that God was calling him to undertake the task of translation himself. Like a good Catholic he resorted to the religious establishment for support in this pious venture. He singled out the newly appointed Bishop of London, Cuthbert Tunstall, as a patron. It seemed to be a very sound choice. Tunstall was a scholar of distinction with clear humanist leanings and a friend of Erasmus. He was also influential at the royal court, was a man 'on the up' and had served on diplomatic missions. But he was no friend of the open Bible. His travels on the continent had brought him into close contact with some of Luther's disciples and he regarded them as a great danger to the church. He urged Erasmus in the strongest possible terms to disassociate himself from the German reformer and he was vigilant in his efforts to rid his own diocese of heretical literature. He turned a deaf ear to Tyndale's request.

It is impossible to nominate a particular single moment as marking the 'start' of the English Reformation but if we were to draw up a shortlist of turning points this would be very near the top. Spurned by the bishop and probably nursing some uncharitable thoughts about the religious establishment, Tyndale settled in the City, and here he fell in with one of the more remarkable organisations in the whole Reformation story. The Christian Brethren were a group of passionately dedicated, Bible-based, evangelical businessmen. Because their activities were, perforce, clandestine we know tantalisingly little about them but we should not underestimate their importance. They were the *practical* link between continental reform and English lay piety. Members of the intellectual intelligentsia exchanged revolutionary ideas in elegant prose. International religious communities provided an important conduit for the dissemination of the new learning and this had some influence on popular preaching. But if the Reformation was to put down deep roots in English soil it would be vital for books promoting evangelical propaganda to be placed in the hands of influential lay people who might respond to it. There was only one group of men who could fulfil this role – men with continental contacts, financial clout, and independent, entrepreneurial spirit. Such were the Christian Brethren.

They were prominent members of the London mercantile community whose commercial activities brought them first-hand experience of white-hot evangelicalism. In Germany and the Netherlands they talked with trading partners on fire with zeal for the new order being proclaimed by Luther and others. In towns and cities where the reform had taken over they attended churches where novel forms of worship had become the norm. Back in London they met ships' captains and German merchants so committed to the spread of 'true religion' that they ran real risks to import contraband books. This little group of respectable English merchants caught the evangelical fervour. Some were City aldermen. Many had aristocratic and court connections. Their status offered them an element of protection from inquisitive episcopal agents and trouble-making neigh-bours. However, discretion was vital. The authorities kept a close eye on people suspected of being tainted with Lutheran heresy. In 1526, Thomas More organised a raid on the Steelyard, the London headquarters of the German Hanseatic League, and several books were confiscated. More was particularly sensitive to the influence of these foreigners; his own son-in-law, William Roper, had been won over to evangelicalism, probably as a result of his contact with the Germans. Roper may stand as an example of the dilemma facing enthusiastic converts. He could not keep his convictions to himself. His new faith was too exciting and, moreover, he believed that spreading the word of salvation by faith only was a responsibility incumbent upon all true believers. But to 'bear witness' was to court persecution. Roper argued with his father-in-law and attracted attention by his unguarded tongue. He was summoned to appear before Wolsey and only avoided serious consequences because the cardinal treated him leniently for More's sake. Other members of the shadowy evangelical underground were fully aware that they, too, courted danger. The fate of Richard Hunne (see above, p. 61), scarcely a decade earlier, lingered long in the corporate memory of the mercantile community. It is therefore significant that the Christian Brethren were prepared to risk money, reputation and even their own personal safety to spread the good news. For years they engaged in a cat-and-mouse game with the bishop's men reminiscent of the Scarlet Pimpernel's fictitious escapades. They smuggled into the country reformist literature and they smuggled out of the country suspected heretics the authorities were searching for. In the 1520s England's capital was, thus, home to a closed and close radical community of 'known men', not dissimilar to the Lollard cells in their adherence to an alternative religion. But, while the Wycliffite networks were largely made up of artisans whom the authorities had long experience of interrogating and, when necessary, punishing, the Christian Brethren were a new phenomenon – men of substance who could not easily be brow-beaten, leading members of City churches to whom the clergy looked for patronage, who traditionally maintained shrines and chapels and who contributed generously to the upkeep of the fabric. It was with a prominent member of this community – Humphrey Monmouth – that William Tyndale became involved soon after his arrival In London.

Monmouth was an alderman and a wealthy member of the Drapers' Company who lived in a fashionable quarter of the City close by the Tower and convenient for the Custom House, through which all woollen exports had to pass. He was a neighbour of Sir John Alleyn who was Lord Mayor 1525–6. He worshipped, along with many other prominent citizens, at All Hallows, Barking, an impressive church which, thanks to its proximity to the Tower, had royal connections. Monmouth was a generous patron of scholars and outwardly gave the impression of being a cultured, orthodox Catholic with an interest in humanist writings. However, he was one of those who, as early as the Hunne case or before, had 'begun to smell the Gospel'.[2] He agreed with Erasmus that the Bible should be available in English and when he met Tyndale it seemed a laudable gesture to offer the young scholar financial aid. So, at least, he would later justify himself. But Monmouth knew perfectly well that to support the unauthorised translation of Scripture was a serious offence carrying the direst penalties and his claim to be innocent of heterodoxy must be taken with a good measure of salt. His official story when under investigation in 1528 was that he had heard Tyndale preaching at All Hallows and had offered him a chaplaincy to say masses for his deceased parents. But that would scarcely explain why Monmouth, in 1524, financed a journey to Wittenberg for Tyndale to meet Luther.

Exactly when the translator's religious conversion occurred we cannot know but occur it certainly did. In later writings he referred to the proper response to the Gospel as 'to turn in the heart and mind . . . to be converted and turn to God with all the heart, to know his will and live according to his laws'. The effect of such a response was such 'that maketh a man's heart glad and maketh him sing, dance and leap for joy'.[3] There can be no doubt that he was describing his own experience. Throughout his sojourn in London Tyndale had been working at his translation and by the time he left for the continent he had virtually completed the New Testament. The principal reason for the trip, organised by Monmouth and his friends, was to find printers courageous enough to risk setting the text and canny enough to avoid detection by the authorities. The work was begun in Cologne but papal snoopers discovered the place and Tyndale had to gather up the pages already printed and make good his escape on a river boat up the Rhine to Worms, a city that had gone over to the reform. Here the books were printed, bound and despatched to England – all 6,000 copies of them.

The fact that Tyndale's backers were prepared to commission such a large print run and face the difficulties of shipping the books and arranging covert distribution, not to mention the risk of prosecution in the church courts, is striking evidence of their dedication and also of the numbers of potential customers who were eagerly awaiting the illicit New Testaments. Thomas More was amazed – and horrified – at the persistence of the colporteurs and their financiers. More, himself an elected member of the Mercers' Company, found it difficult to understand how indifferent the Brethren seemed to be to the profit motive:

> though [the books] cannot be there printed without great cost [nor] none there sold without great adventure and peril, yet they cease not with money sent from thence to print them there and send them hither by the whole vats full at once, and in some places looking for no lucre, cast them abroad by night . . . I was by good honest men informed that in Bristol . . . there were of these pestilent books some thrown in the streets and left at men's doorways by night that where they durst not offer their poison to sell, they would of their charity poison men for naught.[4]

Clearly, what the distributors were involved in was not so much a business as a mission. Some enthusiasts actually bankrupted themselves by distributing the word of God below cost or for free. John Barret, once a prosperous dealer in jewellery and precious metals, fell into poverty and had to be bailed out by the Goldsmiths' Company, and the mercer Thomas Keyle had to seek charity from his livery company because he had beggared himself in the service of the Gospel. George Parker spoke for many of the brethren when he boasted that he and his colleagues had placed 'two thousand books . . . against the blessed sacrament in the commons' hands, with books concerning diverse other matters, affirming that if it were once in the commons' heads they should have no further care'.[5] For such men, what was at stake was nothing more nor less than God's truth, concealed from the people for centuries but now available to everyone who could read the Bible or have it read to them. Their enemies held that the Scripture was a mystery to which only the priesthood were permitted access in order to expound it to the laity. This became within the astonishingly brief space of a few months the central argument of the English Reformation. The line of division was clear and indelible: one was for either the Bible or the church (i.e. the papal hierarchy).

That clash of irreconcilable principles explains the vitriolic tone the debate assumed. Not content with providing a good vernacular text, Tyndale embellished subsequent editions of his New Testament with Lutheran glosses underscoring the doctrine of salvation by faith only and identifying the pope as Antichrist. Thomas More took up the cudgels against him and there ensued a violent pamphlet war between the two protagonists. Here were two educated men, reared in the courtesies of scholarly debate, abandoning themselves to the exchange of insults and the calling down of divine anathemas on each other. They were not alone. Others entered the lists on both sides and, as we have seen, Henry VIII was one of those who contributed to the war of the books.

But by the time Tyndale's second edition came out in 1526 the debate had moved on. The divisions in continental evangelicalism were manifesting themselves among the London brethren. Some, dubbed 'sacramentaries' by their accusers, followed the teaching of Zwingli on the Lord's Supper. Luther maintained a sacramental doctrine not greatly different from that of Catholic tradition. He took literally the words of Jesus recorded in the gospels, 'this is my body', 'this is my blood', and affirmed that some kind of change occurred in the consecrated elements. Zwingli insisted that the words of institution should be understood figuratively; the Lord's Supper was a memorial service and the bread and wine were symbols – powerful, but symbols nevertheless – designed to call to worshippers' minds the sacrifice of Calvary. This understanding of the ancient mystery was similar to the rationalism of many Lollards, whose anti-sacerdotalism prompted them to deny not just the priestly function of the clergy but also the miracle of the mass.

While his people were pondering such theological profundities, the king had other problems to worry about. Catherine of Aragon, his wife of seventeen years, had failed in her primary duty. She had not produced a male heir. A succession of miscarriages and infant deaths had left only one twig on the Tudor tree, the Princess Mary. Now in her forties, Catherine was past child-bearing. She and her husband were sleeping apart and the marriage was, to all intents and purposes, over. Henry had come to the throne firmly believing that God had chosen his dynasty to restore peace and stability to England after decades of civil war. To pass the crown to a daughter would be to invite a return to the chaos of the conflict between the houses of Lancaster and York. There were still potential pretenders around and Henry remembered only too clearly the struggles his father had had to maintain his hold on power. That he had been able to do so was, as far as Henry was concerned, proof of God's favour. Why, then, had God abandoned the Tudors? Why was Henry unable to fulfil his prime responsibility of ensuring the continuance of the dynasty? It grieved the king's conscience sorely to think that everything he was striving for – England's position in Europe, the purity of the English church, national peace and prosperity – would come to naught if he was succeeded by a woman. Even if baronial anarchy was avoided, the queen would, inevitably, marry and England would become part of a foreign empire. Henry told his faithful Cardinal Wolsey that his conscience was deeply troubled by all this. Earlier scholars were inclined to take with a pinch of salt the image of an agonised Henry, wrestling in prayer over his fate and reluctantly impelled to contemplate the formal dissolution of his marriage in the interests of the dynasty and the nation but the balance of opinion now is that the king was quite sincere in his concern.

It was Henry who 'discovered' what had upset his relationship with God: he had married the wrong woman. Catherine had, formerly, been the wife of Prince Arthur, Henry's elder brother. After Arthur's death, Henry had stepped into his shoes – and his bed – for reasons of state. Since this involved marriage within the prohibited degrees, it had been necessary to obtain from the pope a dispensation from canon law. What Henry now 'discovered' was that, in granting the dispensation, Julius II had flown in the face of Scripture. Leviticus 20: 21 stated, 'If a man marries his brother's wife it is an act of impurity; he has dishonoured his brother. They will be childless.' It must have been with a deep sense of relief that the king made this 'discovery' and he turned to his religious advisers for confirmation that his understanding of the Levitical prohibition was correct. Most of them, of course, backed the royal theologian. In fact, Henry's exegesis was flawed but that does not matter; the important point is that he firmly believed it. Having stated it, he stuck by it doggedly. The way out of his problem was, in his eyes, blindingly obvious: what one pope had mistakenly done, another pope could undo. There was nothing unusual about seeking a papal annulment of his marriage. Popes were quite used to obliging royal personages in such matters – for a fee. In 1498, Louis XII had obtained a dispensation to void his marriage so that he could marry Anne of Brittany for dynastic and political reasons. Closer to home, in 1527 Henry's own sister, Margaret, Queen of Scotland, received Clement VII's permission to divorce her second husband. But Henry's luck was completely out.

Henry's future – and England's – was decided by two historic and dramatic foreign events. The Lutheran revolt was one. The sack of Rome was the other. Clement was in no position to grant Henry's request because, in the latest round of Habsburg–Valois competition for control of Italy, he had backed the wrong side. In May 1527, messengers went galloping along the roads of Europe bearing the most sensational and shocking news. The Christian Emperor, Charles V, had sent a motley army of Spaniards and mercenaries to besiege the eternal city. Information arrived home in dribs and drabs from the agents Wolsey had sent to Rome to attend to what came to be known as the king's 'Great Matter'. None of it offered any encouragement. Tearing open one despatch, this is what Henry's minister read:

> What Goths, what Vandals, what Turks were ever like this army of the Emperor in the sacrilege they have committed? Volumes would be required to describe but one of their

misdeeds. They strewed on the ground the sacred body of Christ, took away the cup and trod underfoot the relics of the saints to spoil [i.e. purloin] their ornaments. No church nor monastery was spared. They violated nuns amid the cries of their mothers [i.e. mother superiors], burnt the most magnificent buildings, turned churches into stables, made use of crucifixes and other images as marks for their harquebuses. It is no longer Rome but Rome's grave.[6]

The pope and his entourage sought refuge in the Castel Sant-Angelo and later fled to one of Clement's up-country residences. From there he had to negotiate with the emperor. There was even some talk of him suffering the humiliation of being summoned to Madrid. All in all, he had far more important things on his mind than the English king's matrimonial problems. But what was worse, from Henry's point of view, was that Clement could not afford to upset Charles, who was now in effect his master. Since Charles was Catherine's nephew, family pride was at stake but there were also political implications which determined him to oppose the annulment of the royal marriage. Henry's queen was a valuable Habsburg agent and a means of influencing English policy. Charles, therefore, made it clear that Clement would grant Henry a dispensation at his peril.

By now, Henry was even more deeply emotionally involved. He had fallen in love with Anne Boleyn, one of his wife's ladies in waiting. She must have seemed to him (or he may have persuaded himself that she was) an answer to prayer. She was young, healthy and intelligent. She was no great beauty but what she lacked in physical attributes she more than made up for in personality. She was the sort of woman who made all heads turn when she entered a room and several men about the court were smitten with her. That fact alone was enough to stir Henry's competitive spirit. He warned off all potential rivals and decided that Anne would make an ideal queen. She certainly had the accomplishments necessary to enable her to preside graciously over the court. More importantly, there was no reason to suppose that she would not be able to bear children. Henry, therefore, determined to marry her as soon as the formality of his divorce had been disposed of. He was not, as Catholic historians have traditionally suggested, simply in the grip of lust. Nor was he the frustrated victim of a scheming woman intent of bartering her sexual favours for a crown. Anne certainly declined to become Henry's mistress but Henry was just as intent on marriage as she was: it was the only way he could secure a legitimate male heir. The trouble was that his divorce from Catherine had ceased to be a 'formality'.

The king's Great Matter turned the 1520s into an agony for all concerned. Catherine fought tooth and nail to maintain her own position and that of her daughter. She consorted with the imperial ambassador to ensure that Charles V remained her champion. Anne saw her youth slipping away without the consolation of marriage and children. She accused Wolsey, who was in charge of negotiations with Rome of dragging his feet in his inadequate efforts to secure the divorce. Wolsey (who had been made a cardinal in 1515) intrigued with increasing desperation to achieve the outcome his master wanted, rightly fearing what would happen to him if he failed. At one point he made a thinly veiled threat to the pope which, in the event, proved prophetic: 'The king is absolutely resolved to satisfy his conscience; and if this cannot be done he will of two evils choose the least and the disregard for the papacy must grow daily, especially in these dangerous times.'[7]

Clement dillied and dallied, watching the diplomatic situation closely and reluctant to offend either of the great monarchs concerned. Charles remained as obdurate as his uncle and, in an effort to divert attention from the Sack of Rome, portrayed Henry as a weak king controlled by a minister (Wolsey) who was in the pay of France. This accusation had some potency after January 1528, when England joined with France in declaring war on the emperor. Henry turned this way and that for support in his campaign. Sometimes he trusted Wolsey's strategy; at others he went behind the cardinal's back, sending personal messengers to Rome and hopelessly confusing the progress of his case. And there was one more party which became increasingly involved in the affair – Henry's subjects. In every alehouse and market people eagerly exchanged salacious gossip about the royal 'goings-on'. Public opinion was divided and often became mixed up with religious prejudice; Catherine representing traditional religion and Anne the new learning. Most people felt sympathy for Catherine and Mary and regarded Anne as a malicious home-breaker.

Clement eventually agreed to send one of his cardinals to London to adjudicate the Great Matter in tandem with Wolsey but it was August 1528 before Lorenzo Campeggio set out from Rome and even then he managed to make the journey to England last nine weeks. Procedural haggling and deliberate prevarication by Catherine's representatives ensured that the investigation proceeded at snail's pace throughout the ensuing winter and spring. Then, in June 1529, matters took another turn disastrous to Henry's cause. Charles won a victory over his enemies at Landriano and this was followed by a reconciliation between him and Clement. The pope's options were now drastically reduced. He sent word to England that he had decided to hear the case personally in Rome. That meant that Henry or his proxy would have to appear as a supplicant at the papal court.

The king's desires had been frustrated, his wishes successfully opposed and his person humiliated – all experiences to which he was not accustomed and to which he was not prepared to submit. This explains why he was now disposed to listen more sympathetically to the ideas being noised abroad by reformers and even heretics. He had, albeit unwittingly, already torn a leaf from Luther's book. By taking his stand on the text in Leviticus against the papal dispensation he had implied that an individual's interpretation of the Bible was more authoritative than papal diktat. Now he found in the latest radical literature teaching that seemed to offer sound theological justification for taking a firm attitude against Rome.

The temperature of the debate was rising as more and more writers explored the implications of evangelical doctrine and applied it to the issues of the day. The Sack of Rome had a galvanic effect on many evangelicals. They saw it as a divine judgement on the 'scarlet woman', the new Babylon, as Luther described the papal city. Several felt emboldened to join the print war against the coven of Antichrist. Tyndale, now firmly ensconced in Antwerp, was working on the Old Testament but also becoming adept at evangelical polemic. After his bitter exchange with More he turned his attention to what he claimed was the usurped authority of the clergy. In *The Obedience of a Christian Man* (1528) he proclaimed that persecution marked out the godly minority just as surely as it identified the majority enslaved by papal falsehood:

> the pope's doctrine is not of God . . . and seeketh nothing but
> the possessions of the world, and authority in the world, and
> to bear a rule in the world; and persecuteth the word of God,
> and with all wiliness driveth people from it . . . yea, curseth
> them and excommunicateth them, and bringeth them in
> belief that they be damned if they look on it . . . and moveth
> the blind powers of the world to slay with fire, water and
> sword, all that cleave unto it.[8]

Tyndale declared that all kings were appointed by God and that it was the duty of all subjects – laity and clergy – to obey them. The pope and his minions should have no part to play in the temporal rule of states. 'Is it not a shame above all shames and a monstrous thing that no man should be found able to govern a worldly kingdom save bishops and prelates, that have forsaken the world?'[9]

Ecclesiastical courts should confine themselves to resolving issues of canon law and not impinge on the jurisdiction of the civil law. Clergy should be just as answerable as their lay neighbours in the king's courts instead of having their cases tried in 'biased' ecclesiastical courts. Furthermore, it was an abomination for kings to be summoned to Rome to account for their actions. In the prevailing situation any condemnation of the 'pretended authority of the Bishop of Rome' was likely to go down well with Henry and when the *Obedience* was brought to his attention his reported response was 'This is a book for all kings to read.' But the treatise had a wider potential clientele among all those who smarted at the semi-independence of the clergy, the power of church courts and the siphoning off of money to Rome. Particularly, Tyndale gave voice to the grievances of common lawyers, who resented the intrusion of episcopal jurisdiction in what they considered to be civil cases. This was becoming a major issue and one which was dealt with in a keynote treatise published between 1528 and 1530 by the Warwickshire gentleman and lawyer Christopher St German. *Doctor and Student* was 'the most remarkable book relating to English law published in the Tudor period'.[10] One of the main subjects it covered was the connection between law and conscience. Churchmen insisted that because conscience and morality were the preserves of the church, which administered God's law, the spiritual courts were higher than the common law courts. St German refuted this, insisting that England's legal codes were derived just as much from the divine regulations as those of the canonists.

Tyndale was not the only author to write books for the home market from the safety of foreign havens where reformed regimes were in place. *Rede Me and Be Not Wrothe* was published in Strasbourg in the same year as the *Obedience*. The cloak of anonymity probably covers the identity of William Roye, a headstrong ex-friar who had given Tyndale some assistance with his translation, and John Barlowe, an ex-monk. *Rede Me* is a stinging verse diatribe against the prevailing ecclesiastical regime in England. Their authors spared no one in their 'exposure' of widespread corruption, indolence and false teaching. For example,

> Fryers? Nowe they are worst of all,
> Ruffian wretches and rascall.
> Lodesmen [i.e. 'leaders'] of all knavisshnes . . .

Lyvynge on rapyn and disceyte.
Worshipfull matrons to begyle,
Honourable virgins to defile
Continually they do wayte . . .
Of whordom they are the very baudes [i.e. pimps],
Fraudulent inventers of frauds
Provocacion vnto synne . . . [11]

The prime target for their ire was Cardinal Wolsey, the 'English Lucifer'. Wolsey became in the opinion of many, a resented anachronism. This prince of the church lived in aggrandising opulence, his renaissance palaces York Place and Hampton Court outdoing the splendours of Richmond and Greenwich. He was a glaring symbol – perhaps even a caricature – of the wordly prelate whose lifestyle was at stark variance from the image of Christian ministry presented in the *New Testament*. This was the man who, in the comman perception, 'ruled all' in the king's name.

One more pamphlet among the many illicit pieces of literature being composed by radical English authors in exile was Simon Fish's *A Supplicacyon for the Beggers*, yet another publication of the highly productive year 1528. Fish was a common lawyer currently resident in Antwerp. He, too, exposed the supposed venalities of the clergy but, more importantly, he went for the theological jugular of the old church. The secret of the vice-like grip the pope's minions had on the lives of ordinary people lay in the doctrine of purgatory. The only reason men and women paid for masses and bought indulgences was to provide ease for themselves and their loved ones from the unspecified torments of that shadowy pilgrimage from the grave to the portals of heaven. But, Fish expostulated, 'there is no purgatory'; it is unscriptural, a fiction 'invented by the covetousness of the spirituality'; it is nothing more or less than spiritual blackmail. This little piece of polemic made an impact out of proportion to its size or erudition. It spoke in language which resonated with ordinary people. The *Supplicacyon* of the title was an appeal from the poor folk of England to the king to free them from the financial demands of the clergy. Fish argued that Henry's subjects willingly paid their taxes because they knew that a beneficent king would spend the money wisely for the good of the nation. By contrast, the clergy based their exactions on a fraud and used the income to 'exempt themselves from the obedience of your Grace', to 'translate all rule, power, lordship, authority, obedience and dignity from your Grace unto them'.[12] Proof that this pamphlet struck home is provided by the fact that no less a person than Thomas More was provoked into writing a detailed refutation of it – the *Supplication of Souls*. He understood well how crucial Fish's arguments were and how vital it was to suppress them. Two eventualities must, at all costs, be avoided: the collapse of the entire penitential system which would follow if the king's subjects came to reject purgatory; and the undermining of the delicate church–state balance if the king came to believe that his power was being usurped by the priesthood.

For the moment there seemed to be no danger of that second nightmare becoming a reality. Henry showed no signs of erring from the Catholic straight and narrow. Nevertheless, the circulation of banned books among the free spirits of the court could not be prevented. In April 1529 Cardinal Campeggio grumbled in a report to Rome that Henry's courtiers were reading Lutheran books with impunity and Wolsey instructed Richard Sampson, Dean of the Chapel Royal, to carry out a purge of banned literature at court.[13] One reason why royal attendants were flouting church rules was that they enjoyed the support of the leading lady about the court and her inner group. Anne Boleyn was beginning to emerge as a friend of advanced thinkers. She was an intelligent and sophisticated woman with strong opinions who had made herself mistress of cultured court life during her teenage years. She had been sent by her family to be 'finished' in the entourage of the French king's sister, Margaret of Angoulême. That royal lady, as we have already noted, was the leading patroness of humanist and evangelical scholars, such as Lefèvre and Briçonnet. After her return to England Anne maintained her love of all things French and, in later years, she is known to have possessed French devotional writings and Lefèvre's Bible translation. In January 1530 one of her protégés commended her for her choice of reading matter, such as,

> approved translations from holy scripture, filled with all good doctrines; or equally other good books by erudite men, giving salutary remedies for this mortal life and consolation to the immortal soul. And chiefly I have seen you this last Lent . . . reading the salutary epistles of St Paul, in which are contained the whole manner and rule of a good life.[14]

By the time she became queen Anne was widely recognised as a protector and sponsor of evangelical scholars and preachers. For the moment, however, she had to be circumspect. Bible bashers were viewed with suspicion in the upper echelons of polite European society. By 1528 the Meaux group had been disbanded and one of Anne's favoured authors, Louis de Berquin, had been burned at the stake. Anne's royal lover certainly had a distinct animosity towards heretics and was disinclined to be instructed in matters theological by his womenfolk.

It was, therefore, courageous of Anne to draw Henry's attention to the works of the exiles. In 1528 she commended to the king's study Tyndale's *Obedience* and Fish's *Supplicacyon*. It may have been that an accidental discovery of the former precipitated Anne's approach to the king. According to a well-supported story, she ordered a copy of the *Obedience* as soon as it entered England. Having read it, she lent it to one of her attendants, Anne Gainsford. As the result of some horseplay it fell into the hands of the young woman's suitor, George Zouche. He was discovered reading the book by the vigilant Richard Sampson, who promptly confiscated it. When word got back to Anne Boleyn she had to act quickly before she and her friends could be denounced by the dean. She went to Henry, protesting at the indignity to which she had been subjected and demanding that he should obtain the restitution of her property. The king did as he was bidden but, naturally, wanted to know what all the fuss was about. This was Anne's opportunity to point out certain sections of the *Obedience* which emphasised the authority of kings and denounced the usurpations of Rome. Henry, as we have seen, was impressed with Tyndale's radical argument.[15] He even sent an invitation to the exile to come home and join the propaganda team which was canvassing support for the divorce. Henry also extended his protection to Fish, who returned to England at the end of 1529 and was unmolested, despite having been roundly denounced as a heretic by Thomas More.

The planting of new ideas in the king's mind has to be seen against the background of the faltering divorce campaign. Henry and Anne were both becoming extremely impatient with the non-progress of the cardinals' enquiry into the validity of the royal marriage. Anne especially had turned against Wolsey, convinced that he felt more loyalty to Rome than to the king. On occasions she was heard to lash Henry with her tongue on the not unreasonable grounds that the years of her prime were slipping away without husband or children to show for them. One such conversation reported by the imperial ambassador, Eustace Chapuys, referred to the potential threat Henry believed to be presented by Charles V. Anne was dismissive. 'He can do you no harm,' she said, adding that if the emperor mounted a military challenge the Boleyn family would, at their own cost, put 10,000 men in the field against him.[16] It was as well that this boast was never put to the test. However, the Boleyns were certainly very active in other ways to bring about that change in Anne's status which would make all their fortunes. Since it was increasingly unlikely that the pope would ever decide the divorce issue in Henry's favour, they were seeking means which would enable the king to proceed unilaterally.

They came up with two major initiatives based on the single premise that, to use the phrase that was to become the battle cry of the political Reformation: 'this realm of England is an empire'. In other words, the king was fully sovereign. He owed no fealty to any other human authority and recognised no jurisdiction, spiritual or temporal, as being superior to that of the crown. The Boleyns had their researchers trawl through all the old chronicles, the Bible and works of the church Fathers in search of arguments that could be made to support this assertion. The result was the hotch-potch of proof texts known as the *Collectanea satis copiosa* ('The Sufficiently Abundant Collections'). Henry received it gleefully and went through it, page by page, writing in his own marginal comments. He now had the support of respected antique authors; he did not need to rely on the backing of men tainted with heresy. From this point Henry's campaign against Rome assumed a new, grander appearance. No longer was it merely about untangling himself from an unwanted marriage; it was about his very identity as king. Just as his earlier military adventures had been based on his 'undoubted' claim to the throne of France, so his new mission was to rid his realm of interference by a corrupt foreign power and to purify the English church. And just as his old dreams of battlefield glory had been inspired by the glamorous narratives of Malory et al, so now he was buoyed up by the vision of holy kingship set forth in the ancient writings.

Yet, still he hesitated before the enormity of what he was contemplating. He urged Anne's supporters to explore the other alternative. This was the brainchild of the Boleyns' most important discovery. At Cambridge they had encountered a doctor of divinity and lecturer in theology by the name of Thomas Cranmer. In discussion the academic made the point that the legitimacy or otherwise of the royal marriage was a moral issue, not a legal one. Therefore, the men best equipped to pronounce upon it were not canonists, but theologians. Why not, he ventured, solicit the opinions of Europe's leading doctors of divinity? It was not a sensationally original suggestion but it was timely and when Cranmer's proposal was reported to Henry the quiet scholar found himself whisked out of his ivory tower and established at the royal court before he knew what was happening to him. Within months he was sent off with Anne's brother and father on a tour of leading universities to argue the king's case and collect the opinions of Europe's top theologians.

One ecclesiastic's sudden rise was accompanied by another's precipitate fall. Henry's claim to judicial independence from Rome had placed Wolsey in an impossible position. As Lord Chancellor he was head of the English judiciary. As papal legate he was the pope's representative and the guardian of the church's judicial system. His enemies now gathered like vultures to encompass his downfall. Henry, to do him credit, was reluctant to sacrifice the man to whom he owed so much. For months the cardinal's fate was uncertain. Then, in September 1529, Wolsey was indicted in King's Bench on a charge of *praemunire*. This was founded on an ancient, seldom-cited statute designed to deal with conflicts between royal and papal interests in the courts. It was now stretched to cover Wolsey's use of his legatine authority to adjudicate in certain specified cases against the interests of the crown. But the indictment also included the cardinal's promulgation of his legatine authority. It was not merely the *misuse* of papal authority that was at issue, but its very *existence*. Wolsey knew the score; he did not even bother to plead 'not guilty'. He was condemned, stripped of his office as Lord Chancellor and all his immense wealth was confiscated. He was ordered to take up residence in York, his own archdiocese (which he had never visited). No one in England grasped the immense changes to which the fall of Wolsey was a prelude but many must have looked back in later years to the public humiliation of the most hated man in England as the dramatic turning point of the nation's life. Thousands of spectators lined the river bank and thronged the Thames in boats and barges of every description to witness Wolsey's departure from Westminster. All London was in carnival for the event. Wolsey's ultimate end was an altogether more low-key affair. His enemies, ever fearful of the cardinal's possible reinstatement, dug up evidence against him of a suspected treason. He was ordered to return to London to face trial. But death spared him this ordeal; Thomas Wolsey breathed his last at Leicester during his journey south.

The Boleyn–Cranmer delegation returned from the continent with a useful dossier of opinions from leading theology faculties but Henry and his advisers wanted to be able to present an overwhelming case. This was vital in light of the draconian solution they now had in mind – cutting England adrift from papal obedience. In the continuing search for support Henry and his advisers looked to the great and good of the realm. A 'grand petition' in favour of the divorce was drawn up, supposedly signed by a representative body of top men in church and state. In fact, only eighty-two names were appended to the document and these belonged to men who had been handpicked by the regime. But one body which Henry believed he could rely on in the Great Matter was Parliament or, more specifically, the House of Commons. Its membership was largely made up of courtiers, lawyers, merchants and protégés of the nobility, men who, though not, as a body, subservient to the royal will, were opposed to the kind of clerical power that Wolsey had represented. In the autumn of 1529 writs went out for the summoning of a Parliament which Henry hoped (though at this stage only vaguely) would be useful in his overall strategy for the divorce. At the opening in November the assembly was informed that the fall of Wolsey had necessitated a comprehensive exploration of the laws relating to the position of the clergy.

Unfortunately for the king, the Commons house showed itself to be an unreliable ally. While the laity had several complaints to air about the clergy, they were by no means united in wishing to further the royal divorce. Several MPs were sympathetic to the cause of Queen Catherine, while those who were disposed to back the king were a motley crew of anti-clericals and evangelicals who could be 'managed' only with difficulty. Lords and Commons soon fell to squabbling. The lower house lost no time in pressing for a number of reforms concerning alleged clerical abuses. The Bishop of Rochester took up the cudgels on behalf of the church. 'My Lords,' he complained in the upper house, 'you see daily what bills come hither from the Commons house and all is to the destruction of the church . . . Now with the Commons is nothing but "Down with the church!" and all this me seemeth is for lack of faith only.' Bishop Fisher went on to prophesy the complete collapse of civil order if attacks on the privileges of the clergy were to be seriously entertained.[17] The leaders of the Commons were scandalised by the tone of this attack and protested to the king. Henry summoned Fisher and his allies to account for their behaviour. Wherever poor Henry looked he could see nothing but chaos: his life was being made a misery by his wife, his mistress, their friends at court, rival factions, the bishops, and radical reformers who were getting the bit between their teeth.

At court there was no longer a firm ministerial hand on the tiller. The royal Council was dominated by mediocre minds and riven by rivalries. As England entered the 1530s – arguably the most momentous decade in the nation's history – no one, least of all the king, knew what would happen. Two facts illustrate the confusion of these months. The first was the drafting of a draconian bill aimed at providing for the royal divorce, to be heard by one or both of the English archbishops. This detailed piece of proposed legislation outlined the action to be taken in the event of Rome responding by placing the realm under an interdict – a very real and, for most people, a very frightening possibility. Nothing came of this bill – for the time being. The second indication of confusion at the centre was the repeated prorogation of Parliament. Members were sent home before Christmas 1529 until the following Easter. Then recall was postponed until June, then to October and Parliament did not reconvene finally until January 1531.

Meanwhile nothing stopped the spread of evangelicalism. While courtiers hopped around nervously like cats on hot bricks, more and more people throughout the country were converting to the new learning and bishops were becoming more energetic in dealing with the contagion of heresy. About this time a new word entered the English language or, rather, a new, popular meaning was given to an old word – 'gospeller'. It was applied as a term of contempt to preachers (especially unauthorised preachers) of the new learning and to zealots who read the Bible to their illiterate neighbours. According to the New Testament, Jesus's final instruction to his followers before his Ascension was 'go and teach all nations' and St Paul declared, 'Woe is unto me if I preach not the Gospel.'[18] For many converts, proclaiming the good news was an imperative, a dominical command that could not be ignored. Lollardy had survived largely because its followers shared the Scriptures with their neighbours. It followed naturally that the new breed of evangelicals should do the same.

One of these eager proselytisers was a teenage girl by the name of Anne Askew, living beneath her father's roof at South Kelsey, on the edge of the Lincolnshire fens, and her story provides us with useful insights into how the new learning spread among the upper classes of society, reaching from the hotbeds of London, Cambridge and Oxford into the distant shires. Anne's father, Sir William Askew, was a prominent member of county society, a JP and a man who served on several royal commissions. He was among those chosen for the privilege of accompanying King Henry to the Field of Cloth of Gold in 1520 and he assiduously developed court connections. Askew kept himself well informed about events in the capital and when Thomas Cranmer, member of another prominent East Midlands family, was suddenly elevated to royal service, Askew obtained a place for his second son, Edward, as a page in the cleric's household. Sir William's oldest boy, Francis, had already encountered Cranmer, as a student at Cambridge while Cranmer was lecturing there. News reaching home from the university and London kept the family informed of the clashing ideas and beliefs that were causing such a ferment but the stay-at-home Askews were not ignorant of radical religious beliefs. Sir William had had his children (including his three daughters) well tutored. They could read English and, probably, Latin.

Some time in the mid-1520s a copy of Tyndale's New Testament found its way to the liberal household at South Kelsey Manor and made a particular impression on the middle girl, Anne. She took seriously what she saw as her responsibility to make the Gospel known and read the precious book to domestic and estate servants. This scenario can scarcely have been unique, though no other provincial gentlewoman was destined to make the kind of impact Anne Askew would make on the Reformation in England (see below, pp. 250f). Those captivated by the Gospel passed on the tidings in conversation with trusted friends and letters home to loved ones. In January 1536, Robert Plumpton, a student at the Middle Temple, exhorted his mother in distant north Lincolnshire (modern Humberside), 'I would desire you for the love of God, that you would read the New Testament, which is the true Gospel of God, spoken by the Holy Ghost . . . I write not this to bring you into any heresies, but to teach you the clear light of God's doctrine.'[19]

Hundreds of such transactions took place during the early years of the Reformation and, though we can never quantify them, we should not ignore them. A greater impact, however, was made by the professionals – priests, monks and friars; men with some theological training who had gone over to the radical camp and who spread their message in sermons, pamphlets and books. Before they knew quite what had hit them bishops were ready to grant preaching licences because of the dearth of parish clergy able to preach on a regular basis, and it was armed with episcopal permission that Thomas Bilney devoted his time and energy to hortatory tours in eastern and southern England. He succeeded in stirring up several hornets' nests. What particularly annoyed the ecclesiastical hierarchy, but also local guildsmen, was Bilney's denunciation of the externals of traditional religion. He spoke against the veneration of saints and relics, the pilgrimage industry and the maintenance of shrines and altars, all practices which had been the subject of Lollard invective. Several known men listened to him with approval. This is certainly an indication that native and imported heresies were converging but they never overlapped completely and the emerging evangelicalism would be a broad church.

It took several months for the authorities to respond to the mounting volume of complaints against Bilney and his preaching colleague, Thomas Arthur. This was partly because Wolsey had a fairly laid-back attitude towards heresy, especially as far as academics were concerned. He was prepared to allow latitude to scholars who, by definition, were involved in exploring and evaluating new ideas. Not until the late summer or autumn of 1527 were Bilney and Arthur apprehended on the orders of Bishop Tunstall and imprisoned in the Tower. Their trial lasted from 27 November to 7 December. It took so long because the prosecutors bent over backwards to secure recantations from the accused. Artisans and ill-educated 'bar-room theologians' received short shrift in the ecclesiastical courts and the populace was quite accustomed to the sight of convicted heretics 'bearing their faggot' in marketplaces or even, in the case of those who refused to abjure, being burned at the stake. But the bishops were reluctant to take extreme measures against these two men. They had become celebrities and Bilney, in particular, was recognised as a gentle, saintly character whose devotion and ascetic way of life evoked respect. 'Holy men' were always a source of embarrassment to the church hierarchy. At last, worn down by the entreaties of tearful friends, the accused abjured and were ordered to go in procession to St Paul's Cross, carrying their faggots on their shoulders, and remain standing before the pulpit throughout the sermon. Then they were to be imprisoned at Wolsey's pleasure. It was some time in 1529 before Bilney was released and returned to Cambridge. But he was a broken man. He was convinced that he had compromised his faith and denied his Lord. No one could comfort him or dissuade him from the desperate course on which he was now determined. This was to undertake another preaching tour in order to set right the wrong he had done. Like Jesus, he would deliberately 'go up to Jerusalem', knowing what would await him. He set out for his own county of Norfolk, preaching in the fields because the churches were now closed to him. The inevitable end came on 19 August 1531. Condemned as a relapsed heretic, 'Saint Bilney' (as fellow evangelicals were soon calling him) was burned to death in the Lollards' Pit at Norwich.

The story of 'Little Bilney' is important not just as a tragic tale, or as an example of the courage of Protestant martyrs. It points up the dilemma facing the defenders of traditional religion. When men of obvious intellectual and spiritual stature who enjoyed the respect and affection of their fellows were prepared to die for 'outrageous' beliefs, it might prove difficult to crush the new learning by the age-old intimidatory methods. Its devotees were popping up everywhere – in the royal court, the universities, the legal profession, Parliament, the London livery companies, the ruling families in the shires. The very leadership of society was infected with this disease. It was inconceivable that every prominent subject found guilty of heresy should be shut up in foul-smelling prisons or burnt at the stake in the full gaze of the lesser orders. And it was particularly difficult for members of the ecclesiastical hierarchy to launch a vigorous campaign against lay heterodoxy when they themselves were under attack as agents of a discredited papacy with which the king was at war. Small wonder that they began to panic.

That panic is seen most clearly in the career of the urbane, witty scholar now turned obsessed persecutor, Thomas More. After the fall of Wolsey Henry appointed More to succeed him as Lord Chancellor. It was the most unfortunate decision since Henry II elevated Thomas Becket to the same dignity. 'The clergy doth denounce them . . . the temporalty doth burn them. And after the fire of Smithfield, hell doth receive them where the wretches burn forever.'[20] Such was More's considered opinion of the fully justified fate of all those who defied the Church Catholic and he regarded the suppression of heresy as the most important aspect of his new job. This had become his overmastering passion. He confided as much when writing to Erasmus: 'I find that breed of men [heretics] absolutely loathsome . . . I want to be as hateful to them as anyone can possibly be.' There could be, he insisted, no question of compromise or of a softly-softly approach:

> I am keenly aware of the risk involved in an open-door policy towards these newfangled, erroneous sects . . . some people like to give an approving eye to novel ideas, out of superficial curiosity, and to dangerous ideas out of devilry . . . All my efforts are directed towards the protection of these men who . . . are seduced by the incitements of clever fellows.[21]

On his own authority More issued a list of banned books and demanded of all legal officers in secular courts that *as their first priority* they would seek out and bring to justice anyone suspected of erroneous opinions. The church courts might have their talons clipped but the new Lord Chancellor would make sure that the common law was even more ferocious. This secular inquisitor carried out his own examinations of suspected heretics. There were stories of him imprisoning men in his house at Chelsea, having them flogged and extracting confessions from them under torture. More denied such cruelties but he rapidly gained a reputation as a fanatical persecutor and the moderate legist Christopher St German upbraided him for his excessive zeal.

What particularly frustrated More was the uncertain stance of the king in matters of ecclesiastical discipline. Henry refused to be a slave to principle; personal interest always carried more weight with him than philosophical or theological dogma. Currently he was interested in anyone who might offer support in his Great Matter. In 1531 cautious negotiations were opened with the German Lutheran princes and, although Luther's refusal to back Henry's interpretation of Scripture over the divorce soured English relations with these rulers who had broken away from Rome, the diplomatic door was not closed. In the same year an arch-heretic fell into More's clutches – and was snatched out by the king. John Frith was one of the evangelicals in exile who had worked with Tyndale and he was a very effective controversialist. He was tracked down during a secret visit to England and examined by the Council. They made a list of his – manifestly unorthodox – opinions but, before any further action could be taken, Frith appealed to the king. Henry read the prepared list and noted with approval that the heretic denied the pope's sovereignty over the whole church. As a result Frith was dismissed with a caution. It may well be that Henry thought the able scholar might be persuaded to become a member of his propaganda team.*

So, as the new decade got under way, tension at the centre of national life reached almost unbearable levels. Two things were happening and intermeshing: religious revival and the final achievement of the king's divorce which inevitably involved another divorce, that of the English church from the church of Rome. In 1527 Bilney's colleague, Thomas Arthur, had prophesied that if he was martyred for the Gospel, seven thousand preachers would spring up in his place. In the event he could not face the fire and a clamouring army of evangelists did not emerge to continue the mission. But the numbers are irrelevant. Indeed, those who now identified themselves with the new learning took comfort from the fact that they *were* a minority. Luther had colourfully explained that his followers were guests at an inn whose keeper was a villain. Believers could expect nothing other than hardship in the kingdom of this world whose monarch was the devil. Moreover the true church was an invisible assembly of faithful souls known only to God and was certainly not coterminous with Christendom. Every burning, every imprisonment, every public humiliation of Christ's disciples, therefore, was taken as proof that his 'little flock' was in possession of the truth and that, by logical extension, the enemies of that truth were agents of Antichrist.

---

* Two years later Frith, on another visit home, was again apprehended. Because of the king's interest, More was obliged to handle him with kid gloves. It was only when Frith's obstinacy wore down Henry's patience that More was able to secure the heretic's conviction and execution.

The beleaguered leaders of the church strove mightily in a war on two fronts. They deployed their traditional arsenal against the growing number of heretics and they manned the ramparts to repel assaults on their independence and ancient privileges launched from the royal court and from Parliament. They now found themselves facing an intractable dilemma: the more energetically they tracked down heretics, the more disobedient sons they sent to the fire, the more resentment they stirred among the citizenry who, while not approving of heresy, were deeply troubled by the vicious and inquisitorial demeanour of their spiritual shepherds. No less than the evangelicals, the orthodox clergy were an embattled minority, determined to defend their understanding of Christian truth against the legions of the evil one. Only one event could have delivered them – Henry VIII's capitulation over the divorce. And that was never going to happen.

The 'formal' Reformation was on the point of being brought about by parliamentary statute and royal decree but, because it was very far from being a mere institutional change effected by bureaucrats and politicians, it is important to try to gauge the mood of the times. What were ordinary people thinking and feeling? Religious life in the country at large went its age-old way. Unorthodox opinions and complaints against the clergy there certainly were, but they were mere ripples on the surface of traditional observance and practice. Nevertheless there were sufficient prosecutions in all corners of the realm, noted in ecclesiastical court records or gathered later by John Foxe to indicate the existence of undercurrents of heresy. Thomas Bennet, a teacher, was burned in Exeter for putting up anti-papal posters round the city. When asked why he did not declare his opinions verbally, he reasonably replied that he would have been quickly silenced had he done so, whereas from his placards, 'many should read and hear what abominable blasphemers ye are and . . . might better know your Antichrist, the pope, to be that boar out of the wood, which destroyeth and throweth down the hedges of God's church'.[22] William Tracy, a

Gloucestershire gentleman and Member of Parliament, refused to follow the standard form when making his will, which would have left money for masses and called upon the saints to pray for him. Instead he affirmed his belief in justification by faith. After his death, this was brought to the attention of Convocation in London, which ordered Tracy's body to be dug up, as one not fit to enjoy Christian burial. The local authorities complied with the order but went one better; they had Tracy's remains publicly burned. The man's family (and, doubtless, his parliamentary colleagues) were incensed, appealed against this desecration and gained reparation to the tune of £300.[23]

The connection between Lollardy and the new learning has long engaged Reformation scholars. Was the 'English heresy' of Wycliffe's spiritual heirs a spent force by the 1520s or did it feed into and merge with the new insights coming from the continent? Persuasive answers to these questions must, unfortunately, rest on arguments from silence. There are very few documented examples of old Lollards morphing into new Lutherans. Writing a generation later, John Foxe was intent on demonstrating a connection in order to ward off the accusation of evangelical novelty.

> ... if they think this doctrine be so new that it was not heard of before Luther's time, how then came such great persecution before Luther's time here in England? ... the church of England hath not lacked great multitudes who tasted and followed the sweetness of God's holy word almost in as ample manner, for the number of well-disposed hearts, as now.[24]

Foxe was in no doubt that the same Gospel was professed by pre-Lutheran and post-Lutheran English Christians, but, then, he did have a case to prove.

Lollardy, as we have seen, was a coat of many colours and some overlap of its beliefs with the more sophisticated teachings of the continental reformers was inevitable. Anti-sacerdotalism, dislike of images and, above all, pre-eminence of the Bible were convictions common to both groups. However, some Lollards held extreme opinions and they were never united behind the central doctrine of justification by faith alone.

That said, it would be difficult to assert that the new learning had no appeal for minds already prone to scepticism and Bible-based convictions. If geographical distribution counts for anything it seems that Lollardy did provide a seed bed for the sowing of evangelicalism. The latter spread rapidly in the South East and the home counties. At Amersham Thomas Harding, who fell foul of the authorities in 1506 and 1522, was again in trouble in 1532 – this time for possessing Tyndale's New Testament. In 1527 two Essex Lollards bought a copy of Tyndale's book from the evangelical colporteur Robert Barnes. Such anecdotal evidence is too slight to build a case upon. It must also be admitted that the social framework of Lollardy had little in common with that of the intellectual elites of the universities, inns of court and mercantile communities which responded to the books coming from the continent. But that fact could be pressed into service to make a case for a significant overlap of the two groups: when scholars like Bilney went on tour with the Gospel what they had to say will have struck a familiar chord with some hearers and given a comforting intellectual endorsement to beliefs they had long held.

It was not only the radicals who were disturbing the king's peace. In Kent, a serving girl by the name of Elizabeth Barton drew crowds for several years by her charismatic ravings and supposed miracles. She prophesied horrific divine judgement would fall on the king if he did not abandon his 'whore' and convinced Warham and other leading churchmen that her revelations were genuine. It is significant that Henry did not order proceedings against the popular 'Holy Maid of Kent' until the summer of 1533 (by which time her prophecies had manifestly not been fulfilled). He was always cautious about public opinion and only when she could be thoroughly discredited by public trial and well-honed propaganda did he vent his anger against her. Elizabeth and her mentors were hanged, drawn and quartered as traitors the following April.

It was in the capital and its environs that controversy reached its highest temperature. London was atypical. As the legal, commercial and political centre of the nation's life it could scarcely be otherwise. One result of the general antipathy towards heresy was that many people who fell foul of the authorities or who feared that they might do so gravitated towards London. Here they might hope to be lost in the crowds or to be succoured by the Christian Brethren. Here they could attend secret Bible studies, listen to radical preachers, be provided for out of common funds, take refuge in the Brethren's safe houses, receive legal advice when called before the authorities or, if necessary, be smuggled out of the country. We may reasonably assume that the majority of religious radicals escaped detection.

Some were not so fortunate. They were apprehended, and in increasingly large numbers. Most of them abjured under pressure. Foxe listed forty-six who recanted between 1530 and 1532, when the persecution headed by More and Bishop Stokesley was at its height. This was only a fraction of the evangelicals in the City despite the fact that church leaders used every trick in the book to achieve their objective of showing that erring souls had returned to the truth. They employed torture, argument, imprisonment, false witnesses, informers and even ridicule. They knew the importance of spectacle and entertainment. When four penitents were paraded before the citizens on a November afternoon in 1530 they were made to ride the mile from the Tower to Paul's Cross sitting backwards on their mounts and festooned with copies of Tyndale's books which were then thrown onto a bonfire while the offenders were set in the pillory. Such displays not infrequently, as More admitted, represented a hollow victory for the accusers, for not all the heretics played fair. It was common practice for defendants to submit, carry their faggot and then continue as before – only more circumspectly. The lurid illustrations in Foxe's *Acts and Monuments* give an impression of a vindictive church using

execution as a standard response in dealing with obstinate heretics. The truth is that examiners used every effort to avoid the
final solution. They knew that they were involved in a battle for
the hearts and minds of the people. In this conflict reconversion
was more effective than annihilation. Propaganda triumph lay
in demonstrating that an erring son or daughter had been
restored to the bosom of mother Church. Several suspects were
left languishing (sometimes fatally) in dank prisons – out of
sight and out of mind.

But burnings there were. The place designated for them was
Smithfield, an open space outside Newgate and beside the
church of St Bartholomew. Its regular use was as a horse and
stock market. Every Friday all sorts and conditions of people
came there – farmers to sell pigs and cattle, gentlemen in search
of well-bred steeds, copers marketing stallions, geldings, unbro-
ken colts and amblers for ladies, young tearaways who raced
horses round the field for wagers, blacksmiths with harrows and
ploughshares to sell. In short, Smithfield was where town met
country. On other days of the week it was an area where the
citizenry took part in several forms of recreation – archery,
wrestling, tug-o'-war, casting the bar. But occasionally, and now
increasingly frequently, Smithfield offered spectators another
spectacle. On a November Monday in 1531 an ex-monk,
Richard Bayfield, was led across the field, laden in chains
towards the waiting pile of combustible material. Foxe, as usual,
revels in the detail:

> When the bishop had degraded him, kneeling upon the high
> step of the altar [in St Paul's], he took his crosier-staff, and
> smote him on the breast, that he threw him down backwards,
> and brake his head that he swooned; and when he came to
> himself again, he thanked God that he was delivered from the
> malignant church of Antichrist, and that he was come into
> the true sincere church of Jesus Christ, militant here in earth.
> 'And I trust anon,' said he, 'to be in heaven with Jesus Christ,
> and the church triumphant for ever.' And so was he led forth

through the choir to Newgate, and there rested about an hour in prayer, and so went to the fire in his apparel manfully and joyfully, and there for lack of a speedy fire, was two quarters of an hour alive. And when the left arm was on fire and burned, he rubbed it with his right hand, and it fell from his body, and he continued in prayer to the end without moving.[25]

Bayfield was one among many victims of a church hierarchy determined to meet this new challenge with old weapons. But they found themselves engaged in guerrilla warfare against an enemy who struck in unexpected places and employed unconventional tactics. Pulpit confrontations were becoming frequent. The most notorious was that involving Hugh Latimer. Since his involvement with Bilney he had emerged as the most gifted preacher of the day and one whose forthright denunciations of the papal regime earned him royal protection and the patronage of Anne Boleyn. During Lent 1533 he engaged in a series of sermons in Bristol. He was challenged by local priest, William Hubberdyne, who violently denounced Latimer in sermons of his own. Citizens turned out in force to hear the rivals thundering from their pulpits, a contest which ended with the death of Hubberdyne, whose pulpit collapsed as a result of his ferocious and athletic oratory. As well as questioning orthodoxy in sermons and books, the heretics operated an extremely effective fifth column of colporteurs and gospellers. They pinned inflammatory posters to church doors. They deliberately targeted members of the ruling classes. They indulged in dramatic, sensation-seeking demonstrations. In 1531, a German merchant, Jasper Wetzell, created a stir in Rood Lane, Billingsgate. The church of St Margaret Pattens was being completely rebuilt and, to raise funds, a rood (crucifix) had been erected in the churchyard at which people were encouraged to pray and offer money. Wetzell presented them, instead, with a sacrilegious spectacle. He mounted the cross and stretched out his own arms upon it. 'Don't offer your alms to this lump of wood,' he said. 'You might just as well offer them to me, for I can no more save

you than this idol can.' Images were causes of real offence to the
radicals and frequent targets of abuse. Seven years after Wetzell's
demonstration (for which he was examined and forced to abjure
by the Bishop of London) the rood of St Margaret Pattens was
smashed to pieces during the dark hours of one spring night.[26]
This, then, is the background to the legislative changes brought
in by what has come to be known as the Reformation Parliament.

As we have seen, that body was prorogued in December 1529
and remained so for more than a year while Henry and his
advisers busily gathered together every scrap of support for the
divorce that they could find and tried to decide how to exploit
it. It may be that Henry hoped that the mere threat of new legislation might frighten the pope into acquiescence. Alternatively,
the delay may indicate that the government simply did not know
how to proceed. Certainly, for the time being attention was
focused not on Parliament but on the church's parallel assembly, the Convocation of the southern province. This convened
in January 1531 in a mood of tense apprehension. It was known
that the government were considering ways of using *praemunire*
proceedings against the clergy, on the grounds that, by accepting Wolsey's legatine authority, they had been complicit in a
challenge to the Crown's judicial omnicompetence. Their anxieties were justified. The pope in distant Rome might be able to
defy the king of England but his representatives closer at hand
were about to feel the full blast of Henry's pent-up anger and
frustration. He began by imposing a massive fine to defray the
'great charges' he had incurred over the divorce. They demurred.
He was obdurate. Not only were they going to pay; he was going
to make them grovel. He attached further conditions to the
punishment. The most important was that they must acknowledge him as 'sole protector and supreme head of the Anglican
church and clergy'. It was the first time that the crucial title
'supreme head' had been mentioned and the gathered senior
clergy were not slow to realise its implications. They argued,
they wriggled, they squirmed, they had separate meetings with
the king and with members of the Council. For a week they

tried to avoid the abject surrender Henry was demanding. Eventually, the king accepted a face-saving modification; he agreed to be recognised as supreme head 'as far as the law of Christ allows'. Archbishop Warham and his men knew that the concession was meaningless; there was not one of them who could conceive of standing before the monarch and telling him that he had violated the law of Christ.

Parliament was left with little to do and members must have wondered why they had had to go to the expense of a long and fruitless stay in the capital. They were dismissed in time for Easter. Re-assembly was scheduled for October but, yet again, the summons was deferred until the New Year. These repeated stops and starts do not convey the impression of a government carrying out a clear strategy for reform, or even of a government with a clear vision of what it wished to achieve. Henry, of course, knew what he wanted but as long as Warham was primate there was no chance of bullying him into overriding the pope's decision to try the divorce in Rome. There seemed to be no escape from a stalemate that was frustrating for all concerned.

The impatience of the House of Commons took concrete form in March. They presented their inchoate grievances against the clergy to the king in the form of a petition, known as the Supplication Against the Ordinaries (i.e. the legal officers of the church). This document listed several practices laymen found oppressive but singled out for special mention officious heresy proceedings. The petitioners acknowledged that the dissemination of religious error had prompted the bishops to take firm action but complained that they had gone too far. They had devised canon laws which took no account of the liberties of the subject protected by the king's courts, framed them in Latin which most defendants did not understand, employed unjust inquisitorial methods and imposed harsh sentences out of proportion to the alleged offences. The laity, claimed the Speaker, Thomas Audley, in presenting the petition, 'were sore aggrieved with the cruel demeanour of the prelates and ordinaries, which touched both their bodies and their goods'.[27] Was this an independent action on the part of the Commons or were they set on by Henry and/or his ministers? Scholars differ on the point but what is clear is that the king was more than happy to entertain the complaint of the lower house. His own conflict with the senior clergy had become very personal. Only a few days before Warham had opposed Henry to his face in the House of Lords and Henry had raged at him with swearing and threats. He now referred the *Supplication* to Convocation and promised to be an impartial referee between the two parties. How sincere that offer was became clear at the end of April when Henry summoned a Commons delegation and handed them the clerics' reply. 'We think their answer will smally please you,' he suggested, 'for it seemeth to us very slender. You be a great sort of wise men; I doubt not but you will look circumspectly on the matter.'[28]

But the king and his advisers did not wait for members to debate the issues further. The government wove the Commons' complaint into the fabric of their anticlerical programme, which was, at last, taking shape. On 11 May Audley and his colleagues were once more back in the royal audience chamber to hear the king reveal something which he had just been 'surprised' to discover:

> we thought that the clergy of our realm had been our subjects wholly but now we have well perceived that they be but half our subjects, yea, but scarce our subjects; for all the prelates at their consecration make an oath to the pope clean contrary to the oath that they make to us, so that they seem to be his subjects and not ours.[29]

On the face of it this seems to be an attempt to egg on Parliament to propose legislation to curb clerical power so that Henry could claim that he was responding to the grievances of his people for his moves against the spiritualty, but in fact Henry had no intention of leaving the initiative with Parliament. For one thing, that body was by no means a tame instrument of the royal will. Only days before the Commons had discussed a motion asking the king to take his wife back. Henry was determined to proceed on his own initiative. He ordered Convocation to submit all canon law for review to ensure that it conformed to English common law and to pass no further laws without royal approval.

This was the turning point of the political Reformation. This demand would establish that Englishmen were not only free from papal jurisdiction but that, even within the realm, church law was subordinate to the king's law. The church would completely forfeit its juridical independence. Warham protested. He tried to bargain. But this time the king was in no mood even for a token compromise. He insisted on unconditional surrender and, on 16 May 1532, in a convocation session from which several members had absented themselves, the Submission of the Clergy was ratified. The following day Thomas More resigned as Lord Chancellor. It was not a gesture of protest and the timing was not of More's choosing but the event is significant. Without the unequivocal backing of church law his anti-heresy campaign would be considerably hampered. More feared for the future of the church and understood clearly that the Reformation had not yet run its course. Remaining in office would inevitably involve him in violating his conscience. From Henry's point of view the resignation of More, with whom he had long since fallen out, was the removal of one more obstacle from his path. But still that path was not clear. Still Henry did not have his divorce.

The ongoing crisis brought to the fore the most remarkable servant Henry ever found. Thomas Cromwell was a self-made man who had had a chequered career and ended up as Wolsey's right-hand man. It had seemed inevitable that he would fall into obscurity when the cardinal was disgraced. However, he managed to secure an audience with the king and, almost before royal councillors and courtiers realised what was happening, he became a familiar face around the court. It was Cromwell who took charge of the complex legal arrangements for the transfer of Wolsey's properties and enormous wealth to the Crown and this gave him frequent opportunities to express his own opinions on the crisis between king and church. Exactly what those opinions were at this stage of his career we cannot know but they so much impressed Henry that, in little more than a year, he had been appointed to the Council. By the middle of 1532 he was the leading member of that body. His entry to the corridors of power was as sudden as that of Cranmer and for the same reason: Henry recognised him as a man who could be useful to him.

But the most valuable ace Henry was now dealt was the death of Archbishop Warham in August 1532. This meant that Henry was free to fill the top job in the English church with a man of his choice. He chose Thomas Cranmer over the heads of all the senior bishops who might have considered themselves in the running for the position. Cranmer had shown himself to be a firm upholder of the divorce and that was all that concerned the king as he applied to Rome for the necessary papal endorsement of his candidate. Cranmer was no heretic but he was a questioning academic whose theological position was still undergoing development. His recent travels in Europe had brought him into contact with various leaders of the reform movement and their ideas were rubbing off on him. He had even secretly married a relative of a Lutheran pastor, which was strictly against the official rules of clerical celibacy. At Easter 1533, within weeks of his enthronement, he announced his intention 'to proceed to the examination, final determination, and judgement' of the king's Great Matter.[30] In fact, Henry, now sure of his ground, had already jumped the gun; he and Anne had been secretly married in January and by now she was pregnant.

Now that the situation had changed so drastically there was something for the government planners to get their teeth into. They could employ Parliament to provide the legislative buttressing of Henry's new position. This would demand a prodigious volume of legal paperwork. Fortunately for Henry he had on hand a man for whom such painstaking activity was meat and drink – Thomas Cromwell. It is no coincidence that it was precisely from the spring of 1532 that Cromwell began to receive perquisites that were tangible expressions of his growing importance. He was appointed Master of the King's Jewels in April, Clerk of the Hanaper of Chancery in July and Chancellor of the Exchequer in April 1533. To this portfolio of offices he added several others in ensuing years. His pre-eminence brought him a growing amount of private legal business and he also received payments from suitors who wanted him to use his influence on their behalf at court. He had already been allotted his own quarters in the royal palaces and he began to build himself a magnificent town house on Throgmorton Street, close by Drapers' Hall. He may be said to have 'arrived'. Such men do not lack for clients, protégés and 'friends' and Cromwell had a wide circle of people eager to be in his good books. He was extremely well known in the city among all sorts and conditions of its citizens. Some of them were Christian Brethren. Cromwell had dealings with these evangelical fifth-columnists in the course of his commercial and legal affairs and must have known that some of them held dangerous opinions. But how far did he share those opinions?

Like those of Cranmer and many other thinking people, Cromwell's religious ideas were developing in these years. There is a temptation to put labels on the prime movers of the Reformation age; they were 'Catholic' or 'Protestant', 'traditionalist' or 'radical', 'orthodox' or 'evangelical'. It is almost impossible to tell the story without, for convenience's sake, categorising the men and women who shaped events. The truth, of course, is that people changed. As they struggled with the implications of the new learning they moved along a road from medieval, official lexis and praxis towards full-blown biblicism – and it was a road with many byways. When he drew up his will in 1529, Cromwell used a conventional format which called upon the Virgin Mary and all the saints to pray for him and he left money for requiem masses. In the following year he reported to Wolsey that 'favourers of Luther's sect', were distributing 'pestiferous books' throughout the capital. Yet, by 1532, one of those same evangelical colporteurs was appealing to Cromwell for aid against the authorities, convinced that the minister would understand why he could not 'return again from Christ'.[31] Cromwell had little respect for lazy, arrogant or hypocritical clergy. When he was sorting out the affairs of the fallen cardinal in 1530 he railed against all the clerical hangers-on Wolsey was supporting instead of providing adequately for his devoted lay servants and he shared the resentment felt by most of his fellow common lawyers at the powers of ecclesiastical courts. Anti-clericalism certainly made up one strand of Cromwell's religious convictions – but only one.

When Martin Luther had his historic confrontation with Charles V at Worms in 1521 he famously declined to recant any of his written words unless he could be convicted of error 'by Scripture and *plain reason*'. The italicised words are important because, once the authority of the pope had been replaced by the authority of the Bible, all the dogmas that had been developed to support the institutions and teachings of the medieval church came under scrutiny. Many participants in the Reformation struggle (probably including Henry VIII) did not realise this. They used biblical proof texts to demonstrate the venality of the royal marriage or the deception practised by the papacy in claiming secular power but they did not grasp that the written word of God presented a wholly different way of salvation to that offered by the church's sacramental system. Men of intellectual stature, such as More, Cranmer and Cromwell, saw with growing clarity the implications of Bible-based religion. They lived, worked, reasoned, debated and reflected in the spiritual and intellectual hothouse that was the London of the 1530s and their under-standing of the great issues of time and eternity could not remain static.

Cromwell was all along an enthusiast for the English Bible. He had been one of the earliest readers of Erasmus's Latin New Testament. About 1527 Miles Coverdale, ex-friar and convert to Lutheranism, wrote to Cromwell reminding him of a 'godly communication' (i.e. discussion) they had had and reported, 'I begin to taste of holy scripture; now, honour be to God, I am set to the most sweet and holy letters, with the godly savour of holy and ancient doctors' and he begged his friend to help him acquire books.'[32] This is the sort of language men only use with each other when they share convictions and interests. As early as 1529 there was a motion in the Commons house for the setting forth of an official English Bible which would shoulder aside Tyndale's testaments with their Lutheran glosses. Cromwell cannot have been ignorant of this aborted initiative and the likelihood is that he approved of the initative. In May 1530 the issue had been brought up in Convocation, where Warham pooh-poohed the very idea of an English Bible for the laity. At that time Henry had expressed himself in favour of translation but nothing came of this. There can be no doubt, given Cromwell's later staunch championing of a vernacular Bible, that he followed all these developments closely and waited for a time when the translation project might safely be reignited. He kept himself informed of what the evangelical exiles were up to. His friend Coverdale had had to flee in 1528. He was, as it were, a spiritual grandson of Little Bilney. One of the scholars converted by the agency of that gentle spirit was Robert Barnes, head of the Augustinian house in Cambridge, which Coverdale joined in the early 1520s. As a result of Barnes's influence he abandoned the cloister and, like Bilney, took to itinerant preaching. By 1532 he was in the Low Countries possibly as a member of William Tyndale's travelling circus. He may even have begun at this time work on his own translation of the Old Testament.

Cromwell had contact with the 'arch-heretic' through Coverdale and through an even closer friend and protégé, Stephen Vaughan. Cromwell had helped Vaughan's rise in the commercial world and, by 1530, he was a thriving merchant, a member of the Mercers' Company, the king's factor in the Netherlands – and a card-carrying evangelical. Over the years he carried out various commercial commissions for his old master and acted as a valuable spy whose travels enabled him to collect information about affairs on the continent. Vaughan was enthusiastic about the English Bible project and managed to get into hot water over it. Events in 1530–1 showed just how brittle were the eggshells on which friends of the Gospel were treading. Thanks to the recommendation of Anne Boleyn, Henry read and approved Tyndale's *Obedience of a Christian Man.* The over-eager Vaughan thought that this might be a heaven-sent opportunity to turn the religious tide. He urged the exile to return and wield his pen in favour of the divorce. But, by 1531, Henry's mood had changed. Cromwell was seriously alarmed and wrote desperate entreaties to his friend. Vaughan should 'utterly forsake . . . Tyndale and all his sect' because the king suspected Vaughan of being tainted with the heresy of one 'who nothing goeth about or pretendeth but only to seduce, deceive and disquiet the people and commonwealth of this realm, whose coming into England the king's highness can right well forbear.'[33] Vaughan was slow to take the hint. Despite protesting that he was 'neither Lutheran nor yet Tyndalian', he was soon sending back even more inflammatory evangelical material. It is not clear whether Cromwell was the instigator of the approach to Tyndale or whether he was only with difficulty holding in check a headstrong friend.

Two things are, however, clear. The first is that Cromwell favoured evangelicals. Vaughan would not have written as he did to a correspondent who was indifferent or hostile to the cause of Bible-based reform. The clearest evidence of Cromwell's position in 1531–2 comes from a letter written in 1538 by one John Oliver, a royal chaplain who owed his advancement to Cromwell. He recalled occasions when, as a dinner guest in the Throgmorton Street house, he had taken part in discussions which 'were the very cause of the beginning of my conversion'. The 'conversion' referred to may relate to Oliver's change of opinion over the divorce but, whether it was that or something more spiritual, what impressed him was that he found 'always the conclusions you maintained at your board to be consonant with the holy word of God'. The host and his friends would compare the Vulgate with Erasmus's version and Oliver described how he would go home and check what they had read with the Greek text.[34] Once again the emphasis is on the verdict of Scripture, although there was nothing risky about scholars engaging in sophisticated debate about books which were perfectly respectable in Catholic society.

That brings us to the second aspect of Cromwell's religious attitude: he was not the stuff of which martyrs are made. In matters of theology he dared not run ahead of his royal master. This does not mean that such religious conviction as he had was only skin deep. He knew how delicately matters were poised at court. Ironically it had been Vaughan who had warned him when he first entered royal service, 'a merry semblance of weather often trusteth men into dangerous seas, not thinking to be suddenly oppressed with tempest when unawares they be prevented and brought in great jeopardy'.[35] The truth is that, as Thomas Wyat observed, it 'thunders' round the throne'. There is an unfortunate parallel between the careers of Cromwell and More. Both men had strongly held convictions. Both believed that if they remained in the government they might be able to make a difference. Both had to compromise or, at least, mask their innermost thoughts. Both would eventually fall victim to a king who was no respecter of other men's principles.

For the moment, however, Cromwell was indispensable to Henry. In the summer of 1532 he became, in all but name, the king's secretary. This post was held by Stephen Gardiner, Bishop of Winchester, but he had fallen out with Henry over the Submission and, rather than resign like More, he accepted a foreign diplomatic posting. (Cromwell's position was formalised in April 1534.) It is interesting that Thomas Audley, who now replaced More, was not immediately granted the title of Lord Chancellor. He was nominated Keeper of the Great Seal and only became Lord Chancellor the following January. It looks as though Henry was very reticent about being seen to elevate to major offices of state men known to hold progressive views. Diplomats watched closely and interpreted for their masters such intimations of Henry's intentions.

After the marriage of Henry and Anne in January 1533 and

the discovery of Anne's pregnancy, things moved rapidly – as, of course, they had to. Cromwell had been working assiduously on the piece of legislation which was pivotal to the whole Political Reformation – the Act in Restraint of Appeals. Cromwell made several drafts of the bill and submitted it to a committee of specialists in civil and canon law. Finally it was presented to Henry, who made some additions. King and minister were determined that there must be no loopholes. Its immediate purpose was to frustrate finally and irrevocably any attempt to have the king's Great Matter decided in Rome, but in so doing it defined the new England Henry was forging. Only it was not, according to the preamble, new at all:

> by divers sundry old authentic histories and chronicles it is manifestly declared and expressed that this realm of England is an empire, and so hath been accepted in the world, governed by one supreme head and king having the dignity and royal estate of the imperial crown of the same, unto whom a body politic, compact of all sorts of degrees of people divided in terms and by names of spiritualty and temporalty, be bownden and owe to bear next to God a natural and humble obedience; he being also institute and furnished by the goodness and sufferance of Almighty God with plenary, whole and entire power, pre-eminence, authority, prerogative and jurisdiction to render and yield justice and final determination to all manner of folk resiants or subjects within this realm in all causes, matters, debates and contentions happening to occur, insurge or begin within the limits thereof.[36]

The Act went on to deliver a diatribe against the pretended authority of the pope, enacted that bishops could only be selected if their appointment had royal approval and set out how ecclesiastical courts were to operate in future. Having made the bill as watertight as possible, Cromwell set about ensuring that it would have an untroubled passage through Parliament. Several vacant seats were filled by 'approved' candidates and known opponents of the royal supremacy were warned off. Even so, some Commons voices were raised in protest, not at the religious implications of the Act but against its possible repercussions on trade with Catholic countries. Yet, the passage of the Act through both houses at the beginning of April turned out to be something of an anticlimax.

It cleared the way for Cranmer to convene an archiepiscopal court at Dunstable – well away from any possible protestors – which considered the validity of Henry's marriage to Catherine. On 23 May the judges formally announced their expected verdict. This, too, was a virtual non-event. Few people attended the sessions. The queen and her supporters boycotted the event. In less than seven weeks the affair of the two divorces which had convulsed the nation for seven years was quietly concluded. But this was only round one of the English Reformation.

Chapter 5

Henry's Church

Between 1534 and 1539 the legal framework of the Church of England was constructed. Nine major items of legislation went through Parliament and were supplemented by royal proclamations and archiepiscopal directives. We might easily fall into the trap of treating these official pronouncements as the elements of a preconceived programme but that would be a misunderstanding. The Henrician Reformation *evolved*. It responded to changing circumstances. It reflected the king's fluctuating attitudes to the church, its personnel and its teaching. It was sensitive to events at home and abroad. And it responded to the interplay of what we may loosely call 'court factions' (see below, pp. 222ff). Henry knew full well that his religious policy was balanced on a tightrope and that, if it made a false step, there was no safety net to prevent it crashing to the hard ground of heresy – or the appearance of heresy, which was just as dangerous. The dilemma is evident from the wording of various enactments. For example, the Act of Dispensations (March, 1534) put an end to all payments hitherto made by English churchmen to Rome. But the Act offered this reassurance to potential critics:

> Provided always that this act nor any thing or things therein contained shall be hereafter interpreted or expounded that your Grace, your nobles and subjects, intend by the same to decline or vary from the congregation of Christ's Church in any things concerning the very articles of the Catholic Faith

or Christendom; or in any other things declared by Holy
Scripture and the word of God necessary for their or your
salvation . . .[1]

There are two comments that should be made about such
assurances. The first is that Henry believed them. The second
is that they were nonsense. Logic pointed to the inevitable
consequence of dethroning the pope: the doctrines supporting his rule would be called in question. Indeed, the very
words of the Act of Dispensations indicate that the government was Janus-like in its attitude towards the defining of
Christian truth. It looked both to the 'articles of the Catholic
Faith' and to 'Holy Scripture'. Henry, some members of his
Council and the majority of his bishops may have believed
that there was no conflict between these two sources of
authority but keener minds knew better. More, Fisher and
other leading traditionalist thinkers were as clear about this as
were Cromwell, Cranmer and their supporters. The dramatic
events of the 1530s may be likened to a motor car in which
the king held on to the steering wheel while evangelical advisers pressed the accelerator and their Catholic counterparts
stamped on the brake. At the risk of pushing the metaphor to
absurdity one might comment that no one in the vehicle
possessed a map on which a destination was clearly marked.
In the Act of Dispensations itself there is evidence that, for all
the government's anti-papal rhetoric, Henry was wavering. At
the very last moment he had a clause inserted which hinted
that he might be prepared to abrogate the Act.

The years spent anguishing over the divorce had involved for
Henry a great deal of reading, theological debate and hard
thinking. As a result he had formed strong and firm opinions
about his relationship with the country, with the church and
with God. But he was also a political realist. His policy calculations were based not only upon what he believed but upon what
he thought he could get away with. This makes it difficult to
define exactly what stage the official Reformation was at on any

particular date. As the winter of 1534 slowly elided into spring, two related matters concerned the king and exercised the Lords and Commons assembled at Westminster. They represented two sides of the same coin. Having changed wives, Henry's attention was now fixed on siring a male heir. It was vital that there should be no doubt about this child's legitimate claim to the throne, no possibility of future civil unrest caused by loyalties divided between Henry's children. Any malicious rumours about the divorce, any lingering support for Princess Mary had to be quashed. Thus Parliament was set to pass a Succession Act and at the same time to deliver a strong warning to any malcontents, by showing how dissidents would be dealt with.

The matter that most grabbed public attention was the fate of Elizabeth Barton, the Maid of Kent, and her co-defendants. Henry was determined to make a terrible example of those who had offended his royal dignity, upheld the cause of Catherine of Aragon and, more importantly, had, in pamphlets and public meetings, spread anti-government propaganda. Henry was determined that those at the centre of this pseudo-religious plot should die the hideous death of traitors. Unfortunately, their offences did not come within the remit of the existing Treasons Act. Fortunately, the state always had the fallback of proceeding by a bill of attainder. This was a parliamentary process by which the guilt of accused criminals could be determined without a judicial trial. Henry intended, by this means, to spread a wide net which would scoop up prominent opponents of the divorce as well as those who had actually aided and abetted the Maid. He insisted that More and Fisher should be included in the bill. Only when his legal advisers warned him that the case against More might not stick did Henry relent. As for Fisher, he was eventually condemned on the lesser charge of misprision of treason and escaped with a hefty fine. The Act of Attainder received royal assent on 21 March and, on 23 April, St George's Day, London citizens on holiday were able to watch Elizabeth and six of her co-conspirators dragged through the streets on hurdles to Tyburn, where they were hanged, drawn and quartered. The Maid's fate was unprecedented. As a woman she should have suffered death by burning but that might have given the impression to onlookers that she was being executed for heresy or false divination, whereas Henry wanted it to be made abundantly clear that her crime was treason. What he needed was a propaganda coup and making Elizabeth share the spectacular death of her accomplices certainly had the desired shock value. Others involved suffered terms of imprisonment.

The Succession Act gave statutory backing to Henry's second marriage and pledged all his subjects to allegiance to any issue from it. Nothing was to be left to chance in this matter. In another unprecedented move it was decreed that commissioners should be despatched to every part of the realm to proclaim the Act and to call upon all Englishmen to swear an oath of obedience to it. It was a monumental task, quite unprecedented in the nation's history. Not a single male subject was to be exempted from endorsing the changes in England's religious life or the reasons for it. The taking of oaths ensured that people were impelled by fear, not just of incurring the king's wrath and suffering legal consequences of adherence to Catherine and to papal authority, but also of putting their immortal souls in jeopardy. This was the Act which successfully trapped More and Fisher and other stubborn opponents of the royal supremacy. Its preamble underscored the process by which the divorce had been obtained and denied the right of the pope to interfere in such matters. The Succession Act galloped through Parliament before the Easter closure. Within a month More and Fisher found themselves in the Tower, the most prominent victims among the tiny minority who refused the oath. They declared their willingness to swear allegiance to Henry's children by Anne but not to the assertions in the preamble.

They were joined over the following months by several members of monastic orders whose consciences did not permit them to accept the changes in the religious status quo. They were encouraged in their defiance by the new pope, Paul III. In March he declared that Henry's first marriage was legal and that he was not free to contract another as long as Catherine lived. Then, to rub salt into the wound, in May, he made Bishop Fisher a cardinal. This deliberate insult sealed the bishop's fate. Henry's furious response to the news was that the pope might offer a cardinal's hat but that he would make sure Fisher had no head to put it on. He set his Council on to that examination of the two prominent prisoners which led eventually to their trial and condemnation.

Among the religious who opposed the king over the supremacy and the succession were members of the Observant (i.e. those who rigidly followed the founder's rules) Franciscan and Carthusian orders. Nor was their opposition passive. The Observants had been prominent supporters of Elizabeth Barton's prophesyings. As early as Easter 1532 the leader of the Franciscan Observants, William Peto, denounced the king to his face in a sermon preached at court. Henry bore the reproof patiently, simply ordering Hugh Curwen, one of his chaplains, to preach a contradictory sermon the following Sunday. On the appointed day Curwen vigorously attacked Peto and taunted him with not being present to engage in debate. What happened next caused a furore and helps to explain Henry's strong reaction to criticism:

one Elstow, a fellow friar to Peto, standing in the rood-loft . . . with a bold voice said to Dr Curwen, 'Good Sir, you know that Father Peto, as he was commanded, is now gone to a provincial council at Canterbury . . . In the mean time I am here . . . and will lay down my life to prove all those things true which he hath taught out of the Holy Scripture and to this combat I challenge thee . . . which art one of the four hundred prophets into whom the spirit of lying is entered [a reference to I Kings 22, in which the prophet Micah contradicted the preaching of four hundred official prophets who foretold victory to King Ahab in a forthcoming battle] and seekest by adultery to establish succession, betraying the King unto endless perdition, more for thine own vain glory

and hope of promotion, than for discharge of thy clogged
conscience and the King's salvation.' This Elstow waxed hot,
and spake very earnestly, so as they could not make him cease
his speech until the King himself bade him hold his peace.[2]

Peto was fortunate to escape with exile. He went to Antwerp,
which was becoming something of a haven for English dissidents of all shades of religious opinion. From there he
organised a campaign, sending seditious letters, writing books,
preaching to his fellow countrymen who came to the great
commercial entrepôt, encouraging the activities of a fifth
column in his homeland and spreading the word that Charles
V was ready to invade England to restore it to papal obedience. Peto knew, as all anti-supremacy activists knew, that
there was considerable disquietude throughout the country.
They were encouraged by stories of people who protested, if
not at the disappearance of papal authority, certainly at the
divorce. Queen Anne was hugely unpopular as the 'whore'
who had broken up the king's marriage.

It was the existence of an underground movement (or fear
that such an organised movement might develop) that explains
the prodigious energy expended by the government in extirpat-
ing every last vestige of 'papistry'. The fact that there was no
popular uprising until 1536–7, and then only in the northern
shires (see below, pp. 182ff), should not obscure the fact that
discontent existed throughout the realm or that king and
Council were nervous about it. Rebellion was always the greatest fear of sixteenth-century rulers. Henry knew that isolated
pockets of opposition could be coalesced into a movement
especially when its leaders held out the prospect of support
from foreign powers. He, therefore, insisted on a vigorous 'first
strike' strategy and in Cromwell he had the very man capable of
orchestrating a many-pronged offensive. The king had come
too far and at too great cost to contemplate backing down. He
had got his own way over the divorce. His new wife had
presented him with a child in September 1533 and though that

child was a girl (Elizabeth) the fact that Anne had been safely delivered boded well for the future and the security of the dynasty. It was vital that the government should show firmness by using propaganda to win the argument and by using force to make it quite clear that no opposition would be tolerated.

Henry felt particularly bitter about the opposition of the Observants. This was the order he knew particularly well because there were friaries attached to the royal palaces of Richmond and Greenwich (the former founded by the king's father). The grey-habited figures were a common sight around the court. Only recently Princess Elizabeth had been baptised in the Observant church at Greenwich. Henry may well have felt that, of all the monastic orders, the Observants owed him a special loyalty. Over the summer members of this order were subjected to a veritable reign of terror. Henry was determined that they should either publicly swear their support for the new order or suffer the direst consequences. Scores of them were arrested, imprisoned, interrogated, tortured and killed. Officials at the Tower were kept particularly busy examining detainees. It is no coincidence that Skeffington's Gyves made their first appearance at this time. Leonard Skeffington was the Lieutenant of the Tower and he devised the torture implement which bore his name. It worked on the opposite principle to the rack. Instead of pulling at the victim's joints it compressed them. The simple instrument was clamped to the neck and ankles and forced the wearer to be bent double. By turning the screws more pressure was applied. If the victim did not reveal all that his examiners wanted to know the torture might continue until his back was broken or his internal organs ruptured. It is very doubtful whether many (or any) prisoners met their end in the embrace of the Scavenger's Daughter (to give the contraption its other name). Its significance lies not in its cruelty but in its size. Unlike the rack, which was a fixture, the gyves were portable and could be carried from cell to cell. That suggests that there were, at any one time, several prisoners to be interrogated. We know, for example, that on 17 June 1534 two cartloads of Observants were driven to the Tower. Not all obdurate friars were despatched to royal jails. Some were relocated in the monastic houses of more compliant monks, where they were rigorously handled by abbots and priors eager to prove their loyalty to the king. About forty were confined in this way. Of the others, thirty died, probably as a result of their imprisonment, and thirty managed to escape abroad. In August 1534 the Observant Franciscan order in England was dissolved.

But that did not solve the government's problem. All the members of the Council knew that beyond the ring of conservative champions prepared to resist royal policy lay a multitude of English men and women who resented the changes being foisted upon them. Cromwell received a steady stream of letters from his agents around the country reporting numerous cases of disaffection. The majority concerned little more than alehouse or marketplace grumbling. Some seem to have been the ramblings of people we would today regard as mentally deranged. Several repeated old obscure legends and applied them to the contemporary situation. And there were those who claimed divine inspiration. Few resulted in serious reprisals but that does not mean that Cromwell and his team did not take them seriously. They knew that seditious words did not need to be well founded in logic and cleverly argued to have an effect on the hearers. The culture which had thrown up Elizabeth Barton was one in which people accepted magic and held in awe those who claimed occult powers or prophetic insight or who indulged in ecstatic utterance.

A certain Mrs Amadas was the sort of performer who kept audiences hanging on her words. She had a book of old prophecies including the tale supposedly told by Merlin of the mysterious royal villain pseudonymed the mouldwrap on whom would alight 'the vengeance of God for all evil deeds'. Mrs Amadas now identified this creature as Henry VIII. In her rambling discourse, as reported to Cromwell, in July 1534, she prophesied that the king would be banished from the realm, that the Scots would invade, that 'those that be of the King's part shall be destroyed, for the dragon shall be killed by Midsummer', that Anne Boleyn would be burned 'for she is a harlot', that 'the blazing star [presumably Halley's comet, which appeared in 1531] was toward the island whence the dead man should come', that 'the good Emperor will deliver all good wives when he comes, which shall be shortly', and much more of the same ilk.[3] Mrs Amadas kept all her prophecies in a scroll which was 'painted and written'. Since it contained all manner of titillating revelations about the king's sex life it must have made entertaining reading. If this eccentric lady has been correctly identified, she was not some rural goodwife living in a remote corner of the country but the widow of Robert Amadas, late Keeper of the King's Jewels, and therefore someone who had access to the court and its personalities.

The clergy were more of a problem because they had the freedom of the pulpit to air their views and were influential in shaping public opinion. About the same time that Mrs Amadas was being interrogated, James Harrison, a Lancashire vicar, was being sent up to London under guard, accused of saying that he only recognised Catherine as queen, for Anne had her title from the devil. He had spread the rumour that Henry was going to 'put down the order of priests and destroy the Sacrament' but that God would not permit him to reign much longer.[4] William Inold, curate of Rye in Kent, was a more long-term problem. He first came to Cromwell's attention in September 1533 for prophesying doom and destruction which would fall upon the land as a result of its being placed under papal interdict. When challenged he insisted that the pope was above all earthly kings. He was arrested, examined and let off with a caution. Obviously he was not chastened because, in 1535, he was accused by irate neighbours of taking the oath supporting the royal supremacy (see below) but then preaching against it. This time he was sent up to London to be examined by Cromwell. Again, he got off scot free. Two years later we find him in the midst of a battle royal with a group of parishioners whom he accused of heresy and advocating a return to the 'good old days'. He seems to have deserted his cure in order to go on a preaching tour to stir up opposition to the new learning. Cromwell handed the matter over to the Bishop of Chichester, who eventually removed Inold from his cure. Beyond that, nothing seems to have happened to this turbulent priest.[5] In his review of this case, Professor Elton concluded that the divisions in Rye 'ran not only between adherents of the old and the new way in religion but . . . between the rulers of Rye and the poorer sort, entrenched old conflicts being given a religious and political dressing for the purpose of the moment'.[6] This was undoubtedly the case in many of the local spats sniffed out by Cromwell's agents; personalities and old feuds in England's tight-knit and relatively isolated communities easily took on a religious hue in the 1530s. It was the possible political repercussions of religious or pseudo-religious discord that interested the government. That is why they could concern themselves in cases as trivial as a brawl between an ostler and a customer at the White Horse Inn in Cambridge in May 1534. The stable hand gleefully referred to the demotion of the pope to the status of mere Bishop of Rome. This drew from Henry Kilby the retort that any who said that – including the king – were heretics and that 'this business had never been if the king had not married Anne Boleyn'.[7] The two men fell to blows and Kilby broke the ostler's head with a 'faggot stick'.

Despite the close watch kept on all potential disturbers of the peace and the terrible example made of a small number of prominent opponents of the supremacy, there was no widespread persecution launched in these years – certainly not religious persecution. The government was more interested in law and order than doctrinal orthodoxy and, though Cromwell was more disposed to give the benefit of the doubt to those with evangelical leanings, he was not putting his weight behind religious reformation – not yet. But there is no doubt that the legislation of the Reformation Parliament gave a real boost to radical thinkers. A chronicle kept at St Augustine's Abbey in Canterbury spoke of 'many heretics in sundry places of England which did blaspheme the saints and the worshipping of them, barking against tithes, which neither would have fastings nor pilgrimages'.[8] The king and his councillors underestimated the depth of conviction held by many on both sides of the religious debate. They were complacently satisfied that they could keep the lid on a pot that was coming to the boil.

One obvious means of achieving this was the appointment of new bishops. The powers now vested in the king enabled him to select 'safe' men for the top ecclesiastical jobs. If we want to understand what the government's priorities were we can do no better than consider the type of appointees chosen to fill vacancies on the episcopal bench as they occurred. They were certainly not all devotees of the new learning. Stephen Vaughan, Cromwell's headstrong evangelical friend and agent, was appalled to hear that Rowland Lee was to be made Bishop of Coventry and Lichfield. He certainly did not mince his words. He castigated Lee as 'an earthly beast, a mole [i.e. one who works secretly underground] and an enemy to all godly learning . . . a papist, an idolater and a fleshly priest'. Vaughan had a clear idea of the sort of leaders needed to steer the English church into evangelical truth. Lee did not qualify.

> Such oppress innocents when they be lifted up into the dignities of the world and sit therein as tyrants to destroy realms, people and kingdoms. Who knoweth more of the bishops' iniquity than you? And should you help, in this time especially, to increase the number of wicked men, where there is a lack and so great need of good and virtuous men? Be you sorry for it, and help him with your good counsel; for I am more sorry for this deed done by you, than for all the things that ever I knew you do.[9]

Lee was a king's man through and through and also a long-time colleague of Cromwell. The two men had advanced together through service in Wolsey's entourage. Lee was, as Vaughan knew, a ruthless administrator who gave little indication of humanity in carrying out royal policy. His diocese saw little of him because his most important role in the 1530s was that of President of the Council of Wales. There he devoted himself tirelessly to the business of rooting out lawlessness. He adopted a 'shoot first and ask questions afterwards' policy and was not inhibited by his church office from ordering executions. Nor did he think it necessary to abide by the letter of the law. 'If we should do nothing but as the common law will,' he observed to Cromwell, 'these things so far out of order will never be redressed.'[10]

Of the twelve men to whom mitres were distributed between 1533 and 1537 only five (Latimer of Worcester, Shaxton of Salisbury, Hilsey of Rochester, Fox of Hereford and Holgate of Llandaff) can be identified as favouring religious reform. Three (Rugg of Norwich, Barlow of St David's and Capon of Bangor) actually gained reputations as persecutors of heretics. The remainder probably shared the attitude of Goodrich of Ely, of whom Gilbert Burnet commented that he 'preferred the keeping of his diocese before the discharge of his conscience'.[11] Clearly, when making these appointments, Henry did not have in mind fundamental doctrinal reform of the English church. What all the new bishops had in common was that they had attracted the king's favour by their support for the divorce and the royal supremacy. They were expected to preach against the 'pretended authority of the Bishop of Rome' and to license other clergy to do the same – a responsibility they undertook with varying degrees of enthusiasm.

But the task of proclaiming the new religious regime was not left to the diocesans. In order to ensure that as many pulpits as possible were occupied by men able to persuade the king's subjects to accept change, Cromwell went over the bishops' heads and issued licences in the king's name. He did not lack for willing volunteers ready to preach reform. Some were fired by evangelical zeal. Some were pleased that the English church had broken the corrupt and corrupting shackles of Rome and believed that it could now be purified. And, inevitably, there were those who saw in preaching the king's message the hope of career advancement. One such was Richard Croke, a prominent classical scholar and humanist held in high regard in the Erasmus–More circle. He not only informed Cromwell in 1533 that he had preached sixty sermons in thirty-seven Midlands churches, but also gave the minister a breakdown of their content. He had demonstrated from Scripture, the Fathers and church history that papal claims to any jurisdiction outside Rome were groundless, and also that the Bishops of Rome 'have always, for maintenance of their pomps and fruitless ceremonies, been cause of all the greatest schisms that hath been' in Christendom.[12] It may well be that Croke's zeal was not altogether unconnected with his hope to become Dean of Christ Church, Oxford.

Hugh Latimer was a different proposition entirely. He had been sailing very close to the wind ever since the execution of Bilney in 1531. More than once he had been examined in episcopal courts for proclaiming a raft of heresies – against purgatory, pilgrimage and prayers to saints, in favour of vernacular Scripture. But Latimer had friends at court, including Cromwell, and managed to keep well away from the fire and the stake. However, when, on being condemned by Bishop Stokesley of London in April 1532, he had appealed to the king, Henry had ordered him to submit to his superior and frankly warned him that if he repeated his erroneous views he would be burned as a heretic. Yet, two years later, Latimer was ordered to preach the Lenten sermons at court and, in August 1535, he was appointed Bishop of Worcester. By this time the king needed every talented preacher he could find to proclaim the royal supremacy and Latimer was the most charismatic preacher in the land. Once installed, the new bishop lost no time in spreading evangelical teaching and issuing licences to like-minded preachers.

Latimer's chequered career demonstrates the dilemma in which the government found itself. They wanted to advocate Catholicism without the pope but some of their most effective champions had a far more radical agenda. Pulpits throughout the land became the focal points of doctrinal controversy. St Paul's Cross was the official location for the proclamation of government policy but congregations were by no means passive hearers. When George Browne called for prayers for Queen Anne in 1533 many people walked away. When Edward Crome, another member of the Cambridge 'school', preached there the result was 'variety of opinions and contentions among the people of London'.[13] Cromwell had a running battle with conservative bishops about the licensing of preachers. When, in 1535, Bishop Longland of Lincoln blocked access to pulpits in his diocese the minister got round the problem by enlisting the support of the more accommodating Goodrich of Ely. He happened to have a manor in Longland's diocese and, at Cromwell's behest, put up 'sound' men to preach there. Defenders of the old religion could be as troublesome as alleged heretics. By 1537 Bristol was up in arms again because preachers were attacking Latimer and other proclaimers of 'novelties'. John Kene was reported to Cromwell for abusing those who had the king's licence. He spent twenty days in prison.

What is striking about several of these cases is the leniency with which the government dealt with offenders, whether radical or traditionalist. Terrible examples were made of a few individuals but there was no widespread purge. Several reasons for this softly-softly approach suggest themselves. Cromwell and the other instigators of reform knew that harsh reprisals against ordinary folk who resented religious innovation could be counter-productive, not least because of their effect on the king. Henry was always sensitive to accusations of heresy. Provoking a conservative backlash by arresting large numbers of malcontents might well have deflected the king from the course of reform. It would also have troubled the members of Parliament. They were very sensitive about heresy prosecutions. This was one of their main complaints about the old order. But, perhaps, the main reason why there was no consistency in dealing with preachers of all stamps was that, in these years, there was no hard and fast definition of doctrinal orthodoxy.

That was not the priority at this time. What mattered was securing the dynasty and the new kind of kingship Henry had called into being. There was still legislative work to be done to hedge these about with strong statutes. When Parliament reconvened in November 1534 it had to respond to the anxiety, confusion and unrest that had become manifest during the summer. The government needed to clarify their intentions, close legislative loopholes and give the courts sharper teeth for dealing with disaffection. Both houses quickly passed an 'Act concerning the King's Highness to be Supreme Head of the Church of England and to have authority to reform and redress all errors, heresies and abuses in the same'. The Act offered no doctrinal definition of 'supremacy' beyond stating that the monarch, under God, held sway 'in earth' over the English church. Since he was empowered to suppress all 'errors, heresies, abuses, offences, contempts and enormities' it may reasonably be inferred that he had the authority to define Christian truth but the legislation fell short of actually saying so.

The Act of Succession had, as we have seen, made provision for an oath to be sworn by all the king's male subjects but it had not specified the wording of that oath. This had given some opponents of the king's new powers the opportunity to challenge them by refusing to swear to formulae not specifically set out in the statute. Thomas More famously drove a coach and horses through government policy by refusing the oath presented to him in the Tower because Cromwell and Audley 'did add more words to it'. A new Act now compelled obedience to Henry and his heirs by Anne and rejection of any other oath or allegiance. It remained only to buttress the Tudor regime with a new Treasons Act but here the government ran into parliamentary opposition. The Commons were, as ever, suspicious of anything that increased the power of the state over the individual. The bill before them tightened up and extended existing fourteenth-century legislation, particularly by extending the definition of treason from acts against the Crown to written or spoken criticism. The precise wording of the bill gives us a strong hint about what was troubling Henry and Cromwell in the autumn of 1534. As well as proposing that the Act should cover any who 'wish, will or desire by words or writing' any harm to the king, queen or their children or seek to deprive them of their titles, it included alleged offenders who claimed that 'the King our sovereign lord should be heretic, schismatic, tyrant, infidel or usurper of the crown'. If passed, the Act would imply that it was impossible for the king to err in matters of religion and that his subjects must accept as true whatever he declared to be true. It is not to be wondered that the Commons were uneasy. However, the government were determined and the only concession (easily evaded by royal judges) they made was the addition of the word 'maliciously' to the phrase 'wish, will or desire by words or writing'.

So what were all the king's subjects expected to believe at this juncture? The complex answer is to be found in the vigorous propaganda campaign sponsored by the government. The state-craft of the 1530s was something wholly new in English history. Thomas Cromwell, a man of the world who had studied at first hand the techniques of government practised by Italian Renaissance princes, utilised all available communication media to promote the new image of the king as Christian monarch independent of the pope. As well as preaching, these included published sermons, pamphlets, paintings, prints, songs, plays and pageants. The most striking graphic representation of Henry which has survived and the one which best conveys how the king liked to envisage his new role is a rich miniature high-lighted in gold leaf by Hans Holbein. *Solomon and the Queen of Sheba* (1534–5) may be regarded as a pictorial version of the Act of Supremacy. It depicts Henry in the guise of the Old Testament king, seated on a raised throne and receiving the submission of the Queen of Sheba, representing the English church. Servants of the queen pour rich offerings at the king's feet (a pretty broad hint). In letters of gold above the king's head appears the Old Testament text, 'Praised be the Lord your God. He has shown his pleasure in you by making you king to rule in his name.'[14] Holbein was, in artistic terms, the man of the moment. He had actually been around in London, on and off, for nine years, gradually building up a reputation but he was now brought to Henry's attention by Cromwell and the Boleyns. It was in 1534 that his series of royal portraits with which we are familiar was begun. From this point his fortunes increased dramatically. Not only did he become the king's painter, he was employed by Cromwell to provide various government propaganda images. We may be impressed by the stunning realism of Holbein's portraits of Henry VIII but their impact on contemporaries was even greater. They represented something completely new in royal iconography, depicting the king as powerful, domineering and magnificent – precisely the image the royal egotist wished to convey. And when he was not engaged in taking likenesses of his growing clientele, the artist made woodcut engravings for government-sponsored pamphlets and stand-alone prints. Paintings could only be afforded by the rich but the prints were designed for a larger audience. They made fun of the pope, monks, scholastic theologians and other representatives of the old order. Ever since the invention of printing, political cartoons have been effective tools in shaping public opinion. Holbein was an early master of graphic satire.

Just as Cromwell recognised Holbein's rare artistic talent, so he appreciated and sought to employ scholars, theologians and philosophers of the top rank. He went to considerable lengths to recruit the best brains of the day for the Reformation cause – almost regardless, it seems, of their religious allegiance. At various times he sought to induce Tyndale to come from Antwerp, Philip Melancthon to travel from Wittenberg and Reginald Pole (a firm adherent of the pope) to make the journey from Rome. The supremacy was a fait accompli but the government still wanted to commend it to all literate and well-educated Englishmen. It was for this reason that Cromwell summoned to London Thomas Starkey, an internationally respected scholar and sometime lecturer at Oxford. Starkey was currently studying in Italy but now returned to accept a post as king's chaplain and to put his pen at the disposal of the regime. The result of his labours was *An Exhortation to the People Instructing them to Unity and Obedience.* Starkey stressed the divine nature of kingship and the disastrous consequences which would follow for the nation if people allowed a few scruples over issues such as papal authority to distract them from obedience to their anointed king.

Starkey remained fairly conservative in matters theological. The same could not be said of Cromwell's other leading pamphleteer, Richard Morison. This scholar knew Cromwell well from their days together in Wolsey's household and he hoped for promotion from his old colleague. He was not disappointed. By the time he returned from studying abroad in 1535 he had embraced distinctly evangelical views and had to be somewhat restrained by his employer, who was more interested at this point in urging a disturbed populace to obedience. Morison repeated Starkey's arguments in *A Remedy for Sedition Wherein are Contained Many Things Concerning the True and Loyal Obedience that Commons owe their Prince* . . . but he made a point of stressing that Henry's major concern was for the salvation of his people. He thus neatly bracketed together the need for political stability and the importance of adherence to the official version of the Christian faith.

The writings of these and other propagandists were, in the main, directed at the educated class, the opinion formers of Tudor society. Henry, who liked to think of himself as the perfect Renaissance prince, was a great believer in the power of the written word. He created the first royal library and surviving inventories provide evidence that he owned thousands of volumes, most of them relating to theology and church history. It was natural that he would encourage the development and propagation of sophisticated arguments backing his revolution against Rome. However, just as Holbein and lesser artists were employed to make direct appeal to the lower orders, so writers were found able to make the government's case in ringing journalese, rather than carefully argued academic prose. The anonymous *Little Treatise against the muttering of some papists in corners* was a down-to-earth pamphlet which used scurrilous anecdote, homely style and flattery of its readers to make its points. These and numerous other books touting the official line were published by Thomas Berthelet, the king's printer. He provided an outlet and a distribution system for publications either sponsored by or approved by the regime. Meanwhile, the illiterate masses were not neglected. As well as graphic lampoons, Cromwell's agents made use of music, knowing, as pioneer hymn writers like Luther, Watts and Wesley knew, that the most effective way of insinuating ideas into people's minds is to get them to sing songs. One such was the catchy ballad 'The Fantasy of Idolatry' by William Gray, which debunked the pilgrimage racket. Though few examples of such ephemera have survived we need not doubt that the government propaganda machine made full use of this effective weapon.

The obverse of the explosion of printed propaganda was censorship of material hostile to Henrician policy. When it came to suppressing potentially subversive Catholic literature the government faced several difficulties. England was still officially a Catholic country. Its leaders had not embraced all the implications of the evangelical conviction that every aspect of doctrine and practice must be subjected to the final judgement of Scripture. Its theology was, therefore, in limbo. Advocates of the old way, by contrast, only had to reaffirm what English men and women had believed for centuries. Henry's subjects were, in the main, conservative, suspicious of change. While Cromwell's agents had to persuade them to accept new ideas, their opponents only had to urge them to hold fast to their traditional ceremonies, customs and doctrines. As to dealing with intellectuals, government propagandists were actually inhibited by that very humanist training which was integral to the Reformation. Greg Walker has clearly made this point:

> the rhetorical training, and the sententious, tendentious, habits of mind that it generated ... permeated and influenced

a whole generation of educated men and women that grew up in the early sixteenth century, and can be seen to have influenced informal discussions and improvised speech . . . The schoolboys and students of the early sixteenth century were naturally disputatious . . . willing to argue, to use exemplary stories to justify their claims, to put counter cases, and seek contrary examples to those offered to them in conversation, from the pulpit, or from figures of authority.[15]

The advocates of change in the king's employ, of course, wished to encourage this questioning culture – as long as it led people to the 'right' conclusions. But what if it did not? What if, having weighed up all the evidence, an intelligent man decided that the king could not replace the pope as head of the English church? The government had recent legislation at their disposal and could effectively silence him. But would that not simply put them on a par with the oppressive papal regime they found so obnoxious? The Inquisition and the *Index Librorum Prohibitorum*, the list of banned books, were the tools by which the Roman reactionary regime sought to enforce belief. Cromwell (and, probably, the king) had no desire to emulate it. And, as we have seen, Parliament was particularly sensitive to religious persecution.

For a variety of reasons, then, the government adopted a softly-softly approach. It had the draconian new laws to fall back on and did not hesitate to use them against those it wished to make examples of. In January 1535, Cromwell was appointed to the post of 'Vicegerent in Spirituals', the king's deputy in all religious matters. It was he who, in effect, exercised the royal supremacy and his position placed him above all the bishops. He lost no time in issuing directives to religious and secular authorities throughout the land to monitor preaching and to seek out and report all dissident elements. But the great majority of men and women sent back to the Council for expressing 'non-PC' opinions were dealt with leniently. When More was Chancellor he had issued a list of banned books but the new regime declined to follow this path. In January 1536 a royal proclamation ordered that any publication 'in derogation and diminution of the dignity and authority royal of the King's majesty' was to be confiscated and sent to the Council. Its terms were vague and it was largely ineffective. Two years later another, more detailed proclamation tightened government control of suspect literature. The importation of English books was forbidden except under royal licence. New books could only be printed in England with a similar licence. These restrictions applied as much to evangelical literature as to pro-papal propaganda. Once again, the government resisted the temptation to issue a list of banned books.

However, since the full weight of the state was ready to fall upon any who appeared to challenge the will of the Supreme Head of the English church, critics were circumspect about what they put in writing. John Heywood, a musician and dramatist in the household of Princess Mary, was a staunch traditionalist who was appalled at the chaos into which the drastic changes enforced by the king had plunged the realm. He referred to this in more than one of his plays but was always careful not to lay the blame explicitly at Henry's door. However, audiences could scarcely fail to draw obvious conclusions from such pieces as *The Pardoner and the Friar* (1533), in which a ranting evangelical and an equally obdurate papist engaged in a slanging match which drew in their neighbours and ended in fisticuffs. Although Heywood's criticism was, on the face of it, even-handed, it was obvious to anyone with eyes to see that he blamed the sad state of the nation on those who had disturbed the good old ways with their religious novelties. This was certainly how the authorities came to view his writings. In 1544 Heywood was arrested for denying the royal supremacy and only escaped execution by a public recantation.

On a higher literary plain were the works of Sir Thomas Elyot, courtier, diplomat and humanist scholar. Throughout the 1530s he produced a prodigious number of works on various subjects but it was his treatises on political philosophy, and particularly *The Book Named The Governor* (which went through several editions between 1531 and 1580), that were of most interest at court. Interestingly, Elyot's understanding of the current situation mirrored Heywood's. He envisaged the influence of heresy leading England into utter chaos, just as it had, in his opinion, provoked the Peasants' War in Germany. Elyot was a close friend of Thomas More and shared his religious conservatism but he was careful to conform outwardly and to cloak his criticisms in flattery. More once advised Cromwell to tell the king not what he could do, but what he should do. Elyot made the same point in his counsel to Henry:

> What thou mayest do, delight not for to know,
> But rather what thing will become thee best.

The king's claiming of religious supremacy was, in Elyot's view, a bridge too far, though he could not say so in as many words. Yet the king understood him well. Henry had a genuine respect for Elyot's scholarship and lent him books from the royal library but the writer's fate was eventually to be passed over for promotion and to see his advice ignored. For the depressed and disillusioned scholar, virtue had to be its own reward. All he could claim towards the end of his life was that he had laboured 'with more regard to my last reckoning than to any riches or worldly promotion'.

The government's concern to sell the supremacy and suppress opposition to it for several months took the heat off evangelicals. Under the umbrella of supporting the religious changes radical preachers were able to proclaim reformed doctrine in relative safety from arrest. The respite they enjoyed in 1534–5 was important to the spread of the new learning. The religious debate raging in these years was oxygen to the evangelical cause. People could scarcely avoid taking an interest in the issues involved. Inevitably, some were won over to the new teaching. The fact that gifted preachers such as Latimer stirred up controversy should not blind us to the fact that they made converts. John Hilsey, who went on to become Bishop of Rochester, owed his conversion to Latimer and several ex-friars came to evangelical beliefs as a result of the heated debates at Bristol in the early 1530s. These eager converts formed the nucleus of Latimer's preaching team after he had become Bishop of Worcester and it seems very likely that his evangelistic strategy centred on targeting able preachers. Edward Large was in trouble in 1537 for condemning religious ceremonies. He and other known Latimer disciples fled the country in Mary Tudor's reign or stayed to face persecution and, in some cases, death. As the years passed more and more leaders of provincial society were to be found among the ranks of evangelical believers. Through their patronage evangelicals were appointed to benefices or served as domestic chaplains with a roving mandate to preach. Thus, in Gloucestershire Sir Nicholas Poyntz and Sir John Walsh protected evangelical clergy and in East Anglia ardent proselytisers such as John Bale and Thomas Rose enjoyed the patronage of the Duke and Duchess of Suffolk.

If any evidence is needed to support the contention that popular debate was involving not just the dispute between king and pope but underlying theological issues, it is to be found in an injunction issued by Archbishop Cranmer in June 1534 forbidding for the space of one year all preaching on topics that 'have caused dissensions amongst the subjects of this realm'. Specific items listed were 'purgatory, honouring of saints, that priests may have wives, that faith only justifieth, to go on pilgrimages, to forge miracles'.[16] And tragic proof exists of the depth of feeling on religious matters which existed among some of the king's subjects. As we have seen, in 1530, Cranmer urged the king to authorise an official vernacular translation of the Bible as the best way of overcoming the influence of Tyndale's Testament with its Lutheran glosses, and Henry instructed his bishops to give serious consideration to the proposal. The prospect appalled many conservatives. In 1533, according to Edward Hall's chronicle:

... one Pavier, town clerk of the city of London, hanged himself, which surely was a man that in no wise could abide to hear that the Gospel should be in English, and I myself heard him once say to me and others that were by, swearing a great oath, that if he thought the king's highness would set forth the Scripture in English, and let it be read of the people by his authority, rather than he would so long live, he would cut his own throat, but he brake promise, for, as you have heard, he hanged himself.[17]

1536 was the year that the pot boiled over. It was, by any standards, a most extraordinary year. It was marked by a highly dramatic sequence of events. Indeed, so dramatic were they and so complex that their interrelationships have remained a subject for debate ever since. In our effort to unravel them we may start with three incontrovertible facts – three things that happened in January which caused a flurry of interest at the time and were to be fraught with long-lasting consequences. On the 7th Catherine of Aragon died. On the 24th, Henry, who celebrated his forty-fifty birthday this year, had a bad fall from his horse in the tiltyard. On the 29th Queen Anne suffered her second miscarriage. These misfortunes had profound implications for national and international affairs. Within twenty-four hours of the previous queen's demise, Henry was sending instructions to his ambassadors regarding their attitude towards their French and imperial counterparts. The whole divorce issue could now be consigned to history. There could be a rapprochment between Henry and Charles V. England's diplomatic options had substantially increased. The effects of the king's accident were more problematic but were, yet, crucial to the events that followed. After the fall Henry lay unconscious for (according to one report) two hours. The psychological impact must have been profound. The king had always boasted of his athleticism but, of late, his health had deteriorated markedly. He had become obese and he had developed painful and disgusting leg ulcers. Now, he was forced to acknowledge that his jousting days were over. He was not the kind of man who could easily accept physical disability and its inevitable impact on his public persona. But equally important were the implications of this brush with death for the succession. He still had no legitimate heir. The queen's current pregnancy was, therefore, even more vital. When it ended so tragically the effect on Henry was catastrophic. Once again he had to ask himself why the Almighty appeared to have deserted the Tudor dynasty. In pursuit of what he believed to be God's will he had cut England loose from western Christendom. Had he been mistaken? Henry did not deal well with uncertainty. Mental turmoil coupled with physical pain and the humiliation of needing others to help move his massive bulk played havoc with his temper. His behaviour began to be irrational. This made life very difficult for his courtiers and councillors.

It gave a new urgency to the work of religious reform to which Cromwell and Cranmer were, by this time, firmly committed. They had gone too far to turn back now. Throughout the country there were encouraging signs of the progress of evangelical revival. The law student Robert Plumpton (see above, p. 119) could assure his mother, 'the Gospel of Christ was never so truly preached as it is now.'[18] There was no stopping the influence of illegal English Scriptures. An illiterate London bricklayer had learned by heart several passages of the holy text read to him by others and preached to any who would listen what he had discovered, 'as well as [if] he had studied at the universities'.[19] The Bishop of Hereford was not exaggerating when he warned his colleagues, in 1537, 'Make not yourselves the laughing stock of the world; light is sprung up and is scattering all the clouds. The lay people know the Scriptures better than many of us.'[20]

Cromwell and Cranmer were now committed to the production of an official English Bible. Henry had declared himself theoretically favourable and had handed the matter to the bishops, who had, predictably, done nothing. Cromwell knew that the moment had to be seized; the diplomatic and political situation might change. Luther had claimed, with a large measure of truth, 'I have done nothing; the word of God has done everything.' Cromwell was eager to get the Bible in English out on the streets. Once that happened traditionalists and papists would be powerless to turn the clock back. Vicegerent and archbishop now encouraged their friends abroad to set their minds to a new translation. Miles Coverdale, who had worked closely with Tyndale in Antwerp, completed in October 1535 a version shorn of all contentious glosses and dedicated to Henry. In England the book was provided with a title page and copious illustrations by Holbein. Cromwell showed it to the king and the king had it distributed to the bishops for their verdict. When they reported back Bishop Gardiner tried to pour cold water on the project by pointing out that the book had linguistic faults. 'Does it maintain any heresies?' Henry demanded. 'Well, not actual heresies,' Gardiner was forced to reply. 'Then, in God's name, let it go out among our people,' the king said.[21] It was a moment of high triumph for the reformers. Coverdale's Bible lacked the royal imprimatur but Cromwell was already planning an injunction which would oblige every incumbent to buy a copy for his church.

The reformers also had cause to congratulate themselves on achieving closer ties with reformed churches on the continent. The emergence of the Schmalkaldic League of German Lutheran princes had changed the political map of Europe. It provided England with a new diplomatic option. The choice no longer lay between siding with France against the Empire or with the Empire against France; another alliance now became possible. For much of the year from March 1535 to March 1536 English delegations were hard at work in Wittenberg trying to conclude a formal agreement. Throughout most of the negotiations Henry was content to be represented by one of the extraordinary mavericks of the English Reformation, Robert Barnes. The colourful career of this ex-friar included spells in prison for his brand of eccentric radicalism, recantations, rejection of recantations and escape to the continent by means of faking his own death. The Germans were adamant that their doctrinal statement, the Augsburg Confession, must form part of any contract but Henry, still clinging to the fiction of his orthodoxy, was unwilling to be irrevocably associated with a heretical statement of belief.

Cranmer was also establishing close contacts with the evangelicals of Strasbourg and the Swiss cities. Martin Bucer was greatly impressed by the English primate and was probably the first politician to prophesy that England could become the leader of Protestant Europe. He canvassed his friends in other centres of reform, urging them to use their best endeavours to draw Henry VIII's kingdom into the battle against the papal Antichrist and the extremist Anabaptists. All this was happening in the opening months of 1536 and the English evangelicals really sensed that events were running in their favour. Cromwell stepped up his propaganda campaign and made sure that the pulpit at St Paul's Cross was occupied by reliable men. Cranmer showed the way by preaching against purgatory and denouncing the pope as Antichrist. He and his colleagues were now boldly taking a lead in that pulpit warfare the archbishop had tried to defuse by his injunction of June 1534 preventing preaching about sensitive subjects.

The reason for this deliberate raising of the temperature was the campaign which Henry and his vicegerent were now launching against the monasteries. On 22 February Viscount Lisle, the king's deputy in Calais, received a letter from one of his informants in London:

> touching . . . your request to my master [Cromwell] concerning the Abbey of Bewley, I cannot perceive that the same or any like shall be suppressed, nor any like lands, for as much as at the session of this Parliament they ordain statutes and provisions for the maintenance and good order of the clergy . . . But if any chance shall hap in that case, or any like that may happen to be for your commodity and profit, I shall, as your own poor servant, have vigilant and diligent ear thereunto.[22]

This is the first extant documentary evidence we have relating to the dissolution of the monasteries. It is interesting for at least two reasons. It proves that, by the first weeks of the year, rumours were circulating about action to be taken against the religious orders. And it tells us that landowners 'in the know' were eager to snap up any bargains that might be going. Parliament had recovened on 4 February but it was another month before a bill was introduced into the Lords for surrendering to the king all religious houses with an income of less than £200 per year. There was little opposition to the measure in either house. By 18 March – a mere two weeks from its introduction – Parliament had passed the Act.

That fact is crucial to any understanding we may reach about what was the most momentous change yet to take place in the saga of the Reformation. The disappearance of houses of monks and nuns would affect communities up and down the land. In areas distant from the capital the news would arouse great resentment. Yet the crucial legislation came into being without any strong show of dissent. Why? One ingredient of what must be a complex answer is that the dissolution of smaller houses did not seem to be such a big deal. Western monasticism had had its ups and downs over the centuries and, as we have seen, by the early sixteenth century its halcyon days were behind it. It was quite common for small religious houses that lacked recruits to be closed down and their remaining members to be moved into larger communities. Lady Margaret Beaufort and Cardinal Wolsey were among those who had used the resources of dissolved abbeys to fund their own pet educational projects and the new spirit of humanism generally endorsed such enterprises.

Greed was an obvious motive for parliamentarians and their friends to welcome the 1536 Act. By the beginning of the year and possibly earlier, rumours were circulating (and, as is their nature, becoming distorted in the process) that significant chunks of monastic property were about to change hands. During the preceding autumn a few small religious houses had been persuaded by Cromwell's aides that they were no longer viable and it would not have been difficult to deduce that other establishments would, one way or another, be induced to follow suit. Landowners saw this as an opportunity to extend their estates or consolidate their holdings. They hoped to be able to buy or rent property from the Crown. Cromwell may well have been casting hints abroad that would encourage such territorial ambitions. The prospect of a once-in-a-lifetime business opportunity created what can only be described as a frenzied scramble to take advantage of the bonanza. From early March requests for specific monastic lands flooded into Cromwell's office. Some more devout appellants who had a genuine affection for the religious houses experienced a genuine dilemma. Most, like Sir Simon Harcourt, found ways to assuage their conscience:

> There is a little house of canons in Staffordshire, called Routon, built and endowed by my ancestors, to the intent that they might be prayed for perpetually, and many of them are buried there . . . I beg you will be a mediator to the King for me, that the same house may continue, and he shall have £100 and you £100 if you can accomplish it, and £20 out of the said house. If the King is determined to dissolve it I desire to have it, as it adjoins such small lands as I have in that country.[23]

Even the arch-conservative Duke of Norfolk joined in the scrimmage. He undoubtedly found the process distasteful but, as he wrote to Cromwell, 'where others speak I must speak too'. Since the Act made provision for the dispossessed monks and nuns by relocating them in other houses of their orders or compensating them with pensions and since it allowed the king to exempt any house from closure, many who assented to the Act were able to persuade themselves that no real harm was being done.

Some there were who welcomed the Act as a long-overdue reform. Henry justified his assumption of the headship by taking on the role of the scourge of God, who would purify the English church. He had never been an enthusiast for the religious life and recent events had convinced him that monastic houses potentially harboured supporters of the papacy. He was ready to believe that within many cloisters treason and vice went hand in hand and some of his subjects shared this jaundiced view. Libidinous nuns and pleasure-bent abbots were stock figures of fun. Criticism, from the satires of Erasmus and the lampoons of Holbein to the dirty jokes shared across alehouse tables, featured tales of seduction, sodomy and sleaze. There was certainly some fire amid all this smoke. In claustrophobic, same-sex communities pledged to celibacy, where inmates were often enrolled as children and where some were placed for reasons which had little to do with religious zeal, temptations were great and scandal could scarce be avoided. Henry, through his vicegerent, had carried out a thorough survey of monastic life during 1535. His first priority had been the compilation of the *Valor Ecclesiasticus*. Like an industrialist taking over an old family firm, he had ordered a comprehensive stocktake of all church property and revenues. This had provided him, along with much other valuable information, with an accurate picture of the landed wealth which had been accumulated over the centuries by the monasteries, much of which, he concluded, could be put to better uses. The next step was a visitation of the 850 houses of religion. This was carried out by Cromwell's agents in the autumn. Their instructions were to produce as damning a report as possible of the state of English monasticism. They were careful to register every example of incontinence, every moral lapse, every financial irregularity, every instance of internal discord, every falling away from strict observance of the rules. They readily mixed rumour with fact and gossip with truth and assiduously encouraged unhappy inmates to tell tales about their superiors. The resulting sensational exposé was presented to Parliament in support of the Act of Dissolution.

The means by which this ancient institution was brought

down were shoddy in the extreme and the motives of most people concerned were, at best, questionable. But our scepticism should not deflect us from what was the most important aspect of the campaign against the monasteries. For the first time parliamentary legislation actually became a vehicle for *doctrinal* change. This was the point at which the political and religious reformations began to converge. Cromwell saw that his position as king's deputy in matters ecclesiastical could provide the opportunity to steer the English church firmly in an evangelical direction. His dislike of monasticism was personal (and it was a help to know that the king shared his prejudice). Among the aides-memoires that this most methodical of men wrote for himself some time in December or January was a long list of miscellaneous 'remembrances'. In the midst of it was the following:

> To advise the King to grant few licences for any to be absent from the Parliament. Specially to remember forestallers and regrators, and specially the monopolies used throughout this realm. Specially to speak of utter destruction of sanctuaries. For the dissolution of all franchises and liberties throughout this realm and specially the franchise of spirituality. The abomination of religious persons throughout this realm, and a reformation to [be] devised therein. To send Stephen Vaughan into Flanders. Device to be taken for the purgation of the prisons . . . [24]

Amid actions to be taken to regulate mercantile activities, to remove corruption in the prison service and to ensure a majority for government measures in Parliament, we thus find plans to close traditional ecclesiastical refuges that enabled fugitives to escape royal justice and to tackle the 'abomination of religious persons'. The choice of language is indicative of strong feeling. It was one thing to devise measures to bring all church matters under tighter state control but quite another to launch a moral crusade against monks and nuns.

The projected closure of religious houses and the reduction of the number of men and women dedicated to the cloistered life could not avoid having doctrinal implications. Coupled with the pulpit attacks, the dissolution undermined the age-old teaching about purgatory. Theory and practice came together. If such an intermediate place did not exist there was no need for a special caste of men and women to pray for souls supposedly in transit through it. If religious houses were closed people would come to realise that there was no longer any need to pay for post-mortem prayer. For those dubious about the closures there was a moral carrot: the money currently expended on maintaining the monastic system could be better spent. Cranmer suggested in one sermon that the king would have no more need to tax his people and there was much talk of relieving the poor and making funds available for educational projects. Cromwell, Cranmer, Latimer and other 'new men' now well placed to shape the official belief system of the English church were well aware of the impact of Lutheran teaching about the afterlife. In those parts of Germany where the Reformation had taken hold monasticism had withered on the vine. Luther, the ex-monk, had denounced the unscriptural fiction of purgatory and the way the old church had used its supposed influence over the fate of souls departed to swell its coffers and bolster its power. The results had included mass desertions from the religious life and the secularisation of monastic property. England's reform-ers confidently expected the same things to happen in their own country. But Cromwell was not prepared to wait until the impact of vernacular Scripture acted like a weedkiller in England's fair garden. Hence the parliamentary attack on monasticism.

At the end of March 1536 all was going well for the advocates of reform. Then came the bombshell. Henry turned violently and viciously against Anne, her family and her friends and made it clear to Cromwell that he wanted a change of queen. His eye had alighted upon another young woman of the court, Jane Seymour, and he now intended to marry her. To close observers this looked like a rerun of the annulment of Henry's first marriage; in his desperate search for a legitimate male heir the king was throwing over his current wife for a younger woman. What mattered to most people at court was the latest turn in the carousel of royal favour: Boleyns out, Seymours in. What mattered to the champions of reform and their enemies were the implications of Anne's fate for religious policy. The Spanish ambassador passed on a rumour that the queen's fall would drag down several of her episcopal protégés (he presumably counted Cranmer among this number) who had, allegedly, helped her to conceal the adulteries she was accused of. He also looked forward to seeing Princess Mary rehabilitated.

Historians still argue over the reasons for the end of the Boleyn marriage. Fortunately, that is a minefield we do not need to enter. What we have to record is that the reversal of religious policy which many expected simply did not happen. The two men heading up the reform retained the king's favour – by the simple expedient of falling in with his wishes. Henry wanted Anne dead. He looked to his secretary to arrange it and to his archbishop to pronounce the church's blessing on the judicial murder not only of the queen but of the group of men supposedly implicit in her sexual adventures. Cromwell, with his usual single-minded (and ruthless) efficiency, organised the interrogation of the accused, their trials and their executions. Cranmer was absolutely shattered by the 'revelation' of the queen's misdeeds. He wrote to the king expressing his difficulty in believing in her guilt. But he fell into line and pronounced the annulment of Henry's second marriage on the grounds of Anne's pre-contract to another. (It seems not to have occurred to anyone at the time that if Henry and Anne had not been legally married, Anne could not have been guilty of adultery.) This was certainly not Cromwell's and Cranmer's finest hour but, by submitting to the will of an increasingly tyrannical king, they preserved the religious cause they both held dear. In July a grateful king bestowed on Cromwell the office of Lord Privy Seal, recently stripped from the Earl of Wiltshire, Anne's father, and raised him to the peerage as Baron Cromwell of Wimbledon.

The Reformation had survived but its baptism of blood had inaugurated a new phase in the religious revolution. The leaders of both sides learned from the events of the spring that the nature of religious politics had become red in tooth and claw. They also perceived that their king had changed, that his mood swings were becoming more extreme, that his monumental egotism had lifted him above the sensibilities and moral restraints of ordinary people. Henry as a ruler was, as More had pointed out, like a lion. Someone in his confidence could direct the beast's power and cruelty for his own ends – but would always need to keep a wary eye on those razor-sharp claws.

Doctrinal change – or, at least, redefinition – was in the air and when Convocation met in July the clergy considered the latest information from Wittenberg. Bishop Edward Fox, Henry's envoy, had failed to bring about a formal accommodation between England and the Schmalkaldic princes but he did now return with the Wittenberg Articles, a compromise set of doctrinal propositions which, it was hoped, would pave the way for a treaty. Cromwell now adopted the practice of attending Convocation personally or sending a deputy. He and Cranmer tried to dragoon the assembly into accepting the articles but the conservative bishops united in stalwart opposition. They had seen traditional ceremonies and beliefs dismantled and their own power reduced over recent years and they now pressed their backs firmly to the wall. When the bitter arguments were reported to Henry he was brought face to face with the responsibilities he had tacitly assumed with the headship of the church. He, and he alone, had to define what the Church of England believed.

Henry ordered his bishops to reach a workable compromise. Of course, he dressed up his instructions in pious language. Their articles should be 'most catholic conceived' in order to achieve 'the unity that God's holy word doth require'.[25] The result, known as the Ten Articles, was inevitably a mishmash. Religious conviction cannot be achieved by committees any

176 A Brief History of the English Reformation

more than it can be commanded by royal diktat. If either side could be said to have 'won' it would be the evangelicals. The first five clauses (on essential doctrines) followed fairly closely the Wittenberg Articles. For the first time in England the doctrine of justification by faith alone was set forth as official teaching. Yet as a sop to the conservatives the importance of good works following justification was stressed. The seven sacraments, once so stoutly defended by Henry, were whittled down to three – baptism, Holy Communion and penance. However, confession to a priest was acknowledged as having been instituted by Christ, something firmly denied by Cranmer. On purgatory there was compromise amounting almost to mutual contradiction. The articles insisted that 'it is a very good and charitable deed to pray for souls departed' but then declared about purgatory, 'the name thereof and kinds of pains there . . . be to us uncertain by scripture.' Prayers to the saints were allowed as long as they were 'done without any vain superstition' but votive offerings to and adoration of religious images were now forbidden.

The theory having been established, it remained only to put it into practice. In August Cromwell issued a set of injunctions to the clergy. They were to preach on the Ten Articles but to avoid such contentious subjects as relics, images and miracles. Quite how the conscientious pastor was to walk this tightrope was not explained, nor was there anything to stop partisan preachers labouring articles they approved and neglecting the others. One significant fact about the articles is Cromwell's failure to introduce his pet subject of vernacular Scripture. His first draft contained the requirement that every incumbent should provide, within one year, a copy of the Bible in English and encourage people to read it or have it read to them. Did he have second thoughts or did the king veto the idea? Either way the omission of this vital plank in the evangelical platform is a striking indication of where matters stood in the summer of 1536. The contemporary chronicler Charles Wriothesley was certainly optimistic when he recorded,

This year, in August, the schism ceased here in England of the diversity of preachers, for the King sent a book of certain Articles concerning the articles of our faith and other ceremonies of the Church, the which the bishops of this realm should cause to be declared in their dioces[es] ... the which the King, as supreme head of the Church, with his prelates and clergy of this realm had assented and consented in their convocation to be observed and kept from thenceforth through all this realm of England.[26]

Important battles had been won by the evangelicals but the conservatives had preserved some doctrines which were incompatible with the new learning and the war was far from over. The chronicler was certainly optimistic to claim that the schism had ceased. Within months the country was in armed conflict, caused in part by the religious changes.

Before we move on to consider that it will be useful to take stock of where the English church stood in 1536. Henry VIII had made himself Supreme Head of that church but what, exactly, did that title mean?

You think by subtlety and guile to overthrow the strength of the royal prerogatives which God has given me. I charge you by the fidelity and oath by which you are bound to me that you submit yourself to correction for those presumptuous words against my crown and dignity. And I further beseech the archbishops and bishops here present to do me justice upon you, as appropriate to the rights of the royal crown granted to me by the Most High. It is clear that you oppose my royal dignities and are striving to deprive me of privileges due to me by ancient right.[27]

The outraged words are those of Henry II and were directed against a bishop who had attempted to assert authority over an abbey founded by the king's great-grandfather, William the Conqueror. Henry had already upset the pope and, as a result, his kingdom had been placed under papal interdict. Worse was to follow when Henry had his historic falling-out with Thomas Becket. Conflict between secular rulers and the ecclesiastical hierarchy was far from uncommon; it was the rule rather than the exception. It was so because over the centuries incompatible precedents had been established by contenders for papal and royal authority. The exercise of dominion in church and state depended upon agreed spheres of spiritual and temporal juris-diction but no such spheres were agreed. Both sides could rest their case on holy writ, the writings of the church Fathers and current custom. In asserting his rights against the papacy Henry VIII was doing nothing new, nothing which powerful European monarchs had not attempted from time to time. What *was* new was the comprehensive nature of Henry's claims. Those claims were formulated as a direct result of the long-drawn-out strug-gle over the Great Matter. If Pope Clement had been in a position to reach an accommodation over the royal divorce and if Henry had not been so stubborn, scholars would not have been set to dig out every scrap of evidence they could find. If they had not produced so much material, the king would not have 'discovered' that his God-given powers were so extensive. Yet, by 1536, those powers still lacked precise definition. Henry and his supporters were not working to a clear blueprint. The meaning of the royal supremacy took shape gradually with each twist and turn in the argument with Rome and, as the Ten Articles demonstrates, it still had ragged edges.

When Cranmer and Henry's committee of scholars compiled what would become the *Collectanea satis copiosa* they started out with the conviction that the king was God's deputy in England and that, by virtue of his anointing, he was endowed with an authority that was, in essence, spiritual. Tyndale had obligingly expressed this in trenchant, uncompromising terms:

the king is, in this world, without law; and may at his lust do right or wrong, and shall give accounts but to God only . . . no person . . . may be exempt from this ordinance of God:

neither can the profession of monks and friars, or anything
that the popes or bishops can lay for themselves, except them
from the sword of the emperor or kings.[28]

Henry – and, indeed, his father before him – had always set
great store by his *imperium*. His realm was an 'empire' no less
than the territory ruled by Charles V. It was Henry VII's chroniclers who had drawn up the royal genealogy that linked the
house of Tudor directly to Constantine. As that emperor had
owed no allegiance to any other mortal, so England's king was
at the pinnacle of a social pyramid and all beneath him, whether
clergy or lay, were his subjects and his subjects alone.

But this raised the question of the nature of the king's authority within the church. What was emerging from the royal
propaganda of the early 1530s was a new claim (although, of
course, its defenders insisted that it was not at all novel) that the
king possessed not only *potestas jurisdictionis*, administrative
and judicial authority, but also *potestas ordinis*, sacerdotal and
sacramental authority. Cranmer and his scholers could find
several examples of this 'caesaropapism' in history. Constantine
and Justinian were among emperors who had ruled the church
in all aspects of its life. They had resolved theological disputes
and been involved in establishing orthodox doctrine. Henry's
advisers claimed for him just such a priestly kingship. Henry
had a genuine desire to use his position to purify English religion and he believed himself well qualified theologically to
enforce reform. All the major doctrinal statements of the reign,
from the *Assertio* onwards, provide evidence of his personal
involvement in the form of annotations and marginalia in the
king's own hand. But the fullness of *potestas ordinis* was still not
claimed either by or on behalf of the king. Henry never exercised the obvious priestly functions: he never presided at mass,
or ordained clergy, or heard confession, or even preached. In
1536 the reality of royal supremacy was still evolving.

Henry's reformation had started out as an exploration of his
own power. In defining it he had relied on the only dynamic

'party' within the church, the evangelicals. They shared his
reforming zeal, though what many of them wanted went well
beyond what Henry was prepared to sanction. By the summer
of 1536 he had established his undisputed sway over all the
clergy and laity of his realm. But by then the Reformation
proper had established its own momentum. It was being fuelled
by the talents and enthusiasm of a growing number of people
– both high and low. They still constituted a small minority
within the English church but they were punching above their
weight. What they and the king had signally failed to take into
account was the will of the majority. That majority was about to
make its voice heard.

Chapter 6

England Disunited

Throughout the remaining decade of Henry VIII's reign the government was faced with a singular dilemma. The country was bitterly divided in matters of religion. The king earnestly desired the restoration of peace and harmony. But it was the king who was responsible for the discord; he had freed from restraint the existing rivalries, resentments and conflicting beliefs which had previously been reasonably well contained and the genies he had released could not be rebottled. Henry would use force, threats, statutes, proclamations and direct appeals for unity in his attempts to persuade English Christians to embrace an agreed doctrinal package. What, of course, he could not accept was that he was part of the problem. His councillors and courtiers were certainly not going to point out this unpalatable truth to him.

Henry believed – or managed to convince himself – that the religious changes he was inflicting on his people were for their greater good. Those who disagreed regarded him as a wilful tyrant. Sir Thomas Elyot, in *The Book Named The Governor*, did not dare to say this in as many words. What he did do was urge the king to follow the example of his noble sire. Henry VII was no longer represented as the avaricious despot hinted at by More in his coronation ode of 1509 (see p. 3–4), but as a shrewd and pious monarch who had brought peace and unity to the realm and won the respect of foreign princes. By implication Henry VIII was in danger of throwing away that happy concord. The message was not likely to appeal to the king, whose relations with his father had been less than cordial. The second Tudor *was* a tyrant but he could not be oblivious to the comments made by Elyot and others. He was always concerned about public opinion. He ruled by diktat but he was careful to obtain the support of Parliament. He went to enormous lengths to persuade people that he acted according to the dictates of his conscience. The considerable volume of printed and preached propaganda which he sanctioned was intended to justify his stance on religious matters. For example, in 1526 he published for general view his exchange of correspondence with Martin Luther arising from the *Assertio Septem Sacramentorum*, in order to instruct people in true doctrine and to preserve them from the errors certain to occur if they read Tyndale's New Testament for themselves, instead of being guided by their 'pastoral fathers' (of whom he was, in his own estimation, chief). Henry, aspiring humanist scholar that he was, did not, he assured readers, wish to stifle intellectual enquiry but to 'encourage well-learned men to set forth and translate into our own mother tongue many good things . . . which for fear of wrong taking they dare not yet so'.[1] Like anyone who takes spiritual issues seriously, Henry's religious convictions changed over the years. He apparently thought that his subjects could be encouraged and, if necessary, forced to keep pace with his developing beliefs. He was genuinely oblivious of the contradiction inherent in his position.

He must then have been profoundly shocked, as well as alarmed, when, in the autumn and winter of 1536–7, he experienced for the first time concerted opposition to his religious policy. Hitherto, only a few brave souls – mostly 'professional' religious – had dared to resist the royal will and been prepared to suffer the consequences. The majority, as is always the case, either did not greatly care about the changes affecting society or, if they did, were not prepared to stand up and be counted. But, as those changes increased and as central government was seen to impinge more and more upon the customs and beliefs of ordinary men and women in the shires, the moment arrived when spontaneous revolt erupted.

The Lincolnshire Rebellion and the Pilgrimage of Grace (see below pp.186ff) severely rocked the throne but it has never been a simple matter to determine exactly *why* the people of the northern shires took up arms. What is clear is that there was a deep sense of alienation in the remoter parts of the realm from what was happening at the centre. One of the demands the rebels would make was that the king would hold a Parliament in York and take the opportunity to acquaint himself with the grievances of his northern subjects. But those grievances were many and varied and differed from region to region. Thus, the people of Richmondshire were angry about enclosures while Lincolnshire clergy resented the latest tax imposed upon the church. In a few localities people were genuinely attached to the monasteries which were in the process of being dismantled. Yet people tended to be more worried about their own security when religious houses were closed: those who worked for the monks and nuns or held tenancies feared the loss of jobs or tenure. Henry's subjects had a variety of reasons for being agin the government but they were too circumspect to blame the king. Few people had the boldness (or recklessness) of one Norfolk woman who, in May 1537, declared, 'we shall never have good world till we [come] together and with clubs and clouted shoon [i.e. hob-nailed boots] shall the deed be done; for we had never good world since this king reigned.'[2] It was safer to lay the blame at the door of the king's 'evil advisers'. There was a general feeling that Henry should take his councillors exclusively from among the nobles and bishops, the traditional leaders of rural society, and not from 'new men' like Cromwell, Cranmer and Audley. These were the disruptive elements who wanted to turn the world upside-down with their new learning – as many clergy told their parishioners. Few men and women in the distant shires had had much if any exposure to evangelical teaching but their clergy instilled in them a fear of 'heresy'. Simple people were easily persuaded that the unwelcome changes to which they were being subjected and others that were falsely rumoured to be on the way could all be attributed to 'Lutheranism'. Thus the anti-government movement (or series of movements) north of the Trent gradually took on a religious hue. Its leaders used words like 'pilgrimage' and 'defence of Christ's church' to excuse rebellion, violence and treason.

Having said that, the point also needs to be made that the government provoked reaction by insensitive haste. The super-efficient Cromwell and his over-zealous agents were determined to bring about sweeping changes while tarrying for none. As they rode about the country, examining monks and secular clergy, taking audits of monastic property, setting workmen to dismantle shrines, strip the lead from roofs and load London-bound wagons with the loot taken from abbey churches, they inevitably encountered opposition and provoked the suspicion that unspeakably worse things were to come. Ill-feeling was widespread. Disturbances of the peace were reported in Somerset, East Anglia and elsewhere. No outbreaks reached the proportions of those in the North but there is no telling what might have happened had the Lincolnshire and Yorkshire rebellions not been so speedily suppressed. It was false rumours that lit the blue touchpaper of the northern risings. The injunctions following on the Ten Articles had made inroads into the people's leisure activities by abolishing lesser holy days which fell during harvest time and ordering that all church dedication days were to be celebrated on the first Sunday in October. This innovation was meant to do two things, ensure the efficient gathering in of the year's crops and restrict the veneration of images, but most people saw it simply as an unwarranted interference with their traditional way of life. Then came stories of the dismantling of lesser abbeys. Who could doubt that these upheavals were but the beginning of a programme which would destroy all that ordinary folk held dear? When people saw cartloads of altar furnishings, vestments and precious reliquaries trundling south-wards they could easily believe that parish churches would be next on the government's list for spoliation. If lesser monasteries were to be closed and their inmates moved to other houses how could anyone doubt that parish life would not be similarly rationalised, some churches closed and their treasures confiscated by the king? Such morbid speculation was fanciful but some people who knew that used common fears for their own ends. The clergy did nothing to prevent growing panic. Quite the contrary. Many grabbed the opportunity to strike against those who, they believed, had been the cause of their humiliation.

They were the members of society who had already suffered most from religious change and they stood to lose even more if the trend of government policy continued. Ever since 1531, when the attack on the clerical order had begun, they had seen their status and authority dwindle. They were incensed by the heretical influences which seemed to be gaining the upper hand in the distant capital and particularly resented the new orders they were under to remove images from their churches and preach against revered local customs now designated as 'superstitious' by Cromwell and his men. Fewer altars meant fewer masses to be said for the souls of the departed and fewer masses meant fewer mass priests. Several rural priests felt threatened by the coming of commissioners to enquire into the educational standards of the clergy. They now disobeyed the injunctions by using sermons to urge their people to unite in defence of their ancient ceremonies. It was the clergy who allowed their churches to be used as rallying points for the rebels. It was the clergy who had their steeple bells rung to summon men to defence of the old traditions. In the aftermath of the rising several witnesses singled out the clergy as the principal instigators of trouble:

> The parson of Stewton, 2 parsons of South Somercotes [and] of Biscathorpe, the vicar of Haughton with the great club and many other priests were at Louth on the Monday, and but for them the people had been stayed . . .
>
> The priests were the occasion of this business. The

parsons of Helloff offered them £40 and the parsons of
Somercotes and Welton and the dean of Muckton aided and
encouraged them.[3]

The insurrection began at Louth. The people of this prosperous, medium-sized town in the fen country east of the
Lincolnshire Wolds had particular reason to be sensitive to
change. They were justifiably proud of their parish church. For
two generations they had planned, raised funds and laboured to
rebuild, redecorate and re-equip St James's, Louth. Their
crowning achievement had been the erection of a soaring
95-metre spire which remains one of the finest of such construc-
tions in England. Louth folk were proud of their achievement
and naturally defensive about any threat to it. During the
summer they had seen the Cistercian abbey of Louth Park and
the nunnery of Legbourne dissolved. Then, at the end of
September, news came of the approach of two more sets of
commissioners: the bishop's chancellor, Dr Raynes, was coming
to conduct a visitation of the clergy and ensure their adherence
to the Ten Articles, and Henry's tax collectors were on their way
to collect the second part of the subsidy voted in 1534. As the
strangers appeared in their midst bent on carrying out their
duties it only took a few minor clashes between the London
sophisticates and the 'rude' commons to ignite the air already
thick with the combustible fumes of resentment.

Michaelmas (29 September) was an important landmark in
the rural year. As well as being a church festival and holiday, it
was a quarter day when landlords (or their reeves) met with
tenants for the payment of rents and the settlement of other
accounts, and it was a day on which certain local officials were
traditionally elected. In other words Michaelmas was a time
when communities were particularly self-conscious about their
identity. When the Louthians congregated for high mass in St
James's on the feast day of St Michael and All Angels and
witnessed the impressive ceremonial of clergy in sumptuous
vestments processing behind the choir, carrying silver crosses

and lavishly embroidered banners; when they later gathered for the traditional goose feast; when they sat over their ale long into the evening, their thoughts and conversation must have been of their anxiety for the continuance of all these things. The mood continued over the weekend. Back at the church on Sunday 1 October one of the choirmen spoke for many when he called out, 'Let us have all the crosses before us this day for we cannot tell when we shall see them before us again.'[4]

During Sunday and Monday the priests of the district began to gather in obedience to the summons of the diocesan chancellor and it was this concentration of angry clergy which turned vague grumbling into violent action. The parishioners of Louth seemed content for the moment to collect together all the church treasures and remove them to a place of safety. It was their spiritual leaders who sent to the surrounding villages for all able-bodied men to come to the town and who, as their people congregated, distributed the poison of hatred. One clerical orator proclaimed that, if he could come face to face with Cromwell, he would dash out the heretic's brains and he was not the only one to indulge in frenzied rant. Faced with events such as the rebellions of 1536–7 historians usually seek to identify 'causes' but the quest for rational motives can miss the point. Eastern Lincolnshire was a remote and introverted region, partially cut off by fenland quags from the 'outside world'. Its community now felt under threat from a government that was as distant emotionally as it was geographically. All that was holding people back from violent protest was fear of the consequences. When the clergy offered holy justification and absolution the people simply threw caution to the wind and gave free rein to their hatred. By Sunday evening they had chosen one Nicholas Melton, henceforth known as 'Captain Cobbler', to be their leader.

From this point mindless mob rule took over. During the ensuing few days the outrages perpetrated by the rebels rapidly grew worse. Bands roamed the countryside, urging and forcing others to join them. All clergy (whether supporters of the insurrection or not) and other men of substance were sworn to be loyal to 'God, the king and the commons'. The rebels broke into mansions and abbeys demanding food and weapons. They captured some of Cromwell's agents and imprisoned them. They made a point of rounding up as many of the local gentry as possible and obliging them, under threat of violence to themselves and their families, to assume the leadership of the rebellion. When Dr Raynes fell into their hands they tore him limb from limb. Other unfortunates who opposed them or who simply found themselves in the wrong place at the wrong time were also summarily despatched. Within a week most of the county was up in arms. A messenger sent from London to assess the situation reckoned that some forty thousand Lincolnshire men were in revolt and that messages were already being exchanged with potential allies beyond the Humber. As reports of the disturbances reached the Tudor court it seemed to many that England was about to experience its own version of the German Peasants' War.

Not surprisingly, it was only after long hours of ill-tempered debate that the leaders of the rising were able to agree on a list of 'grievances' (no longer demands) to be sent to the king. They were eventually able to whittle them down to four. They asked for remission of the latest agreed taxation. They requested that no more abbeys should be dissolved. They complained about the king's choice of councillors. And they demanded the repeal of the Statute of Uses. This latter was a clause added by gentlemen who were incensed by a government measure which complicated the process of property inheritance. Thus, while the menace of the rebellion was growing, the actual demands of the insurgents were being watered down. Cooler heads were prevailing and divisions were appearing in the rebel ranks. By 8 October the host, with their gentry prisoners, had moved to Lincoln and there an uneasy truce was established. Captain Cobbler and his associates reluctantly agreed to wait for the king's reply to their articles before taking any further action.

With the benefit of hindsight we can see that from this point everything depended on timing. The rebels needed to maintain their impetus. The king needed to muster his forces. The captive gentlemen and their freer friends needed to sow doubt and fear among the rank and file of the insurgents. Every day that passed without some definite move by either side increased the probability that the situation would get beyond anyone's control. There can be little doubt that Henry VII would have taken the field in person and crushed the revolt with a display of royal power and courage. Henry VIII, by contrast, shut himself in his strongest castle at Windsor, ordered all his leading councillors to convene there and responded to the crisis with rage born of fear. Having recently killed his own wife for suspected betrayal, he was disposed to see disloyalty everywhere. The actions of the Lincolnshire gentlemen aroused his suspicion. So did the attitude of people closer to the king. Having instructed the Earl Marshal, Thomas Howard, Duke of Norfolk, to lead an army to the North, he quickly rescinded the order, believing (with reason) that the duke sympathised with some of the grievances expressed by the rebels. It took Henry several days to devise a suitable military strategy. He ordered leading nobles to join a force heading for Lincolnshire but also mustered a reserve army to encamp at Ampthill in Bedfordshire in case of trouble nearer home. Reports flooding in to Windsor suggested that if, as seemed likely, the rebel host marched southwards they would find considerable support. Only eight kilometres away from the royal headquarters a priest was arrested for declaring from the pulpit that the Lincolnshire dissidents were 'God's people, who did fight and defend God's quarrel'.[5]

The inconsistency of orders issued, then reversed or changed indicates a measure of panic. Henry faced the possibility of that horror from which his father had freed the realm – civil war. Yet what seems to have angered him more were the veiled accusations of heresy. The rebels blamed the new religious policy on his close advisers but Henry refused to accept this escape route from responsibility. A decade before, when there had been a revolt against an unpopular tax called the Amicable Grant, the king had not hesitated to make Wolsey his scapegoat but now he refused to disassociate himself from the dissolution of the monasteries, the assumption of headship of the church, the breach with Rome or the reforms announced in recent months. These were *his* policies and he was proud of them. So, while his military response had about it a shambolic air, his answer to the rebels' articles was defiant and could not have been clearer. He castigated them as 'the rude commons of one shire, and that one of the most brute and beastly of the whole realm, and of least experience . . . you like traitors and rebels have behaved, and not like true subjects, as ye name yourselves'. Henry upbraided them for their presumption, then went on to answer their objections, point by point. Finally, he demanded that they hand over for trial a hundred ringleaders and threatened that further obstinacy would 'put yourselves, lives, wives, children, lands, goods and chattels . . . in the utter adventure of total destruction, and utter ruin by force and violence of the sword'.[6]

The firm stance seemed to work. Charles Brandon, Duke of Suffolk, entered Lincolnshire at the head of a royal army, the captive gentlemen held in Lincoln escaped and the host disintegrated. But by now there were disturbing signs of disaffection spreading across the Humber. Brandon, who reached Lincoln on 17 October, lowered the temperature by declining to carry out the draconian retribution demanded by the king but at the same time he sent for reinforcements. The prologue might be over but the main drama was only just beginning. Even as Brandon re-established royal authority in Lincoln, malcontents under the leadership of a lawyer called Robert Aske took possession of York. The Pilgrimage of Grace that now convulsed all the northern shires was a more complex movement than the Lincolnshire revolt and involved all strata of society. Norfolk and the Earl of Shrewsbury were sent, with all the men they could muster, to face the new menace.

But before we consider the apotheosis of popular, involuntary traditionalism we need to reflect on events at the centre of power. Feelings among the clergy of the capital were every whit as bitter as those of their provincial brethren. Cranmer was often sneeringly dismissed as 'the ostler', a reference to his brief first marriage in Cambridge to a girl from one of the city inns, and similar insults were hurled at other advocates of the new learning. Tension in London was raised to new levels by the events of 1536. The fall of the hated Boleyns had raised expectations of a return to the old ways and when hopes were dashed the atmosphere of resentment became almost tangible. The Ten Articles further fuelled the anger of the traditionalists. Reactionary clergy had their own information network and when news began to arrive that church people in England's rural hinterland were resisting religious innovation bolder spirits in London proclaimed that the time had come to make a stand. There were many priests who would cheerfully have echoed the threat of their Lincolnshire colleague to dash Cromwell's brains out. The vicegerent was beyond their power. His accomplices were not.

On 13 November, at about five o'clock in the morning, the prominent mercer Robert Packington set out from his house in Soper's Lane, as was his pious habit, to walk the short distance to the chapel of Mercers' Hall for early mass. As he crossed the still-quiet thoroughfare of West Cheap he was shot down in cold blood by a hired assassin, who immediately disappeared in the misty darkness. Such an atrocity would not fail to make the headlines in the twenty-first century. Its impact on Tudor London was many times greater. This was the first time in the City's history that a firearm had been used for murder. Despite a substantial reward offered for information, the perpetrator and his hirer were never brought to book but suspicion fastened on the conservative clergy and especially on John Incent, Dean of St Paul's. He was a vociferous enemy of the evangelicals, and Packington was not only an evangelical but one of the Christian Brethren involved in the forbidden book trade and a member of Cromwell's network. Whatever else it was, this vicious act was one in the eye for the government; a statement that the northern rebels were not on their own.

Knowledge of this brooding hostility created problems for the Tudor propaganda machine. Threats and bluster might work with ignorant rustics but not with the heterogeneous population of the overcrowded capital. As soon as possible after the defeat of the Lincolnshire insurrection (5 November) Cromwell had appointed Hugh Latimer to preach at Paul's Cross. The bishop was to endorse and explain the official response to the Lincolnshire uprising. He took the opportunity not only to justify the firm suppression of the rebellion but to criticise all those who refused to stand four-square behind the Ten Articles. Habitués of Paul's Cross sermons were used to Latimer's robust evangelicalism but in the nervous atmosphere it could only inflame traditionalist opposition. Hastily the government backtracked. When Latimer preached again at St Paul's Cross, a month later, he was under orders from Cromwell to proclaim 'unity without any special note of any man's folly'. Other evangelical firebrands were kept well away from London pulpits. Some, including Robert Barnes, were actually placed under virtual house arrest to stop them increasing the heat under a pot already dangerously close to boiling over. The king's old fear of being labelled a heretic now surfaced again. In a round robin to the bishops he pointed out that the Ten Articles were, in fact, a statement of orthodox belief and not an evangelical Trojan horse. Henry disavowed Latimer's take on the latest doctrinal statement.

This caution was partly prompted by international developments. The northern revolts were an encouragement to England's enemies. Chapuys had long been inciting Catholic clergy to make a concerted attempt to overthrow the regime and there had been much clandestine talk of foreign aid in the form of money, troops and materiel. Fortunately, talk was all it was but Henry and his Council were not to know that. At the end of 1536 there seemed to be a real possibility that imperial help for the rebels might be forthcoming. Pope Paul III certainly used his influence to bring England's heretical monarch to heel and what particularly infuriated Henry was that he used

Reginald Pole in his schemes. Pole was one of the limbs on the flourishing Yorkist tree and, therefore, of the king's cousinage. Henry had always treated him with great favour, contributing to his education and foreign travels. But Pole was also a darling of Catholic activists. As a pro-papal scholar with a distant claim to the throne he was an obvious focus of interest for those who sought a permanent solution to England's religious problems. At one time there had been talk of marrying him to Princess Mary. Early in 1536 Pole expressed his own opinion of Henry's divorce and the breach with Rome in *Pro Ecclesiasticae Unitatis Defensione*, in which he reluctantly concluded that, if Henry's subjects were pressed to decide between obedience to the king and obedience to the pope, they should choose the latter. In October Paul III summoned Pole to Rome and discussed the English situation with him. He urged on the diffident scholar the duty of playing a prominent part in the English crusade. Francis I was designated as the military leader of this venture and Pole would be made a cardinal-legate (he was at this time still a layman) to oversee the reconversion of his country. Pole resisted any involvement in this scheme. Not only did he flinch at treason, he feared for the safety of his mother and brothers who were in England and, therefore, at the king's mercy. However, in mid-December, he gave in to the pope's demands. He was ordained, made a cardinal and despatched to the Low Countries to co-ordinate plans for the invasion. To Henry this was yet another betrayal and a particularly bitter one. He sent agents to the continent to fetch Pole home to face trial, with the instruction that if they could not engineer his abduction they were to assassinate him.

The rebellion in the northern counties ebbed and flowed during these weeks. It was on 4 October that the lawyer-gentleman Robert Aske came into contact with the Lincolnshire rebels and recognised their grievances as ones shared by many people in the neighbouring county. In all probability he also realised that the rising in Lincolnshire was likely to be doomed by its own disorganisation and the rifts between commons and gentlemen. Certainly, when he hurried home it was to take control of the incipient outbreak in what is now Humberside. Here he was a man of consequence and he knew that the people would follow him. He gave the uprising a clear religious identity, calling it the Pilgrimage of Grace and having banners displaying the five wounds of Christ raised as the battle standards of the Yorkshire host. York fell to the rebels with only a token resistance on 16 October and, on the 21st, Pontefract Castle was yielded up by Thomas, Lord Darcy, a royal servant of long standing, but one divided between his loyalty to the king and his religious convictions. With Darcy there fell into the rebels' hands the Archbishop of York and several gentlemen who had sought refuge in Pontefract. The fire of rebellion spread rapidly over a wide area, engulfing Durham, Northumberland and Lancashire. By 24 October some 30,000 or more 'pilgrims' had gathered at Doncaster, not far from the Nottinghamshire border. This was an army, poised ready, it seemed, to march south.

Henry's military resources were stretched to the uttermost. The Duke of Suffolk had just enough men to contain the East Midlands. The Earl of Shrewsbury was busily recruiting supporters in Nottinghamshire and Derbyshire. But the government's main hope was reposed in the Duke of Norfolk, at last trusted with an 8,000-strong army and instructed by the king to deal firmly with his disobedient subjects. He rightly assessed that a military solution was impossible. Not only were the king's forces heavily outnumbered, their own loyalty could not be assumed and they certainly had no stomach for fighting against their fellow countrymen. There was no alternative to diplomacy. Norfolk held talks with Aske and Darcy, promising to relay their grievances to the king. To say that Henry was not amused would be a serious understatement. 'We marvel much,' he protested, 'that you do all write to us in such extreme and desperate sort, as the world should be, in a manner, turned upside-down, unless we would, in certain points, condescend to the petitions of the rebels'.[7] It was one thing for him to take stock of the situation in

London and make conciliatory gestures to the opposition but, apparently, quite another for his generals in the field to do the same. But what the duke had done, in strategic terms, was to buy time. He managed to drag out talks with the rebel leaders for several weeks, thus halting the impetus of the rising. Norfolk knew that the encamped rebels would find life increasingly difficult as winter approached.

Aske and his colleagues were equally aware of this. They did not want to lose the initiative. But they did not want to fight either. They were intent on finding a peaceful solution; on presenting to the distant government, as a basis for negotiation, a clearly worded ultimatum on which all the 'pilgrims' were agreed. For this reason they were prepared to risk delay and to hold in check the wilder spirits within the movement while they held talks with the various interest groups. But the northern leadership now ran into the same difficulty that had confronted the Lincolnshire rebels: how to present the heterogeneous discontents of the people in a coherent programme which the king could be persuaded to accept.

Aske was particularly concerned to emphasise the religious tone of the rebellion and not allow demands for economic and social reforms to dilute what was, for him, a defence of fundamental Christian truth. For this reason he insisted that a committee of learned clerics should meet to draw up a catalogue of religious grievances. Aske was a man of strong traditionalist convictions and, as a member of the inns of court, he was well aware of the theological debate which lay at the heart of the Reformation. He was intent on preserving the image of the rising as a holy campaign in defence of the ancient faith. He drew up articles for the clergy to discuss and tried – unsuccessfully – to have them endorsed by Archbishop Lee. Despite the pressure put upon him, the primate insisted that the Ten Articles had already defined English church doctrine and that there was no more to be said on the matter. That pro-government stance satisfied neither Aske nor the majority of the clergy. When the representatives of the 'pilgrims' gathered in

Pontefract over the weekend of 2–3 December the committee of clerics met separately to give their responses to a series of articles drawn up by Aske.

What the priests came up with horrified even the traditionalist Robert Aske. Given free rein, they attacked existing government policy in no uncertain terms. Nothing would please them but a complete restoration of their own status and of the church's pre-1529 position in relation to the Crown. Their list of innovations to be reversed is a reminder of just how far England had come in seven years. Papal headship, purgatory, veneration of images, pilgrimage, benefit of clergy, papal dispensations, canon law, the heresy law of Henry IV, abrogated saints' days, the law of sanctuary, alienated church property – the clergy demanded restitution of all these. They wanted draconian punishments to be imposed on preachers and writers of what the church deemed to be heresy. Clergy who had been imprisoned or who had fled into exile for opposing religious change they wanted to see reinstated. Monks and nuns who had accepted pensions to renounce their vows should, they insisted, be forcibly returned to their religious houses. They denied the king's right to collect ecclesiastical tenths and first fruits. When Aske saw the results of the clergy conference he realised that they had gone too far. What they were presenting was not a basis for peaceful negotiation; it was more like a declaration of war. They were demanding that Henry VIII do a humiliating U-turn. That, as Aske well knew, was never going to happen.

When the official list of grievances was drawn up by the rebel council the religious issues were watered down. Aske was still far from happy with the document presented to Norfolk to take to the king and it is not difficult to see why. It was a jumble of assorted complaints which gave the impression of being hastily cobbled together by various parties who were by no means in complete agreement.

The specific religious points were as follows: The 'Anabaptist' heresies of Luther, Wycliffe, Hus, Tyndale and other radicals (fifteen English and continental reformers were specifically listed) were to be outlawed. To the majority of the pilgrims the names of these evangelical writers would have been completely unknown. The inclusion in the list of the legist Christopher St German, who was certainly no heretic, is strongly suggestive of Aske's particular prejudices. St German's textbook, *Doctor and Student*, had opened up the relationship between common and canon law and was a matter of eager debate at the inns of court but it can scarcely have been of great import to the rank and file of the 'pilgrims'. What St German had done and what would have annoyed the better-educated priests among the rebels was enter into controversy with Thomas More over the shortcomings of the clergy and this may explain why he was singled out for denunciation at Pontefract. The list of 'heretics' was both vague and all-embracing. The king would certainly have had no difficulty, in 1536, of sharing the rebels' rejection of most of those named.

The same could not be said of the next religious grievance: 'The supremacy of the Church touching "cura animarum" to be reversed to the See of Rome as before.' This fell some way short of complete rejection of the king's headship of the English church. It drew a distinction between spiritual and temporal jurisdiction, reserving the former to the Bishop of Rome (who, interestingly, was not called 'pope'), including the right to appoint bishops, as long as he did not demand first fruits and other financial dues.

The rebels went on to demand the restitution of suppressed abbeys and singled out for special mention the houses of the Observant Friars. The 'pilgrims' next focused their ire, in a generalised way, on 'the heretics, bishops and temporal, and their sect', and called for such to be burned. Specifically, they wanted to be revenged on 'the Lord Cromwell, the Lord Chancellor, and Sir Richard Rich, knight [who, as Chancellor of the Court of Augmentations, was responsible for the disposal of confiscated monastic property], . . . as the subvertors of the good laws of this realm and maintainers of the false sects of those heretics and the first inventors and bringers in of them'.

The rebels called for the restitution of ancient religious traditions, though in terms that lacked compelling specificity: 'the liberties of the church [i.e. places enjoying certain exemptions from royal jurisdiction] to have their old customs . . . the privileges and rights of the church to be confirmed by act of parliament and priests not suffered by sword'. The rebels demanded the restitution of sanctuary and the right of clergy to be tried by ecclesiastical courts. Of the twenty-four articles in the document only ten related specifically to religious issues. They were still demands to which the king was not going to accede but they avoided, as far as was possible, head-on collision between Henry's view of the church and that of the traditionalist clergy.[8]

On 6 December Aske presented the 'pilgrims' articles to Norfolk and received in return an assurance that the king would readily give ear to the complaints of his loyal subjects and pardon their presumption if they did but lay down their arms. The Doncaster host disbanded within days. Some of the rebels were relieved that the tumult had ended peacefully and were ready to trust the king's promises but others departed to their homes with great misgivings. They had nothing to show for all their labour and they had been talked into abandoning their position of strength. On 9 December, Henry despatched heralds to read the terms of his pardon in all the disaffected towns. It was a mildly chiding document, offering royal forgiveness to all who submitted to the king's generals or their deputies but it asserted, *en passant*, the claim that lay at the heart of the conservative clergy's protest: their sovereign, it declared, had 'the chief charge of you under God both of your souls and bodies'.[9]

Henry's next move was to invite Aske to spend Christmas at court – secretly. This seems to have been a divide-and-rule ploy aimed at creating suspicion among the leaders of the Pilgrimage. Other northern gentlemen were making their way to London of their own volition, anxious to establish their loyalty, and the government's intelligence brought news of rifts between gentlemen and commons. Henry probably wanted to encourage the suspicion that Aske, too, was interested in making his own peace with the king. The leader of the 'pilgrims' set off about 20 December (though he was careful to let his colleagues know that he was going) and was cordially received by the king. According to Edward Hall, Henry gave his guest 'apparel and great rewards'.[10] If the chronicler knew that it must have been common knowledge and if it was common knowledge the story will have reached Yorkshire. When Aske returned home his welcome was mixed and the activists were looking to other leaders who had not been compromised.

The hot embers of revolt that flared up again in January reveal just how disparate the rebellion was. In Cumberland local feuds were as influential as general principles and it was the absence of leading gentlemen (who had hastened to the royal court) which created an authority vacuum and allowed the commons around Carlisle to renew the revolt. As the rebels mustered once more they did not hesitate to plunder the tithe barns of the monasteries. On the east of the Pennines new seditious outbreaks were led by the unlikely collaboration of John Hallam, a traditionalist yeoman farmer committed to the old ways, and Sir Francis Bigod, a sophisticated gentleman with court connections who was a follower of the new learning. Bigod's alienation sprang not from rejection of the Cromwellian reform programme but his disillusion with its practical outworking. He had hoped that money raised from the dissolution of the monasteries would be ploughed back into the economy and, particularly, into new educational projects. Discovery that the government was playing the people false and that the northern shires could expect no succour from the Henrician regime enraged him. The plans of Hallam and Bigod to seize Hull and Scarborough and use these strongholds to raise all the surrounding country failed because their strategy was betrayed; because the social leaders had escaped from the clutches of the commons and wanted to reassert their control; because the psychological moment had passed and the bulk of the population no longer had any stomach for serious rebellion.

Loyalty and betrayal – that was what the crisis of 1536–7 came down to for the leading participants. Was a man to be true to king or conscience; to identify with his class or to maintain the peace; to follow his priest or his Bible; to be stalwart in defence of age-old custom or to open his mind to modern influences? True, there were those who did not find these distinctions easy to make. They were swayed by orators or coerced by neighbours. Some were motivated to action, inaction or changing of sides by unambiguous self-interest. But most believed in something or believed they believed in something. What doomed the protestors of Midland and northern England was their lack of cohesion. Participants were committed to and cared about many things. There was no firm common core, no ideological glue to hold the movements together. Certainly there was no shared conviction among the more substantial men strong enough to drive them to embrace treason. Even a forceful ideologue like Robert Aske could not keep control of the motley mob.

Thus, when Norfolk and Shrewsbury returned to clear out the last centres of resistance their task was not difficult. The rump of the rebels had played into Henry's hands. By taking up arms again they had forfeited their right to pardon and the 'gracious' promises made by the king in December. He now ordered his generals to exact savage reprisals and to terrify the troubled counties into permanent submission. Norfolk, anxious to demonstrate his loyalty to a royal master baying for blood, oversaw the execution of 178 rank and file rebels whose bodies were exhibited on public gallows and suspended from church steeples, while a few prominent leaders were sent to London for state trials and subsequently despatched in various locations where the spectacle of their last moments was calculated to have maximum effect. Last to suffer was Robert Aske, hanged at York on 12 July 1537. Henry had triumphed in the worst crisis of his reign by a combination of determination, guile and luck but the hidden hand behind his success was that of his father. It was Henry VII who had broken the power of the great magnates and augmented the authority of local magistrates whose loyalty was to the Crown. Thanks to these fundamental changes in the politics of the shires, popular discontent was denied effective leadership. Probably some credit should be given to Thomas Cromwell. The prospect of acres of confiscated monastic land passing into secular ownership made acquisitive noble and gentry families complicit in the fate of the abbeys. They were unlikely to support any movement seeking to reverse the dissolution of the monasteries.

Henry was cock-a-hoop at the crushing of the northern rebellions and, by the spring of 1537, he had another reason to celebrate: his new queen, Jane Seymour, was pregnant. He could now believe that his years of trial were over and that God had vindicated his righteous cause. This was the moment when the Henry VIII of history was created – the image of the king frozen for all time in the self-assertive posture of the majestic icon created by Hans Holbein. The Whitehall wall painting was commissioned for the privy chamber of Henry's palace and was meant to impress all personal attendants, English dignitaries and foreign ambassadors admitted to the king's inner sanctum. The life-size fresco tells us everything we need to know about how Henry VIII saw himself and wanted to be seen by others. The painting depicts the Tudor dynasty as it was in the spring of 1537. There were only four members – Henry, his parents and his current wife (Mary and Elizabeth both having been bastardised). They are grouped around a marble plinth but it is Henry who dominates the ensemble. He stands four-square, hands on hips, and stares straight out at the viewer. (From a surviving preliminary sketch we know that this pose was deliberate; the sketch presents the king three-quarter face.) The thrusting codpiece is a direct affirmation of Henry's virility (which had been called in question during the Boleyn trials). The puffed sleeves, broad shoulders and outthrust elbows cunningly conceal the subject's obesity. It is an awesome image and, if one early commentator is to be believed, those who beheld it were 'stricken with fear' – precisely the response Henry wanted to evoke in anyone who might be tempted to contemplate fresh rebellion. Equally significant is the fact that Henry VII is thrust into the background, nervously clutching his gown in a very unheroic pose. This was the second Tudor's answer to those who were looking back to his father's reign as a golden age of peace and harmony.

But there is more for us legitimately to read out of the painting. The plinth bears a Latin inscription which may be translated:

> If it pleases you to see the illustrious images of heroes, look on these: no picture ever bore greater. The great debate, competition and great question is whether father or son is the victor. For both indeed were supreme. The father often overcame his enemies and the conflagrations of his country, and finally brought peace to its citizens. The son, born indeed for greater things, removed the unworthy from their altars and replaced them by upright men. The arrogance of popes has yielded to unerring virtue, and while Henry VIII holds the sceptre in his hand religion is restored and during his reign the doctrines of God have begun to be held in honour.[11]

There could not be a more complete graphic commentary on the supreme headship, vindicated now by triumph over subjects who had dared to question it. Unlike his father, Henry VIII had no great military triumphs of which to boast. So he deliberately played down Henry VII's warlike accomplishments and claimed that his superior achievement was the reform of the English church. He prided himself on the break with Rome, on freeing the church from centuries of accumulated error and appointing bishops committed to true doctrine and loyal to the Crown. The fresco seemed to suggest that Henry had been singled out for a divine mission and given himself wholeheartedly to its accomplishment but, of course, few if any of the momentous changes he had sponsored would have come about if he had not run into personal matrimonial difficulties.

Henry's new marriage at last delivered the prize he had struggled so determinedly to obtain. In October 1537 Queen Jane presented her husband with a son. The fact that she died days later of post-natal complications was a sadness to Henry but one from which he was quick to recover. It was almost as though Jane's death was the last sentence in a long and unhappy book that Henry could now close and move on. It brought the obvious advantage that the king was free to enter personally into the international marriage market. With the succession secure, sex (theoretically, at least) could take second place to diplomacy in Henry's quest for wife number four. He was in a strong position to gain maximum advantage from Europe's turbulent politics. The government had several options when deciding where to place England in relation to France, the Empire, the Schmalkaldic League and the trading nations of the Netherlands and the Baltic. Religion, of course, was a significant element in those calculations but the spectacular failure of the religious reaction gave Henry freedom to continue shaping the national church as he wished.

Between 1537 and 1540 the process of consigning English monasticism to history was completed. Although several of the smaller houses earmarked for closure in the 1536 Act were spared for reasons of local politics, a number of larger abbeys were closed as a result of their involvement (or alleged involvement) in the northern rebellions and others went into voluntary liquidation because their superiors correctly read the writing on the wall. The lessons of the 'commotion time' were easy to learn: the Crown intended to appropriate all monastic property; it was dangerous to oppose this policy; and responsible landowners would be foolish to ignore the opportunity to participate in the nation's biggest-ever land grab. A second dissolution Act was passed in 1539 which gave statutory authority for the confiscations that had already taken place and to those which 'hereafter shall happen to be dissolved'. By January 1540 all eight hundred or so English monasteries had disappeared. The Crown was the richer by some £90,000 a year as well as the massive haul of jewels and precious metal torn from shrines and altars. Courtiers, nobles, gentlemen, merchants and yeomen the land over were applying to the Court of Augmentations for grants of land or buildings, consolidating their estates and converting conventual buildings into mansions.

The scramble for the ancient demesnes of the monks can only be described as 'feverish'. By way of illustration we might cite the opportunism of Thomas Wriothesley, an upwardly mobile young man (born 1505) with court connections who, by 1536, was a member of Cromwell's secretarial team. By being serviceable to John Capon, one of Henry's new bishops, he received a long lease on the parsonage of Micheldever, near Winchester, in 1533, whereupon he set his sights on becoming a leader of Hampshire society. As early as 1534 the priory of St Faith's, Horsham, was surrendered to the king by its prior, John Salisbury, a Cromwellian nominee who had earlier suffered mild persecution for his heretical opinions. Salisbury's lavish rewards from a grateful regime included the office of commend-atory abbot of Titchfield Premonstratensian Abbey, which (surprise, surprise) became one of the first of the larger monas-teries to be voluntarily surrendered, in November 1537. Wriothesley got in his bid early for this prime site on the Hampshire coast. He immediately moved in an army of masons, carpenters, tilers and glaziers and, within nine months, had turned the abbey into 'a right stately house, embattled and having a goodly gate and an enclosed conduit in the middle of the court'.[12] At the same time Quarr Abbey on the coast of the Isle of Wight fell into Wriothesley's hands. The following April Beaulieu Abbey was up for grabs and, despite fierce rivalry from other bidders, Cromwell's clerical assistant was able to add this to his property portfolio for £1,305. 6s. 8d. He raised the cash for this and other purchases by ruthless asset stripping; when many new owners were building themselves impressive country houses there was an excellent market for stone, lead, glass, furniture, wall hangings and other useful materials. Still Wriothesley was not satisfied. In 1539 he obtained the abbey of

Hyde, near Winchester, where his old friend John Capon was the last commendatory abbot. These were only the more impressive of his many acquisitions. By the end of the decade Wriothesley, a 'new man', was the biggest landowner in Hampshire and one of the county's members of Parliament.

Nor was the appropriation of monastic property confined to the wealthier sections of society.

> the poor people thoroughly in every place be so greedy upon these houses when they be suppressed that by night and day, not only of the towns, but also of the country, they do continually resort as long as any door, window iron or glass or loose lead remaineth in any of them. And if it were so done only where I go, the more blame might be laid to me, but it is universally that the people be thus greedy for iron, windows, doors and lead. In every place I keep watch as long as I tarry and imprison those that do thus abuse themselves and yet others will not refrain.[13]

So complained one of Cromwell's agents. This should warn us against simplified judgements about the dissolution and its aftermath. The people were not so attached to the monasteries that they thought it sacrilege to join in the work of plunder. Nor was the enthusiastic stripping of holy sites merely the work of acquisitive fat cats. The boom market in building materials made scrap merchants and stolen goods' receivers out of some of the humblest (and most devout) of Henry's subjects.

The monks themselves were not averse to making private gain from the closing down of their houses.

> upon the examination of divers of the monks here . . . I well perceive that divers precious stones, [such] as emeralds and others to a great value taken out of the jewels of the house here privily by the prior and four or five monks of his affinity, without consent or knowledge of the convent, were sold to one Bestyan, a jeweller, who, as I hear say, is in London in

some family of the Strangers there . . . he hath been in divers religious houses throughout the realm for a like purpose.[14]

The dissolution created a business opportunity par excellence and few people, it seems, from foreign dealers to the ousted inmates themselves, failed to take advantage of it. Petty and not so petty crime flourished in the unique confusion of the 1530s.

What heightened this sense of disorientation was the increased pace of evangelical reform. Cromwell, Cranmer and their supporters took full advantage of the king's reaction against the recent insurrection. Henry was intent on demonstrating his religious authority – the supremacy in action. He was in favour of change – for the present, at least. Therefore the reformers could go confidently on to the offensive. 'Religion is making favourable progress among us.' So reported an English evangelical to the Swiss reformer Heinrich Bullinger in September 1538. 'By order of the king,' he continued, 'persons are sent to preach the truth in all parts of England. You have, I suppose, heard long since respecting the lady of Walsingham, and the breaking of other idols.'[15] What the writer referred to was the destruction of the shrine of the Virgin at Walsingham, Norfolk. This was England's most famous shrine and one of the most frequented pilgrimage centres in Europe. In more settled times Henry VIII had been among the pilgrims who had made offerings there. Now his opinion had changed.

> the images of Our Lady of Walsingham and Ipswich were brought up to London, with all the jewels that hung about them, at the King's commandment, and divers other images, both in England and Wales, that were used for common pilgrimages, because the people should use no more idolatry unto them, and they were burned at Chelsea by my Lord Privy Seal.[16]

More information on this event comes from a letter written to Cromwell a few weeks earlier by Hugh Latimer from his diocese:

I trust your lordship will bestow our great Sybil [the image of Our Lady of Worcester] to some good purpose, that her memory may perish with a great clamour. She hath been the devil's instrument to bring many, I fear, to eternal fire; now she herself, with her old sister of Walsingham, her young sister of Ipswich, with their other two sisters of Doncaster and Penrith, would make a jolly muster in Smithfield; they would not be all day burning.[17]

The most gruesome spectacle of the summer occurred on 22 May. John Forest, one of the imprisoned Observant friars, was executed, not, interestingly, for treason, like others who had denied the royal supremacy, but as a heretic. This was a dramatic signal that England now had a new orthodoxy and that any supporters of the pope's religion were just as far beyond the pale as sacramentarians who denied the presence of Christ in the bread and wine of the mass. Forest was, therefore, burned at Smithfield. Into the same fire went the statue of a saint brought all the way from North Wales. This demonstration that idolatry and the old religion were one and the same was watched by leading councillors, churchmen and City dignitaries as well as a crowd estimated at ten thousand.

1538 might well be called 'the year of the burning statues'. In every corner of the realm familiar objects of devotion were being torn down, some by government order, others the result of spontaneous iconoclasm. The visitations by Cromwell's agents had given the government a very clear idea of the nature and extent of people's reliance on visual religious stimuli and the beliefs that were associated with holy images. Reports came in steadily to the vicegerent's office, like the one reporting the confiscation of two Midlands statues. Thomas Thacker related the despatch to London of 'the image of Saint Anne of Buxton, and also the image of Saint Modwen of Burton upon Trent, with her red cow and her staff, which women labouring of child in those parts were very desirous to have with them to lean upon and to walk with it and had great confidence in the same staff.'[18] Cromwell knew the psychological importance of 'holy things' and realised that their disappearance was a necessary precursor to establishing biblical truth in people's minds. In September he issued fresh injunctions which reinforced those of 1536. They had urged the clergy not to encourage their people to venerate objects of superstition. The tone of the new instructions was different:

> such feigned images as ye know of . . . to be so abused with pilgrimages or offerings or anything made thereunto, ye shall, for avoiding that most detestable sin of idolatry, forthwith take down and delay, and shall suffer from henceforth no candles, tapers or images of wax to be set afore any image or picture . . . [19]

It was particularly important to Henry to write Thomas Becket out of English history. This was the archbishop, later canonised, who had defied his king in the name of holy church and had, ever afterwards, been revered as England's foremost martyr. Becket's shrine at Canterbury had been high on the list of pilgrimage centres and tourist attractions since long before Chaucer's motley caravan made its way thither. By 1538 it was laden with an enormous amount of precious votive offerings placed there by generations of pilgrims. In September the work of dismantling was begun. If contemporary records are to be believed, two enormous chests of jewels and twenty-four wagon-loads of plate were soon on their way to the royal treasury. More important to Cromwell was the dispelling of the Becket myth.

> the bones of St Thomas of Canterbury were burned in the same church by my Lord Cromwell. They found his head whole with the bones, which had a wound in the skull, for the monks had [en]closed another skull in silver richly, for people to offer to, which they said was St Thomas skull, so that now the abuse was openly known that they had used many years afore; also his image was taken down that stood

at the high altar at St Thomas of Acre in London . . . and all
the glass windows in the said church that was of his story
was taken down, with the image of his putting to death that
was at the altar . . . so that there shall no more mention be
made of him never.[20]

The king followed this up personally in a proclamation of
November which ordered all images of Thomas in all
churches to be destroyed and all rites associated with his
memory to cease.

It was with particular glee that the regime was able to expose
fraud and chicanery practised at some pilgrimage sites. The
Rood of Boxley was an image of the crucified Christ whose eyes
and lips supposedly moved. On Cranmer's order it was taken
down and the mechanism employed to work the 'miracle'
revealed. It was then displayed in the marketplace at Maidstone
before being taken to St Paul's Cross, exhibited to the London
citizenry and ceremoniously broken up. Later in the year Bishop
Hilsey demonstrated from the same pulpit the imposture of the
Sacred Blood of Hailes, Gloucestershire, which was reputed to
be Christ's blood, capable of liquefying on demand. He

showed plainly that it was no blood, but honey clarified and
coloured with saffron, and lying like a gum, as it . . . had been
proved and tasted afore the King and his council, and did let
every man behold it there at St Paul's Cross, and all the way
as he went to dinner to the mayor's, to look on it, so that every
person might well perceive the abuse of the said thing.[21]

Such revelations were intended to arouse popular indignation
and they did not fail. It is not surprising that many people,
whether or not they bought into the new learning, were so angry
at being duped by advocates of the 'Old Superstition' that they
took the law into their own hands: 'the 22nd of May after
midnight the image of the Rood at St Margaret Pattens [Lane]
by Tower Street was broken all in pieces with the house [i.e.

tabernacle] he stood in by certain lewd persons, Flemings and Englishmen and some persons of the said parish.'[22] Such spontaneous acts of vandalism were becoming frequent. One mob pulled down the image of Thomas Becket on London Bridge and, doubtless, excused their action by official anti-Becket policy. Another wrapped tarred rags around the figures on the rood loft of Rickmansworth parish church and set them ablaze, which may have been an easier act of sacrilege than dismantling the images but, presumably, put the church at some risk. The chronicles report other non-violent, unauthorised activities. Priests at certain churches in London and East Anglia began to celebrate mass in English. Others got married. The evangelical leaders were certainly sympathetic to such unlicensed activity but they were nervous about headstrong partisans whose actions threatened to bring their movement into disrepute. Cromwell was happier organising events aimed at ridiculing the enemies of the faith, such as the riverain pageant he staged in the summer of 1539. This was a contest between a royal barge and a papal barge which took place on the Thames at Westminster, the two vessels noisily firing off guns at each other until, inevitably, the pope's men received a thorough ducking.

The most solid achievement of the evangelical leadership was the official promotion, at long last, of an English Bible. This was something to which they were totally committed, as is indicated by a letter from Cranmer to Cromwell of 13 August 1537:

> These shall be to give you the most hearty thanks that any heart can think – and that in the name of all of them which favoureth God's word – for your diligence at this time in procuring the King's highness to set forth God's word and his Gospel by his Grace's authority. For the which act, not only the King's majesty, but also you shall have perpetual laud and memory of all them that be now, or hereafter shall be, God's faithful people and favourers of his word. And this deed you shall hear at the great day, when all things shall be opened and made manifest.[23]

The 1538 injunctions instructed every parish to equip itself with a copy of the vernacular Scriptures before the following Easter. Every incumbent was to see the book installed 'in some convenient place within the . . . church that you have cure of, whereas your parishioners may most commodiously resort to the same and read it'.[24] This time there were no second thoughts; no message from the king that the initiative was inopportune. But there were other obstacles to be overcome. The chronicle of the English Bible is an oft-told adventure story and this major episode in that story lacks nothing in terms of exciting conflict. The conservatives in the Council and on the episcopal bench recognised the open Bible as the threat it was to the religious establishment. The danger lay, not just in the Lutheran glosses of the currently banned versions, but in the very text and the freedom given to laymen to inter-pret it for themselves. Within its pages readers would find a concept of 'Church' which differed markedly from the institu-tion which had developed over the centuries. The Duke of Norfolk proudly boasted that he had never read the Bible for himself and never would. In September 1538, Stephen Gardiner, traditionalist Bishop of Winchester, returned to court after three years as ambassador in France. Both these men loathed the 'upstarts' who currently controlled policy but as long as Cromwell and Cranmer remained high in royal favour their enemies were powerless to stop the Bible project. However, their opposition remained firm and they watched for opportunities to silence the word of God written.

There were clandestine ways in which they could interfere with the production of the new book. One was to enlist the aid of friends abroad. Cromwell had employed his protégé Miles Coverdale to make the translation which would be called the 'Great Bible'. It was, essentially, a revision of the scholar's earlier work and was to be printed in Paris, where the typesetters were the best in Europe for large-format books. But to have the work done under the nose of the French inquisitor-general was risky. Cromwell's confidence and passionate commitment to the project are indicated by the fact that he sank £400 of his own money in it. In December, informers revealed to the French church authorities that an English heretical book was being produced in their territory and the print shop was raided and closed down. Was it a coincidence that Gardiner's close friends in the French ecclesiastical hierarchy got to hear of the undertaking to which he was so violently opposed? Cromwell's colleagues responded to the challenge. Workmen were smuggled across the Channel with whatever printed pages could be salvaged. New presses were set up in London where, racing against time, the printers just managed to run off copies by the Easter deadline.

The response was immediate. Most parish priests dutifully obeyed the injunction and so did enthusiastic laymen. Within three years the Great Bible went through seven printings. The appearance in a parish church of this official book with its ornate title page displaying King Henry handing the word of God to Cromwell and Cranmer for further distribution to the people, who gratefully cried out, 'God save the King,' obviously aroused much curiosity. People who could not read asked their better-educated neighbours to recite passages to them. This led to the emergence of several gospellers who took it upon themselves to read aloud and expound from the sacred text to people who gathered in the church for this purpose. At Chelmsford, according to one evangelical, people gathered 'in the lower end of the church . . . to hear the reading of that glad and sweet tidings of the Gospel'.[25] At St Paul's Cathedral, Bishop Bonner had to put up a notice telling people to read quietly to themselves, not to attract crowds for unlicensed expositions and certainly not to read aloud during church services. Evidently some gospellers were performing at the same time as the mass, so that while the priest was at the altar someone else was running a rival show in the nave.

This response was not universal. A priest in Kent staunchly refused to buy a Bible, telling his parishioners that they might wait till doomsday for a copy. The vicar of Wincanton, Somerset, angrily dismissed a delegation of his people with the words that 'the new-fangled fellows with their new books . . . be heretics, knaves and pharisees'. Richard Bush, a priest of Hastings, went so far as to tell his congregation that the English Bible should be burned.[26] It would be impossible to exaggerate the impact of the cultural revolution taking place in these years. An image-based religion was being replaced by a word-based religion. Zealots promoted the change by vandalising churches or by translating the mass into English to encourage greater congregational participation or by eagerly exhorting their neighbours from the printed page. Lovers of the old ways responded by refusing to allow the Great Bible into their churches or by hiding away much-loved images to preserve them, in the hope of better times to come. All was not conflict; apathy is not a twenty-first-century invention, as one reformer mournfully observed:

> The most sacred and holy Bible is now had among us in our vulgar tongue, and freely permitted to be read of all men universally, at times convenient, without any let or perturbation, even in the churches. But how many read it? Verily a man may come into some churches and see the Bible so enclosed and wrapped about with dust, even as the pulpit in like manner is both with dust and cobwebs, that with his finger he may write upon the Bible this epitaph: *ecce nunc in pulvere domino,* that is to say, 'behold I sleep now in the dust'. So little pleasure have these filthy swine and currish dogs in that most sweet and singular treasure.[27]

Not even the celebrated Bishop Latimer could always be assured of an audience. He described in a sermon how, overnighting in a certain village, he had let it be known that he would preach the following day (1 May). Duly arriving at the church, he found it locked and not a soul in sight. When, at last, one of the locals appeared he explained, 'The parish are gone abroad to gather for Robin Hood.' Latimer was outraged that the people would rather go maying and commemorating

Robin Hood, 'a traitor and a thief', than come to receive 'the ministration of God's word'.[28]

Thus, the picture of English religious life in the late 1530s is one of vivid and violent contrasts. The chronicler Charles Wriothesley considered it worthy of record that when the wealthy mercer Humphrey Monmouth (Tyndale's erstwhile patron) died, in November 1537, he left money not for requiem masses but for the preaching of sermons by Latimer, Barnes and other evangelicals and for the singing of Te Deums, 'to give laud and praise to God for the King, that hath extinguished and put down the power of the Bishop of Rome and hath caused the word of God to be preached that we may have the very true knowledge as Christ taught and left to his apostles'.[29] Six months later he had to describe the death of John Forest who, when invited to recant, declared, 'That if an angel should come down from heaven and show him any other thing than that he had believed all his life . . . he would not believe him'.[30] The bulk of Henry's subjects found themselves somewhere between these two extremes of certain and confident faith.

As for the king, he was determined to project an image of himself as demigod, above the conflict except when he chose to step down into the world of mere mortals to offer wise guidance. The *Bishops' Book* provides a case in point. In February 1537, while the mopping up of the last pockets of northern resistance was under way, Henry had his vicegerent convene a committee of bishops and senior clergy to draw up a doctrinal and liturgical manual. This was something important for every national church that had embraced reform. The Lutherans had the Wittenberg Articles and Calvin had just published the first edition of his comprehensive *Institutes of the Christian Religion*. Other state churches had similarly found it necessary to define in what ways they were distinct from Rome (and, indeed, from each other). What was needed was a document more detailed than the Ten Articles which would, Henry hoped (and might, just possibly, have believed), unite all his subjects. Cromwell set the discussions in motion then left Edward Fox, Bishop of

Hereford, in charge of subsequent meetings. Fox was dubbed by Chapuys 'among the most perfect Lutheran in the world' but he was also a born diplomat, well versed in patient, irenic chairmanship. The fact that the divines were able to come up with an agreed text by the end of July was largely due to his sensitive guidance – that and the fact that all the participants were impatient to escape the plague-ridden city. Latimer was not the most tolerant member of the episcopal team but he spoke for many when he observed, 'it is a troublous thing to agree upon a doctrine, in things of such controversy, with judgements of such diversity, every man (I trust) meaning well, and yet not all meaning one way.'[31]

The result was *The Institution of a Christian Man* or *Bishops' Book*. Inevitably, it was a compromise document, but one leaning well in an evangelical direction. Some tenets were expressed in conventional Catholic terms; others borrowed heavily from Lutheran formularies. Cromwell had laid down the basic tradition that arguments put forward must be based on Scripture, not tradition, nor was it to advocate the reversal of any recent reforms. 'If men will indifferently read these late declarations,' Cranmer affirmed,

> They shall well perceive that purgatory, pilgrimages, praying
> to saints, images, holy bread, holy water, holy days, merits,
> works, ceremony and such other, be not restored to their late
> accustomed abuses; but shall evidently perceive that the word
> of God hath gotten the upper hand of them all, and hath set
> them in their right use and estimation.[32]

What the *Bishops' Book* emphatically did not set out was a clearly stated *Anglican* theology. Here was no *media via*. Unlike the Ten Articles, it recognised seven sacraments but was careful to point out that only three – baptism, penance and the Lord's supper – were 'dominical' (instituted by Christ). Marriage, auricular confession, extreme unction and confirmation were downgraded to the second rank. In discussing the Ten Commandments the new book placed great emphasis on the condemnation of idolatry. On the central theological issue of free will and divine grace (whether man, unaided, can please God), over which Luther and Erasmus had locked horns, the *Bishops' Book* was cautiously Lutheran: the commandments 'teach us what is good and what we should do to please God, yet they give not unto us strength and power to do the same; but all such strength cometh of God, by his singular grace and gift'.[33] Henry saw at least portions of the *Institution* and made annotations on them but when Cromwell asked permission for the book to be printed on the king's authority he replied that he had not had time to read it properly. He knew that it would not command universal acceptance and determined to remain above the fray. One of the bishops reported Henry as saying that he was content for the book to be set forth until he 'shall otherwise order some things with a more mature and deliberous counsel'.

One problem facing the king was that English theology and church order were not subjects that could be discussed in a vacuum. The pope was intent on isolating England and using all diplomatic means to bring it back into the Catholic fold. His machinations and the efforts of Reginald Pole were ineffective as long as France and the Empire maintained their longstanding enmity. Henry could pursue his quest for a royal bride in a leisurely fashion and bargain for a marriage treaty with one or other of the major powers. At the same time he had his ambassadors counter papal propaganda by asserting that his religious position was still orthodox. To this end he organised an elaborate heresy show trial in November 1538 and presided over it in person clad all in virgin white. The unfortunate singled out for destruction was the sacramentarian John Lambert. This high-profile event was an embarrassment for the evangelical leadership. They were all agreed in rejecting the extremist interpretation of the sacrament of the altar but several of their followers were headed in that direction and their Catholic enemies took every opportunity to assert that heresy was the inevitable destination of all those travelling the new learning road. At the same time as the king was haranguing Lambert and parading his theological knowledge he issued a proclamation denouncing the sacramentarians and distancing his church from these extremists. In recent months a number of Dutch Anabaptists had sought sanctuary in England. They were now warned to vacate the realm or face the inevitable consequences of their erroneous beliefs. Henry made it clear that certain marks of 'Catholicity' such as the age-hallowed 'laudable ceremonies' of creeping to the cross, bearing candles to mark the purification of the Virgin and using holy bread and holy water still had a valued place in English devotional life. By such occasional personal interventions Henry was pointing out that his bishops had not said the last word on Christian doctrine. He was the fountainhead of religious truth. Whatever he approved was orthodox. Radical extremists and supporters of papal pretensions were equally in error.

Paul III was not slow to respond. Within weeks he activated the long-threatened excommunication of the English king and renewed his appeal to Francis I and Charles V to sink their differences and unite against heretical England. In January 1539, the emperor and the French king signed the Treaty of Toledo. It fell short of what the pope was demanding but it did commit the signatories to make no unilateral alliance with England and both monarchs duly removed their ambassadors from London. This was enough to generate in Henry's kingdom a real fear of invasion. The king directed his energies to building up coastal defences and ordering troops, ships and equipment to be put in readiness. All this was, of course, expensive. Henry spent more money on fortifications than any king since the castle-building Edward I. To pay for these projects he had to cash up a substantial part of the proceeds of the monastic spoliation and he still needed to summon a Parliament to grant more taxes.

Diplomatic isolation meant that Henry had to say goodbye to his hopes of marrying a Habsburg or Valois princess. This gave

Cromwell the chance to revive his plan for an alliance with the Protestant states of northern Europe. That option was never very much to Henry's taste but he sanctioned a fresh exchange of scholars with the Schmalkaldic League. The Germans arrived in April but stayed only a few weeks. The major stumbling block to agreement was the League's insistence that Henry sign up to their definition of faith, the Augsburg Confession. Henry, always his own man in matters of dogma, declined to be dictated to.

In fact, he was in the process of doing something that would distance him further from other Reformation states. He pressed Cromwell for more precise definitions of some points which had been deliberately left vague in the *Bishops' Book*. When the minister dragged his heels the conservative caucus at court grabbed the initiative. Gardiner was the brains behind the campaign which was now developed and, though Cromwell was able to have 'Wily Winchester' excluded from the Council for several months, he effectively marshalled his colleagues. Norfolk led the attack in Parliament by pressing for an Act which would define some major points of doctrine and practice. However, the legislation would not have been passed in its final form without the direct involvement of the king. He attended several sittings of the Lords and gave them the benefit of his theological knowledge. The evangelical bishops put up a stiff resistance and the bill had a very difficult passage but ultimately Henry's determination carried it through. The Act of Six Articles was a triumph for the conservatives. It affirmed transubstantiation, clerical celibacy, auricular confession, private masses, the permanence of vows of chastity and communion in one kind only for the laity. Moreover it ring-fenced this regressive measure with savage punishments for disobedience.

This new hard line in religious policy was, in part, the result of deep and bitter rifts at court. The two factions were locked in a life-and-death struggle. Gardiner and Norfolk were now backing a French alliance and warning the king against the danger of alienating himself from the Catholic powers. Cromwell and Cranmer, as we have seen, pointed out the advantages of forming a strong alliance with the Protestant states based on some kind of evangelical confession of faith. It was this acceptance of a new kind of Christian polity which Henry baulked at. Hitherto he had been able to justify the widening gap with Rome by asserting that he was correcting errors and malpractices that had crept into the Church. He was adamant that his realm remained a part of historic western Christendom. Not until now, it seems, did he recognise the logical conclusion towards which evangelical reform was heading. If the policy urged by Cromwell was leading him to tie himself irrevocably to a group of states in revolt against the emperor and the pope and, moreover, if that trend was making England a haven for devilish heretics then it definitely represented a bridge too far. On 26 May, when the German ambassadors had an audience with Henry, a violent argument broke out over the legislation going through Parliament and the Lutherans were sent packing. About this time complaints reached court of a sacramentarian cell in Calais that Cromwell was, allegedly, protecting. The minister's enemies made sure that Henry was well informed of this stain upon the life of England's continental outpost. Several matters were, thus, trying the king's – always limited – patience in the middle months of 1539 and we should, perhaps, remind ourselves that he was a sick, overweight widower who had no confidants he fully trusted, with the possible exception of Cranmer, and whose suspicions against anyone were easily aroused.

One result of the passage of the Act of Six Articles which was the icing on the cake for Gardiner and his friends was the resignation of Hugh Latimer and Nicholas Shaxton (Bishop of Salisbury). They could not in good conscience continue working as bishops if that meant enforcing the new legislation. Latimer claimed that the king had demanded his resignation and, though Henry later denied this, there can be no doubt that he was pleased to see them go. Like More and Fisher (though for different reasons), the two prominent men had parted company with royal policy and might well have counted themselves fortunate to escape severe reprisals. Both were placed in custody in the London homes of fellow bishops (Chichester and Bath and Wells respectively). The silencing of Latimer, the most celebrated preacher of the age, was a particular triumph for the enemies of reform.

It is impossible to be certain to what extent the dramatic events of the next year were driven by the king and how far they were brought about by his squabbling councillors. Cromwell pursued his plan for a Protestant royal marriage. He really had no choice. Given the current diplomatic situation Henry's search for a bride would otherwise have directed his attention to the eligible young ladies of England's leading families. That would have put fresh pressures on the complex faction-balance at court. The choice had narrowed to the two sisters of the Duke of Cleves-Julich, and on the face of it this looked like an alliance with which Henry could have been well satisfied. Duke William's Rhineland territory was strategically situated on the commercial and diplomatic crossroads between the Netherlands and Italy. Moreover, he was not a Lutheran. Like Henry, he had renounced papal allegiance and, though he had not sought admittance to the Schmalkaldic League, he was on good terms with his brother German princes. If England was to avoid isolation the Cleves match was the only game in town. In October the marriage treaty was signed and Anne arrived at the end of the year. Bride and groom met on 1 January and the king did not like what he saw. Based on the reports of his diplomats and the portrait provided by Holbein, he had actually been looking forward to having this woman share his bed and board. When he encountered the reality he believed that he had been betrayed into a disagreeable union. It was not just that Anne was plain; she was *dull*. She spoke only German, had no courtly accomplishments and, most importantly of all, she knew nothing of the arts of the bedchamber. Henry liked his women vivacious and feisty. It seems that only with such partners was he able to perform sexually. The marriage was never consummated and the king immediately looked to Cromwell to get him out of it.

What made matters worse was that the European situation

had changed. France and the Empire had resumed their traditional bad relations. That meant that Henry's immolation on the altar of matrimony now carried no diplomatic advantages. It had all been for nothing. And, of course, Henry did what he always did when life was treating him badly: he blamed someone else. This time Cromwell was the fall guy. His enemies were not slow to take advantage. Norfolk's teenage granddaughter, Catherine Howard, was dangled before the king. She was all that Anne was not – pretty, lively and extremely experienced sexually for her tender years. As the next consort in waiting Catherine opened the door wide to the influence of her grandfather and his allies. Throughout the late spring a fierce battle went on at court. Accusations and counter-accusations were bandied back and forth. But, at the crucial moment, it was the conservatives who gained the upper hand. On 10 June Cromwell was arrested in the council chamber on confused and confusing charges of heresy and treason. On 28 July 1540 Thomas Cromwell met his end beneath the headsman's axe on Tower Hill. Thus perished the man who, more than any other, merits the title 'Father of the English Reformation'.

Chapter 7

Building a Christian Commonwealth

Any triumphalist Catholic who thought that the fall of Thomas Cromwell was the prelude to a far-reaching purge of evangelicals, a return to traditional orthodoxy and a rapprochement with Rome soon learned that these were not the king's intentions. Henry's religious policy was governed by two concerns. It would be no exaggeration to call them passions. He was determined to maintain the royal supremacy and he urgently sought the unity of his people. One way of achieving the former was by dramatic demonstrations against religious deviants, whether radical or reactionary. Two days after Cromwell's execution, a gruesome assertion of the royal will was enacted at Smithfield. Three recalcitrant papists were hanged, drawn and quartered, while Robert Barnes, sometime emissary to the Lutheran princes, and two other evangelicals were burned. The only offence uniting the six victims was that they had, in various ways, challenged the royal supremacy. Debate might rage over some points of doctrine but Henry's subjects were not allowed to doubt that he was their father in God.

Henry still assumed that bullying would work and, for many people, such deterrents were effective. But there were, by now, enough men and women of conviction in England to thwart negative policies. Some of them were in Henry's own household. A conversation that occurred on 15 September 1540 provides us with a fascinating glimpse of backstairs court gossip. Three members of the chamber staff were discussing recent events. John Lascelles, just returned from a spell of leave, asked his colleagues Johnson, Maxey and Smithwick, 'What news . . . pertaining God's holy word, seeing we have lost so noble a man, which did love and favour it so well?' The response was not encouraging. Maxey reported that Norfolk now ruled the roost and that he was a sworn enemy of reform. In the great chamber the duke had declared that he had no intention of ever reading the English Bible. 'It was merry in England before this new learning came up,' he said. Norfolk clearly took no pains to conceal his religious sentiments. Maxey also narrated an exchange the peer had had with an Exchequer official. Norfolk had upbraided the man for marrying an ex-nun. He had replied that he recognised 'no nuns nor religious folk in this realm, nor no such bondage, seeing God and the King have made them free'. To this Norfolk had snapped, 'By God's body sacred, it will never out of my heart as long as I live.' Smithwick was all for confronting the court traditionalists but Lascelles advised caution: 'If we would let them alone and suffer a little time, they would overthrow themselves, standing manifestly against God and their prince.'[1] Eventually it was agreed that a written deposition would be presented to Sir Nicholas Hare, a senior judge and Speaker of the late Parliament. This zealous group were sufficiently serious about causing trouble for Norfolk to have their evidence weighed by a leading legal authority.

John Lascelles was one of Cromwell's agents and had been used by the minister as a messenger between the court and the Midland shires where his family estates lay. In all probability the other parties to this conversation were also Cromwell's protégés. If that is the case it indicates just how effectively Cromwell had insinuated evangelicals into the royal entourage at several levels, from the Council board and the privy chamber to various household departments. Evangelicals were established in important positions around the king. Sir William Butts was the royal physician and in almost daily attendance on the ailing monarch. Sir Anthony Denny was Groom of the Stool and the senior gentleman of the privy chamber with a seat on the Council.

Edward Seymour, Earl of Hertford, was an increasingly influential member of the Council. In 1542 he was joined by his friend and comrade in arms John Dudley, on the latter's appointment as Lord Admiral. Cranmer was, of course, the premier advocate of reform. He took the lead in urging further change and, though he lacked Cromwell's political acumen, he was devising a programme which would have considerable liturgical and doctrinal implications. Of Thomas Cromwell it might well have been said that 'he, being dead, yet speaketh' (Hebrews 11: 4). Many who had clustered around him in the years of his power had been inspired by his ideas, his industry, his clear thinking, his political and administrative methodology, his commitment to building a Christian commonwealth which would be a part of the northern European Protestant world. Several of Cromwell's disciples and admirers were now well placed to continue his work.

The Council from this point was a different body from the one that had existed in the earlier years of the reign. Its members were determined not to be dominated by another Wolsey or Cromwell, a 'chief minister' who passed information to his colleagues on a need-to-know basis and restricted debate. What had emerged by 1540 was, in fact, the Privy Council, a small body of advisers (about fifteen), comprising household officials, officers of state and senior ecclesiastics. They took corporate responsibility, met several times a week, kept their own register and were served by a professional secretariat. Since members had other responsibilities it was rare for them all to be present at meetings; the business of king and country was usually conducted by eight or nine men. It was this concentration of power in a few hands that made faction fighting inevitable in the 1540s. For the first time we can speak accurately of rival groups within the Privy Council which took on clear religious identities. Anyone who has worked on a committee knows the intriguing, lobbying and deal-making that go into achieving majority votes. Such activities can take on almost fanatical urgency when issues arise about which people feel passionately. Such was the situation which prevailed at the centre of English government between 1540 and 1553, when England was, increasingly, run by a committee.

Throughout Henry VIII's last years, when it seemed increasingly likely that a sick, prematurely aged king would be succeeded by a minor, what was at stake was nothing less than the religious identity of England. In their determination to set the country's faith agenda conservative and radical councillors strove mightily to bring each other down. Lascelles had hit the nail on the head when he had accused Norfolk and his party of working 'against God and their prince'. The strategy of the radical councillors was to show that their opponents hankered after Rome and were intent on subverting Henry VIII's religious settlement. At the same time, the strategy of the conservative councillors was to embroil their evangelical adversaries in charges of heresy and to expose them as men intent on subverting Henry VIII's religious settlement. All were, of course, exaggerating for effect and we have to guard against being caught up in their rhetoric. It would be inaccurate to paint the adversarial groups in hard black and white. Terms such as 'conservative', 'traditionalist', 'reformer', 'evangelical' and 'radical' all too easily mask the differences which existed *within* rival camps. Thus, few traditionalists favoured returning to the pope all the powers, rights and privileges he had enjoyed in the early 1520s. Most conservatives agreed that the Church was in need of some reform. All evangelicals were not Lutherans; their leaders were in touch with the diverging streams of continental reformed religion and were influenced by Calvin, Zwingli, Bucer and even revolutionary Anabaptists. We need also to bear in mind that people's beliefs developed as a result of private meditation and public debate. For example, in 1540, Cranmer was a staunch believer in the real presence. Like Luther, he rejected transubstantiation but understood literally Christ's words of institution, 'This is my body . . . this is my blood.' Several English evangelicals, however, in their rejection of the sacerdotal power and authority of the Roman priesthood, were moving towards the Zwinglian position which asserted that Christ's identification of his body and blood with the sacramental elements was figurative. Within a decade Cranmer had moved to a position which was virtually Zwinglian. '[The papists] teach that Christ is in the bread and wine: but we say, according to the truth, that he is in them that worthily eat and drink the bread and wine.' So the archbishop explained in his *Defence of the True and Catholic Doctrine of the Sacrament of the Body and Blood of our Saviour Christ* (1550).[2]

King Henry's views were also developing and it was his opinions alone which really mattered. Historians of these years have tended to focus on such questions as 'Did religious policy derive from the king or from the interplay of court factions?', 'Did the Reformation come to a halt in the mid-1540s?', 'Was the eventual "triumph" of the evangelical group the result of a definite policy shift or did the conservative opposition simply self-destruct?' The see-sawing fortunes of the Gardiner–Norfolk axis and the Cranmer–Hertford alliance certainly pose problems for anyone trying to chart the evolution of religious policy. Trusted royal servants could fall out of favour in the blink of an eye. A pain-distracted king could make sudden decisions which defy analysis and, probably, defy logic. Accordingly, we should avoid looking for symmetrical patterns in the fabric of policy-making. We are more likely to understand the tos and fros of fortune if we keep ever before us the fact that the central characters were all men who sincerely and, in many cases, passionately believed the faith-truths they were contending for and that principles, personalities and power-seeking conflicted on a daily basis.

However, while we keep our eyes on the framers of policy, we must not lose sight of the broader realities of these unquiet years. 'Reformation' means something wider than movement from a priest-centred belief system to a Bible-based belief system. By 1540 'change' was very much in the air. No one, from the highest to the lowest in the land, could be unaware of it. What concerned most of the king's subjects on a day-by-day basis was not dispute over doctrine but how to make ends meet in a time of unprecedented inflationary pressure. A price index based on the cost of a basket of basic foodstuffs and taking the figure of 100 at the beginning of the reign as its starting point registers 158 for 1540 and 248 for 1546.[3] This drove landowners to maximise agricultural yield and to reduce the numbers of people working the land. Inevitably, social problems such as vagabondage, begging and wayside crime increased. This is not the place to explore the causes of such dislocation or to assess the inadequate government response. Some contemporaries looking for answers identified the secularisation of church property as a root cause for their misery. Others believed that the bringing of monastic and other lands under Crown control was a basic step in the right direction. Those in the latter group believed – or hoped – that the sufferings they were enduring were the birth pangs attendant on bringing forth a better world. Even among those who found it difficult to come to terms with the 'stripping of the altars' there were many whose hopes, aspirations and expectations had been raised. That is why one of the buzzwords of these years was 'commonwealth'. From pulpit and printed page (and also from alehouse and marketplace) campaigners pressed for a raft of social changes. They urged the government to carry on the work of reformation.

Those who occupied what we would now call a 'liberal' platform were concerned about the injustice of a society which was still manipulated by the rich and powerful to the detriment of the poor. They pointed to old ills such as enclosures, money-grubbing lawyers, usury and clergy who demonstrated more zeal over the collection of their tithes and fees than over the pastoral care of their parishioners. Robert Wisdom, a prominent evangelical preacher, forced to recant in 1543, revealed himself as a proto-Puritan in his outraged written denunciations of materialism. He condemned the uncaring rich for

> their pride and ambition; their excess and vain apparel; their banqueting and drunkenness till every place be full of vomit; their vain buildings as though they would live here [for] ever;

their laying house to house and coupling field to field till poor men be eaten out of their [neighbourhood]; their engrossing of farms . . . their raising of rents unto the utter impoverishing of the poor.[4]

Although exacerbated by the worsening economic conditions of the 1540s, there was nothing new about class-based resentment. What was new was the way some writers and preachers linked it with a wider platform of reforms based upon the demands of a just and holy God, as revealed in Scripture. Just how intertwined religious conviction, social concern and personal grievance could become is illustrated by the fate of a certain Mr Collins, a gentleman and student at the inns of court, who was burned in 1541, having previously languished in prison for a couple of years on Bishop Gardiner's authority.

Once, as he was passing by a crucifix, to which processions had sometime been made . . . he aimed an arrow at the idol, and striking its foot, called out to it to defend itself, and punish him if it were able. Many persons, however, say that this was not the cause of his imprisonment; but rather because he was wont to exclaim against the nobility and great men of the kingdom, and rashly to bring against them many passages of holy scripture . . . wherein there was any mention made of unrighteous judgements, or the cruel treatment of neighbours and dependents.[5]

Collins's sanity had, apparently, been undermined by the conduct of an unfaithful wife but he was a fluent exponent of the Bible and had firm opinions on the social and economic problems of the day. He may well have had much to say about prison conditions for these frequently came under attack, as did inadequate care for the sick and poor. The deployment and remuneration of the clergy were subject to much scrutiny: pluralism and the tithe system were condemned; it was argued that parish priests should be adequately stipended and obliged to serve in their cure, rather than accumulate benefices and appoint unlearned curates to perform their duties. Education was earmarked as a special concern. The dissolution of the monasteries presented a God-given opportunity to use confiscated wealth for the founding of schools and the support of poor students. Moral issues were seldom far below the surface. Campaigners inveighed against drunkenness, foul language and sexual immorality. It did not escape the notice of evangelicals that the Southwark stews, London's red light district, were under the control of Bishop Gardiner, whose rents derived in part from the income of the brothels. The government did take sporadic action against prostitution and, in 1546, Henry ordered the closure of all houses of ill repute. Inevitably, this only drove prostitutes out of their premises and on to the streets.

Many promoters of the social gospel were circumspect in their attitude to the establishment but the logical conclusion of what the 'commonwealth men' were urging entailed criticism of the leaders of church and state. They were frustrated when the powers that be neglected to proceed with reforms that seemed to them logical. For example, those who rejected propitiatory masses and the doctrine of purgatory could only regard chantry priests as a waste of space – 'lusty lubbers' as 'Bilious Bale' called them. He demanded that such men be put to honest labour and the chantry endowments used for charitable purposes. Another writer expressed indignation with churchmen who were heedless of the Gospel injunctions to good works while commanding parishioners 'to build them goodly churches with high steeples and great bells to wring our pence into their purses when our friends be dead'.[6] It was very difficult for advocates of social reform to avoid overt or covert criticism of king and Parliament. They could hardly avoid pointing out that Henry was spending the fruits of ecclesiastical spoliation on war rather than educational reform or that royal patronage supported several absentee and pluralist clergy who were employed on the king's business and drew their income from benefices they never visited.

But it was a fundamental difference of attitude towards

poverty which set most commonwealth men at variance with the government. The glaring inequalities of wealth and the absence of charitable sentiment turned even moderate reformers into anti-establishment figures. They regarded people forced into vagrancy, mendicancy and crime as victims of the system and looked to government to come to their aid. This was not the view which prevailed in Westminster. Like modern reactionary politicians who lambast 'scroungers' and 'benefit fraudsters', Henry, supported by the House of Lords, insisted that most poor people were responsible for their own plight; they were too lazy to work. It was the responsibility of the law to make sure that all 'sturdy beggars' settled down to honest labour. Legislation passed in the 1530s instructed all unemployed men, on pain of public flogging or, after three offences, death, to return to their own native towns or villages, where private charity might come to their aid until they found honest work. Church and state authorities were quick to pounce on commonwealth writers and preachers who, as they believed, were encouraging public unrest by their 'seditious' criticism of the government. In 1547 a balladeer lamented,

> And yet not long ago
> Was preachers one or two
> That spake it plain enough
> To you, to you, and to you,
> That it was right time to repent
> This devilish intent,
> Of covetous accumulation.
> From Scotland to Kent
> This preaching spread;
> And from the east coast
> Unto St Michael's Mount,
> This saying did sound
> Abroad to all men's ears . . .
> That from pillar to post
> The poor man he was tossed . . . [7]

Henry VIII had no intention of repenting or reversing the course on which he was set. As he progressed along that course he veered from side to side, sometimes accelerating and sometimes braking, but always moving in the same general direction. If he sought the advice of his councillors – and sometimes even took it – he never let any of them forget that his will would prevail.

It may be no coincidence that Cranmer was able to push ahead with reform in 1541. Henry was in the habit of discussing doctrinal issues with his archbishop, and Gardiner, the only councillor who was Cranmer's intellectual equal in such matters, was once more absent on a diplomatic mission for much of the year. In May Henry agreed to issue a proclamation strengthening the earlier edict on the Great Bible. Now financial penalties were announced for any parish which failed to buy a copy of the book and display it prominently. This certainly applied an effective spur to recalcitrant priests and churchwardens. Furthermore preachers were instructed to confine themselves to expository sermons, i.e. explaining and basing exhortation on the plain words of Scripture without reference to any other church doctors, past or present. This was, in effect, an assertion of the Lutheran doctrine of *sola scriptura* and was a major plank in the evangelical platform. Cranmer was demonstrating – in the king's name – that the authority of Scripture stood above that of the Church and not vice versa. This did not stop conservatives grumbling about the English Bible. They represented to Henry that the Great Bible contained errors and, early in 1542, he ordered the bishops to form a revision committee for improving the text. But only a few weeks later he informed Convocation that he was taking the matter out of the bishops' hands and giving it to the universities. This was, in effect, a blocking measure and we can surely see here the influence of Cranmer. When an official translation had first been mooted in 1534 the bishops had been placed in charge of the work. Most of them had sat on their hands. It was the resulting deadlock that had obliged Cromwell and Cranmer to make their own arrangements.

Perhaps the archbishop now reminded Henry of the earlier fiasco. However it came about, Henry changed his mind, realising that nothing useful could be expected from church leaders whose hearts were not in the enterprise of creating an effective English Bible. Since no instructions were given to the universities, there the matter ended. Cranmer must have relished using his adversaries' tactics against them.

The iconoclastic campaign continued. The king ordered his bishops to remove and destroy all remaining local shrines. Another proclamation further limited the number of saints' days, allowing only memorials of holy men and women who appeared in the Bible. For the first time adoration of the Cross came under fire. Most churches had a rood screen dividing nave and chancel upon which stood an effigy of the crucified Christ attended by the figures of St Mary and St John. This impressive ensemble was a powerful focus of devotion. Now, worshippers were to be discouraged, not only from worshipping saints, but also from exalting the Cross itself as an object of adoration. The removal of visual stimuli was slowly – in remoter areas very slowly – changing the nature of English religion.

As pilgrimage centres, shrines and images disappeared and fraudulent miracles were exposed people ceased reposing trust in invocation of saints and the existence of purgatory. Fewer and fewer testators left provision in their wills for the beautification of altars or the recitation of requiem masses. The stock formula used in wills, whereby men and women facing death besought 'Our Blessed Lady and all the saints' to pray for them, began to be replaced by other words. As yet few testators adopted a full-blown evangelical formula such as 'trusting only for salvation in the merits of Christ my Saviour' but surviving evidence supports a weakening of belief in traditional soteriology. On a practical level few people were prepared to leave money for shrines and altars if there was a real chance that they would be abolished and their adornments confiscated.

In the autumn of 1542, Norfolk and his friends suffered a serious setback and the originator of their discomfort was that humble waiter at the king's table, John Lascelles. In the summer Henry had, after thirty-three years on the throne, made a progress to the northern parts of his realm. He was attended by an enormous retinue and he was, of course, accompanied by his young, new wife, Catherine Howard. Lascelles was one of the chamber staff members not selected for the expedition and he took the opportunity to ride into Sussex to visit his recently married sister, Mary Hall. He had an ulterior motive. Gossip was flying around the court about the queen's sex life. Mary had spent some years in the household of the dowager Duchess of Norfolk, mother of the current duke, Thomas Howard, whom Lascelles so much detested. During her time of service, young Catherine Howard had been among the noble ladies billeted out to the duchess's establishment to learn the accomplishments of a lady destined for the royal court. The stories Mary could tell about the goings-on between the adolescent girls and their gallants suggested that Catherine had been no unspotted virgin when she married her royal husband. Lascelles probed – and made careful notes – of his sister's reminiscences. He soon had details of names and places which, carefully used, might severely damage the Howard clique.

That clique was currently enjoying great favour on the northern tour. Now, the fact that Norfolk and his friends were with the itinerant court meant that the rump of the Privy Council left to hold the fort at Westminster was headed up by Hertford, Cranmer and Lord Chancellor Audley. John Lascelles sought an audience with the archbishop and poured out his story. Once Cranmer knew about the queen's alleged fornication, he was in an unenviable position. He scarcely dared to inform the king but neither did he dare to keep the information back and become, in effect, an accessory after the fact. He waited until the court's return and then, at Hampton Court on 2 November, he handed Henry a carefully worded letter. The king gave permission for the allegations to be examined and, within four days, confessions had been wrung from two of Catherine's former lovers. The story of Henry's heartbreak, of fresh revelations exposing Catherine as an adulterous wife, of her trial and eventual execution the following February is too well known to require repetition.

Lascelles must have hoped that Catherine's fall would have dragged down her uncle and the whole Howard faction, just as Anne Boleyn's execution had ended the ascendancy of the Boleyn caucus. This did not happen. Norfolk frantically extricated himself from the ruins of Henry's fifth marriage and performed a skilful damage limitation exercise. The effect this unhappy episode did have on the faction struggle at court seems to have been to heighten still further the personal animosities that were inextricably entwined with the evolution of religious policy. Gardiner and the conservative bishops had not been inactive since Cromwell's death but their efforts had not met with unqualified success. A planned widespread purge of five hundred London evangelicals for offences against the Act of Six Articles had been halted by royal command in the summer of 1540. Early in 1542 Bishop Bonner of London had issued a ban on all books by English evangelicals but when he and his friends tried to make this a nationwide prohibition announced by royal proclamation they failed. The place where the conservatives were most effective was Convocation, because in the church's parliament they had a decisive majority. Thus, for example, Cranmer's episcopal opponents blocked his attempt to issue a set of homilies – approved sermonets to be used by clergy lacking the skill or education to preach effectively. Any initiative by Cranmer which smelled of evangelicalism was blocked by the archbishop's rivals.

1543 was the year that witnessed a major conservative campaign on several fronts. Those involved were aided by the fact that Henry was distracted by foreign policy. He had decided to go to war again. Gardiner's patient diplomacy had resulted in a fresh treaty (ratified in February 1543) with Charles V which committed both monarchs to a military campaign against France. It was now in the king's interest to project an image of himself as thoroughly orthodox in matters of religion. While

Henry busied himself with the invigorating preparations for war, the Bishop of Winchester took immediate advantage of the situation and of his own high standing in the king's esteem to wage a furious campaign against those intent on pressing the Reformation further. His objective was to destroy as many of the most influential evangelicals as he could lay his hands on. At the top of his list came several members of the privy chamber. The king's inner circle bristled with men whose religious ortho-doxy would not bear close scrutiny. As well as Denny and Butts, already mentioned, there were accomplished courtiers such as Ralph Sadler, Thomas Caradine, Philip Hoby and George Blagge. Some had reached their favoured position via Cromwell's patronage and all were intelligent, well-read, cultured sophisti-cates – the sort of men Henry had always welcomed to his household and who were valued even more now that he needed pleasant company to divert his mind from his pain. If such companions tended to veer towards the new learning it was because they were men of independent mind, conversant with the latest intellectual fashions. To break up this evangelical caucus at the very centre of national life and to replace Henry's current companions with 'safe' men would be no easy task, but without control of the privy chamber other policy successes might well count for nothing. Doctrines could be promulgated, proclamations issued, parliamentary Acts passed but all these things could be undone if the king wished (or if those in power in the next reign so wished). And it was by no means certain that Henry would permit the downfall of his friends, be they ever so heretical. Past experience had shown that direct action against men the king liked and trusted could prove fruitless: personality often counted for more than dogma with Henry.

The strategy the conservatives now adopted was to have lesser men arrested and condemned for heresy and then to show that these offenders had close contacts with the people they were really aiming at. In March 1543 Gardiner set his agents to weed out members of a heretical cell in Windsor. The result, in the summer, was the burning of Anthony Parsons, a preacher and colporteur of banned books, Henry Filmer, a local churchwarden, and Robert Testwood, a singing man of the chapel royal. The organist of the chapel royal, John Marbeck, was also arrested but only suffered a period of imprisonment. Marbeck's name is known to students of church music as a composer of chants for the first English services as well as mass settings but he was no mean theological scholar. Gardiner's bloodhounds found copies of Calvin's works as well as some pages of a concordance to the English Bible upon which the accused was working. The case against him was watertight. Yet, after several interrogations, he was set at liberty. Gardiner claimed to have ordered Marbeck's release because he was a good musician but it is more probable that careful calculation lay behind the decision. It was very unlikely that Henry would countenance so prominent a member of the royal religious establishment being publicly punished for heresy. It would not have done much for his credentials as a Catholic monarch if it had become known that there were Calvinists in his own chapel.

Gardiner was not too worried; he had other fish to fry, including the biggest fish of all. 'The Bishop of Winchester would give six thousand pounds to pluck down the Archbishop of Canterbury' – so it was rumoured among a band of conservative activists in Kent.[8] Canterbury was a focal point of opposition to Cranmer. The large staff of the cathedral and other city clergy were, like all establishment men, resentful of change and they acted as a magnet for priests and prominent laymen throughout a wide area who shared their dislike of evangelical preachers and sympathisers. It was here that what has been called the 'Prebendaries' Plot' originated. It started out as a disorganised attempt to purge the diocese of radical preachers but Gardiner saw in it the possibility of tarring his arch-enemy with the brush of heresy for supporting and encouraging men found guilty of subversive teaching. From London he tried to give the emerging plot the cohesion it would need when it came to presenting accusations before the Privy Council. Throughout the early spring information came in from Windsor, Kent, London and even Calais about evangelical activists. Gardiner sifted it all carefully and, by the last week of April, he had an adequate case to set before the king. Just as, five months earlier, Cranmer had been responsible for originating a discreet official enquiry into the conduct of Catherine Howard, so now a similar royally sanctioned investigation was launched against the archbishop. That, in itself, must have given the Gardiner–Howard clique immense satisfaction.

All this coincided with a new formulation of official doctrine. For some months the bishops had been working on a replacement for the *Bishops' Book*, which had always been regarded as an interim statement of doctrine for the English church. Henry was closely involved in the preparation of *The Necessary Doctrine and Erudition of a Christian Man* and its preface clearly reflected his genuine concern. The new manual was set forth so that 'all men may uniformly be led and taught the true understanding of that which is necessary for every Christian man to know'.[9] In April Convocation was working on the final draft. They were doing so amid all the kerfuffle of alleged heresy in high places being stirred up by Gardiner's agents. It is scarcely believable that the two activities were not closely linked in the bishop's mind. With various heterodoxies breaking out at all social levels like pustules on a smallpox victim it was virtually certain that Henry would be eager to excise any Lutheran elements that might have crept into the *Bishops' Book*. So it proved.

The volume, published in May, was commonly known as the *King's Book* and reasonably so, for Henry checked every page and made various changes. This was a statement of what he believed – or, at least, what he believed in the spring of 1543. The *King's Book* struck at the heart of the Reformation by denying that justification was by faith alone and that good works played no part in salvation. On the contrary, human effort to achieve divine approval (including auricular confession and penance) was vital and no one could be assured beforehand of God's acquittal at the day of judgement. The book supported transubstantiation and the sacrifice of the mass, although it was less than coherent about the fate of the faithful departed because it was lukewarm about purgatory and rejected the efficacy of private requiem masses. The *King's Book* was undoubtedly a severe blow for the advocates of further reform, yet in one respect its style of argument was a vindication of what Cromwell and Cranmer had already achieved: every point of doctrine was advocated on the basis of Scripture and not on the unsupported testimony of traditional teaching.

However, the conservatives had an answer even for that. The Bible, they agreed, was the final authority in all matters of Christian faith and conduct. The problem was that not everyone was capable of interpreting it properly. This was always the argument that had been advanced in opposition to the rendering of Scripture into the vernacular. Now that the English Bible had been officially set forth it could not be banned. But access to it could be restricted. This time the conservatives used Parliament to achieve their objective. The bishops introduced a bill in the Lords in April which, within a month, reached the statute book as an Act for the Advancement of True Religion. This piece of regressive legislation forbade any men or women below the rank of yeoman to read the Great Bible, either publicly or privately. Noblemen, gentlemen and merchants were to restrict such activity to quiet study at home with their households. If this measure was intended to stamp out what a later age would condemn as religious 'enthusiasm' it was a nonstarter. If, as seems more likely, it was designed as one more weapon in the conservative armoury to flush out evangelicals by provoking them to angry response and flouting of the law it stood some chance of success. Their inquisition, stepped up throughout the summer, was aimed not at lesser fry but at prominent men and women of the court. They knew that the real problem with heresy was that what had once been a 'disease' of the lower orders was climbing the social scale.

Preachers and writers were not slow to react against the new legislation, which they saw as an attempt to muzzle the word of God. William Turner, theologian and botanist, lampooned the new law from the safety of Basle in his pamphlet *The huntyng and fyndyng out of the Romish fox*. In answer to the argument that the wealthier members of society were cleverer than their underlings, he retorted, 'Well, in answer I say besides that there are more gentle fools than yeoman fools, number compared to number . . . whoever thou art that for any cause would keep poor men from the Scriptures, I say that thou art one of the Pharisees' fools.'[10] The granting of a right (freedom to read the Bible) which was then snatched away caused widespread offence and not only to evangelicals. It helped to raise the political temperature in the shires during the summer of 1543. Early recorders of the events of this year, such as John Foxe and John Strype, collected several anecdotes which indicate a frenzy of activity. When Sir Thomas Caradine of the privy chamber heard that one Robert Ockham was on his way up from Kent with evidence against him and some of his colleagues to lay before Gardiner he had the man waylaid at Woking and roughed up. Ockham persisted and, a couple of days later, had reached London. As he was making his way along the Strand in the company of a servant of Robert Bennet, another of Gardiner's men, 'coming by the Earl of Bedford's lodging Ockham was pulled in by the sleeve and no more seen of Bennet's man, till he saw him in the Marshalsea [prison]'.[11] This arrest had been arranged by Caradine with Bedford. Now that Ockham was out of the way, Caradine broke into the man's rooms and confiscated his papers. These turned out to contain complaints against no less than eight members of the court. The matter was brought to the king's attention. He readily pardoned the accused and instructed that Ockham's behaviour should be looked into. The end result was that Ockham and his fellow inquisitors were tried and found guilty of perjury. They were 'Appointed to ride through Reading, Windsor and Newbury . . . with their faces towards their horses' tails and a paper upon their heads setting forth their crime. Also they were to stand upon the pillory in each of those towns.'[12] Thereafter they were lodged in the Fleet prison, where one of them died. Both sides were equally guilty of playing dirty.

It was not only suspected evangelicals who were under investigation. Where reformers were in the ascendant it was traditionalists who had to watch their step. Colchester was one such place. Several members of the town council were of the new learning and closely supervised the running of their churches. In 1543 they indicted two local clergy, Thomas Kyrkham and Henry Beck, for preaching neither 'the Gospel of God nor the statute of the Lord King'. The offence of these conservative priests was not reciting the latest royal injunctions quarterly, as they were instructed to do.[13]

Meanwhile, no action had been taken against Cranmer. Information had been assiduously gathered by his enemies in Canterbury and other parts of Kent but Henry had not seen fit to act upon it. When he did do so the result was not what the conservative group had envisaged. One afternoon in September the king was being rowed up the Thames in his barge and, stopping at Lambeth, he summoned Cranmer aboard. 'Now I know who is the greatest heretic in Kent' was his surprise greeting. He handed the archbishop a paper containing a summary prepared by Gardiner from all the bits and pieces of damning evidence that had been gathered. Clearly, Henry intimated these serious matters would have to be looked into. The best person to take charge of the enquiry, he said, was Cranmer himself. Thus it was that, during the autumn, a wide-ranging investigation took place into the activities of both evangelicals and their opponents. Nocturnal raids on the homes of Canterbury clergy now revealed details of the Prebendaries' Plot to destroy the archbishop. Incriminating letters led the investigators straight back to the Bishop of Winchester's office and, especially, to his secretary and nephew, Germain Gardiner. This committed, zealous and scheming traditionalist had been foolish enough to keep papers linking him with Cardinal Pole, Henry's number one *bête noire*. There was immediate panic within Winchester's camp and it was this which precipitated an ill-advised direct assault on Cranmer. The famous incident, which probably occurred in late November, is only explicable as a desperate attempt to distract the king from the outfall of the Prebendaries' Plot.

What Gardiner and his associates planned was a rerun of the tactics that had brought down Cromwell. Charges against the archbishop were to be laid before the Privy Council who would, then, order him to be held in the Tower pending enquiry. The king's permission for this was received but on the night before Cranmer was summoned to appear before his conciliar colleagues Henry sent Sir Anthony Denny to fetch him from Lambeth. The archbishop's secretary, Ralph Moris, recorded the conversation. Henry told Cranmer what was about to happen.

> My lord answered and most humbly thanked the king that it would please his highness to give him that warning afore-hand, saying that he was very well content to be committed to the Tower for the trial of his doctrine, so that he might be indifferently heard, as he doubted not but that his majesty would see him so to be used. 'Oh, Lord God,' quod the king, 'what fond simplicity have you, so to permit yourself to be imprisoned, that every enemy of yours may take vantage against you. Do not you think that if they have you once in prison, iii or iv false knaves will soon be procured to witness against you and to condemn you, which else, now being at your liberty dare not once open their lips or appear before your face. No, not so, my lord,' quod the king, 'I have better regard unto you than to permit your enemies so to overthrow you. And, therefore, I will that you tomorrow come to the council, who, no doubt, will send for you, and when they break this matter unto you . . . then appeal you from them to our person and give to them this ring (which he delivered unto my lord Cranmer then), by the which', said the king, 'they shall well understand that I have taken your cause into my hand.'[14]

That was exactly what happened, to the confusion of Gardiner and his supporters. Cranmer was now safe from any further attempts to dislodge him. As for Germain Gardiner, his trial went ahead and, the following February, he was hanged, drawn and quartered as a traitor. His uncle almost followed him to Tyburn a few months later, for his enemies on the Privy Council tried to do to him precisely what he had tried to do to Cranmer. The bishop managed to obtain an audience with the king and the proceedings were stopped. If Henry was unwilling to be deprived of the services of his archbishop, he was also not prepared to lose those of Cranmer's arch-rival. No English monarch was more profligate with talented servants than Henry VIII. Wolsey, More and Cromwell had all been thrown to the wolves by a king who had every reason to be grateful to them. Perhaps now, rather late in the day, he had come to appreciate the talents of others. He had certainly regretted the loss of Cromwell and soundly berated his councillors for talking him into the minister's trial and execution. Perhaps he hesitated about making the same mistake again.

It makes little sense to try to provide Henry with a rationale. He was a moody semi-invalid, long accustomed to acting on a whim. What is important about his refusal to be manoeuvred into destroying Cranmer or Gardiner is that it highlights for us an important fact about the Henrician Reformation – the gap between lexis and praxis. Church doctrine was clearly established by statute and proclamation. Had the law been rigidly enforced in the last years of Henry's reign England would have been an orthodox Catholic country – without the pope, to be sure, and drastically reformed but nevertheless, as to doctrine, impeccably traditional. It would have had its own version of the Inquisition, as heretics were rounded up, burned or driven into exile and as all evangelical books were banned. This was how state religion was protected and enforced in England's near neighbours – Spain, France and the Netherlands. It did not happen in Henry's realm because the king kept a tight rein on persecution. The Act of Six Articles was available, the *King's Book* was available and their provisions could have been driven home with ruthless efficiency. They were not. More importantly

Henry's protection of prominent evangelicals and, also, his placing the education of his heir in the hands of devotees of the new learning kept the reform movement alive.

While church politicians schemed and vied for power the evangelicals were quietly building up their influence in places where it really mattered. One of those places was the household of Prince Edward. In the summer of 1544 Henry's only son was approaching his seventh birthday and the time had come for him to leave the nursery and begin his education and training for his future role. The king naturally wanted to hire the best tutors available. Three of the scholars he chose were Cambridge men. John Cheke had been Regius Professor of Greek. Roger Ascham also taught Greek. Richard Cox, after his university days, had been a very distinguished headmaster of Eton. The only non-Cambridge member of the quartet, Anthony Cooke, had been privately tutored but subsequently earned for himself a distinguished reputation as a teacher. (His daughters, Mildred and Ann, were reputedly the most learned women in England.) All were gifted educationalists dedicated to the then 'trendy' principle that learning should be enjoyable. There is no doubt that young Edward could not have been in better hands, nor that his tutors well merited their royal appointment. What is remarkable is that they were all advocates of religious reform. Furthermore, the man chosen to teach the prince French was Jean Belmain, a staunch Calvinist. It is inconceivable that Henry did not know the religious proclivities of the pedagogues to whom he was entrusting the upbringing of his heir. Yet he made no attempt to balance the influences on Edward by placing in his son's entourage scholars of a more traditionalist bent. It may be that he was too busy planning and waging war when the crucial decisions were made. Henry was with his army in France from early July to the end of September 1544, and the preceding and ensuing months were dominated by foreign policy issues. The king invested an enormous amount of personal energy in the ruinous and fruitless campaigns which marred the last years of the reign. Perhaps the training of his son paled into insignificance beside the glorious and 'kingly' tasks of mustering armies, building ships and staking a claim for England in the military conflicts of the continent. Perhaps he did no more than seek the advice of his close attendants. That would certainly have accounted for the radical composition of young Edward's household.

All the new appointees had friends at court who were in a position to recommend them. Thomas Cranmer, Dr Butts, Anthony Denny and their chamber colleagues were all part of the humanist-evangelical network which was spreading wider and wider among the educated classes. Many members of England's intellectual elite, who now held important positions at court, in Parliament, in the diplomatic corps and in the government of the shires, had been students at Cambridge and the inns of court in the 1520s and 1530s – years when smuggled New Testaments had been circulating among them, when Thomas Bilney and other pioneer evangelical martyrs had gone to the stake and when Hugh Latimer's electrifying sermons were attracting large audiences to St Edward's church in Cambridge. Such men were now prominent among the movers and shakers of the realm. It is not difficult to imagine the letters that may have been written, the hasty journeys from Cambridge to London that may have taken place, the conversations that may have been held in palace antechambers. However it may have transpired, the selection of Edward's tutors was momentous for its significance in the story of the Reformation.

Perhaps we should also consider the part which may have been played by another participant in the life of the court. In July 1543, Henry had raised one evangelical sympathiser to the pinnacle of English life. This was the year in which he married his sixth and final wife. Catherine Parr was thirty-one and already twice widowed when she became queen. She accepted Henry's offer, which can scarcely have seemed wholly attractive, because she believed God was calling her to an exalted role which would enable her to advance the Reformation. Catherine was an intelligent and pious woman with the gifts of humanity, patience and kindness which had matured during the years spent caring for her previous elderly husbands. In all probability she had not yet embraced evangelical certainties but she was well advanced on a pilgrimage that would bring her to that position and one which she later described in the book she wrote herself: *The Lamentation or Complaint of a Sinner, Bewailing the Ignorance of her Blind Life led in Superstition.* Catherine found among the prominent ladies of the court a coterie of like-minded women, some of whom were more theologically advanced than herself. Prominent among them were Catherine Brandon, Duchess of Suffolk, an outspoken critic of the ecclesiastical establishment who kept a pet lapdog named 'Gardiner', Lady Hertford, wife of Edward Seymour, and Lady Lisle, wife of John Dudley. These gathered with her in a pious routine of regular devotional exercises and Bible study. These, it seems, were open meetings to which other ladies and gentlemen of the court were welcomed.

The religious life of England had an appearance of calm during the years that Henry was obsessed with war in France and Scotland. Foreign policy complications meant that, once more, the king had to open communications with the Protestant princes and did not wish to offend them by harrying Lutherans at home. Conflict in the Privy Council was at a minimum because the principal contenders were often absent – Gardiner on diplomatic missions and Seymour and Dudley on campaign. However, the rarity of heresy trials and the absence of vitriolic pulpit warfare certainly did not mean that religious conflict had subsided. In December 1545 Henry treated Parliament to a dressing-down on the subject of unity. It was a speech many of the hearers found moving and it is not difficult to understand why. The king was very obviously ill. His familiar oratorical bluster seemed to be wearing thin and exposing a monarch depressed by the failure of his religious policy. For all his 'supremacy' in matters ecclesiastical he could not enforce doctrinal concord. All he could do was sanction the punishment of extremists of all stamps. Yet he shared the distaste felt by many of his subjects for religious persecution and did not hesitate to halt prosecutions when he thought they were getting out of hand or too close to royal circles. He complained about the party strife that revealed itself in name-calling: 'Papist!', 'Heretic!', 'Hypocrite!', 'Anabaptist!' He condemned both clergy and laity for mishandling the word of God. He denounced preachers who propagated their own doctrinal opinions instead of simply opening up the Scriptures. He upbraided congregations who presumed to refute what they heard from the pulpit. He came close to acknowledging that, from a political point of view, the Englishing of the Bible had been a mistake. He pointed out that he had taken this step 'only to inform your conscience and to instruct your children and family' and not to have Scripture 'disputed, rhymed and jangled in every alehouse and tavern, contrary to the true meaning and doctrine of the same'. He warned that, if these abuses did not cease, 'I, whom God hath appointed his vicar and high minister here, will see those divisions removed and those enormities corrected, according to my very duty'.[15]

Henry's entreaties fell on deaf ears. In the last year of his reign there was no easing of religious tension; quite the reverse. If we were to attempt some sort of snapshot of English church life in 1546 the most obvious fact would be that the majority of the king's subjects remained loyal to traditional beliefs and practices. John Hooper was undoubtedly right when he observed gloomily, in January,

> Our king has destroyed the pope, but not popery; he has expelled all the monks and nuns, and pulled down their monasteries; he has caused all their possessions to be transferred into his exchequer ... The impious mass, the most shameful celibacy of the clergy, the invocation of saints, auricular confession, superstitious abstinence from meats, and purgatory, were never before held by the people in greater esteem than at the present moment.[16]

Yet radicals continued to make inroads into traditional religion in various places. In March the curate and churchwardens of the London church of St Martin Pomeroy removed the crucifix and other images, adorning the walls instead with the royal coat of arms and Bible texts. Even where zealots were not taking such initiatives there was a gradual movement away from a religion based on visual stimuli to one in which truth was imparted through words – English words – read, preached, sung and recited. Fewer testators now left bequests for the maintenance of altars or the saying of masses. No new devotional images were commissioned. As the traditional elements gradually faded from people's regular experience of church the psychology of worship slowly but inevitably changed. There was a tiny minority of English men and women for whom that change was either too fast or too slow to be endured. They became part of what was a growing European phenomenon: religious migration. Some of Henry's subjects who were unable to compromise their belief in papal supremacy or who found their interpretation of Scripture leading them to reject the miracle of the mass – both equally anathema to the regime – went into voluntary exile. This was not an option open to many. Most ardent believers were too attached to their families and communities to remove – perhaps permanently – to a foreign land, even if they could afford to do so.

There cannot have been many of Henry's subjects who suffered the kind of crisis of conscience which prompted them to quit their homeland – or even to wish they could quit their homeland. Most accepted the changes imposed on their communities. Some because they were loyal to the Crown. Some because they lacked the courage to protest (especially after the crushing of the Pilgrimage of Grace). Some because they were largely indifferent. Some because they were enthusiastic about reform. Since there were no opinion pollsters in sixteenth-century England we can never evaluate the 'success' of Henry VIII's Reformation.

The quiescence of the mid-decade proved to be the lull before the storm or, at least, before the next squall. Religious policy was, as ever, tied up with foreign policy. Anglo-French peace talks got under way in the spring of 1546. The younger councillors, Seymour and Dudley, had proved themselves as generals in the recent fighting and were high in royal favour. The imperial ambassador accurately summarised the political situation when he reported gloomily,

> If the King favours these stirrers of heresy, the Earl of Hertford, and the Lord Admiral [Dudley], which is to be feared . . . because the Queen, instigated by the Duchess of Suffolk, the Countess of Hertford, and the Lord Admiral's wife, shows herself infected, words and exhortations, even in the name of your Majesty, would only make the King more obstinate to show his absolute power and independence and might engender a coolness towards your Majesty, which is at present undesirable.[17]

The leading court evangelicals certainly seem to have been on the offensive. They openly supported partisan preachers, including Latimer and Shaxton, who now re-entered the limelight. If the conservatives were to change the situation, they would have to act quickly.

The social dislocation Henry had described in his Christmas address was very real but we should be careful not to isolate religious discord from the other ills afflicting the king's subjects. As well as the appalling poverty which we have already considered, England was involved in a very unpopular war. Hundreds of her men died in the mud of the Pas de Calais (neither the first nor the last in the history of the nation's relations with her neighbours to perish in this 'foreign field'). Their situation was hardly worse than that of many of their comrades:

> The soldiers coming from Calais and Boulogne were dying along the road from Dover to London and all along the roads from London to every quarter of the kingdom while

trying to go to their homes. After they had come home, those who were well fell sick, and those who were sick got worse and from this sickness and feebleness and pest they died in every part of England.[18]

In the previous summer England had suffered a bad invasion scare when a French fleet sailed into the Solent. The cost of the war affected everyone. Trade with the Low Countries was crippled and that rebounded not only on the merchants but on the households which supplied the cloth and the farmers who reared the sheep. Rampant inflation was made worse by new war taxes and debasement of the coinage. The imperial ambassador, for once, did not exaggerate when he reported, 'every man of wit in England blasphemes against the war.'[19] Naturally, the disaffected looked around for people to blame. Priests were attacked on suspicion of being fifth columnists working for Catholic France. Some preachers blamed heretics for calling down God's wrath on a wayward nation, while others attributed divine judgement to England's half-hearted reform. Religion was only part of the country's deep malaise but partisans eagerly focused on it for their own purposes.

Conservatives learning of Henry's determination to remove 'enormities' were encouraged to renew their attack on evangelicals, and to do so as a matter of urgency. Earlier in December they had tried to obtain a new, tougher heresy law but the Commons threw the bill out. Thanks in large measure to Cromwell's reforms many religious issues, hitherto the preserve of Convocation, were being taken over by Parliament; in other words, they were being decided by the laity. Evangelical patrons and activists ensured that their interests were well represented in the lower chamber. Among newly elected members there were a high proportion of evangelicals, including seven of the privy chamber staff. However, the Act of Six Articles was still available and a bout of fresh prosecutions was under way by the spring of 1546. In several towns the inhabitants were treated to the sight of human bonfires. But the conservative leaders knew

that such piecemeal persecution was of limited value if the religious balance *at the centre* was not changed. They therefore fell
back on an old strategy – that of entangling their prominent
evangelical opponents with the fate of convicted heretics. They
found a tool fit for their purpose in a young Lincolnshire gentlewoman we have already met – Anne Askew (see above, p. 119).

This vivacious, headstrong twenty-six-year-old daughter of
one of the leading members of county society was, by the standards of most rural womenfolk, well educated. She certainly
knew her Bible and, probably, some of the evangelical writings
currently in circulation. Her contacts with the reform movement may well have come through two of her brothers.
Christopher had been a gentleman of the privy chamber until
his death in 1543 and Edward held a highly prestigious place as
a member of the Gentlemen Pensioners, Henry's ceremonial
guard. She was no stranger to the court and may well have
hankered after the glittering and exciting life of the royal household, instead of being confined to a humdrum existence in the
provinces. Matters became unpleasant for her after her arranged
marriage to a fenland squire, Thomas Kyme. The couple did
not see eye to eye on many things, particularly religion, and
Anne was not the sort of woman to submit meekly to male
domination. She defied her husband to go about 'gospelling',
and Kyme must have been justifiably irritated by his wife's
neglect of her domestic responsibilities. After two years of
married life Anne left her husband and sought a divorce. Her
grounds were, in her own eyes, absolutely compelling. Had not
St Paul counselled, 'A woman which hath to her husband an
infidel . . . if the unbelieving depart, let him depart. A brother or
sister is not in subjection to such.' (I Corinthians, 7: 13–15,
Tyndale). The bishop's court was not impressed with this argument and ordered Anne back to her husband. Instead, she took
the road southwards, towards the end of 1544, either to present
her case in the court of Chancery or simply to seek the comforting presence of fellow believers.

It did not take her long to meet up with her Midlands

neighbour and brother in the faith, John Lascelles, and to be introduced by him to other evangelicals at court and in the City. If Anne found her new friends congenial company, they were no less taken with her. Her knowledge of the Bible was impressive, as was her devotional life. According to one observer, 'at midnight she beginneth to pray and ceaseth not for many hours after.'[20] She quickly became something of a celebrity in the evangelical world of the capital. Someone as pert and deliberately provocative as Anne Askew could not fail to attract the attention of the authorities and, in the spring of 1546, she was subjected to a series of examinations by the City council and the Bishop of London. According to the one-sided accounts which Anne wrote of her trials and which subsequently circulated among her fellow believers, she tied her august interlocutors up in knots and made them look foolish. The truth seems to be that Bishop Bonner suspected her of sacramentarianism and tried to shake from her a clear expression of her belief about the mass. Finally, tiring of her smart answers and her refusal either to confess to heresy or to state unequivocally her orthodox faith, he allowed her to be bailed and ordered her back to her husband at the end of March. The bishop had learned that one had to be very cautious in any heresy proceedings which involved people who had friends at court. Bonner would have had little hesitation about sending a fishmonger's wife to the stake.

Paradoxically, it was her connections in high places that persuaded Anne's enemies to reverse their decision. Her dismissal coincided exactly with Gardiner's return from his latest diplomatic mission. He will have been shocked by his first sight of the king. Henry suffered several bouts of fever during the winter and was more often in bed than out. His features were heavily lined by pain. Fewer people were allowed into his presence and that gave his smaller inner circle more power. One vital instrument of that power was the 'dry stamp'. Henry now avoided the fatigue of signing documents in person. A special stamp impressed his signature on official papers and was then inked in by one of his chamber staff. Anthony Denny had charge of this vital implement. 'Wily Winchester' (one of the more polite nicknames bestowed by Gardiner's opponents) summed up the situation very quickly. Unless immediate action was taken the conservative cause would be lost. The only circumstance in his favour was that his most effective enemies on the Privy Council, Seymour and Dudley, were still on active military service abroad. He orchestrated an immediate attack on the evangelicals of the royal inner circle. Troublesome London preachers were arrested and examined on the subject of their court contacts. John Lascelles was one of the first to be brought in for questioning as a result of these interrogations. Another was Robert Huicke, the king's new physician (Butts had died the previous November, his tomb in Fulham church being provided with a Latin epitaph by John Cheke). As Lord Chancellor, Thomas Wriothesley, an arch-trimmer who currently saw his advantage in helping the conservative reaction, gathered jigsaw pieces of evidence. From his interrogations one name that cropped up as having been succoured during her imprisonment by certain ladies of the queen's establishment was that of Anne Askew. At the end of May she and her husband were summoned to appear before the Privy Council.

June was a month of frenzied activity. London prisons filled with suspected heretics and much of the Privy Council's time was taken up with questioning the more important of them. Anne had to endure several more bouts of interrogation concerning her beliefs. Eventually it was clear to her examiners that she rejected the doctrine of the real presence and that she had not the slightest intention of recanting. She was, accordingly, sentenced to death by burning and sent to the Tower. This was the place where royal prisoners could be subjected, in privacy, to whatever methods of interrogation seemed most likely to produce results. Here she was visited by Wriothesley and his assistant, Richard Rich. To understand the line of questioning to which Anne was now subjected we need to understand what was happening at court. When Henry and his wife were together the conversation sometimes turned to religion and, on one such occasion, Gardiner was present and overheard a slight disagreement between the royal couple. He grabbed the opportunity to suggest to the king that Catherine, encouraged by members of her entourage, was flirting with heresy. Henry gave him permission to investigate. It was for this reason that Wriothesley was set to extract from Anne Askew information which would lead to members of the queen's inner circle. In the words of Anne's own written account, 'they asked me of my Lady of Suffolk, my Lady of Sussex, my Lady of Hertford, my Lady Denny and my Lady Fitzwilliam.'[21] When she refused to name names, Wriothesley and Rich resorted to the extraordinary expedient of stretching her on the rack, a barbarous act even for those times. So appalled was the Lieutenant of the Tower that he hurried to report personally to the king and to disassociate himself from the proceeding. That royal councillors personally wielded the instruments of torture can only indicate the desperation of the conservative faction. Their strategy failed because Anne Askew withstood her suffering and because Queen Catherine, learning of the plot, threw herself on Henry's mercy and received his gracious forgiveness.

The whole sequence of events provided its instigators with spectacular but short-lived triumph. Anne Askew and John Lascelles perished in the same fire on 16 July, the former carried to the stake on a chair because her racking had damaged her legs. In the aftermath of the latest outbreak of persecution a diplomat reported from the Low Countries, 'About 60 Englishmen are fled over here for fear of death . . . so that here are tales of persecution by the bishops, and the King is slandered for suffering it. These things are spoken by the best in the land.'[22]

On 8 July the king had been induced to issue a proclamation against heretical books which gave the conservatives the success they had failed to achieve in Parliament. Several prominent evangelicals buckled under pressure and recanted. But by now the dynamic of the Council board had changed with the return of Seymour and Dudley. Once again conservative successes were balanced by contrary government activity. Condemned prisoners were released on orders from the king. In discussions with French representatives in August Henry actually proposed that the two nations declare their intention to have the mass translated into vernacular languages. Domestic religious policy was, as ever, being strongly influenced by events abroad. Charles V had, at long last, gone to war with the princes of the Schmalkaldic League. This was the big showdown, long expected, between the champions of traditional and reformed Christianity and it was far from clear how it would all end. John Hooper, one of the evangelical exiles, had the measure of the king and explained to a foreign friend what the royal turn and turn about meant:

> There will be a change of religion in England, and the king will take up the gospel of Christ, in case the emperor should be defeated in this most destructive war. [However] should the gospel sustain a loss, he will then return to his impious mass, for which he has this last summer committed four respectable and godly persons to the flames.[23]

Charles's winter campaign was successful and so nothing eventually came of the liturgical initiative but it is a further indication of just how bewildering the state of English church life must have seemed to many of Henry's subjects. There was certainly tension at the top. In September a furious argument in the Privy Council led to John Dudley slapping Gardiner's face.

Towards the year's end Henry experienced fresh bouts of chronic illness that confined him to his privy chamber but the strength of the royal lion's will was unabated and two of his most senior advisers now felt the lash of his claws. The timing could not have been more crucial. Henry 'requested' an exchange of royal property with estates belonging to the diocese of Winchester. (This was not an unusual proceeding for the consolidation of Crown lands.) Gardiner, concerned to assert a degree of independence for the church, asked permission to discuss the deal with the king. Henry, who by this stage was not welcoming visitors, chose to interpret this as a refusal and angrily banned the bishop from court and Council. One result was that Henry changed the provisional arrangements made for a regency council in the event of the accession of a minor. He ordered Gardiner's name to be removed from the list. When a colleague spoke up for the bishop Henry silenced him sharply. 'I myself could use him and rule him to all manner of purposes, as seemed good to me; but so shall you never do,' he snapped.[24] Henry knew his man. (Thomas Thirlby, Bishop of the brief see of Westminster, another adamant religious conservative, was also struck off the list of regency body members.) The other councillor to be brought down in the last days of the reign was none other than the Duke of Norfolk. He was destroyed by the folly of his son, the Earl of Suffolk, who, unable to contain his aristocratic pride and ambition, was adjudged to have antici-pated the king's death by asserting the 'right' of the Howards to govern the person of Edward during the forthcoming minority. Suffolk was beheaded for treason and Norfolk, languishing in the Tower, would have shared that fate had Henry not died within hours of the moment scheduled for his execution.

Thus, by a combination of the folly of leading conservatives, the domination of the privy chamber by evangelicals and the inscrutable will of the old king, the fate of the nation was placed in the hands of a predominantly evangelical council when Henry VIII died in January 1547. Now there was nothing to stop the progress of the Reformation. But it was by no means clear what form the transformation of English life would take. What kind of evangelicalism would hold sway? As long as the religious radicals had been fighting the forces of reaction there had been a fairly well agreed theological manifesto – at least among those at the centre of national life. The open Bible, justi-fication by faith only, vernacular worship, and the abolition of propitiatory masses and veneration of images – these had been the objectives which Cranmer and his allies had hoped to achieve. Those who held more extreme beliefs had no input to official policy. They had either kept silent or had openly professed opinions widely condemned as heretical. But now all evangelical activists contended for their own version of the faith and tried to shape what would emerge as English Protestantism.

Henry's will entrusted the child king, Edward VI, to a regency Council with an evangelical majority. The result was the first government in English history which may be said to have had a 'programme' for the reshaping of society; for the creation of a Christian commonwealth; for what was, in effect, an officially sponsored and coordinated revolution. The Bible was the manifesto for policy and God's agent in implementing it was young Edward, hailed now as another Josiah, like the boy-king of ancient Judaea who had carried out sweeping reforms of the national religion, purging it from the idolatry which had arisen by the infiltration of pagan worship. The comparison was considered by Cranmer and his associates as particularly apt because Josiah had based his reconstruction on the discovery of the long-lost book of Deuteronomy with its exposition of the Mosaic law. Edward and his ministers would now reshape English life and religion in accordance with the newly set forth vernacular Scripture. The intellectual and spiritual force behind the new policy was Archbishop Cranmer who, now free from the constraints imposed by a 'difficult' king and a divided Privy Council, displayed an 'inflexible determination to further the evangelical goal by fair means or foul'.[25]

Purging the church of the remaining elements of 'superstition' and establishing 'right doctrine' was always going to be a Herculean task. The majority of the bishops were set in the old ways and the new learning was very far from being established in the hearts of the people. However, the reformers held in their hand three aces (and were quite convinced that God was in charge of the game). The king was a genuine upholder of evangelical truth; the Privy Council majority were committed to further reform; and the new establishment had the support of an impressive array of continental scholars and church leaders.

We have a king who is firm, learned and pious beyond his age. [He was ten in 1547]. If there has ever existed a Josiah since the first of that name, this is certainly he ... a more holy disposition has nowhere existed in our time. He alone seems to sustain the gospel by his incredible piety, most holy manners, prudence altogether that of an old man, with a firmness at this age altogether unheard of.[26]

That encomium from an exile recently returned from Geneva may appear to be somewhat excessive but is well supported by the testimony of others who had access to the court of the young king. Edward, they reported, read several chapters of the Bible daily, received thankfully the writings of contemporary reformers and discussed them with his peers, had sermons preached before him every Sunday and made notes on what he heard.

The task of turning pious doctrine into workable politics was largely in the hands of Edward Seymour and John Dudley, who dominated the Council. Henry VIII's will had entrusted his heir and the kingdom to a regency panel of equals but, with little difficulty, Seymour, the king's uncle and newly appointed Duke of Somerset, was able to establish himself as Lord Protector. However, the increasing high-handedness with which he forced through policies his colleagues considered ill-advised, if not downright dangerous, opened up a rift which resulted in his downfall in the autumn of 1549 and his execution two years later. John Dudley, Duke of Northumberland, took up the reins and, as President of the Council, ruled as *primus inter pares* until his own downfall in 1553. Both pursued aggressive evangelical policies, though they differed in their precise aims and methods.

The strong links now forged between English and foreign theologians had their origin in major events on the continent. In February 1547 Charles V won a convincing victory over the Protestant princes at Mühlberg and set about eradicating Lutheranism from his dominions. The task ultimately defeated him but the years 1547–51 were bleak years for the cause of reformed religion in Europe. The migration pattern went into reverse and England now became the haven for many evangelicals fleeing persecution. In 1545 Pope Paul III had summoned a council to meet at Trent to make the Catholic church tougher, leaner and more determined to see off the evangelical challenge. Various Reformed leaders dreamed of a counter-council which would gather all evangelical communions under one doctrinal umbrella and make them stronger to face the enemy. Cranmer now took up this idea with great enthusiasm.

> We are desirous of setting forth in our churches the true doctrine of God, and have no wish to adapt it to all tastes, or to deal in ambiguities; but, laying aside all carnal considerations, to transmit to posterity a true and explicit form of doctrine agreeable to the rule of the sacred writings; so that there may not only be set forth among all nations an illustrious testimony respecting our doctrine . . . but that all posterity may have a pattern to imitate. For the purpose of carrying this important design into execution we have thought it necessary to have the assistance of learned men, who having compared their opinions together with us, may do away with all doctrinal controversies, and build up an entire system of true doctrine.[27]

It was a big, bold scheme and destined never to be realised, but Cranmer did welcome to England many of Europe's leading evangelical thinkers with whom he entered into discussion and for some of whom he found benefices or employment as university teachers.

One result was a doctrinal shift among many of England's clergy and scholars. For twenty years Europe's evangelical leaders had sought agreement on the major Christian doctrines. They had achieved a large measure of success and it is certainly realistic to speak of an evangelical consensus. However, the one topic on which agreement still proved impossible was the nature of Christ's presence in the Holy Communion service. At the Last

Supper Christ had declared, as he distributed bread and wine to his disciples, 'This is my body' and 'This is my blood.' Lutherans held fast to the literal understanding of these words. Christ was present corporeally in the elements. Catholics made the same claim and explained the mystery by teaching that the transformation was effected by the priest at the moment of consecration. The problem for Swiss and Germans in the Reformed tradition was how to remain true to Scripture, while rejecting sacerdotalism. Zwingli and his successor at Zurich, Johann Bullinger, insisted that the words of institution were to be understood figuratively. Christ's presence at the holy table was not localised in the elements; these were simply aides-memoires. It was this sacramentarianism which had taken many English men and women to the stake and which could not be openly professed during Henry VIII's reign. The old king would accept no denial of the miracle of the mass. But now Cranmer and some of his colleagues felt free to engage in dialogue with their continental brethren on the vexed problem of how Christ met with believers in the Lord's Supper. The archbishop's voyage of exploration ended up in the theological new world located by the Strasbourg scholar Martin Bucer. Bucer had laboured hard and long to bring all the principal evangelical leaders to agreement and one result had been his development of a form of words which he hoped (in vain) would be acceptable to all. What he – and Cranmer – held true was that Christ's real presence in the sacrament was not ingested in the elements but apprehended *by faith*. Communicants became 'partakers of his body and blood', *spiritually*. This distinctive position would, in the fullness of time, become official Anglican doctrine. It would be fair to say that its theological subtlety would be lost on most ordinary believers, who, if pressed, would probably have been content with the simple logic that the Lord's Supper was a memorial feast in which bread and wine were symbols of Christ's passion. From a historical point of view the importance of Cranmer's shift in doctrinal allegiance was that the reformed English church had not only distanced itself from Rome; it had also moved on from its Lutheran beginnings.

However, before the new administration could set out its religious stall radical elements welcomed it with euphoria. Evangelical exiles hastened to return and to be part of what they confidently expected would be the completion of the English Reformation. Within the realm impatient evangelical activists took matters into their own hands. In May Bishop Gardiner received a disturbing report that in Portsmouth the rood had been 'contemptuously pulled down and spitefully handled'. At the same time students at Magdalen College, Oxford, went on an iconoclastic rampage. Such unauthorised activity created a dilemma for the government. While sympathising with the motives of headstrong zealots, they could not encourage controversial activity which might lead to breaches of public order. It is significant that when the reformists at St Martin Pomeroy church were hauled before the Privy Council for their removal of images the previous year they were released with a caution. Somerset and Cranmer knew that they faced an uphill task in purifying English religion but they also knew that they had eager potential agents in various parts of the country.

Like Thomas Cromwell a decade before, their first step in official reformation was to make a visitation of all the nation's churches. The main objective of this spiritual stocktaking was to discover how far the campaign against 'idolatry' had progressed since the injunctions of 1538. And, like the Cromwellian surveys of monasteries and parishes, this was far from being a mere fact-finding exercise. The chosen visitors were almost to a man passionately committed to 'decluttering' churches. Although their instructions, set forth in new injunctions, were to remove only objects which were venerated and thus detracted from the worship due only to God, it was left to them to decide what items fell into this category. Having identified what constituted offensive 'shrines, covering of shrines, tables, candlesticks, rolls of wax, pictures, paintings or other monuments of feigned miracles, pilgrimages, idolatry and superstition',[28] they were to instruct parishioners to remove and completely destroy them 'so that there remain no memory of the same in walls, glass windows, or elsewhere within their churches or houses'.[29] Not only were churches to be stripped bare of almost every vestige of Catholic ritual, houses, too, had to be cleansed. The ultimate object, of course, was to rid people's minds of the old ways – 'so that there remain no memory'.

Parishioners in the capital and the provinces watched with mixed feelings as the instructions were carried out:

> the 5 day in September began the king's visitation at Paul's, and all images pulled down; and the 9 day of the said month the said visitation was at Saint Bride's, and after that in divers other parish churches; and so all images pulled down throughout all England at that time, and all churches new whitelimed, with the commandments written on the walls.[30]

By the time Parliament met at the end of the year the government were ready to give legal force to religious change. They swept away the old heresy laws and, with great relish, dumped the Act of Six Articles. The most important aspect of traditional religion to go under the axe in this thorough *renversement* of English devotional life was prayer for the dead. In December 1547 an Act was passed for the dissolution of chantries, colleges and guilds established for the purpose of intercession for souls in purgatory. This had been contemplated by Henry's last Parliament but the Henrician regime had shrunk from dismantling this major pillar of popular religion. The new regime judged the time to be right. If any piece of legislation may be said to have marked the transformation of England from a Catholic to a Protestant country this was it.

> The outright proscription of purgatory, and of the whole gamut of traditional means of assisting the repose of the souls of the dead, must rank as one of the most audacious attempts at the restructuring of beliefs and values ever attempted in England, a kind of collective cultural de-programming.[31]

This revolutionary activity taking place not at distant pilgrimage sites or abbeys remote from human habitation but at the heart of every rural and urban community poses two interrelated questions: what drove local people – in many cases with great enthusiasm – to destroy age-hallowed devotional aids; and why was there no immediate outcry against an attempt at national brainwashing of a kind we now associate with extreme totalitarian regimes? Certainly there were places where images were kept from the flames; hidden away by pious protectors, perhaps in the hope of better times to come. There were also places where the traditionalists insisted that their statues did not provoke idolatrous worship. Such protests obliged the government, in February 1549, to toughen the royal injunction by simply ordering *all* images to be removed. It is also true that protest against the attack on images was one reason for rebellious activity which broke out in a few places in 1549 (see p. 271ff). However, not only did the vast majority of priests, churchwardens and layfolk order in the demolition men and pay for the necessary repainting, reglazing and structural repairs, in many places they actually went beyond what the government ordered.

In 1550 Parliament found it necessary to issue a restraining order. A new Act pointed out that removal of church furniture 'shall not extend to any image or picture set or graven upon any tomb in any church, chapel, or churchyard only for a monument of any king, prince, nobleman, or other dead person, which hath not been commonly reputed and taken for a saint'.[32] Surely people were not desecrating graves, ripping up memorial brasses and smashing tombstones which marked the resting places of their own ancestors, were they? The answer is 'Yes, that is precisely what they were doing.' At Holy Trinity, Long Melford, a Suffolk church spectacularly well endowed with carvings, sculptures, paintings, gilded ornament and jewel-bedecked altars – of which the parishioners were presumably very proud – three hundredweight (151 kilograms) of memorial brasses were sold off in 1548. The church officers of St Martin's, Leicester, did not wait for the arrival of government commissioners before disposing, in 1547, of nine hundredweight (453 kilograms) of brass which had commemorated earlier town worthies. These were very far from being isolated examples of excessive zeal or sheer vandalism. The government, as it were, placed its seal upon these actions by the most dramatic demonstration of all. On the north side of St Paul's Cathedral there was a cloister within which were numerous tombs of once-prominent Londoners. A charnel house and a chapel decorated with Dance of Death paintings completed this site given over to commemoration of and prayer for the dead. It was a powerful statement of the communion of the living with the dead and the priesthood's authority on both sides of the grave. In April 1549, perhaps emboldened by attacks on funerary monuments in many places, the Duke of Somerset resolved that it should be totally effaced. Gangs of workmen moved in with picks and shovels. Within days this ancient necropolis at the heart of the City had been dug over and levelled. Some onlookers reckoned that a thousand cartloads of bones were hauled out to Finsbury Field for dumping.

Much as we might deplore the incalculable loss of thousands upon thousands of beautiful medieval artefacts, the story of this cultural rape cannot be told in terms of 'Protestant Philistines' versus 'Catholic Aesthetes'. It is not that simple. All over the country cash-strapped (or just plain greedy) churchwardens were grabbing the opportunity to turn an honest buck. Just as traditionalist landowners had petitioned the Crown for ex-monastic property and local profiteers had raided conventual buildings for stone, lead and timber when the monasteries came tumbling down, so, now, loyal churchmen with an eye to the main chance competed for the endowments of chantries and the saleable stone and metal coming out of 'purified' churches.

Why do the records provide us with no tales of churches being locked or barricaded to prevent desecration? Why did no local activists stir their neighbours to resist the commissioners, as the parishioners of St James's, Louth, had in 1536? Why do state and church archives for these years not bristle with letters of outraged protest? Fear must certainly have played a part in the widespread non-resistance. The Pilgrimage of Grace and the fate of those who had instigated it were still fresh in the communal memory. But that, in itself, would be insufficient to explain why prayers for the dead, once so central to people's understanding of eternal reality, were given up without much of a struggle or familiar and beautiful objects of devotion surrendered to the flames. It certainly does not account for parishioners participating in the removal of brasses commemorating their parents and grandparents.

Logic may have been just as persuasive as fear. For twenty years (longer if we count Lollard scepticism) the existence of purgatory had been called in question. It had been as long ago as 1528–9 that Simon Fish's *A Supplicacyon for the Beggers* had provoked a lively debate by denouncing requiem masses as a money-making racket. Since then, evangelical books and sermons had stressed that assurance of salvation came only from personal faith in the once-for-all, finished work of Christ. Even Catholic apologists were less than enthusiastic in defence of such a blatantly unbiblical doctrine as purgatory. For those who accepted the authority of Scripture it was axiomatic that people who died without faith would not go to heaven and no amount of prayer by priests or intercession by saints could change that. It followed, with inescapable logic, that if there was no purgatory there was no need for chantries or altars maintained by guilds where sacrifice was made on behalf of the departed. It may even be that distorted logic appeared to justify rejection of all commemoration of the dead.

Doubt must also have been a powerful solvent of commitment to the old ways. One did not need to buy into the whole justification by faith package to be influenced by scepticism about sacerdotal priesthood and the power wielded by clergy over their parishioners by virtue of their ability to influence the fate of the dear departed. For those who now became convinced that priestly authority did not extend to the afterlife it was difficult to avoid the conviction that they and their forebears had been conned. It was indignation which fuelled some of the indiscriminate attacks on church property. Iconoclasts vented their fury on the clergy by smashing any appurtenances of the religion they represented. In the old church of the London Grey Friars, sweating zealots 'pulled up all the tombs, great stones, all the altars, with the stalls and walls of the choir and altars in the church'.[33]

Nationalism, doubtless, also had its part to play in acquiescence to change. Government propagandists represented the new wave of iconoclasm as a continuation of the campaign against foreign (i.e. Roman) control of English religious life. Cranmer and other writers and preachers, following the pattern of earlier Tudor royal historians, emphasised England's continuity with a heroic past. They eulogised Celtic Christianity and identified the corruption of the faith with the arrival of papal envoys and the increasing domination of native religion by Roman falsehood. It was important for sixteenth-century evangelicals to rebut the charge of 'novelty'; to assert that, so far from reinventing Christianity, they were rediscovering the original Gospel. It was in these years that an Oxford graduate, John Foxe, began his researches in church history which would, within a decade, come to fruition in the monumental work which defined and, more than any other single influence, established English Protestantism, the *Acts and Monuments of the Christian Martyrs and Matters Ecclesiastical passed in the Church of Christ, from the Primitive Beginnings, to these our Days* . . . In one of the prefaces to this book Foxe identified the slender thread of true believers who had kept the faith alive over the centuries:

> the true church of Christ, although it durst not openly appear in the face of the world, was oppressed by tyranny; yet neither was it so invisible or unknown, but, by the providence of the Lord, some remnant always remained from time to time, which not only showed secret good affection to sincere doctrine, but also stood in open defence of truth against the disordered church of Rome.[34]

Those who now took the lead in eradicating the last vestiges of Romanism from the national church believed they were standing on the shoulders of spiritual giants. That is why the purging of churches could sometimes take on an atmosphere of carnival. Bonfires of images, books and even of saints' bones tipped out of reliquaries attracted cheering crowds, just as, only a few years before, similar conflagrations consuming heretical books had been attended by enthusiastic throngs. For many evangelical activists, convinced that the truth had been kept prisoner for centuries, this was pay-back time. Priests led a rampage through the churches of Norwich in September 1547, exultantly ridding them of the garish symbols of doctrinal error. In Durham one of the visitors threw a processional monstrance to the ground and gleefully jumped up and down on it. Such demonstrators were possessed by an intoxicating sense of freedom. It is difficult for us to comprehend the euphoria felt by those who believed that, after generations of foreign, papal oppression, the solemn symbols of priestly authority were now being exposed as the accoutrements of fraud. The sacerdotalists' bluff had been called and they had no answer.

Most modern narrators of these turbulent events have focused on the 'shocking' destruction of masterpieces of medieval art and shocking the iconoclasm certainly was from an artistic point of view. But the artistic point of view was not available to Edward VI's subjects. In our secular age we can look objectively at paintings, sculptures and stained glass windows and appraise them by aesthetic criteria. This was something our sixteenth-century ancestors could never do. Church furniture consisted of items which were both functional and symbolic. According to the attitude of the worshipper, they either brought one close to the divine or acted as brick walls preventing access. If the latter, then the only safe thing to do was to sweep them all away.

The Reformation of 1547–53 was not just about getting rid of the old; now that they enjoyed almost unlimited authority to change English religious life, Cranmer and his associates laboured hard and long to provide the nation with doctrinal and liturgical tools for constructing a purified and Bible-based church life. Preaching was the most immediate way of reaching ordinary people with the Gospel and here the reformers were confronted by the obstacle of clergy who were either too poorly educated to present the evangelical message or were actually opposed to it. The immediate answer to this problem was to provide set sermons which were to be read to all congregations and which left no doubt about official doctrine. The *Book of Homilies* was something Cranmer had been working on since 1542 and he was able to gain input from other bishops and publish in July 1547. The twelve topics covered the principal points of evangelical doctrine (conservative bishops were only invited to contribute addresses on such uncontroversial subjects as Christian charity and against swearing and perjury):

1   Holy Scripture
2   Universal sinfulness
3   Justification
4   Faith
5   Good works
6   Christian love and charity
7   Swearing and perjury
8   Apostasy
9   Death
10 Obedience to rulers
11 Whoredom and uncleanness
12 Civil disorder

All restrictions to Bible reading were now withdrawn – and in quite unequivocal terms:

Here may all manner of persons, men, women, young, old, learned, unlearned, rich, poor, priests, laymen, lords, ladies, officers, tenants, and mean men, virgins, wives, widows, lawyers, merchants, artificers, husbandmen, and all manner of persons, of what estate or condition soever they be, in this book learn all things what they ought to believe, what they ought to do, and what they should not do.[35]

When dealing with faith, Cranmer sought to scotch two common misconceptions. The first was that faith was an intellectual exercise, believing *about* God and his plan of salvation. Such activity he called 'dead faith'. True faith was identified as personal 'earnest, trust and confidence in God'. Cranmer's second concern was to reject the charge of antinomianism – that since salvation is obtained by faith, there is no need to perform good works. He countered with the assertion that true faith would show itself in good works, since human response to a loving God was to obey his commands.

The ninth homily presented a counter-balance to the desecration of tombs and the paraphernalia of purgatory. It affirmed that the Christian had no need to fear death or agonise about what lay beyond. Hearers were urged to lay hold on the assurance of eternal salvation, something impossible to them under the old dispensation. They were to take comfort from the Bible's promises that those who died in the faith of Christ would go to heaven. The reformed emphasis now began to appear in the formulas used by testators when drawing up their wills. A growing number abandoned the old invocation of 'the blessed Mary and all the saints' to pray for their soul and stated that the person preparing for death trusted 'only in the merits of Christ my Saviour'.

The remaining homilies reflected the uncertainty of the times. They upheld high moral standards, stressed the scriptural principle that kings derive their authority from God and must be obeyed and anathematised rebellion. This sent a clear message into every parish that, though a powerful king had died, no one should doubt that the boy on the throne possessed the plenitude of royal power.

The next step in the reformers' programme was to change the pattern and doctrinal content of church worship. In any campaign to win over the hearts of the people to evangelical truth, shaping what they encountered every Sunday and saint's day was vital. The constitutional problem faced by the reformers was the absence of any authoritative church body which could pronounce upon and enforce liturgical change. Since Cromwell's fall there had been no Vicegerent in Spirituals effectively wielding the royal supremacy on the king's behalf. The governing ecclesiastical bodies were the convocations of Canterbury and York, but these both had conservative majorities and would be of no use at all in bringing about that wholesale and rapid transformation on which the government were determined. Cranmer, Somerset and their allies got round this problem by appointing committees to draw up new formularies and by using Parliament to enforce their adoption. Throughout much of 1548 Cranmer consulted with a hand-picked team of theologians to provide a uniform worship book to replace the various services currently in use.

Before the result of their deliberations was presented to the nation a remarkable debate was held in Parliament. For four days in December Lords and Commons discussed the meaning and significance of Holy Communion. Attention focused on the central issue of the nature of Christ's presence. One member of the lower house, Bartholomew Traheron, hastened to report the outcome to Bullinger:

The argument was sharply contested by the bishops. The archbishop of Canterbury, contrary to general expectation, most openly, firmly, and learnedly maintained your opinion upon this subject . . . Next followed the bishop of Rochester [Nicholas Ridley], who handled the subject with so much eloquence, perspicuity, erudition, and power, as to stop the mouth of that most zealous papist, the bishop of Worcester [Nicholas Heath]. The truth never obtained a more brilliant victory among us. I perceive that it is all over with Lutheranism, now that those who were considered its principal and almost only supporters, have altogether come over to our side.[36]

The writer was allowing his optimism to run away with him. The parliamentary debate generated more heat than light and it is doubtful whether any participants were converted to a new opinion. The doctrine of the Holy Communion liturgically expressed in the new worship book, published a few months later, was not as clear cut as Traheron and his friends would have liked. Richard Hilles, another of Bullinger's correspondents, described the new rite as 'after the manner of the Nuremberg churches and some of those in Saxony, for [the government] do not yet feel inclined to adopt your rites'. [Ibid, I] Stephen Gardiner (safely locked up in the Tower) claimed that he could find the old mass enshrined in Cranmer's prayer book.

That book was endorsed by Parliament on 21 January 1549 in the First Act of Uniformity of Edward's reign. It came off the press in March and was ordered to be universally employed by 9 June. Hilles was probably right in his assessment of government policy:

'our bishops and governors seem, for the present at least, to be acting rightly; while, for the preservation of the public peace, they afford no cause of offence to the Lutherans, [they] pay attention to your very learned German divines [e.g. Martin Bucer], submit their judgement to them, and also retain some popish ceremonies.[37]

The Book of Common Prayer was not designed as the final word in English evangelical worship. Cranmer and his allies wished to wean people off esoteric rituals performed by priests on behalf of their parishioners to 'common' worship in which congregations were involved. The services were in English, so that everyone could understand what was happening. The main sacramental service was cautiously retitled 'The Supper of the Lord and holy Communion, commonly called the Masse'. Priests were enjoined only to celebrate when there were communicants present to receive the elements; the mass was no longer to be a private action to which lay people were only admitted as spectators and occasional participants. The services were all 'soaked' in the English Bible; not only were there public readings of scheduled lessons, psalms were recited and other scriptural passages became the basis of canticles. Anything that was sung was to be 'in plain tune after the manner of distinct reading', an instruction designed to outlaw elaborate settings which might obscure the meaning of the words. The intention was that, through the repetition of set vernacular prayers, canticles, versicles and responses, illiterate worshippers were to become familiar with the essentials of the faith. Until such time as there should emerge a body of ministers well equipped to preach and teach, this, together with the delivery of homilies, was the only way to spread evangelical Christianity at grassroots level.

However, the events of 1549 were to show that the government's cautious moves towards the establishment of a fully reformed English society did not meet with universal approval. Serious civil disorder occurred in centres as far apart as Cornwall, Yorkshire, Hampshire and East Anglia. It is impossible to identify a common programme among all these dissidents. They were not united in a shared cause, unless the underlying desire for a just Christian commonwealth may be said to have been a unifying factor. Two aspects of the risings made them a particular challenge to the government. One was timing. What made various dissatisfactions come to a head in the summer of 1549 was an atmosphere, a widespread mood of impatience bordering on desperation. The disastrous policies of Henry VIII's last years were coming home to roost. Inflation, taxation and trade recession reinforced old resentments about social injustices, and disputes over land use now reappeared. A disastrous harvest in 1548 was, for many, the final incentive to protest. They had hoped that the end of Henrician tyranny and the beginning of government by a noble clique who spoke earnestly about the 'common wealth' would deliver meaningful reform. But the new regime had been in power for two years and, although it had made sweeping changes, as far as the sufferings of ordinary people were concerned it had changed nothing. So it was that the king's subjects in various parts of the kingdom gave vent to their frustration, their spokesmen highlighting what seemed to them to be those problems most urgently crying out for solution. The other bothersome aspect for the government of these revolts was the religious gloss put upon them by their instigators. It was inevitable that those challenging the Crown, while protesting loyalty to the Crown, should claim to be acting in the name of a higher power. They were contending not just for a fairer society, but for a truly Christian society. There was no consensus as to what this Christian society would look like. Thus, while the men of the South West, egged on by their parish priests, were incensed by the abolition of the Latin mass and the loss of traditional ceremonies, the Norfolk rebels insisted that evangelical reform had not gone far enough. The law, as the controversialist Robert Crowley pointed out, needed to be brought into line with the Gospel and directed against evil landowners who 'live as though there is no God at all'.

Popular demonstration, as we know only too well, covers everything from banner-waving to arson, property damage and deliberate confrontation with the forces of law and order. In the latter part of 1548 there were several such outbursts. Breaking down hedges to express their anger with landowners was the fashionable tactic of the day employed by the protestors. The fact that this escalated into something more serious was, in large measure, the fault of the government. The Council became steadily more concerned about public disorder and advocated firm measures to nip it in the bud. But the Duke of Somerset, eager to be seen as a friend of the people, distanced himself from his colleagues and made the mistake of trying to appease the troublemakers. He left policing to the local gentry and nobility while he promised to address the protestors' complaints.

For the most part the leaders of shire society were able to deal with the problem but in two areas popular unrest got completely out of hand. It may have been lack of resolution at the centre that emboldened malcontents in Bodmin to assemble in June and dragoon some of the gentry into joining them. They drew up a list of social and economic issues which, in their opinion, needed redress. However, once some of the clergy took a hand in matters, what came to be known as the Prayer Book Rebellion assumed a conservative religious complexion. A second set of articles was drawn up which focused entirely on rejection of the Reformation and restoration of sacerdotal authority to the priesthood. The style of the articles, sent as a petition to the king, reflected the arrogance of a clerical elite who, in their far-western enclave, had become accustomed to exercising unquestioned control over the lives of their parishioners. It was peremptory in the extreme and hardly likely to elicit a sympathetic hearing. Each clause began with the words 'We will have' and the whole document demanded nothing less than a return to the pre-1529 situation. The rebels insisted on the restitution of the Latin mass, on the grounds that many Cornishmen did not speak English, so that the new liturgy meant nothing to them. But the demands were much more comprehensive; every aspect of traditional religion was to be restored. The articles went dangerously further and trespassed on political matters: the Act of Six Articles was to be reinstated, confiscated church lands were to be restored, prayers for souls in purgatory were to be reintroduced and Cardinal Pole was to be called home and given a seat on the royal Council. The nub of the rebels' position (and the real giveaway) was the article which declared, 'We will have the Bible and all books of scripture in English called in again, for we be informed that otherwise the clergy shall not of long time confound the heretics.'[38]

It is hard to see this as anything other than a desperate *cri de coeur* by traditionalist clergy. Such a demand for complete capitulation by the government was certainly not a realistic proposal for reform or even an opening gambit for negotiation. Somerset, replying in the king's name, had no hesitation in identifying the real troublemakers: 'We believe your complaints about the blindness and unwillingness of your curates to set forth our proceedings, and think much of this dangerous stir comes from them.'[39] For several weeks the initiative lay with the rebels because Somerset had difficulty accumulating a sufficiently large force to combat them. But, though a large area of Devon came under their control, they wasted precious time and resources in a fruitless siege of Exeter, instead of pressing on eastwards where they might have found other groups of dissidents prepared to make common cause with them. It was the end of July before a force, comprised partly of mercenaries and troops diverted from the Scottish campaign, was ready to confront the rebels. In pitched battles on 4 and 16 July the troublemakers were routed with losses of more than four thousand dead and several prisoners who were later executed or died in prison.

Meanwhile, a worse situation was brewing in Norfolk. Here the instigators, led by yeoman farmer Robert Kett, took a very different stance. They were able to do so because they thought that what they were doing was in line with government policy. Somerset had set up commissions to enquire into agrarian grievances. This gave the impression that he was on the side of the lower orders against the grasping gentry, a conviction reinforced when it was revealed that Parliament had thrown out draconian anti-enclosure measures sponsored by the Protector. Kett's men, like other 'defenders of the commonwealth', did not march menacingly across the land. They set up a camp outside Norwich, requisitioned food – in the king's name – to feed their followers and proposed a dialogue with the government for the settlement of their grievances. Among those grievances were complaints against ignorant or recalcitrant clergy, who either would not or could not lead the new services. They attacked excessive tithes, absentee incumbents and clergy who accumulated personal landholdings. They demanded that 'priests and vicars that be not able to preach and set forth the word of God to his parishioners may be thereby put from his benefice, and the parishioners there to choose another, or else the patron or lord in the town'.[40]

The opinions of the 16,000 men camped on Mousehold Heath might be politically correct but they were still rebels and the regime was very jittery about civil disturbance. Somerset sent envoys to negotiate with Kett but the rebel leader refused to break up his camp. By now he and his associates were in the grip of class hatred, convinced that any attempt to dislodge them was further proof of a plot by the gentry and nobility to keep them suppressed. As the days and weeks passed their mood worsened. On 21 July they attacked York Herald, the Protector's latest emissary, and the following day they overran a large area of Norwich. On 1 August they routed a force sent against them. The government now had no alternative but to send the best army at their disposal under their best general, John Dudley (later Duke of Northumberland). The result of seasoned troops and German mercenaries being launched against the rebels' ramshackle defences was never in doubt. The 'Battle of Dussindale' was nothing other than a massacre in which more than 2,500 champions of the commonwealth perished.

It was a bloody proof of Somerset's incompetence. The impatience of his conciliar colleagues had reached breaking point. His old friend and colleague Sir William Paget expressed what they all felt when he wrote a private memorandum to the Protector:

> Society is maintained by religion and laws: you have neither. The old religion is forbidden and the new not generally imprinted. The law is almost nowhere used: the commons are become king. You should have followed the first stir hotly and used justice to the terror of others.[41]

Somerset was headed for a palace coup, which took place in October. The man who emerged to replace him was John Dudley. He lacked Somerset's ambition and had no desire to assume semi-regal status. He was given to bouts of illness and the burden of office weighed heavily upon him. He looked forward eagerly to the time when Edward would achieve his majority and he could retire from active politics. His immediate priorities were the solving of England's chronic economic and foreign policy problems and the training of the young king to assume full power. He freed the monarch from his uncle's tutelage and had no desire to step into Somerset's role of puppet-master. Quite the reverse; he steered Edward towards assuming his full responsibilities. Northumberland's own political training had been at the court of a domineering king. This was the pattern of monarchy he understood and it was the pattern for which he groomed Edward. He initiated him into the discussions of the Council and treated him as an adult. The obverse of this was his devotion to those policies closest to the king's heart. Young Edward was growing into an opinionated teenager who seemed to need little encouragement to become a strong king and one who knew his own mind. It would be some time before he mastered all the intricacies of foreign and domestic policy but the one aspect of his role as king that Edward fully understood was his headship of the church. He was determined to press on with the evangelical revolution and Northumberland backed him to the hilt. England's religious policy from 1550 to 1553 was, in a very real sense, the king's policy.

Kett's rebellion and associated disturbances posed a dilemma for the evangelical cause. Opponents of reform could and did make capital out of them, pointing out that individualism, emphasis on personal salvation and a social gospel, explicit in evangelical preaching and teaching, led inevitably to libertinism and the breakdown of law and order. In a sermon Cranmer delivered in St Paul's at the height of the troubles he found himself walking a tightrope between roundly condemning the rebels for manifest and unscriptural treason and acknowledging that behind their protest lay social evils, including the greed of wealthy landowners and their oppression of the poor, to which they were justified in drawing attention. The blueprint he set out for achieving a Christian commonwealth involved national repentance, support for the government of England's godly king and a programme of legal reform. The disturbances of

1549 had been a nasty shock but their successful suppression had cleared the way for centrally organised reform. The regime assumed that it had plenty of time to turn their plans into reality. Edward would grow into a king who would lead Protestant Europe. England, relatively free from invasion or interference by Catholic princes, would be a beacon of gospel truth. Cranmer kept alive his plan to host an ecumenical Protestant council. The only thing that prevented this happening, as John Calvin lamented to Cranmer in a letter of April 1552, was that

> the churches are so estranged from each other, that scarcely the common intercourse of society has place among them; much less that holy communion of the members of Christ, which all persons profess with their lips, though few sincerely honour it in their practice . . . Thus it is that, the members being scattered, the body of the church lies torn to pieces.[42]

Cranmer knew all about division. The conservatives, though firmly on the back foot, could still make trouble. For resisting the injunctions and the book of homilies and for denying the authority of the Council in matters ecclesiastical Gardiner was confined for most of the reign, first in the Fleet and then in the Tower. In February 1551 he was deprived of his see. The actions against him were, at best, of questionable legality. Bonner of London had already been sacked for letting it be known that he did not support the doctrinal and liturgical changes introduced by the Somerset regime. Three other conservative bishops were removed from office and Thirlby, bishop of the new diocese of Westminster, was put out to grass in the distant episcopal centre of Norwich by the expedient of ending the brief history of Westminster diocese. Sound evangelicals were instituted to the empty offices and Cranmer looked forward to changing the complexion of the episcopal bench as death or more demonstrations of intransigence removed the existing incumbents. This was the best way of ensuring the permanence of the Reformation.

But, while keeping an eye on traditionalists, the archbishop also had to deal with extremist and over-exuberant members of his own party. From the correspondence of English evangelicals with their friends in the Reform centres of Europe it is clear that the differences over niggling points of theological detail which Calvin pointed out as dividing the churches of Germany and Switzerland were also undermining Protestant unity in England. What the depapalised churches were discovering more and more was that taking the Bible as the sole benchmark for faith and order actually meant following the interpretations of various Bible expositors. The fixed 'Reformed' doctrine on such matters as Holy Communion for which Cranmer longed was a chimera. His own views were undergoing development so it was scarcely logical to expect that other evangelicals would not also think through their understanding of the more intricate aspects of the faith.

There was emerging a group of ardent evangelicals who would later be dubbed 'Puritans' because they determined to purge the English church of every last vestige of papal impurity. In the spring of 1550 the member of this group who was hitting the headlines was John Hooper, an ex-monk who had learned his reformed theology during a two-year exile in Zurich. He was a dogmatic, unyielding public figure who was revered as a stickler for truth by those who happened to agree with him but disliked by virtually everyone else. Hooper was totally out of sympathy with Cranmer's softly-softly approach. He criticised the new prayer book for not going far enough and drew large crowds to his London sermons by his fearless demands for out-and-out reform. Cranmer was incensed by this sniping from within the evangelical ranks and had the troublesome zealot hauled before the Council. But Hooper enjoyed the support of both Somerset and Northumberland, who recognised him as a valuable propagandist, and he came off best in the confrontation. Not only did he emerge triumphant, he was also nominated by Northumberland to the vacant see of Gloucester. Then, not content with this little victory, he made it known that he would only accept preferment on his own terms. He took exception to the oath he was expected to swear and to the 'popish' vestments he would have to wear for the ceremony. This brought archbishop and bishop-elect into sharp conflict. The result was a draw; the oath was reworded (after intervention by the king in person) but Hooper agreed (after eight months of argument and a spell in the Fleet) to wear the prescribed episcopal dress.

However, further radical changes were being made in routine church life of which Hooper and his sympathisers certainly approved. Bonfires had already been made of old Latin service books but further reforms were considered necessary if worshippers were to be allowed nothing reminiscent of the popish mass. In the autumn of 1550 the order went out from the Council that the main altars in all churches were to be removed from the east end and replaced by wooden tables set lengthwise in the chancel. This change was completely logical, given the doctrinal shift of the Edwardian regime, as Nicholas Ridley, the new Bishop of London, was at pains to point out: 'the use of an altar is to make sacrifice upon it; the use of a table is to serve for men to eat upon'. But the visual impact would have been enormous. Ultimately this particular reform failed to survive, not so much because Reformation doctrine was rejected but because the change to the internal geography of churches simply did not work. In medieval buildings erected to express the concept of mass sacrifice, removing the high altar deprived them of a focal point and installing the new tables, especially in churches with narrow chancels, was awkward in the extreme. Logically, new doctrine called for new buildings (such as, for example, the non-conformist chapels of the seventeenth and eighteenth centuries), or at least considerably modified buildings.

Other innovations affecting many parishes concerned education. The dissolution of chantries and guilds had been carried out with the promise that the money raised would be ploughed back into schools. Where chantry priests and guild officers had taken in hand the education of the young, provision would be made for the continuance of their work. In addition, new

grammar schools would be set up. Such principles were close
to the hearts of commonwealth men but not a few of them were
sceptical about the implementation of the declared policy. They
knew what had been promised – and not delivered – at the time
of the dissolution of the monasteries. Governments in the
sixteenth century, as now, were very good at declaring good
intentions but less so at carrying them into effect. The vast hole
in Crown finances needed plugging as a matter of urgency and
the temptation to use for general purposes money notionally
ring-fenced for education was strong. In April 1548 the Council
decided to sell £5,000 worth of chantry lands. A few weeks
later a sweetener was issued, the government declaring their
intention 'to erect divers and sundry grammar schools in every
county in England and Wales, for the education and bringing
up of youth in virtue and learning and godliness, and also to
make provision for the poor'.[44] But they covered themselves by
explaining that this laudable programme could not be imple-
mented immediately. By the year's end commonwealth men
were growing impatient. They introduced a bill into Parliament
urging the founding of schools. It was defeated in the Lords
and another attempt a year later fared even worse. It took a
campaign of sermons and pamphlets to hold the regime to its
promises. In 1550, twenty-four educational establishments
were endowed. Some were re-foundations; others new 'Edward
VI grammar schools'.

Considering the extent of the government's problems such
modest social reforms were laudable. Northumberland was
working hard to dig the nation out of its financial hole. He
reached peace agreements with France and Scotland. He began
paying off the government's debts and he stopped the ruinous
devaluation of the currency. Inevitably, there was a price to be
paid for the beginnings of recovery and the regime's tough,
sometimes unscrupulous measures won it few friends.
Merchants were obliged to make loans available to the government at low interest and every opportunity was taken to fleece
the church of yet more of its property.

By the autumn of 1551 Edward, now fourteen, was beginning to assert his authority. Writing from the court to the Council majority in Westminster, he delivered a sharp rap over the knuckles. They had presumed to return a document, drawn up by the king and the Council members in attendance on him, without endorsement. Edward was furious:

> We think our authority is such that whatever we do by the advice of our council attendant, although much fewer than eight, has more strength than to be put into question. You are not ignorant that the number of councillors does not make our authority. If you . . . should be of other opinion, as may be conjectured from your letter, that is not convenient and might be harmful where our affairs, for lack of speedy execution . . . might take great detriment.[45]

The issue in question concerned proceedings against the bishops of Worcester and Chichester, who were refusing to implement some of the recent changes. Edward was very sensitive about such disobedience and, as head of the church, he was determined on the recalcitrant bishops' dismissal. The young king has sometimes been presented as John Dudley's puppet. It is easy to imagine the Lord President of the Council as a Svengali figure, using his royal charge to bolster his own authority and power. This had certainly been true of Somerset but the Edward of 1551 was not the Edward of 1547. He was a strong-willed adolescent, a Henry VIII in the making, and he was determined to assert his will, especially in matters of religion. Dudley saw himself as the servant of that will – an attitude that would eventually destroy him. Cranmer, for his part, was subservient to his royal master but he was also the representative, under the Crown, of the church. He had a grasp of theological issues that neither Edward nor Dudley could aspire to, which meant that he saw national affairs from a different perspective.

The dynamic of court politics that dominated the remainder

of the reign was created by the king, Cranmer and Northumberland and it was a highly unstable dynamic. The first cause of dissension was the downfall of the Duke of Somerset. He had been re-admitted to the Council but was unable to accept his reduced importance and made plans for a comeback. Northumberland decided on a pre-emptive strike. In October 1551 he had Somerset arrested. The proceedings against him, as with most Tudor state trials, were not noted for impartial justice and the end result was inevitable. On 22 January following he was beheaded on Tower Hill. The action was very unpopular, particularly with those who still regarded Somerset as a champion of the common man. Cranmer and several of his colleagues opposed the execution.

Further causes of dissent emerged during 1552. The main problem was money. The government was scrabbling for every penny they could find. Northumberland was far from happy when his commissioners calculated the total landed wealth of the church at over £3,500,000. Yet what galled him even more was a mounting chorus of attacks by clergy against government policy. The Council were repeatedly condemned by common-wealth preachers for being on the side of the rich against the poor commons: Dussindale cast a very long shadow. Northumberland might have felt particularly hard done by because the government was doing its best to deal with the nation's social problems. New legislation, replacing the Vagrancy Act of 1547, instituted alms boxes in every church and ordered weekly collections for the relief of the poor. The Crown set an example by making over the palace of Bridewell as a house of correction for vagabonds and harlots and endowing St Thomas's Hospital, not to mention the new schools. It seemed to Dudley that the biggest obstacle to the establishment of a Christian commonwealth was the church leadership which whinged at every sacrifice demanded of them for the common good.

Throughout the remaining months of the reign many of the achievements of the regime were undone by state and church bickering, personalised in the figures of the archbishop and the duke. By the spring of 1552 a new prayer book was ready to be issued. It had been assiduously worked over by Cranmer and his aides to remove any last vestiges of the old religion and it had been approved by Parliament. The congregation were now expected to participate even more than before. Prayers such as the general confession were to be repeated after the minister, phrase by phrase. The creed also was to be said by 'the minister and the people, standing'. The word 'mass' was now dropped, the central service being named 'the Lord's Supper or Holy Communion'. It was to take place around a table set in the chancel or the body of the church with the celebrant standing at the north side (i.e. not facing eastwards with his back to the people). Special instructions were given for the administration of the elements. Communion wafers were not to be used: 'To take away the superstition, which any person hath or might have in the bread and wine, it shall suffice that the bread shall be such, as is usual to be eaten at the table . . . the best and purest wheat bread that conveniently may be gotten.' It was to be delivered into the hands of the communicants (i.e. not into their mouths) and any bread or wine remaining was to be taken away by the minister for his own use (i.e. not reserved as objects of worship).

The framers of the new order must have felt that they had closed every loophole. They had reckoned without John Knox, a Scottish evangelical even more extreme than Hooper. He took exception to the instruction that people were to receive communion kneeling. To Knox this smacked of popish adoration of a physical presence within the elements. Northumberland agreed with him and demanded that printing of the prayer book be halted until the offending text had been altered. Cranmer refused point blank and a fierce argument ensued. It was only resolved, after several months had been lost, by the addition of the 'black rubric' which pointed out that kneeling was a sign of humble and reverent reception and not idolatrous worship.

It was in the spring of 1553 that relations between church and Council broke down almost completely. The latest confiscations of ecclesiastical property provoked some incredibly violent pulpit denunciations. Several popular preachers rounded on the government and the landed interest the government was accused of supporting. Northumberland and his allies were accused of greed, corruption, pride, ambition and neglect of duty. Understandably, the duke responded angrily and threatened to silence those who did not know their place. It was probably out of petulance that he torpedoed in Parliament Cranmer's pet project of canon law reform. The archbishop retired to Kent in a huff and was absent from the Council for several weeks.

The regime could not have chosen a worse time to give way to internal rifts. Their young Josiah fell ill with a pulmonary infection. By the early summer those closest to him knew that he was dying.

Chapter 8

Sealed in Blood

Exactly when Council members knew – or were forced to acknowledge – that the king was terminally ill is not clear. On 7 June, Sir John Cheke, now secretary to the Council, could inform Bullinger that Edward was 'scarcely yet restored to health' and, on the same day, Jan Utenhove, leader of the Dutch exiles in London, reported that the king, who had been 'in the most imminent danger from a most severe cough' was now 'somewhat better'.[1] Such opinions may well have been the triumph of hope over experience. It is fully understandable that those with access to the royal sickbed should have grasped at every sign of apparent recovery and we do not need to interpret the activities of the regime leaders in the tragic summer of 1553 as being completely governed by self-interest. Cheke listed, and attributed to the king, the evangelical reforms of the reign and opined that in the future he would 'contribute very greatly to the preservation of the church' and the increase of godly learning. He concisely expressed the attitude of the evangelical establishment, which looked both backwards and forwards. Over the preceding seven years the religious life of England had been changed out of all recognition. The veteran diplomat and erstwhile Cromwellian agent Sir Richard Morison expressed no more than a truth which seemed obvious to his contemporaries when he wrote, 'The greater change was never wrought in so short space in any country sith the world was.'[2]

The architects of reform also looked forwards. Until that

early summer of 1553 they had been able to do so with confidence. They had a king who was not only committed to continuing the work begun, but had the necessary years ahead of him to bring it to full fruition. Edward would establish a Protestant dynasty (plans were already being made for his marriage) and oversee the firm establishment of a godly commonwealth. Natural wastage would gradually remove all 'enemies of the Gospel' from the episcopal bench. Preachers would educate those who still hankered after the old ways. Even among the unconvinced, familiarity with the new services would establish at least a formal unity of belief. There was plenty of time to achieve all this. But, on 6 July 1553, the sands ran out. Edward VI's pain-racked body yielded up his spirit.

The king had made a desperate attempt to prevent the crown falling into the hands of his fanatically Catholic half-sister, Mary, by making a will bestowing it upon his first cousin once removed, Jane Grey, who by her recent marriage to Northumberland's youngest son had become Jane Dudley. The tortuousness of his 'devise for the succession' reveals how perilously fragile the Tudor dynasty had become. Of all the descendants of Henry VII, Edward was the only surviving male and the next generation also was made up entirely of girls. Whatever happened, the crown was destined to pass to a woman, something akin to disaster in the minds of most members of the political class. The closest in succession were Henry VIII's daughters, Mary and Elizabeth, both solemnly bastardised by their father and subsequently named in his will as successors after Edward. Despite Edward's personal attempts at persuasion, Mary remained quite uncompromisingly Catholic and it was for that reason that the dying king believed it would be a mortal sin to bequeath the nation into her papistical and vengeful hands. From his bed he forced his councillors and lawyers to honour his wishes for the succession. Northumberland lent his weight to this appeal and did his best to secure Jane's recognition as queen. Or, rather, he did not do his best: he badly bungled the arrangements. Jane was proclaimed on 8 July and installed in the Tower, together with the bulk of her Council. Mary's entourage were quick off the mark. They got her away into Norfolk, where she summoned all loyal Englishmen to her standard. Northumberland, uncharacteristically, dithered and by the time he set off for East Anglia support for Mary was building up. The duke was cordially hated in eastern England as the butcher of Somerset and Kett and the enemy of true commonwealth men. Mary, by contrast, had always enjoyed a great deal of public sympathy because of the appalling way she and her mother had been treated by Henry VIII. Northumberland's erstwhile colleagues almost to a man followed the policy of *sauve qui peut*, leaving the duke and the sixteen-year-old queen isolated. On 18 July Jane's officers proclaimed Mary and transferred their allegiance to her. On 3 August the new queen was duly welcomed in London with great rejoicing as a saviour, just as her father had been in 1509 and her half-sister would be in 1558.

But among men and women of conviction nothing had changed. It took only a few days for the capital that had warmly welcomed the queen to erupt in sectarian violence. A priest who ventured to say the Latin mass in his church narrowly escaped being torn limb from limb. The preacher at St Paul's Cross was pulled from the pulpit and the government had to order troops there on subsequent days to control crowds intent on preventing the new party line being proclaimed. What everyone wanted to know was what balance of exhortation, persuasion, propaganda and main force Mary would employ in her attempt to return her country to papal obedience and pre-Reformation orthodoxy. She was hampered by one disadvantage that had not troubled Henry or Edward. She was caught in a constitutional trap. Her father and half-brother had enjoyed supreme headship of the English church and had had no doubt that they were able to determine what their people should believe. They had proceeded by proclamation and statute. Mary regarded as blasphemy the assumption of spiritual authority which rightfully belonged to the pope. She would have to work from within a situation she did not believe in if she was to undo the evangelical revolution which had fundamentally changed the workings of government.

That revolution had, by now, been more than two decades in the making. It had begun when Henry had set about severing the link with Rome and making the English church a department of state. During those twenty years the outward signs of the medieval church had, one by one, disappeared. The monasteries were no more. Shrines and pilgrimages were but a fading memory. Saints' days, holy days and the many ancient customs that had given shape to community life were things of the past. Chantries and, with them, the whole paraphernalia of prayers for the dead had been scrapped. The cowled friar with his well-practised sermon and scrip full of pardons no longer made his appearance at the market cross. The terms 'cleric' and 'layman' had taken on new meaning. Priests were no longer performers of arcane rituals; they were expected to be 'ministers of the word' and, even if few had as yet mastered the art of preaching, the people now had to look to their incumbents for that 'pulpit entertainment' once provided by visiting Franciscans and Dominicans. As for parishioners, they were no longer expected to be passive participants in holy rites, turning up in church to 'hear' the priest perform 'his' mass. They were required to sit through services, understand what was being said and share in the liturgy by reciting the creed, canticles and prayers.

But it was the transformation of the local church which made the greatest impact on villagers and townspeople throughout the realm. The wholehearted purging of interiors had removed the accumulated devotional objects of centuries. These were the images which had shaped parishioners' thinking and had worked upon them subliminally to impart a 'feel' of what Christianity was about. They were not replaceable – certainly in the short term. It was the silent language of church interiors which impacted most powerfully upon worshippers. For example, the disappearance of the 'doom' from chancel arches meant that people were no longer constantly reminded of the pains of hell awaiting those who were disobedient to their spiritual superiors. Many churches had replaced their whitewashed pictures with painted texts, such as the Commandments and the Lord's Prayer. Their officers were in no hurry to go to the expense of effacing them. In many parishes new pulpits and reading desks had been installed, providing focal points which attested to the primacy of God's word written. When, in response to Marian directives, communion tables were removed and altars reconstructed at the east end of the chancel they appeared to be in competition with those pieces of furniture which attested to the primacy of Holy Scripture. Again, cost-conscious churchwardens baulked at moving pulpits and lecterns. The Henrician and Edwardian iconoclasts had done their work so well that many churches had lost their ancient mystique and holy magic. Although some churchwardens had clandestinely preserved condemned 'idolatrous' objects and others commissioned replacements for their lost treasures, it was quite impossible to re-create the pre-Reformation atmosphere. By 1553 the only people who could remember the medieval church in all its splendour were, by the terms of the mid-sixteenth century, old or middle-aged.

Many of the old 'sermons' in stone, fresco and stained glass which had shaped people's thinking had proclaimed the power and authority of the church and the fate of those who rejected official doctrine and this teaching was dramatically supported by the punishment of heretics. Forced recantations, public humiliation of men and women who presumed to think for themselves, and the lurid spectacle of offenders burned at the stake had made it clear to past generations that the definition of faith by the ecclesiastical hierarchy was not to be questioned. But the 1530s had ushered in a questioning age. The fallout from Henry's defiance of the pope was the encouragement of his subjects to do what only despised Lollards and cloistered scholars had done previously: hold church doctrine and practice up to scrutiny. In Edward's reign public burnings had come to virtually a complete halt. Only two extreme radicals had been done to death for stubbornly holding to beliefs that were well outside the canon of trinitarian Christianity. Anabaptists had still been examined and obdurate bishops like Bonner and Gardiner had been imprisoned but otherwise there had existed in England an unprecedented freedom of debate. The presence of foreign exiles and the close connection with Reformation leaders on the continent encouraged a remarkable openness in matters of doctrine. Scholarly disputation filtered down to ordinary people via books, pamphlets and, primarily, pulpit oratory so that unorthodox opinions which it had once been prudent to air only in private became matter for open discussion. It is true that, by the closing months of the reign, mounting criticism had prompted the government to reintroduce a measure of censorship but this was only because the intoxicant of intellectual freedom had proved too potent.

The main ingredient in the heady cocktails of ideas being served to the people was, of course, the open Bible. What the old church authorities had always insisted and what Henry VIII had discovered too late was that the Bible was a manual of revolution. When Luther had been commended for his work in unleashing the Reformation he had routinely replied, 'I have done nothing; the word of God has done everything.' A vital truth was but thinly veiled by this apparent modesty. Easy access to vernacular Scripture was both the strength and the weakness of the European evangelical movements. It established the fundamentals of New Testament Christianity and demonstrated how official Catholicism had deviated from it but it also provided a text which doctrinal nit-pickers could squabble over, thus permanently dividing the Protestant world into rival camps. Yet, despite their divisions, it was the evangelicals who were in possession of an exuberant dynamic which their enemies found it difficult to match. As Diarmaid MacCulloch has said, 'The difficulty for the leaders of conservative opinion in resisting the evangelical message was to present a coherent and exciting alternative.'[3]

But where in all this theological toing and froing were the English people? How many had embraced evangelical faith?

How many wanted to see the nation restored to papal obedience? How many were so irritated by years of religious argument that they no longer bothered their heads with the search for spiritual truth? Attempts to 'get to the heart' of the English Reformation often resolve themselves in partisan answers to 'what if' questions: 'What if Edward had lived a full adult life and left a son to inherit his Protestant crown?' 'What if Mary had survived into old age, having provided the Tudor dynasty with a Catholic heir?' The process of proffering answers rests on asserting that the English people either were, or were not, responsive to religious change and that, in the last analysis, they either would, or would not, have accepted whatever religious settlement the government imposed. The questions are false – or, at least, unhelpful – because they are posed by chroniclers with points to prove. Roman Catholic and Anglo-Catholic writers try to persuade us that England has always been a nation wedded to the ancient faith and that the Edwardian experiment was an aberration. Their opponents assert that, between 1547 and 1553, the English people were delighted to be liberated from an oppressive and spiritually bankrupt medieval church and would never have allowed themselves to go back into bondage. To reduce the events of the mid-sixteenth century to a game between two teams in distinctive and easily recognisable Catholic and Protestant colours is simply bad historiography. The reality is immeasurably more complex, if not, in fact, utterly bewildering. English religious life before the Reformation was a patchwork of beliefs and customs. English religious life in 1553 was a patchwork of beliefs and customs. English religious life in 1558 was a patchwork of beliefs and customs. English religious life after the Elizabethan Settlement was a patchwork of beliefs and customs. The sets of patterns were different, though they had certain squares in common. The doctrinal seamstresses went about their work in response to personal conviction, national pressures and international events. So, let the reader beware, all attempts at analysis – including the present one – must be regarded with caution.

The English church with which Mary had to deal when she came to the throne was predominantly Catholic because reform had not had long enough to gain widespread accept-ance, because preachers were few, because a largely illiterate population had not yet had their thinking shaped by the Bible and because it was difficult for people to accept the different mindset required by the new faith. Evangelicalism demanded personal conversion, leading to earnest moral endeavour. It was not sufficient to clamber aboard the good ship *Church* and trust her to convey the passenger safely through this world and purgatory to the heavenly haven. When the worshipper listened to the homily on True and Lively Faith, he/she heard that personal commitment was required, not the prayers of living clergy or dead saints. The man or woman justified by faith was exhorted:

> Thy deeds and works must be an open testimonial of thy faith: otherwise thy faith (being without good works) is but the Devil's faith, the faith of the wicked, a fantasy of faith, and not a true Christian faith . . . If you feel and perceive [a true and lively faith] in you, rejoice in it and be diligent to main-tain it, and keep it still in you, let it be daily increasing, and more and more by well working, and so shall you be sure that you shall please God by this faith . . . and receive the end and final reward of your faith.[4]

No longer could the believer rely on the 'treasury of saints', that heavenly bank balance available, according to the old schoolmen, to improve the credit rating of less holy mortals. No longer could a routine confession to the priest and the perform-ance of an allotted penance wipe the sinner's slate clean. The evangelical Christian was called to a more introspective religion. In other words, he/she was expected to make a commitment to a more demanding faith, the sort of faith that ardent pre-Refor-mation souls had sought in the cloister or in clandestine Lollard fellowships. It is hardly surprising that comparatively few people understood or were prepared to accept such a formidable regimen. Edwardian bishops complained about falling church attendance but, then, so did Marian bishops. It is difficult to draw clear-cut conclusions from such evidence about the attitude of the 'average parishioner'. While commitment to the old ways and eager embracing of the new were results of the Reformation thus far, so was the spread of scepticism. There were many whose response to the religious conflict was 'a plague on all your houses'.

One fact that is reasonably clear is the geographical distribution of adherence to the reformed faith. It was strong in London and the South East, much of East Anglia, in port towns and major commercial centres. It tended to become progressively weaker with every mile from such places. However, that analysis by no means represents the complete picture. Where evangelical congregations were established they tended to be very firmly established and prepared to 'stand up and be counted'. Unlike members of the old Lollard cells, most of whom feigned orthodoxy when challenged and were ready to make 'recantations of convenience', several of the new evangelicals proved obdurate, in some cases to the point of death.

It would be hard to exaggerate the difficult position in which Mary found herself. The divine gift for which she had prayed so long, so ardently and often without hope was now hers. She had the joy and the responsibility of bringing back the entire English nation to papal obedience. It was only as she unwrapped this gift that she became aware of the enormity of her task. Hers was a unique constitutional position. It was four hundred years since a woman had attempted to rule England in her own right and Matilda's reign had seen the nation plunged into civil war. Neither the queen nor her advisers were in any doubt that exercising rule in the kingdoms of God's world was a male prerogative. Mary needed men to support and guide her. She had a Privy Council and a Parliament but both were divided on religious issues. She had bishops, who, by virtue of the Act of Supremacy, were answerable directly to her. By removing dissidents from the bench and installing reliable Catholics she could acquire a compliant Convocation. She had her court and could surround herself with loyal and devoted Catholics. But there were no Englishmen with whom she found herself 'on the same wavelength'. For real confidants she had to look outside the realm.

Mary had always aligned herself with her mother's family. During the long years of her rejection by Henry VIII and by those who governed the realm for Edward she had maintained a clandestine correspondence with the head of that family, the Emperor Charles V, through his envoys. In 1550 she had actually planned to escape to the imperial court. Her bags had been packed in readiness before the vigilance of royal officers forced her to abort her exodus. She had pledged herself to be guided by Charles in all things and she now renewed that vow. Within days of her accession, Simon Renard, the imperial ambassador, became her closest confidant. He had access to the royal apartments at all times and the queen sent for him frequently, often advising him to come concealed in cloak and hood, under cover of darkness. She discussed with Renard matters which she could not or would not share with her ministers. This was not well received by experienced councillors such as Gardiner, now appointed Lord Chancellor, who claimed to have at heart the best interests of queen and country. And when Mary concealed herself behind a wall of Spanish and English devotees this did not please the leading English families, who regarded membership of the royal entourage as their birthright.

As the queen gathered together an executive to carry out her will she had to go public about her intentions. She used her first, deliberately circumspect proclamation to assuage the anxieties of her subjects. She would, she asserted, remain loyal to the religion in which she had been nurtured and 'would be glad the same were all of her subjects quietly and charitably to embrace'. However, she declared that 'of her most gracious disposition and clemency her highness mindeth not to compel any her said subjects thereunto unto such time as further order

by common assent may be taken therein'. This was an acknowledgement that further religious change would have to be
brought about with parliamentary consent. The Reformation
had been established by Parliament; it would have to be overthrown by Parliament. The problem was that the preceding
regimes had failed to create religious unity and harmony. We
are left to wonder whether Mary really believed that she could
impose that religious conformity which had eluded her father
and half-brother.

The answer was not long in coming. Parliament was
summoned quickly to endorse the new regime, reverse the
divorce of Mary's parents and dismantle the Edwardian religious legislation. Lords and Commons obliged by getting rid
of the prayer book, reinstating clerical celibacy and restoring
all pre-1547 rites and ceremonies. But over two issues members
dug their heels in: they would not reinstate papal authority or
countenance the restoration of ex-monastic property. It very
soon became clear to the regime that the two most threatening
rocks between which they would have to steer were xenopho-
bia and self-interest.

The government did try to learn some lessons from the
Edwardian Reformation. While convinced that it had been an
alien imposition forced on the nation by a government influenced by foreign heretics and while believing that there were
many who hankered after the old devotional ways, they were
realistic enough to acknowledge that evangelical success could
largely be attributed to the ignorance of the people. Bishop
Bonner, now restored to his old position in London, took the
lead in ordering his clergy to preach regularly 'the significance
and true meaning of all . . . laudable and godly ceremonies used
of old time in this Church of England to the best of their power,
in such sort that the people may perceive what is meant and
signified by the same'.[5]

Bonner produced his own set of homilies to explain the
significance of the rituals and festivals which were now being
reinstated. His exposition of traditional Catholicism in the light

of recent controversy reflected changed doctrinal emphases. Thus, while not detracting one iota from traditional teaching on the mass, he also asserted the all-sufficiency of Christ's once-for-all sacrifice in words which were almost Protestant in tone. The emphasis on instruction of the laity in their mother tongue and on the need for a better informed clergy, now adopted by all the Marian bishops, was an unwritten acknowledgement of failings which had been identified by John Colet and others at the beginning of the century and passionately urged by Erasmian humanists ever since. It was late in the day for conservatives to start putting their own house in order but a consistent educational programme might have achieved its objective – given time. Hand in hand with the reassertion of Catholic doctrine went rehabilitation of the rituals which gave visual expression to that doctrine. Every church was ordered to recover or acquire a holy water stoup and sprinkler, an antiphoner, service books, a chalice and patten, vestments for all the clergy, altar cloths and furniture, processional candles and crucifix, a sacring bell, a censer and incense boat, a pyx for the reserved sacrament, banner and bells, a rood and rood loft, chrismatory for holy oil, a paschal candle and, of course, all altars had to be rebuilt. The order provoked an outcry. Churchwardens across the land protested that they simply could not afford this wholesale reordering. Their dismay emphasises just how thorough the Protestant purge had been. The obligatory shopping list was extensive but, even so, it did not include all the images, side altars, shrines, tabernacles, paintings, windows and sacred furnishings churches had lost. Bonner and his colleagues probably believed they were being reasonable in demanding the bare minimum of liturgical exotica necessary for the conduct of seemly worship but the burden they were imposing was, for most churches, intolerable.

Nor was that the only handicap imposed on parishes by the zeal of the Catholic regime. The reintroduction of clerical celibacy led to about eight hundred priests being deprived. The impact on understaffed dioceses was considerable. London and Norwich lost a quarter of their parish clergy. In an attempt to limit the damage many priests were moved – wifeless – to localities where they were not known. This merely opened the church to scandal when clergy were cited in church courts for continuing to consort with their wives or when bishops, of necessity, turned a blind eye to breaches of the rules. We can only guess at the impression such manoeuvring made on lay people who expected their spiritual leaders to set examples of honesty and probity. Mental attitudes had changed since the days when a sacerdotal priesthood had enjoyed a seldom-questioned status protected by canon law. Another indication of changing attitudes is the reluctance of testators to make bequests for church furnishings. Bonner urged his clergy to impress on their parishioners the imperative of private charity to make good the damage done by the iconoclasts but there was little response. Benefactors were more likely to leave money for poor relief, a form of liberality which had been urged by the Edwardian reformers.

With education and persistent pressure from the bishops it might have been possible to restore the pre-Reformation ambience – given time. But time was something the Marian regime did not have. The governments of Edward's minority had calculated on his survival and his ability to secure a Protestant succession. By contrast, those backing Mary's bid for restoring England to the bosom of Rome were reliant not only on the queen's longevity but on her ability to give birth to a Catholic heir. Since she was thirty-seven and, as yet, unwed this could only be regarded as problematic. They also had to face the fact that the dynastic logic which had brought Mary the crown would convey it, in the event of her death without heir, to her half-sister Elizabeth, a princess who had had a humanist-evangelical upbringing. Pragmatism as well as zeal suggested to Mary and her bishops the need for haste. And haste occasionally gave way to panic. The fragile nature of Catholic recovery always lay at the back of their minds and must explain the drastic nature of some of their policies.

The queen's cautious approach to changing English religious life lasted scarcely more than a few weeks. Gardiner, Bonner and others who had suffered ignominy in the previous reign, no less than the queen, were determined to make examples of their enemies, and especially of those ecclesiastical celebrities who enjoyed public popularity. By mid-September Cranmer, the evangelical bishops and several evangelical preachers had been rounded up and thrust into prison. The bishops were deprived by edict of the queen in her capacity as supreme head. There was, as yet, no new heresy law by which they could be condemned so other devices had to be engineered to prevent their escape until such time as Mary's vengeance could be lawfully deployed against them.

John Hooper was among the first prominent evangelicals to be arrested. He had not supported the attempt to place Jane Grey on the throne but that fact did not protect him. He was sent to the Fleet prison on a charge of alleged debt. It was the following March before further proceedings were taken. Then he was deprived of his bishopric on the basis of being married. He arranged to get his family away to Frankfurt and his wife's letters provide a glimpse of the movements of the exiles:

> since the Lord . . . conducted me safe to Antwerp, I availed myself of an opportunity of accompanying a party every way suitable, and joined my female relative at Frankfurt, where now, by the mercy of God, the senate has granted liberty to the foreign church for their whole ecclesiastical ministry . . . I shall prefer remaining here in my own hired house, until I see how the Lord shall deal with my husband, concerning whom, as I have not yet received any intelligence, I am not a little anxious.[6]

Hooper, if we are to take his complaints at face value, was suffering the ministrations of jailers who made the conditions of his confinement as unpleasant as possible. The treatment of evangelical captives contrasted greatly with the relatively comfortable earlier detention of Bonner and Gardiner. Months followed relentless months for Hooper and his colleagues during which they received no definite news of their fate. This was deliberate psychological warfare designed to bring them to recantation and provide the government with valuable propaganda coups. On 11 December 1554, Hooper informed Bullinger in a letter smuggled out of prison:

> We are still involved in the greatest danger, as we have been for almost the last eighteen months. The enemies of the gospel are every day giving us more and more annoyance; we are imprisoned apart from each other, and treated with every degree of ignominy. They are daily threatening us with death, which we are quite indifferent about; in Christ Jesus we boldly despise the sword and the flames.[7]

Meanwhile the government were occupied with major affairs of state. From the very beginning of her reign Mary was determined to marry. The choice of husband she left entirely in the hands of the emperor. Charles proposed his son, Philip, whom he had already designated to assume the crown of Spain and the government of the Netherlands. By early October it was all decided. Mary was delirious with joy, overwhelmed by the honour bestowed upon her. Not so all her political advisers. Gardiner headed a group of councillors who feared a patriotic reaction to a foreign marriage and tried to persuade the queen to seek a husband within the realm. On 16 November a Commons deputation went to court to express their concern. Mary was not to be moved. She brushed aside the arguments of the Parliament men and told them in no uncertain terms not to meddle in matters that did not concern them. To her the advantages of the Spanish match were obvious: backed by the most powerful Catholic power in the world her God-inspired mission would be sure to succeed. Mary was not a political animal. As John Guy has observed, 'she saw the future in terms of the past'[8] and her *idée fixe* prevented her from assessing calmly the realities of international politics. The reconversion of England was not high on Charles V's list of priorities. The Schmalkaldic princes had staged a comeback since 1547 and imperial control of Germany was far from complete. Habsburg territory was, in effect, divided into two parts, Spain being separated from the Netherlands by France and the Protestant Rhineland. Bringing England's queen into the family would provide him with valuable harbours from which to keep the Channel free of enemy shipping and safe-guard his lines of communication. As long as anyone could remember, England's foreign policy had been based on play-ing off the Habsburgs and the Valois against each other. Mary, it seemed, was bent on discarding this diplomatic ace.

Opposition to this policy very soon went beyond words. In January 1554 Sir Thomas Wyatt raised the standard of rebellion in Kent and marched towards London with 3,000 men. His action had been planned as part of a much wider protest but the plot was uncovered, so that contingents from Devon, Wales and the Midlands were prevented from mustering. Even so, Wyatt's little army was sufficiently determined and enjoyed enough support in the capital to give the government some heart-stop-ping days. When push came to shove Londoners declined to open their gates to the rebels and when, on 7 February, hastily gathered royal forces engaged with the rebels in the western approaches to the City they secured an easy victory.

The immediate effect of the rising was to endanger all who might be seen as presenting a threat to the regime. Jane Grey and her husband, Guildford Dudley, who had hitherto been spared the fate of Northumberland and his chief supporters, were executed within days of the rebellion. In March, Princess Elizabeth was locked up in the Tower of London. She protested that she had had no contact with Wyatt but one of the aims of the rebels had been to remove Mary in favour of her half-sister. Elizabeth was subjected to rigorous interrogation but, when no proof of her complicity could be discovered, she was moved into the country and placed under house arrest. Mary would happily have sent to the scaffold the daughter of the hated Anne Boleyn and we may wonder – Tudor state trials being what they were – why Elizabeth was not charged with treason. The answer is that the Council, and probably Mary herself, realised that this would be counter-productive. Juries had failed to convict some of Wyatt's fellow conspirators and when the traitor's head was stuck on a pole at St James's a sympathiser stole it. In the prevailing atmosphere the Council decided that to take drastic action against Elizabeth, who was very popular with the people, might well provoke another, more dangerous rising. For her part, the princess was circumspection itself. She occasionally heard mass and asked for books so that she might learn 'true' doctrine. When the two ladies met Elizabeth protested her affection and obedience and Mary responded with words of kindness. It was all a *pas de deux* of hypocrisy, the gracious moves and gestures concealing real feelings. The queen knew from those employed to report on the events and personalities of the princess's household that Elizabeth remained wedded to her evangelical faith. She did not deviate from her mistrust of her half-sister and, according to Renard, she contemplated emulating Edward in barring Elizabeth from the succession because 'it would burden her conscience too heavily to allow a bastard to succeed'.[9]

By mid-April, when Wyatt's putrefying body parts were on display in various city locations, another and ultimately more effective protest was under way. Prominent evangelicals were leaving England in significant numbers. Courtiers, gentlemen, members of noble families, merchants, clergy, university lecturers, lawyers and students, together with their dependants and servants, to the number of at least a thousand made their way across the Channel in 1554, most of them to seek refuge in established centres of reform. As we have seen, there were strong connections between English evangelicals and the leaders of churches in Zurich, Strasbourg, Geneva and other centres under the control of Protestant regimes. Edwardian England had provided havens for brethren fleeing from persecution in

France and the Empire. Now the evangelical network served English exiles.

But this exodus was no 'flight' of poor believers on the run from an English version of the Inquisition. The religious migrants were, for the most part, well-to-do activists backed by an efficient organisation which looked after their finances and travel arrangements. Nor were they harried from the land by cruel vigilantes, eager to bring them to prison or the stake. The attitude of Catholic pragmatists was 'good riddance'. And no one was more pragmatic than Gardiner. He confided to Renard his strategy in dealing with suspected heretics: 'When he hears of any preacher or leader of the sect, he summons him to appear at his house, and the preacher, fearing he may be put in the Tower, does not appear, but on the contrary absents himself.'[10] The most striking example of this policy in action was the departure of Catherine Brandon, the termagant dowager Duchess of Suffolk, who had been an outspoken court evangelical for almost twenty years. She made a leisurely five-week progress from London to the coast, accompanied by a major-domo, a personal maid, a kitchen-maid, a laundress, a brewer, a joiner, a fool and 'a Greek rider of horses'.

The delay in dealing with the imprisoned evangelicals can be explained by the government's need to secure their political position. Wyatt's rebellion had been anti-Spanish rather than anti-Catholic but Mary and her councillors were well aware that the two strains of protest might fuse. Negotiations for the marriage settlement were, therefore, particularly delicate. At the height of Wyatt's rebellion Mary had made a public declaration that she would only proceed to the altar with Philip if Parliament concurred with her that the marriage was 'for the high benefit and commodity of all the whole realm'. Such reassurances were vital in the light of the widespread hostility to the proposed marriage. The suppression of rebellion had not disposed of the resentment underlying it. The Spanish treaty negotiators were snowballed on their arrival in London. Because public feeling was so hostile and because the alliance was crucial for the Habsburgs the English representatives actually found themselves in a strong bargaining position. Thus, while Philip was permitted the title 'King of England', his actual powers were restricted to those of a consort. In the event of the queen predeceasing her husband, all his rights in England would cease. As to the succession, that was limited to the children of Philip and Mary; existing and future offspring of Philip were specifically excluded. Crucially, the terms of the alliance exempted England from automatic involvement in any foreign wars on Philip's behalf. The king was not to appoint foreigners to English offices and he was not to take his wife out of the realm. On paper it looked as though national interests were thoroughly ring-fenced. In fact, Philip accepted the terms with his fingers firmly crossed behind his back. He secretly made it known to the queen and her close advisers that he would regard the treaty terms as flexible. However, it achieved its immediate objective; both houses ratified the treaty in April 1554 and on 25 July the wedding took place.

The man designated to lead the reconversion of England was Cardinal Reginald Pole, who, for the past twenty years, had proved himself to the governments of Henry and Edward the most troublesome Englishman abroad. He returned from Rome to his native shore at the end of 1554, to take up the Archbishopric of Canterbury, from which Cranmer had been ejected. He also came as papal legate, with authority to lift the interdict and restore the nation to Roman obedience. In November he made a speech to Parliament, his words being carefully chosen to allay fears:

> I come not to destroy but to build. I come to reconcile, not to condemn. I come not to compel, but to call again. I come not to call in question anything already done [a message directed at the holders of ex-monastic lands], but my commission is of grace and clemency to such as will receive it . . . all matters that be past . . . shall be as things cast into the sea of forgetfulness.[11]

On the last day of November a solemn ceremony was held at Westminster. The king and queen, together with representatives of Lords and Commons, knelt before Cardinal Pole to make their humble submission and to receive from him absolution for all the nation's past sins and full restitution to the Catholic church. Parliament ratified this move, went on to repeal all religious legislation after 1529 and restored the ancient heresy laws.

Yet, the representatives of the political nation were not prepared to yield on all matters and, particularly, not on property rights. Only days after the moving submission ceremony the government introduced a parliamentary bill sanctioning the confiscation of exiles' lands. This touched members closely; many of them had relatives and friends living on the continent who were dependent on receiving income from their English estates. When the bill came up for second reading, its opponents in the Commons barricaded the chamber door and forced the Speaker to take a vote. The measure was defeated and, though the ringleaders of the coup had to endure a spell in the Tower, no attempt was made to reintroduce it.

Such setbacks were small in comparison to the changes which Mary had introduced and she was euphoric. She had been delivered from her enemies, she had forged a permanent link with Europe's most powerful dynasty and she had placed most prominent heretics behind bars. She had overseen the restoration of her land to papal obedience. But, best of all, she was already pregnant – or so she believed.

The pope's representative wasted no time in instituting a programme of church reform. He realised that permanent transformation would depend on changes at grassroots level. This meant not only restoring the sights, sounds and smells of worship with which the legate had been familiar in his youth, but instructing the laity more effectively than the pre-Reformation clergy had done. In effect, he faced the same problem as Cranmer and his friends had faced and he tackled it in much the same way. He set in train the publication of devotional aids and educational material for the laity and the provision of a well-trained clergy. Service books, primers and catechisms poured from the presses and – most revolutionary of all – plans were made for an official vernacular New Testament.

That was the easy part of Pole's strategy. What would take longer and be more difficult would be the recruiting and equipping of an army of revitalised parish clergy. He summoned a legatine synod in the autumn of 1555 and impressed upon the bishops the need for firm discipline. There was to be no more nonsense about priests or people reading the Bible for themselves and devising all manner of personal heresies. 'Control' was to be the buzzword. Regular episcopal visitations were to take place. Canon law was to be rigidly enforced. Seminaries were to be founded in every diocese for the training of priests. Bishops and clergy were to be resident in their places of work. Pole's approach was visionary. It was also set out with crystalline logic. It was the kind of reform programme which had been advocated by John Colet and other pioneers of reform almost half a century earlier. But since the early days of Catholic humanism ideological storms had swept across the nation, radically transforming the landscape. Pole failed to grasp just how changed England had become. Not only were there now stubborn heretics prepared to endure suffering and claiming loyalty to a religion which had, until recently, had the backing of law. Not only were there numerous secret conventicles armed with the hitherto official Bible and prayer book. Not only were there slippery customers who conformed outwardly but privately held to the evangelical faith and, as they were able, succoured prisoners and exiles. Not only was there a new influx of anti-Catholic literature produced by the refugees and smuggled into England from their continental havens. What added to Pole's problems was the situation prevailing in most of the parishes. He and his royal mistress may have convinced themselves that the bulk of the population were simply waiting for a return to the 'good old days' but the reality was much more complex. The numerous changes and counter-changes had left people confused. The old oral traditions surrounding holy images, relics, shrines and chantries were fast evaporating. The guilds which had involved lay people in activities designed to maintain church fabric as well as maintain intercession for the dead had been abolished. Layfolk were no longer involved in church life in the ways that their forefathers had been and, though they were now expected to take a more active part in regular worship, new habits had not had time to form themselves. In many parishes clergy were either non-existent or inadequate to help their people through the bewildering intricacies of change. This left devout souls wondering where they were to look for authority. Was it to be found in the Bible or in Catholic doctrine? And in either case who was to expound truth to them?

One notable failure of the regime was its disinclination to engage in printed controversy with exiled Protestant propagandists. They preferred to concentrate on educational and devotional manuals. But, significantly, they faced a practical problem: half of the London publishers had fled abroad.

For Pole, as for Mary, the sword which would cut this Gordian knot was power. During his long years in Rome Pole had witnessed a shallow-rooted evangelical revival successfully crushed by the Inquisition. He believed the same uncompromising attitude would work in England. Being people of conviction, the queen and the legate never questioned that doubt, unorthodox belief, scepticism and rebellion could all be overcome by the ruthless exercise of the church's authority. Their solution to dissidence did not involve debate; people had to be coerced into truth for their own sake and for the sake of the nation. This black and white attitude was constantly fed by the personal emotions shared by the queen and the cardinal. Both had suffered intolerably at the hands of Henry VIII. Both had been exiled from their rightful position in society, for, although Mary had remained in England, she had been for years relegated to the position of a non-person. Most important of all, both of them had mothers whose shades were crying out for vengeance. Catherine had died in lonely misery. Reginald's mother, the Countess of Salisbury, had been imprisoned by

Henry in a round-up of extant Yorkists and executed in 1541. There were scores to be settled and Catholic revival provided the justification for retributive justice.

It was on this policy that the queen and the legate parted company with their Habsburg allies. For them ends justified means. For all Pole's reassurances to Parliament, the velvet glove soon came off the iron fist. Philip and Charles, by contrast, were pragmatists. They needed the support of the English aristocracy and the merchant community and were concerned that unyielding religious policy would play into the hands of anti-Spanish elements. Charles's instructions to his son could not have been clearer: 'Stay where you are and be with the queen my daughter, busying yourself with the government of England, settling affairs there and making yourself familiar with the people, which it is most important you do for present and future considerations.'[12] The emperor, well informed by Renard, was aware of just how difficult the bridge-building process would be. Anti-Spanish demonstrations continued. Exiles were conspiring with the French court to disrupt English political life. The French ambassador, Antoine de Noailles, was running an effective fifth column. English ships, operating out of Normandy harbours, were preying on Philip's vessels. The king had already persuaded the pope to backtrack on the reclamation of church property from those who had benefited from the dissolution. Now, with the prospect of more campaigning on the continent, he needed to persuade his new territory to contribute men and money. A softly-softly approach on religion would be more likely to yield the results he wanted.

If events had followed the script devised by Pole and Mary, a few show trials and spectacular executions of England's arch-heretics would have been followed by the surrender of rank-and-file evangelicals who were either convinced of the error of their ways or were terrified into submission. Things did not work out quite like that. Dealing with the imprisoned senior clergy began in January 1555.

On the 22nd, John Hooper was among the first to be put on

trial for heresy. The outcome being inevitable, he was moved to Gloucester to be burned before an audience of his own erstwhile diocesan flock. A large military contingent were also turned out for the event to prevent any sympathetic demonstrations. The bishop's end, on 9 February, was, according to Foxe, particularly harrowing. It was a windy day and the fire was badly set. The flames played about his legs but not until more faggots had twice been thrown on the pyre did they reach his torso.

> and then the bladders of gunpowder brake, which did him small good, they were so placed, and the wind had such power. In which fire he prayed with somewhat a loud voice, 'Lord Jesus, have mercy upon me; Lord Jesus have mercy upon me: Lord Jesus, receive my spirit!' ... when he was black in the mouth, and his tongue swollen, that he could not speak, yet his lips went till they were shrunk to the gums: and he knocked his breast with his hands, until one of his arms fell off, and then knocked still with the other, what time the fat, water and blood dropped out at his fingers' ends, until by renewing of the fire his strength was gone, and his hand did cleave fast, in knocking to the iron upon his breast. So immediately, bowing forwards, he yielded up his spirit.[13]

But the regime's sights were fixed not on such relatively small fry but on the major celebrities of the Edwardian church. These were Nicholas Ridley, the man who had displaced Bonner as Bishop of London, Hugh Latimer, the Reformation's star pulpit performer for more than twenty years, and, top of the list, Thomas Cranmer. He was the arch-heretic who had imposed evangelical doctrine and liturgy on the church and he had to be publicly brought to book. But Mary had a personal score to settle with Cranmer. It was he who had colluded with her father and become the source of all her misery. These three Protestant champions had to be not only destroyed but thoroughly discredited.

In the spring of 1554 they had been moved to Oxford in order to enter into disputation with a team of theologians selected by the government. The purpose of this academic sparring match was that 'their erroneous opinions, being by the word of God justly and truly convinced, the residue of our subjects may be thereby better established in the true catholic faith'.[14] The prisoners were presented separately with questions about the nature of the mass and instructed to state their opinions. Then followed a week of sessions at which each in turn was subjected to attack on his stated faith by a barrage of questions and assertions from the massed battery of academics. 'The atmosphere of the Marian disputation was unusually hysterical, both among the Catholic participants and the packed audience.'[15] The inevitable verdict was that the opinions of the three men had been soundly trounced and exposed as rank heresy. The prisoners were now kept in confinement for the rest of the year. They had to wait until the arrival of Pole with full papal authority to proceed against them and the uncertainty as to their fate would, it was hoped, help to destabilise the underground evangelical movement. The strategy seems to have been effective. John Cheke, Edward VI's old tutor, writing from his Strasbourg exile, commented that the three men

> are either, I understand, already burned or are shortly to experience the power of the flames and the cruelty of their tyrants. It is most painful and distressing to us to be deprived of those, whom, if God should be pleased to effect any alteration of affairs in our wretched and now greatly ruined England, we should not be able, or at least should hardly be able, to dispense with.[16]

However, the strategy was not without its risks. The longer the ex-bishops remained in custody the more their celebrity was enhanced – and not only among members of their own party. By the autumn it was necessary to tighten the security of the prisoners to prevent people trying to make contact with them.

On 16 October 1555 Latimer and Ridley were burned together outside the city gate, near the spot where a memorial to their memory was raised almost three centuries later. One onlooker noted Latimer's last oratorical gem and passed it on to John Foxe: 'Be of good comfort, Master Ridley, and play the man. We shall this day light such a candle, by God's grace, in England, as I trust shall never be put out.'[17] After this the conditions of Cranmer's confinement were eased. He was moved to the college environment of Christ Church and the familiar company of fellow academics.

His enemies knew that the ex-archbishop was, at heart, a scholar, accustomed to developing his ideas as the result of reasoned debate. By surrounding him with clever intellectual Catholics with whom he could talk in comfortable surroundings they hoped to persuade him to see the error of his ways. It was so vital for the regime to break the principal architect of the English Reformation that they were prepared to invest whatever time and effort it took to achieve their objective. Cranmer was now sixty-six years of age and probably suffering from a heart condition. He was alone. He had been made to watch from a window the burning of his old friends Latimer and Ridley. He received news of the scores of executions now taking place and his captors lost no opportunity to point out that God was visiting his judgement on a nation which had fallen into heinous sin – a sin for which Cranmer was largely responsible. For two months – from 11 December 1555 to 14 February 1556 – Cranmer was engaged in theological debate on an almost daily basis with some of the most skilled dialecticians (most of them Spanish) the Catholic church could produce.

The brainwashing techniques worked. Cranmer became disorientated. He wavered. He began to question some of his beliefs. Particularly he re-evaluated his understanding of royal and papal authority. All the reforms he had instigated had been on the basis that kings were God's representatives on earth in all matters, temporal and spiritual. Now England's new monarch decreed that in all religious affairs she and her subjects were under the authority of the pope. Did not Cranmer's duty to God's anointed queen oblige him to accept the papal supremacy? But if he did so would that not mean that he had been misguided in his obedience to Henry VIII? These and other questions tortured his brain as he tried, in all honesty, to discover what he should do in his current circumstances. That he would be executed he was in little doubt. He made appeals to Mary for clemency but she turned a deaf ear. Since, then, death was imminent, it was important that Cranmer should face it with a clear conscience. Day after day and night after sleepless night he agonised over this, while his enemies kept up their relentless onslaught of argument, cajolery and threat. The result was a series of written recantations, each one more abject (though not progressively more extreme) than the last. In these documents he tried to give the regime a submission they would accept and each time they upped the surrender terms.

One reason for the delay in dealing with Cranmer was that his case had to be heard in Rome. Unlike Hooper and Ridley, the archbishop had been appointed by a pope and only a pope could reverse this decision. As soon as the necessary documents arrived the final proceedings got under way. On 14 February Cranmer underwent the humiliating, elaborate ceremony of being degraded of all his clerical orders. He was dressed up in imitation vestments of sub-deacon, deacon, priest, bishop and archbishop, one atop the other. Then, placed high on the rood loft, in order to give the audience an excellent view, he was solemnly stripped of each layer of clothing. His head was shaved and Bishop Bonner symbolically scraped his fingers over the victim's scalp to undo his anointing. It was as a mere layman that he was afterwards taken from Christ Church back to his former prison.

But the arguments, theological debates and aggressive interviews did not cease. On 26 February, Cranmer, by now mentally exhausted, set his name to his fifth and most detailed recantation. In it he accepted transubstantiation, purgatory, the seven sacraments and the primacy of the pope. He rejected the teachings of Luther and Zwingli, begged forgiveness for his former errors and threw himself on the mercy of Mary and Philip. His triumphant enemies rushed the document to the printers – and realised too late that, in their haste, they had blundered. The recantation was confirmed and countersigned by two Spanish friars. Feelings against the regime were now running so strongly that the document was received in London with scorn and anger as a put-up job. The government hastily called in all the undistributed copies, an unspoken acknowledgement that their propaganda coup had backfired.

The final events in Cranmer's life were played out against a religious backdrop that was changing rapidly. During 1555–6 the campaign to eradicate Protestantism got into its stride. Persecution spread like a stain from Bonner's diocese of London, where 113 men and women went up in flames during the purge, to most of the South and the Midlands. Between 280 and 300 victims in total perished and, thanks to John Foxe's determination that they should not be forgotten, we know the details of most of them. His *Acts and Monuments* makes painful reading and, though contemporaries lived in a harsher world than ours, many incidents caused revulsion and resentment at the time. Public executions were a common sight. Crime was an assault on community life and it was important for communities to observe and thus to share in the punishment of criminals. But there was no precedent for the execution by burning of large numbers of men and women, many of whom were respected members of their communities who had committed no obvious offences against their neighbours. Many onlookers could not be convinced that what was being done was being done on their behalf. They could only see the burnings as part of a programme being carried out by 'the church' or 'the government'. When, in Guernsey, a pregnant woman dropped her child at the stake, an onlooker rescued it, only to have it snatched from his hands and thrown back into the flames. By contrast, at Colchester, the deputy sheriff dismissed a condemned woman because she was suckling an infant.

The demeanour of those who endured this most horrific of deaths made an impact on spectators. Evangelical activists certainly knew how to turn their suffering to propaganda advantage. Their valedictory speeches and statements of forgiveness for their persecutors may have impressed audiences but often actions spoke louder than words. Doubtless some of the condemned went wailing and fearful to their fate but such have left no trace in the records. What made more impact was the sight of Cranmer running to the stake so fast that his guards were hard pressed to keep up (see p. 318f), or John Rogers washing his hands in the flames as though it were cold water, or Laurence Saunders embracing and kissing the stake. One Protestant woman told Bonner that the Catholic overkill had 'lost the hearts of twenty thousand that were rank papists . . . twelve months [ago]'.[18] The statistic is quite unreliable; but the general impression conveyed by the assertion cannot be ignored.

What we can never know is how many convinced (or even partially convinced) evangelicals covered their belief with outward conformity. Lollards had been adept at such dissembling for a century and a half. After Elizabeth's accession many crypto-Protestants came out of the woodwork, some seeking public office at local or national level in the more favourable atmosphere. During the reign of the last Tudor it was the turn of covert Catholics to conceal their real faith beneath outward acceptance of the official religion. This is the most natural stratagem for people who find themselves in a persecuted minority. Between 1553 and 1558 thousands of Mary's subjects experienced exile, imprisonment, interrogation or death because of their opposition to the queen's religion. It is reasonable to suppose that there were many more who kept their heads down in the hope that better times would come.

No common pattern emerges from the trials and executions. Some officials carried out their duties with enthusiasm. Others had to be reminded of the penalties for showing leniency. (Fines were levied for a first offence. Anyone persisting ran the risk of also being identified as a heretic.) People might fall foul of the authorities in a variety of ways. One man refused to have his child baptised. Another expressed sympathy for Latimer, Ridley and Cranmer. Here a family were conspicuous by their absence at mass. There an unlicensed preacher took it upon himself to exhort his neighbours from the Bible. Inevitably, some martyrs were the victims of local feuds or malicious neighbours who denounced them for personal reasons. Inevitably also, the majority of the accused made their submission, avoided the harsher penalties and returned to the fold of mother church. They were the regime's success stories. Yet, among those who buckled under pressure there were not a few who (like Little Bilney years before) were broken by remorse and were eventually consigned to the flames as relapsed heretics. Those who died for their faith were a minority of those who were tried and those who were tried were a minority of those who believed. But that fact only highlights the size of the active evangelical community. If about 300 were prepared to pay the ultimate price for their faith, how large must the entire Protestant community have been? Persecution was, in fact, contributing to the consolidation of that community. Those brought to book by Mary's bishops espoused a variety of unorthodox views. Some could be labelled as 'Lutheran', 'Zwinglian' or 'Anglican' but others held Anabaptist or idiosyncratic beliefs which would have been denounced in any Christian country. Some of those brought into the episcopal courts were simply ignorant countryfolk who could not describe basic official doctrines. In their cases any fault lay with the clergy who should have better instructed them. Subjecting all unorthodoxies to the same treatment gave their holders a spurious common identity as 'anti-Catholic' and that sentiment now began to feed into the mainstream of English religious life.

Resentment showed itself in the frequent manhandling of priests and in demonstrations against the regime. It was in the closing months of the reign that one of Bonner's commissioners could write from Harwich, 'Would to God the Council saw the face of Essex as we do see. We have such obstinate heretics,

Anabaptists and unruly persons as never was heard of.'[19] However, the Council had more than adequate evidence of the strong resentment felt by dissidents at the heart of national life. One bold protester even managed to gain access to the queen's apartments and scatter copies of a crude caricature depicting Mary as a withered hag suckling a brood of Spanish 'infants'. Anti-Catholicism and hatred of Spanish influence were becoming inextricably linked.

The only answer to the problem that Mary could see was 'more of the same'. She never reached the point of acknowledging that her religious policy was failing; that different, more subtle tactics were called for. As late as February 1557 the king and queen appointed new commissioners with instructions which could not have been more comprehensive or urgent:

> We ... do give full power and authority unto you ... to inquire ... of all singular and heretical opinions, lollardies, heretical and seditious books, concealments, contempts, conspiracies, and all false rumours, tales, seditious and slanderous words or sayings, raised, published, bruited, invented, or set forth against us, or either of us, or against the quiet governance and rule of our people and subjects, by books, lies, tales, or otherwise ... within this our realm of England or elsewhere, in any place or places beyond the sea, and of the bringers-in, utterers, buyers, sellers, readers, keepers, or conveyers of any such letter, book, rumour and tale, and of all and every their coadjutors, counsellors, comforters, procurers, abettors, and maintainers, giving unto you ... full power and authority ... to search out and take into your hands and possession, all manner of heretical and seditious books, letters, and writings, wheresoever they or any of them shall be found, as well in printers' houses and shops, as elsewhere ... And also to enquire, hear and determine all and singular enormities, disturbances, misbehaviours, and negligences committed in any church, chapel, or other hallowed place, within this realm ... And also to inquire and search out all

such persons as obstinately do refuse to receive the blessed sacrament of the altar, to hear mass, or to come to their parish churches . . . and all such as refuse to go on procession, to take holy bread, or holy water, or otherwise do misuse themselves in any church or other hallowed place.[20]

Mary was trying to do the same thing as her father – enforce religious unity on her people – but she was prepared to go much further than Henry VIII.

It was not only the religious situation which caused her frustration. In fact, she had several other worries on her mind and plenty of cause for despair. Her greatest sorrow concerned her 'pregnancy'. It began as a mistake, grew into a delusion and ended as a farce. Mary announced her good news in late November 1554, believing that her child had been conceived in the first days of her marriage. The child was expected in May and in mid-April the queen moved to Hampton Court for her lying-in. On the 30th steeple bells were rung in London and other southern towns in celebration of the birth of a prince. Descriptions of this beautiful and perfectly formed royal personage were even circulated before a correction went out from the palace to indicate that the rejoicing was premature. In the queen's chamber several of her attendants were sceptical but the physicians continued to reassure their patient that all was well, the date had merely been miscalculated. May came and went and then June. Still the doctors stuck to their diagnosis and still Mary hoped against hope. Meanwhile there was a flurry of Protestant pamphlets poking fun at the queen's predicament. Some even suggested that there was a plot afoot to smuggle a healthy baby into the palace and pass it off as the heir to the throne. Not until late July did Mary order the court to leave for other premises and concede that she had deluded herself. What she could not know was that her distended belly and other symptoms were the signs of stomach cancer.

At the beginning of September Philip made good his escape from England. He had been longing to leave for the Low

Countries and had only stayed his departure to await the expected birth of his child. Charles V had decided to abdicate, dividing his vast dominions between his brother, Ferdinand, who succeeded him as emperor, and Philip, who was to receive the crown of Spain and the Netherlands. The transfer of power occurred on 25 October 1555. From this point English affairs have to be understood in the context of European power politics. His island kingdom was only of interest to Philip as a supplier of men and money for the contest with Henry II of France. Mary had come to lean heavily on her husband for emotional and political support and felt bereft by his 'abandonment'. She was left with only Pole's support to fight her battle against the heretics and her conflict with the Privy Council, whose members strongly resisted England being dragged into war with France. Then Fate added another, wholly unexpected load to the burden she was carrying. On 9 April 1555, Marcellus II was elected pope. Twenty-two days later he died. The hastily formed conclave conferred the papal tiara upon Giovanni Carafa, who assumed office as Pope Paul IV. He was an ascetic of awesome personal purity who would tolerate in others nothing but the highest standards of moral rectitude and doctrinal orthodoxy. It was Carafa who had reinvigorated the Roman Inquisition and now established the Index of Banned Books (which included the writings of Erasmus and even Henry VIII's defence of the seven sacraments). He was the sworn enemy of Jews and homosexuals, he cleansed the Augean Stables of the Vatican by forbidding any women to set foot there and he outlawed from its works of art all representations of the nude. Of heretics of all stamps Paul IV was the most determined and energetic enemy.

This should have made him an obvious supporter of the Marian regime. Unfortunately for the English Counter-Reformation, very high on the pope's long list of hatreds came the Habsburg regime and Cardinal Pole. Carafa was a Neapolitan and Naples was a part of the Spanish empire, a situation he was determined to change. Accordingly, he called upon Henry II to help him rid the Italian peninsula of Spanish dominion and threw his support behind France in the war. He recalled his envoys from Habsburg lands and raised an army for the invasion of Naples. As for Pole, the pope held a long-cherished aversion to him as a Catholic negotiator who had, at one time, sought a rapprochement with Luther. He was considering summoning the cardinal to Rome to face charges of heresy. Mary desperately needed a good news story; something that would vindicate her policy and persuade the Catholic world that she was determined to make a reality of her country's reconversion. That was why the abject and detailed recantation of Thomas Cranmer was important to her. Cranmer was an international figure, one of the celebrities of the Protestant world. To have him defeated, crushed, and renouncing every heresy with which he had deceived the English would have repercussions that would be felt through all the Protestant communities of Europe and all the way to Rome.

The story of how Cranmer thwarted her is well known, though it has been variously interpreted by historians. That his long, lonely ordeal had left him disorientated and emotionally spent is beyond doubt. Having made a comprehensive recantation and been reconciled with the pope's church it is possible that he might have believed he had done enough to escape a heretic's death. On 17 March he learned that there was to be no reprieve and that the date for his execution had been set for the 21st. Some time in those few remaining days Cranmer's mind cleared. The academic fog lifted. The fear of death similarly evaporated. He developed a new resolve. When he came to the stake he would proclaim what he really believed.

On the morning of 21 March he was taken to the university church for the elaborate formalities preceding his execution. A packed congregation listened to a sermon by Dr Henry Cole, Provost of Eton. All this time the prisoner had been placed on a specially constructed stand in full view of the people. When Cole had finished Cranmer was invited to make his farewell address. He was to speak from a prepared script which had been vetted by his captors. This was to be the climax of all their work on him over the last two years. He would declare that the Edwardian Reformation, for which he had been largely responsible, had been a diabolical error drawing many people away from the safety of the Catholic church. All began well. With tears in his eyes, the archbishop asked the people to pray for him, to be obedient to their superiors, to remember the poor and to show love to all. He confirmed his belief in 'every article of the catholic faith, every word and sentence taught by our Saviour Jesus Christ, his apostles and prophets, in the New and Old Testament'. Then he declared that there was one sin above all others which weighed heavily on his conscience, 'more than anything that ever I did or said in my whole life': he had spread abroad false writings. What the authorities were expecting to hear now was a denunciation of Cranmer's books on the subject of the mass and other orthodox doctrines. Not until it was too late did they realise that the prisoner had departed from the approved text. He explained that 'the writings contrary to the truth, which now here I renounce' were

> All such bills or papers which I have written or signed with my hand since my degradation, wherein I have written many things untrue. And forasmuch as my hand offended, writing contrary to my heart, my hand shall first be punished thereafter; for may I come to the fire, it shall be first burned. And as for the pope, I refuse him, as Christ's enemy, and antichrist, with all his false doctrine. And as for the sacrament, I believe as I have taught in my book against the bishop of Winchester.[21]

Now his words were drowned out by the uproar of the congregation and the angry protests of the officials. Cranmer was pulled from his place, jostled out of the church and along the street to the place of execution. But if the authorities were anxious to make an end they were not as enthusiastic as the prisoner. He ran towards the stake, pursued with difficulty by his guards. When the fire was lit he kept his promise by holding out his right hand to the flames, calling the bystanders to witness the 'punishment' of his errant member. It was excellent theatre and it was highly effective. The publicity torpedo which should have blasted the Edwardian Reformation out of the water had missed its mark.

To add to the government's woes the Oxford fiasco coincided with the discovery of a plot which had the alarming potential of developing into a serious revolt. It was led by Sir Henry Dudley, a distant cousin and former agent of the late Duke of Northumberland. Hatched at the French court, it involved the landing of an army of exiles on the south coast in ships supplied by Henry II. The carefully planned enterprise was to be funded by £50,000 stolen from the Exchequer and it had the backing of a worrying melange of highly placed traitors, including members of Mary's court, an ex-lord mayor of London, the master of the Tower mint, the keeper of the Star Chamber and the customs officer at Gravesend. Within days the Venetian ambassador suggested that, had the conspirators succeeded, they would have 'placed the Queen and the whole kingdom in great trouble'. That and the execution of Cranmer had produced a widespread anti-government backlash, 'as demonstrated daily by the way in which the preachers are treated, and by the contemptuous demonstrations made in the churches'.[22]

Thus, in the spring of 1556, Mary, who had come to rely on Philip for political guidance and emotional support, found herself alone and frightened. She was facing widespread resentment, threats of rebellion, actual rebellion and hostility from the head of her own church. She responded to this isolation by clinging to Pole, whom she scarcely let out of her sight, and becoming increasingly reclusive. She did not show herself in public and the French ambassador gleefully reported that she 'rages against her subjects'.

It may have been the unsatisfactory outcome of Cranmer's ordeal that provoked an event a few weeks later. The Marian regime were determined – perhaps, by now, desperate – for triumph in the intellectual arena. In their search for fresh scalps they targeted Sir John Cheke, the highly respected academic and one-time tutor to Edward VI. He had been given permission in 1554 to leave the country and had eventually taken up residence in Strasbourg. The government, apparently reversing now the policy towards religious exiles instituted by Gardiner (who had died the previous November), decided to proceed against this harmless scholar. Cheke received an invitation from members of the Privy Council (apparently at King Philip's instigation) to visit Brussels, where his wife was currently residing. On his way there in May, he was seized, bound, thrown into a wagon, conveyed to the nearest harbour and ended up in the Tower. Thus began a five-month ordeal during which he was subjected to repeated attempts by various Marian clergy to induce him to recant. Worn down by privation and psychological pressure, Cheke at length gave his enemies what they wanted. In October he was taken to the royal court where, in the presence of the queen and an invited assemblage of notables, he was obliged to read a detailed recantation. His death within a year was, inevitably, attributed by Protestant reporters to a broken heart. Who is to say that they were wrong?

The summer of 1556 was one of the worst on record. Severe drought withered the crops, reduced their yield and forced up basic food prices. Economic hardship only added to public discontent. This was reflected in Mary's letters to her husband, whom she begged to return. She even appealed to Charles V, claiming that if Philip did not come back quickly 'to remedy matters, not I only, but also wiser persons than I fear that great danger will ensue'.[23] Government control was faltering badly.

It was March 1557 before Philip returned and when he did so, it was not for the pleasure of being reunited with his wife but to demand her country's support in his continental conflicts. He was fighting a war on three fronts against virulent Calvinism in Flanders, against France on their common border, and against the pope in Italy. The previous September Philip's general, the Duke of Alva, had led his forces up to the very walls of Rome.

Paul IV responded by excommunicating the king. In April 1557 he revoked Pole's legatine commission and summoned him to Rome to face the Inquisition. This was all very distressing for Mary, who felt, not without reason, that, having restored her renegade nation to full communion with Rome, she deserved better of the holy father. Philip, however, was more interested in the military situation. Henry II had sent troops to relieve Rome and it was now a matter of urgency for Philip to create a diversion in order to force the French king to call some of his troops home. He planned to launch a major attack on France across its northern border. For that he needed money. He had none. His treasury was bankrupt and he had reneged on his massive loans with his Italian bankers. His only hope was England. He demanded help from his wife and she turned to her Council.

They opposed her to a man. They had no intention of allowing England to be dragged into Philip's war, especially as it involved forming an alliance against the pope. The queen did her best, cajoling and threatening her recalcitrant advisers. Eventually, in June, she forced them to agree to a declaration of war against France, to provide Philip with cavalry and foot soldiers, and to contribute heftily to his war chest. As soon as he had got what he wanted the king left for the Netherlands. This behaviour was exactly what the opponents of the marriage had always feared. Mary and her government lost virtually all credibility with her people.

But the severest blow to pro-Spanish policy occurred in the following January. During the autumn Philip's generals had chalked up important victories. In France they had taken the commercial and pilgrimage centre of St Quentin on the Somme and in Italy Alva had forced the pope to come to terms. Philip thankfully called a halt to the campaign and disbanded much of his northern army. This had an unforeseen and catastrophic result. It allowed Henry to turn his attention to the achieving of a long-standing ambition: the recovery of Calais. Bombardment began on the first day of the year. When news reached London, Mary made desperate, urgent appeals

to the powerful men of the south-east counties to send reinforcements across the Channel. But within a week the citadel
had fallen and, by 21 January, the French had taken the outly-
ing garrisons of Hammes and Guisnes.

The shock to English pride was considerable, although it
must be said that the Council were not prepared to expend
more resources in an attempt to win the town back. As for
Mary, devastated though she was, she did have one consolation: once again she fancied herself to be pregnant. She waited
until January to make the announcement, by which time she
reckoned that she was entering her seventh month. Was this a
frenzied clutching at straws or was she really convinced that
God had, at long last, come to her aid and to the aid of his
church? What is certain is that few people believed her. No one
was surprised when the date of her supposed delivery passed.
The failure of the queen's womb became symbolic of the
barrenness of government. The finances were in a terrible
mess. Stringent economies in the royal household only made
the dire situation more obvious to foreign observers. Mary was
constantly at odds with her Council, which contained no men
of sufficient intellectual calibre or administrative skill to
propose and effect a comprehensive rescue package. It took
little time for Philip's newly arrived envoy, Gómez Suárez de
Figueroa, Count of Feria, to assess the state of the government:
'from night to morning and morning to night they change
everything they have decided, and it is impossible to make
them see what a state they are in, although it is the worst any
country has ever fallen into.'[24] It must have seemed to Mary
that whatever could go wrong did go wrong. The winter of
1557–8 brought a severe influenza epidemic. In April the
marriage took place of Mary, Queen of Scots to the French
dauphin. Reginald Pole, broken by illness and by the pope's
treatment of him, was no longer a staff for Mary to lean on.
She had refused to allow him to leave for Rome and had
entered on a long and fruitless correspondence aimed at securing her friend's reinstatement. Now the cardinal shuffled round

the court like a ghost. These hammer blows of Fate were evidence to Protestants of God's punishment of the enemies of the Gospel. While the queen could not possibly embrace this analysis of the situation, she did, in the depths of her despair, beseech her spiritual advisers to tell her what she had done or failed to do that had so much displeased the Almighty.

In the summer Mary grew weaker in mind and body. In August she succumbed to influenza. She was forced to recognise that the issue of the succession had to be addressed. Her problem was the mirror image of that which had faced Edward five years before but Mary did not repeat her half-brother's mistake of trying to leave the crown to someone whose religion she approved. There was only one person who would be acceptable to the people. The events of 1553 had demonstrated the weight they placed on orderly succession. Even Philip was making overtures to Elizabeth. He sent envoys to her residence at Hatfield to offer her his protection. Mary can have entertained little hope that her half-sister would maintain her own religious policies. The princess had openly embraced the Catholic faith but there was little doubt where her real sympathies lay. An earlier attempt to marry her off to a suitable husband had come to nothing. In the autumn of 1558 there was no more room for manoeuvre. Ambitious courtiers were already gravitating towards Hatfield. Yet Mary held out until the last moment. Only on 6 November did she nominate Elizabeth as her heir. Eleven days later she died.

Unlike some of their continental counterparts, the English are not much given to providing their monarchs with nicknames. Aethelred the Unready, Alfred the Great and John Lackland seem to be the only kings whose sobriquets have stuck, providing a quick (not necessarily accurate) indication of their characters. Mary Tudor has the dubious distinction of being added to this select company. She will forever be known as 'Bloody Mary'. Is this altogether fair? History provides us with many monsters whose crimes were worse than hers; men, and occasionally women, whose actions we need not hesitate to characterise as evil and who carried them out quite deliberately. Clearly, Mary Tudor did not set out to murder some three hundred of her subjects in the name of religion but that was the end result of what she did and what she did not do.

Can it be urged in her defence that 'Those were crude and cruel days and human flesh was cheap'? Capital punishment was imposed in sixteenth-century England for a variety of what we would call minor offences. No one – certainly no town dweller – was unfamiliar with the sight of decaying bodies swaying on gibbets or severed heads speared on poles. It would certainly not have seemed strange to Mary that heresy, that most heinous of offences, should carry the most severe of penalties. That was a principle to which the vast majority of people – Protestant as well as Catholic – subscribed (although for Protestants there was an inherent contradiction between this concept and the individualism which was explicit in the principle of freedom to read the Bible). Mary's imperial hero had set the pace. In Charles V's Netherlands territories the Inquisition had been given full rein. A decree of 1550 had established the most savage punishements for convicted heretics: men were to be beheaded, women buried alive and particularly persistent offenders were condemned to the stake. In all cases the victim's property was to be confiscated by the Crown, thus effectively impoverishing his/her family. It has been calculated that, between 1523 and 1565, thirteen hundred people suffered death in the Habsburg Low Countries for refusing to renounce beliefs at variance with those of the Catholic church.

That sobering statistic leads to another question: should not any intelligent ruler have grasped the fact that persecution – particularly on such a dramatic scale – was counter-productive? In the Netherlands, where Calvinism went hand in hand with hatred of Spanish domination, heresy was spreading and there were regions where the church had become so unpopular that attendance at mass had fallen by a half. In 1555, while his daughter-in-law was still imposing her religion on her subjects, Charles V was forced to acquiesce in a religious settlement in

Germany by which he abandoned the attempt to eradicate Lutheranism. Those who still believed in the church's traditional way of dealing with dissent could point to other parts of Europe where it had been successful, such as Italy and the Iberian peninsula. However, there were specific reasons for Catholic triumph in those countries. The only fact that an objective analyst could have recognised was that violent coercion in the name of religion worked in some places and not in others.

Mary was not an objective analyst. Neither was she a pragmatic politician like her father. Henry had provided himself with the legal mechanism to hold heresy in check but he had known when to use it and when not to use it. He was aware of public opinion and had not allowed his bishops to wield indiscriminately the 'bloody whip with six strings'. Mary was surprised and distressed that England's autos-da-fé did not have their desired effect but she could not claim that no one had warned her. In February 1555, when the burnings were only just getting under way, Philip's Spanish confessor, preaching at court, denounced the policy of killing prisoners of conscience as contrary to the Gospel. And Renard made it clear that, in his opinion, such a policy was politically ill advised: 'I do not think it well,' he told Philip, 'that your Majesty should allow further executions to take place unless the reasons are overwhelmingly strong and the offences committed have been so scandalous as to render the course justifiable in the eyes of the people.'[25] The queen knew that there were divided opinions over the efficacy of persecution.

The hounding to death of almost three hundred men and women is one of the most lurid episodes in English history and no amount of explanatory overpainting can obliterate it from the record. It has been argued that contemporary Protestant regimes advocated the 'final solution' in dealing with Anabaptists and extreme religious radicals. Certainly the laws against religious deviants were harsh everywhere in Europe. But there was always a conceptual divide between the Catholic and evangelical position on coercion. No Protestant government unashamedly carried out a comparable purge. It is, for example, significant that the hounding of Catholics in Elizabeth's reign was justified under the treason laws. No official record listed men and women done to death because they were Catholics. In seeking to account for something so out of place even in such a violent century we cannot avoid fixing the blame where it has always traditionally lain; in the heart of a woman whose beliefs and personal experience made her over-zealous. The handful of state trials was inevitable. What was not and what could at any time have been stopped was the impetus they gave to bishops and Catholic vigilantes to continue the persecution in all parts of the realm. Mary and Pole, supported by most of the Council, let slip the dogs of war and made no attempt to call them off. If the hounds inflicted a disproportionate amount of suffering or used religion as a cloak for personal vendetta the responsibility ultimately remained with the kennel-masters. What took the regime by surprise was the number of men and women ready to die for their faith. This should have been something Mary easily understood; few people had suffered more than she for what they believed in and, had the situation been reversed, there can be little doubt that she would have readily gone to the stake. But to have called a halt would have meant to compromise and that is something she could not bring herself to do.

With the benefit of hindsight we can see what she could not. There were two fundamental reasons for the failure of the Marian reaction. One was that the dismantling of medieval English Catholicism among the educated and semi-educated sections of the population had been too thorough to be reversed in the short time available to the queen and her bishops. The other was that Mary, instead of assessing what was politically possible, attempted to undo *everything* that had happened in the quarter of a century preceding her accession. She assumed that all her subjects shared her desire for a return to the church of her childhood. While some, predominantly those of an older generation, undoubtedly did, many did not. It was not only evangelicals she had to contend with. Religious conservatism covered a wide spectrum of belief and included many people who welcomed some degree of reform. On this fundamental misunderstanding Mary erected the Spanish alliance which swelled the ranks of those who opposed her regime and fused together religion and patriotism. England was on the way, albeit tentatively, to becoming a Protestant nation before Mary Tudor breathed her last.

Chapter 9

Commitment, Compromise and Conflict

Elizabeth Tudor, like her half-sister, had not been trained for the throne in her mid-twenties. Like Mary, she had to cope with the odd situation of being a woman in supreme power. Like Mary, she was called upon to make sense out of the mess that was the English church. And that is where any similarity between the two queens stops. What we now know as the 'Elizabethan Settlement' was possible, in part, because the new ruler had the good fortune to enjoy a long life and this enabled her to put policies in place, to carry them into effect and to see them accepted by the bulk of her people. That was a blessing denied to Mary. But we should not discount Elizabeth's genuine religious faith and her considerable intellectual gifts. Mary was nobody's fool and she certainly was passionate about her own beliefs but her successor possessed something that Henry's elder daughter lacked: a balance of conviction and political realism. It was this that enabled her to rule a divided nation effectively and to enjoy the respect and even the affection of her subjects. Pragmatism was something Elizabeth had learned during her half-sister's reign. Indeed, it almost certainly saved her life. By conforming outwardly and keeping her distance from zealots who plotted ostensibly in her name she gave Mary no excuse for taking serious action against her.

There was more than seventeen years' difference in the ages of the two princesses and the gap is highly significant. Between 1528, when Mary celebrated her twelfth birthday, and 1545, when Elizabeth reached the same age, life in royal circles had changed enormously. Mary had received a conventional upbringing, strongly coloured by her mother's Spanish brand of Catholicism. The education provided for Elizabeth was dominated by the newly fashionable humanism. Nothing indicates more clearly the changed religious orientation which moulded the thinking of the younger princess than the gift this twelve-year-old girl worked at to present to Queen Catherine Parr. Within handsomely embroidered covers featuring the intertwined initials HR and KP (Henry Rex/Katherine Parr) Elizabeth offered an English translation of a current theological treatise which had taken the Protestant world by storm. In her covering letter she commended the book's argument:

> the majesty of the matter surpasses all human eloquence, being privileged and having such force within it that a single sentence has power to ravish, inspire and give knowledge to the most stupid and ignorant beings alive in what way God wishes to be known, seen and heard.[1]

The text was none other than the first chapter of John Calvin's *Institution of the Christian Religion, comprising almost the whole sum of piety and whatever it is necessary to know about the doctrine of salvation* . . . more conveniently known as the *Institutes*. First appearing in 1536, this work of systematic theology went through several revisions and enlargements in Latin and French. The first chapter, which followed closely a catechism written by Luther, was not the most controversial part of the book. It established the basis that human wisdom consists in knowing God and knowing oneself, an exploration which inevitably leads to a realisation of human sinfulness. Such propositions would have been perfectly acceptable to the most dyed-in-the-wool papist. But the *Institutes* was anathema to Catholics. Its author was a religious exile from his French homeland who, after various adventures, had become the leader of the Reformed commonwealth of Geneva and was, by 1545, recognised as the intellectual leader of international evangelicalism. He was the Aquinas of the Protestant world, the scholar who attempted to tie up all the loose ends of Christian revelation and create a watertight exposition covering every aspect of doctrine and ecclesiology. It is extremely unlikely that Elizabeth read the whole of Calvin's latest edition but it is remarkable that this twelve-year-old girl could master the opening arguments of what was already being recognised as the most detailed and effective statement of Protestant dogmatic theology.

She was, indeed, a precocious child and one thoroughly versed, from her earliest years, in Christian humanism. Elizabeth grew up with very little memory of her mother and, until she entered teenage years, she seldom saw her father. Although she had a genuine affection for him, her really strong relationships were with the members of her household. She shared tutors with Edward, who was only four years her junior, and, because she was bright, she genuinely enjoyed the challenges and discoveries of mastering other languages and studying a wide curriculum of ancient and modern literature. Her thinking was shaped by the coterie of Cambridge scholars – Cheke, Cox, Ascham and William Grindal, her personal tutor – who were responsible for her half-brother's education. Her French teacher was the ardent Calvinist Jean Belmain, of whom she was especially fond. It is reasonable to suppose that it was Belmain who directed her attention to the *Institutes*. Other people to whom Elizabeth felt particularly close were Queen Catherine Parr and Sir Anthony Denny, both, as we have seen, committed followers of the new learning.

Elizabeth's early years had, thus, been secure and happy ones, during which she had been able to develop those beliefs, attitudes and convictions which she carried into adult life. In 1548 she had set up her own household and, thanks to a generous allowance made to her in Henry's will, she was able to be very much her own woman. During Edward's reign she was always welcome at court and enjoyed her status as the second lady of the realm (after Catherine Parr's death in 1548). Thus, by the time Mary came to the throne, Elizabeth was an independent and self-assured young woman. She was determined enough not to capitulate on religion after 1553 and clever enough not to parade her convictions. Like many other convinced evangelicals of social standing, she espoused 'Nicodemism', so named from the timid Jewish leader, Nicodemus, referred to in John's Gospel (Chapter 3), who visited Jesus secretly by night. She ostentatiously attended mass and avoided any open expression of religious opinion. This alone would not have saved her. There were several at Mary's court who wanted Elizabeth disposed of. There were moves to bring her to trial for treason and also suggestions that she be removed to some distant place of confinement where she might succumb to 'illness' or 'mishap'. But Elizabeth refused to allow her enemies to keep the initiative. She protested her innocence by letter and in personal encounters with the queen and she ensured that her agents publicised her troubles. The princess was popular in the country at large and it was this, combined towards the end of the reign with Philip's desire to remain in her good books, which sowed doubts in Mary's mind about how to handle her half-sister.

So Elizabeth survived to become the last monarch of the House of Tudor. She had none of her half-sister's hang-ups about the headship of the English church. (The title of Supreme Governor was confirmed by Parliament the following April.) Indeed, she was determined to use her authority to settle all matters of religious dispute and to pursue the Holy Grail of unity which her father and siblings had sought in vain. It would be a long and frequently bitter quest. She got down to work straight away. The first few days of the reign were spent in choosing her new Council. It was cut down in size from thirty to about twenty and the partisan Catholics of the Marian body were removed. Elizabeth chose for the most part experienced advisers who had served Henry and/or Edward, brought in some who had been out of favour in the previous regime and appointed two – Sir Francis Knollys and Lord Bedford – who had spent time among the exiled Protestants. The Council contained no bishops. Indeed a major characteristic of the new body was that it was dominated, probably for the first time in history, by university-trained laymen, the kind of keen-minded humanists Elizabeth most easily related to. However, the inner core of royal advisers, as also the dominant members of the court, could not be characterised as eager religious reformers. 'The keynote of the new court was a political rather than an evangelical Protestantism, in which hostility to the old faith and the regime which had promoted it was as potent an ingredient as enthusiasm for the Gospel.'[2]

The leading member of the Privy Council and the man who now became Elizabeth's secretary was Sir William Cecil. He was destined to remain at the queen's side for forty years and to be a formative influence on the character of the emerging Protestant state. He was another member of the Cambridge 'connection' who had enjoyed a position among the intellectual and political elite during Edward's reign. He was married to Mildred, daughter of Sir Anthony Cooke, tutor to the young king, one of the foremost educationalists of his day, and, as secretary to Protector Somerset and privy councillor, had become accustomed to handling the administration of the state. He was well acquainted with England's leading evangelicals and was at the London end of the network which supported the exiles and kept them in touch with affairs at home. For himself, Cecil preferred the role of Nicodemite and, while continuing to live in the capital during Mary's reign, he studiously avoided the political limelight. Cecil was a consummate survivor who enjoyed a wide circle of friends in both camps. For this reason and also because he was careful not to express his innermost thoughts in writing, it is difficult to assess the depth of his religious commitment. It would be wrong to dismiss him as an ambitious politique who changed his religious coat at will. As an exceptionally clever and experienced administrator in his mid-thirties he might well have sought a path back into government during Mary's reign. He did not. However, as soon as it seemed likely that the old queen would soon be dead, he made a beeline for Elizabeth's entourage. The ex-councillor and the queen-in-waiting evidently hit it off and Cecil's was the first appointment of the new reign.

It would probably be reasonable to say that for Cecil, as, indeed, for Elizabeth, religion, no less than politics, was the art of the possible. The new secretary has been described as 'active, reforming and moderately Calvinist'.[3] However, whatever his own convictions, the queen's secretary had a responsibility to queen and country. He had seen the devastating results of conviction politics and knew that in order to establish a Protestant commonwealth it was necessary to take the long view. England's future hung on the slender thread of one young woman's life. That woman, though obviously strong-minded and strong-willed, would need wise guidance. She would obviously marry – almost certainly with a foreign prince. Please God, she would have children. The nation's long-term fate would, thus, inevitably be tied up with the balance of Catholic and Protestant powers abroad. Bearing in mind the violent contemporary clashes of religious parties on the continent, England might find itself caught up in costly warfare. A new religious settlement, therefore, was not a simple matter of putting down a confessional marker or of negotiating appropriate alliances or of establishing England's right to determine its own religious identity or of reinforcing the supremacy of the Crown in matters ecclesiastical or, even, of steering rival religious streams into the channel of Christian unity. It was all these things. The government was facing a Herculean task. For almost a generation English society had been repeatedly shaken to its very foundations. The time had come for the restoration of peace and harmony within the context of a new national identity.

1559 was a critical year. Continental statesmen and Elizabeth's own subjects watched anxiously to see how the regime would set out its stall. It was clear to all reasonably well-informed observers that there would be a resumption of Protestant reformation but it was far from clear what kind of reformation would emerge. Would Elizabeth take up the baton which had fallen from Edward's lifeless fingers and move still closer to the doctrinal and ecclesiological positions of Geneva or Zurich? Would she backtrack and found her realm on a Lutheran or Erasmian understanding of the Christian faith? Did she even have a clear vision of the kind of English church she did want or would that church evolve, in an almost haphazard fashion, as interested parties manoeuvred, argued, struggled and jostled for power? Bitter infighting began within days of Elizabeth's accession. The Marian bishops and their followers dug their heels in very firmly, clinging to the hope that the new reign would be as short as the two which had preceded it. As long as they formed part of the decision-making process there would be no abandonment of papal allegiance or Catholic doctrine or the ceremonial attached to that doctrine. But exiles were now scurrying back from the Protestant hotspots of the continent with a variety of versions of what reformed Christians should believe and how they should organise the church (see below, pp. 340ff). Acrimonious rivalry between the various parties ruled out the possibility of compromise. Yet, compromise there would have to be if the desired goals of peace and unity were to be achieved.

No one was more aware of the difficult task facing the government than Elizabeth herself. She could not yet feel secure on her throne and it is scarcely surprising that her behaviour during this disturbed and disturbing year wavered between firm assertions of authority and anxious seeking of advice. One thing the queen and her Council were agreed upon was the necessity of working with Parliament. Mary's first proclamation had pre-empted parliamentary debate by asserting her own Catholic faith and her desire to see all her people embrace it. All unlicensed preaching and publishing had been censored upon pain of severe punishment and, though subjects had not been directly forced to confess their Catholicity, any leniency on this score had been declared temporary, 'unto such time as further order, by common assent, may be taken therein'.[4] The tone of Elizabeth's first proclamation, issued at the end of December 1558, was markedly different. Preachers were exhorted to restrict their matter to the exposition of the gospels, the epistles and the Ten Commandments. That was the extent of the new regime's censorship. Liturgy was to be restricted to 'that which is already used and by law received'.[5] This holding operation was to be in force, 'until consultation may be had by Parliament, by her majesty and the three estates of this realm, for the better conciliation and accord of such causes, as at this present are moved in matters and ceremonies of religion'.[6]

Less than a month later the first Parliament of the reign was convened. The religious debate began on 9 February and, by the 21st, was focused on consideration of a composite bill covering the royal supremacy and conformity to a new prayer book. A letter written by John Jewel, one of the returning exiles, provides a lively indication of the tensions existing at the political centre:

> The bishops are a great hindrance to us: for being . . . among the nobility and leading men in the upper house, and having none there on our side to expose their artifices and confute their falsehoods, they reign as sole monarchs in the midst of ignorant and weak men, and easily overreach our little party, either by their numbers, or their reputation for learning. The queen, meanwhile, while she openly favours our cause, yet is wonderfully afraid of allowing any innovations: this is owing partly to her own friends, by whose advice everything is carried on, and partly to the influence of Count Feria, a Spaniard and Philip's ambassador. She is, however, firmly and prudently, and piously following up her purpose, though somewhat more slowly than we could wish. And though the beginnings have hitherto seemed somewhat unfavourable, there is nevertheless reason to hope that all will be well at last.[7]

The impression is of an administration walking on eggshells – and with good reason. Mary had done a thorough job of ridding the church of progressive bishops and parish clergy.

Her restoration to the parishes of as much of the pre-Reformation ceremonies and customs as could easily be salvaged had
been popular in most areas. Senior ecclesiastics did, indeed,
make up the dominant faction in the House of Lords and the
nobility were generally conservative by nature. While the court
certainly influenced several elections to the lower house, the
Commons was very far from being 'packed' in the government's
favour. The Council did receive some help from returning
exiles. Chief among the political figures now taking their place
in society once more was the Earl of Bedford and he pledged
himself to use his patronage in the interests of evangelicals. In a
letter to a friend in Zurich he wrote:

> I can truly promise that this our religion, wounded and laid
> low as it were with a whirlwind by the tyranny of the time,
> and now, by God's blessing, again beginning by some meas-
> ure to revive, will strike its roots yet deeper and deeper; and
> that which is now creeping on and advancing by little and
> little, will grow up with greater fruitfulness and verdure. As
> far as I can, I am exerting myself in this matter to the utmost
> of my poor abilities.[8]

As well as being a privy councillor, Bedford was the most
powerful man in the South West. One of his more enduring
contributions to the evangelical cause was the securing of a
Cornish parliamentary seat for a certain Francis Walsingham.

Any experienced schoolteacher knows that it is vital, when
faced with a new class, to establish authority immediately. One
can always relax later but display weakness at the first encounter and it becomes very difficult to regain control. Elizabeth
and her Council adhered to this principle at the opening of the
1559 Parliament. Dr Richard Cox, recently returned from the
continent, was appointed to preach the inaugural sermon.
Calvin was being charitable when he described Cox as possessing 'a proud and confident manner'. His ninety-minute
harangue lambasted the leaders of the Marian regime and set

a militant tone for change. This was followed up by Nicholas Bacon, the new Lord Keeper of the Great Seal, when he read the session's opening speech. He succinctly stated the primary task facing Parliament: the 'well-making of laws for the according and uniting of the people of this realm into a uniform order of religion'. The basic concerns of government had not changed since the days of Henry VIII. Bacon even borrowed the rhetoric employed by the old king in his famous speech of 1545, delivered in the very same chamber. Members, he instructed, were to debate without resort to 'sophistical, captious and frivolous arguments' more suited to theologians than parliamentarians. Nor were they to hurl back and forth terms of abuse, such as 'papist' and 'heretic'.[9]

The speech was based on two government assumptions. The first was that matters of religious belief and practice could be settled by the monarch in Parliament. Cromwell had anchored the Reformation in statute law and Mary had been obliged to go through Parliament in order to abrogate the right of Lords and Commons to settle issues of doctrine and liturgy. Now the government was reclaiming the rights their Henrician and Edwardian predecessors had gained. (This would later pose problems for Elizabeth. When she and the Commons majority parted company on religious issues she found it expedient to restrict decision-making to herself and her bishops in Convocation.) The second assumption was that in such deeply felt affairs touching belief and conscience government could dictate the mood of debate. If Bacon thought that the men assembled to hear him would restrain themselves in the forthcoming religious discussions he was deluding himself.

The legislation which would establish for all time the legal basis of the Church of England was tossed back and forth between Commons, Lords and Council from 9 February to 29 April. Debate took place in an atmosphere of mutual hostility and fear. It was not simply a matter of Protestant versus Catholic. The bishops and their allies were very sure of themselves. England was ringed by Catholic nations. It seemed

scarcely feasible that it could maintain its religious independence in the long term. If anything were to happen to Elizabeth,
the last of the Tudor line, there would be no one to come to the
country's aid. Some members of the Commons sympathetic to
reform were nervous about being seen to support it. The
stench of the Smithfield fires was still metaphorically in their
nostrils. Commitment and conviction there certainly were but
there was also a miasma of apprehension wafting about
Westminster. What added to the tension was the sheer
complexity of the task facing Parliament. All the religious
legislation of the previous three reigns had to be examined,
sifted and either repealed or reworded to fit the new situation.
Small wonder that the parliamentarians found themselves
drafting, redrafting and amending the measures that came
before them. Foreign diplomats watched with some bemuse-
ment the labyrinthine activities of the legislators:

> Parliament has not yet come to any decision about a 'Bill', so
> called by them . . . whereby it is proposed to give ecclesiasti-
> cal authority to the Queen, and to annual almost all public
> and private Acts enacted and ordained by the late Queen. As
> the 'Bill' contains very many clauses, an order became neces-
> sary for its examination, clause by clause . . . These
> examinations and debates are made by the Lower House, and
> when they are concluded, the Bill will be sent to the Upper
> House, to which however as yet nothing has been sent.[10]

The commons had first proposed two separate bills, one
establishing the royal supremacy, the other imposing uniformity
based on adherence to the 1552 prayer book. By 21 February
this scheme had been abandoned in favour of a composite
measure. Opposition to royal headship had been voiced not
only by Catholics but also by some evangelicals, on the basis
that the Bible forbade women from exercising authority in the
church. The debate was not helped by the publication a few
months before of a book which had raised a storm in Protestant

lands. The Scottish cleric John Knox published in Geneva *The First Blast of the Trumpet against the Monstrous Regiment of Women*. When the fiery Scot asserted that 'to promote a woman to bear rule, superiority, dominion or empire above any realm is repugnant to nature, contrary to God, and, finally, it is the subversion of good order, of all equity and justice', he had in mind the Catholic queens and regents, Mary Tudor, Mary of Guise and Catherine de' Medici.[11] Knox stated that subjects were under no obligation to render obedience to such harpies. It was unfortunate that the *First Blast* hit the bookshops shortly before Elizabeth's accession. She took the broadside personally and was very wary of any returning exiles who might be tarred with the Knoxian brush. Sir Anthony Cooke, Cecil's father-in-law, seems to have been one of those who disagreed with the proposal to recognise the queen's headship of the church. His speeches in Parliament certainly upset the evangelical apple cart. John Jewel complained that Cooke 'defends some scheme of his own, I know not what, most obstinately, and is mightily angry with us all'.[12] This warns us against the assumption that the returning exiles constituted a united 'Puritan party' with an agreed agenda for further reform. Indeed, we need to pause in the narrative at this point to consider just what had been happening in those evangelical refuges where English exiles had sojourned during Mary's reign.

The strongest theological magnets drawing English evangelicals in the 1550s were Peter Martyr in Strasbourg, Heinrich Bullinger in Zurich and John Calvin in Geneva. Several other municipalities had set up Reformed constitutions but it was the Protestant 'stars' that all exiles wanted to hear. Such politically active theologians had established versions of the godly commonwealth that appealed enormously to those shaking the dust off their shoes against Marian England. To them it must have seemed that the portals of heaven on earth had been opened to them; they found themselves in well-ordered Christian communities that were as near perfection as anything to be found in this life. However, all was very far from being sweetness and light among the exiles. Not unnaturally, they aspired, as soon as Antichrist was overthrown in England, to bring home the revelations they had received. The problem was that not all Englishmen abroad agreed about what those truths were.

In 1554 William Whittingham, Oxford scholar and former fellow of All Souls, arrived in Frankfurt. He became a pastor to the English church there, which was led by John Knox, and set about providing a prayer book for the use of his fellow countrymen. As a committed Calvinist, his liturgical and theological thinking differed from those who shared a commitment to Cranmer's second prayer book. Some of them refused to accept Whittingham's worship manual and they found a champion in Richard Cox, who arrived early in 1555. Cox and his friends were determined to remain faithful to the 1552 liturgy. Both sides appealed to Calvin and Cox's letter gives a good impression of the issues which were dividing the refugee church:

> we freely relinquished all those ceremonies which were regarded by our brethren as offensive and inconvenient. For we gave up private baptisms, confirmation of children, saints' days, kneeling at the holy communion, the linen surplices of the ministers, crosses, and other things of like character. And we gave them up, not as being impure and papistical, which certain of our brethren often charged them as being; but whereas they were in their own nature indifferent ... we notwithstanding chose rather to lay them aside than to offend the mind or alienate the affections of the brethren ... [13]

The civic authorities at Frankfurt were annoyed by the illtempered squabbling of their guests and expelled Knox, who headed for Geneva in March 1555. Whittingham tried to live with a form of worship he regarded as an unholy compromise with Rome but, six months later, he followed Knox.

This conflict proved to be a precursor to the divisions which were to trouble the Elizabethan church. They fall into two overlapping categories, liturgy and ecclesiology. There were those who, like Bishop Hooper in Edward's reign, objected to anything in religious ritual, such as vestments and ornaments, that to their minds smacked of Rome. They refused to regard the 1552 prayer book (dismissed by Knox as a 'mingle-mangle') as the last word in Reformed worship. They looked for their model to Geneva, with its simple, unadorned church interiors which were, essentially, preaching halls. In whitewashed, plain-glassed interiors the pulpit took pride of place and no ornamentation, in the form of either pictures or music, distracted worshippers from the word of God. For guidance in church government these 'Puritans' (This term of oprobium now became common) looked to the New Testament. What they read there of the life of the first Christian communities seemed to be much at variance with the episcopal ordering of national churches which had developed throughout the Christian epoch. In the first century local churches survived in an environment which was, in many respects, hostile. The development of regional overseers – bishops – and of the papacy had brought into being a different concept of the 'visible church'. When Christianity became the official religion of the Roman Empire and when missionary activity led to the conversion of whole tribes complex issues of church–state relations inevitably arose. It was only extremists who took the New Testament pattern to its logical conclusion and argued for a complete separation of the two spheres; for independent, autonomous congregations in which spiritual and moral discipline would lie entirely in the hands of ministers. Anabaptists regarded admission to church membership as voluntary and marked by adult baptism. Such teaching horrified all mainstream Protestant leaders. Non-conformity was not an option in the mid-sixteenth century. Quite apart from the challenge such radicalism presented to existing episcopal organisation, there was the uncomfortable fact that the Protestant churches needed the protection of the civil powers. The battle against 'Roman tyranny' had, over the centuries, been fought by emperors, kings, princes and municipal authorities. Godly commonwealths could only be established and maintained by civil law.

The followers of Calvin and Zwingli were basically in agreement that the magistrate and the minister should work together in the ideal Christian community to sustain and, where necessary, enforce high moral standards and the unhindered teaching of gospel truth. They upheld a collegial style of church leadership in which pastors and their overseers met in synod to encourage, exhort and support one another in the work of ministry. But what was possible to achieve in the small urban centres of Switzerland and South Germany was far from easy to impose on England's ancient and multi-layered governmental system – particularly if the reigning sovereign was not in full accord with Puritan principles. The exiles were returning to a church but half reformed and many were perplexed as to what attitude to take. Should they seek office in the hope of effecting further change or hold aloof and, by so doing, make their point?

> Let others have their bishoprics; my Cleeve is enough for me. Many of the bishops would most willingly change conditions with me; though one or two, perhaps a little ambitious, might decline doing so. And you must know that I myself was to be enrolled among their number; but I implored some of our leading men, and my intimate friends, that my name should be erased from the list . . . When I was lately in London, one of the privy councillors and Parker, the archbishop of Canterbury, threatened me with I know not what bishopric. But I hope for better things; for I cannot be ambitious of so much misery. I am king here in my parish.[14]

So wrote John Parkhurst, vicar of Bishop's Cleve, Gloucestershire, and late of Zurich, in December 1559. Sadly, he was unable to resist preferment indefinitely and was, the following September, consecrated as Bishop of Norwich, in which office he suffered to the full the frustrations and pressures he had feared. The queen, for her part, was just as trapped as ardent reformers like

Parkhurst, when it came to staffing her church. The sacking and resignation of Marian clergy left large gaps in the parishes and on the episcopal bench and many of these had to be filled with men of what one commentator called a 'Germanical nature'.[15]

Absence from England during Mary's reign had enabled exiles to take a detached view of what was happening in their country. They wrestled with such questions as 'Why did God allow the western church to fall into such serious error?', 'Why was he permitting so many English saints to be slaughtered?' and 'What role was he preparing England to play in the restoration of true religion?' The humid religious climate of the Reformed havens nurtured a whole scholarly literature destined to have a profound effect on the development of Elizabethan Protestantism. John Bale was a prolific writer and controversialist who spent most of his refugee years in Basle, a major publishing centre and a home to reformers of widely differing views. Here Calvin came to study and here Erasmus was buried. The English community in the city was not immune to the rivalries which were disturbing Frankfurt but Basle was a more congenial centre for scholarly study. The university enjoyed an excellent reputation and free debate was encouraged. Bale's most influential work was *Scriptorum Illustrium maioris Britanniae Catalogus*, a monumental volume of more than a thousand pages. Ostensibly it was a catalogue of over fourteen hundred writers, scholars and others who had contributed to the evolution of English culture but Bale's primary objective was to 'justify the ways of God to men' by demonstrating how Bible prophecy, and particularly the apocalyptic vision of the Book of Revelation, had been worked out in the history of the British people. England, he sought to demonstrate, had been singled out by God for a special role in the preservation, manifestation and propagation of Gospel truth.

John Foxe had also found a home in the agreeable atmosphere of Basle and it was here that he brought to fruition his grand design of producing a comprehensive church history. The first edition, in Latin, was superseded in 1563 by an English version, whose partisan and nationalistic purpose, as we have seen, was clearly stated in its title: *Acts and Monuments of these latter perillous days touching matters of the Churche, wherein are comprehended and described the great persecutions and horrible troubles that have been wrought and practised by the Roman Prelates speciallye in this realme of England and Scotland* ... Implicit in this title are three fundamental truths as understood by the English reformers: the Christian church is not to be identified with any human organisation, but is the invisible congregation of true believers throughout time and space. By identifying itself as *the* church and persecuting true believers, Rome has shown itself to be the abode of Antichrist. In the providence of God Britain has a special and important role to play in the Christian story. Foxe worked assiduously at his task. Just as Bale had visited many of the monastic libraries at the time of the dissolution and later tirelessly tracked down rare copies of books in order to compose his impressive catalogue, so Foxe was constantly interviewing and corresponding with men and women who had witnessed or personally experienced acts of persecution. Both of these books accumulated massive volumes of evidence to demonstrate that the Reformation was not some newfangled thing, some passing fashion, some latter-day aberration, but, on the contrary, was in the mainstream of human history – or, more importantly, of divine history. If it appeared new and exciting and turbulent it was only because it was rediscovering what had been new, exciting and turbulent in the era of the New Testament church.

One more book written during the years of evangelical exile must be mentioned. It was the work of William Whittingham, whom we have already met as a follower of Calvin and Knox. It was while he was in Geneva between 1555 and 1560 that he masterminded a new English translation of Holy Scripture. What came to be known as the Geneva Bible was a team effort. Whittingham and his colleagues drew on the very latest work done by continental scholars on the best available Hebrew and Greek documents to produce a version which was as accurate as possible. They furnished their text with woodcut illustrations, maps, charts and philological, geographical and historical notes. For the first time they divided the chapters into numbered verses. The Geneva Bible was a study Bible and everything was done to make it as informative and easy to read as possible. This included providing the original with a running commentary which was Calvinistic, partisan and, in many places, controversial, especially in its exegesis of the book of Revelation. For example, the beast from the bottomless pit of Revelation 11: 7 was unhesitatingly identified with 'the Pope which hath his power out of hell and cometh thence'. Early in Elizabeth's reign the Geneva Bible established itself as the most popular version available. It never received the royal licence because the Queen insisted that it should be submitted to the archbishops for their approval, an imprimatur Whittingham was not disposed to seek. This did not prevent the book running through forty editions during Elizabeth's reign.

These three books were immensely influential in shaping the religious life of England after 1558. However, a case could be made for suggesting that another was even more effective in moulding the thinking of ordinary people. Congregational singing has been called the 'secret weapon of the Reformation'. It was the means by which – almost subliminally – the words of Scripture and Protestant doctrine entered the consciousness of illiterate and semi-literate worshippers. The story of congregational singing began in the reign of Edward VI, when Thomas Sternhold, a member of the royal chamber, produced a collection of nineteen psalms arranged to be sung metrically. These were used in the exiled evangelical communities and more psalms were added by Whittingham and others. The number of the Old Testament hymns used in Protestant worship gradually increased and it was in 1562 that the publisher John Day brought out the first complete metrical psalter. The principal contributor to the new book was John Hopkins, a Suffolk schoolmaster who had not been numbered among the exiles. The new collection soon became known as 'Sternhold and Hopkins' and proved to be a runaway bestseller. It had always been an objective of the reformers to involve the laity more in regular worship, and psalm singing proved to be the most effective tool. Many of the tunes used came from Geneva and some were appropriated from popular ballads of the day. Elizabeth disliked what she called these 'Geneva jigs' but they were immediately popular with many of her subjects. As early as March 1560 John Jewel could report:

> The people are everywhere exceedingly inclined to the better part. The practice of joining in church music has very much conduced to this. For as soon as they had once commenced singing in public, in only one little church in London, immediately not only the churches in the neighbourhood, but even the towns far distant, began to vie with each other in the same practice. You may now sometimes see at Paul's cross, after the service, six thousand persons, old and young, of both sexes, all singing together and praising God.[16]

Over the next couple of centuries 'Sternhold and Hopkins' was outsold only by the prayer book and the Authorised Version of the Bible. English hymnody had arrived.

After this excursus we must return to the fraught situation existing in England in the first half of 1559. The revised Supremacy-cum-Uniformity bill bumped its way uncertainly through the Commons but when it was sent to the upper house the sparks really began to fly. Bishops and conservative peers resisted the abandoning of papal and episcopal control of church affairs. Argument became heated and personal. At one point Bedford denounced the Bishop of Ely and Viscount Montague for consorting with whores in Rome. Such slanging matches set the tone and made it clear that the necessary legislation would not get through before Easter. Queen and Council had wanted to prorogue Parliament but, in urgent, last-minute consultation, they realised that different tactics would have to be applied. Lords and Commons were instructed to reconvene after Easter and, meanwhile, arrangements were made for a special event to take place in Westminster Abbey. This would be a full debate between doctors of the church about the theological issues involved in the proposed new policy. This had the appearance of being fair to all parties. Christian truth would be openly debated in an appropriate setting without any political strings attached. In reality, the disputation was a piece of theatre to distract attention from the government's determination to have its own way. It was staged as much for the benefit of foreign observers as for English partisans. Elizabeth could not be unaware that the eyes of the continental Catholic powers were upon her. As well as their own rivalries, they were waging their own internal wars against heretical minorities and there was always a possibility that, urged on by the pope, they might sink their differences to prevent the emergence of another Protestant power. A further advantage of the delay was that it gave the Council time to do some number-crunching in order to ensure majorities when Parliament reassembled.

The disputation began on Friday, 31 March and was scheduled to be completed before Parliament reassembled on 3 April. Two teams of eight disputants were appointed and a crowd gathered in the abbey to cheer on their champions or to hear for themselves the arguments presented by each side. The three points for debate were the need for services in the vernacular, the freedom of national churches to decide their own ceremonies and the nature of Christ's presence in the communion service. In fact, the event never got much further than the first day. When the parties reconvened on Monday, 2 April, the Catholic bishops complained, probably with some justification, that the rules of debate had been rigged against them; they had been ordered to present their case first, which gave the opposition the advantage of answering all the points against them without the Catholics being able to counter-attack. Whether or not, as Protestant commentators alleged, the conservatives ruined their own case with weak arguments and resort to invective, they were completely outmanoeuvred. Not only did the

debate break up in unseemly bickering over procedure, but also
two of the most effective Catholic controversialists, the bishops
of Winchester and Lincoln, played into the government's hands
by refusing to be bound by the rules. 'The two good bishops,
inflamed with zeal for God, said most boldly that they would
not consent nor ever change their opinion for any fear. They
were answered that this was the will of the queen, and that they
would be punished for their disobedience.'[17] In their unguarded
anger, they had either stated or implied that the queen was a
schismatic and for this they were conveyed to the Tower on the
very day that the Parliament men returned to their chambers.
According to Jewel, 'The rest are bound in recognizances to
appear at court from day to day, and await the determination of
the council respecting them.'[18]

The message was not wasted on opponents of the government's policy. A new Supremacy bill naming the queen as
'Governor' rather than 'Head' of the church was introduced
and passed through Parliament with little difficulty. However, a
fresh Uniformity measure fared less well. The 1552 prayer
book had been tweaked in one or two places in the hope of
satisfying traditionalists. Crucially the words of administration
at the communion were deliberately fudged in order to accommodate those who believed in the real presence. In the second
prayer book the recipient was enjoined to 'remember that
Christ died for thee and be thankful'. Now, words from the first
prayer book were reintroduced: 'The body of our Lord Jesus
Christ which was given . . . the blood of our Lord Jesus Christ
which was shed for thee preserve thy body and soul unto everlasting life'. It seems that Elizabeth had personally endorsed
this change, believing, as she said, 'In the sacrament of the altar,
some thinks [one] thing, some other, whose judgement is best
God knows.'[19] Even so, the bill only scraped through the upper
house by three votes. Had the imprisoned bishops been present
to add their voices to those of all their colleagues who opposed
the bill the outcome would have been different. As it was, the
Act of Uniformity made history by being the first doctrinal

measure to become law without a single episcopal vote being cast in its favour.

The change was revolutionary; its implementation was evolutionary. Church doctrine was enforceable by law. Ministers had to use the revised prayer book. Parishioners had to attend divine service regularly, on pain of a fine. Clergy who refused the oath of Supremacy were deprived. This included several bishops, who were now replaced with safe Protestants. Anyone convicted of upholding the authority of the pope risked imprisonment and, on the third offence, prosecution for treason. Yet enforcement was cautious. Recalcitrant bishops were allowed to retire into private life as long as they behaved themselves. Elizabeth went slowly about the work of finding replacements. Several had to be selected from among the returning exiles, for they were obviously men of vision and erudition, but the queen did her best to select moderates, rather than zealots who might not prove malleable to the royal will. A visitation of every parish in the summer led to the deprivation of only around three hundred priests. Ardent reformers were frustrated by the leniency shown to open or covert papists. John Jewel (who became Bishop of Salisbury in January 1560) contrasted their fate with that of evangelicals in the previous reign:

> Our adversaries always acted with precipitancy, without precedent, without authority, without law; while we manage everything with so much deliberation, and prudence, and wariness, and circumspection, as if God himself could scarce retain his authority without our ordinances and precautions.

Of the queen, Jewel observed:

> excellent as she is, and earnest in the cause of true religion, notwithstanding she desires a thorough change as early as possible, [she] cannot however be induced to effect such change without the sanction of law; lest the matter should

seem to have been accomplished . . . in compliance with the
impulse of a furious multitude.[20]

The instinct of Elizabeth and Cecil was, undoubtedly, correct.
They had experienced at first hand the bitter divisions caused
by the religious persecution of the Marian regime. They desired
openly to distance themselves from the kind of oppression,
justified by religion, currently prevalent in the Spanish
Netherlands. They knew how important it was to carry public
opinion with them. That is not to say that they would have
ascribed to the aphorism *vox populi vox dei*; they had both lived
through times of working-class revolt and believed wholeheartedly in a divinely ordained hierarchic society in which every
subject knew his/her place and, when necessary, had to be kept
in it. But it was important to carry the political nation with them
and trust that the leaders of local society would, in their turn,
ensure the compliance of the populace.

Much has been written about the religious opinions of
Elizabeth. She who had carefully kept her beliefs to herself in
Mary's reign did not parade them ostentatiously once she had
acquired the crown. There was certainly sound political reason
for this; danger for queen and country had certainly not gone
away. The royal regimes of France and Scotland were closely
allied and staunchly Catholic. In July matters took a dramatic
turn for the worse. Henry II of France was killed in a jousting
accident. His son became king as Francis II and the fact that
he was married to Mary Stuart meant that the crowns of
England's closest potential enemies were united. It was part
of their diplomatic stance that Mary was the rightful queen of
England by virtue of her descent from Henry VIII's sister,
Margaret, and they blatantly quartered the royal English arms
with their own. The Stuart regime was opposed in Scotland by
a caucus of Protestant nobles (fired up by the preaching of
John Knox) who called themselves the Lords of the
Congregation. Cecil supported them diplomatically and was
eager that England should provide more tangible aid. That

created a dilemma for Elizabeth: helping Mary's enemies might deflect her from any possible cross-border activity but it would be encouraging rebels in their actions against their divinely anointed sovereign. As well as being a risky precedent, that went against Elizabeth's firm belief in the sacredness of Christian monarchy. The same dilemma confronted her in later years when she was pressed to support the Protestant subjects of Philip II in the Low Countries.

Successful politics demands pragmatism. Politically the queen had to be all things to all men. She told the Spanish ambassador that her understanding of the communion service differed little from his. She repeatedly assured foreign diplomats that she would not take the title of Supreme Head of the church. When writing to Protestant German princes she urged brotherly love between all those who had escaped the 'darkness and filth of popery'. In her public appearances Elizabeth showed herself to be a consummate actress who studied her role diligently in order to present to her audiences the image of the queen they wanted to see. At her first appearance in London on the eve of her coronation she graciously received the gift of a Bible at the Little Conduit in Cheapside. 'At the receipt whereof, how reverently did she with both her hands take it, kiss it and lay it upon her breast, to the great comfort of the lookers-on.'[21] In her private chapel she ordered the celebrant not to elevate the host and, when he ignored this prohibition, she swept out. That was a Protestant statement more effective than any sermon. Yet, she persistently, to the distraction of her anti-ceremonial advisers, persisted in having her communion table decorated with cross and candlesticks. John Jewel, knowing how people looked to the queen for an example, was appalled:

> That little silver cross of ill-omened origin, still maintains its place in the queen's chapel. Wretched me! This thing will soon be drawn into a precedent. There was at one time some hope of its being removed; and we all diligently exerted ourselves, and still continue to do so . . . But as far as I can

perceive, it is now a hopeless case. Such is the obstinacy of
some minds [i.e. the queen's].[22]

The writer gloomily regarded this royal peccadillo as symbolic
of a lack of enthusiasm for reform: 'The slow-paced horses
retard the chariot,'[23] he grumbled.

Elizabeth's 'obstinacy' sprang not from doctrinal conviction
but from cultural preference. She had been brought up in the
colourful atmosphere of royal courts and loved beautiful things.
Symbolism had always been a part of her life – the royal coat of
arms on the canopy of her throne and the ceremonial livery of
her guards; the illuminated capitals of the charters she signed;
the heraldic designs engraved on the costly gifts she received at
New Year from her wealthier courtiers. These things were
important to her and she expected to continue enjoying them
when she attended divine service. Most ornate trappings had
been stripped from the royal chapel but Elizabeth would not be
deprived of all religious symbols. She could never identify with
the austere worship of Calvin's disciples. One aspect of the
reformed faith she particularly loathed was clerical marriage.
She could not force ministers and bishops to remain celibate;
that would have sent out unacceptable pro-Roman signals. But
she could and did withhold her favour from those who offended
by taking wives – as most did. In the day-to-day life of the
church the existence of young families in the vicarage was one
of the most obvious signs of change but Elizabeth could never
accustom herself to it. It must be said that she also resented
members of her own household taking wives or husbands.
Having, herself, foresworn the married state, she seemed to
expect others to make the same sacrifice.

Elizabeth's personal religion was a compound of humanistic
Protestantism, aesthetic indulgence and a strong sense of duty.
She was still able to keep it separate from the official religion of
the nation, as she had done in the dark days of the mid-1550s.
For that reason we are still unable to penetrate to its core. If we
can find any word that, at least partially, throws light on her

inner feelings that word is 'peace'. It figures prominently in *Precationes privatae*, a book of prayers and Scripture extracts published in 1563, perhaps in emulation of Catherine Parr's *Prayers or Meditations*. One typical extract reads,

> God of peace and concord, who hast chosen me Thy hand-maid to be over Thy people that I may preserve them in Thy peace, be present and rule me with the Spirit of Thy wisdom, that according to Thy will I may defend a Christian peace with all peoples. In Christ Thy Son (who is our peace) make us all be of one accord, so that Thy enemies may be ruled by Thy hand, and confound them with Thy outstretched arm. Thou Thyself give us Thy peace, because there is no other who fights for us if not Thou, our God.[24]

Peace in the confrontational realities of the 1560s could only be achieved by doctrinal fudge and a great deal of turning of blind eyes, a state of affairs which satisfied very few of Elizabeth's subjects who cared about religion. The *media via* which the queen is sometimes said to have brought into being, creating a church with a Calvinist theology and Catholic liturgy, is a fiction. She and her advisers were not engaged in an exercise of constructive compromise; they were trying to find a path through a minefield so as to detonate as few explosions as possible.

In June a set of injunctions was issued for the use of parish clergy. They were based on those produced in 1547 in the name of King Edward, with a few omissions but with several new instructions added. In all there were fifty-two separate clauses, plus an extensive coda. All these were to be read in every church twice a year! The Elizabethan additions make interesting study because they indicate some of the things which were happening throughout the land and which were disturbing the government. We are not surprised to discover censorship of religious books; every regime did its best to muzzle the underground press. Prohibition of unlicensed preaching and public debate of religious issues are also restrictions we would expect to see. But now every parish was to appoint 'three or four discreet men' to enforce church attendance on all Sundays and holy days. They were to see that worshippers 'there continue the whole time of godly service'. Moreover, people were to support their parish churches and not to 'resort to any other church in time of common prayer or preaching'. From all this we can infer that there were two extreme reactions to religious controversy: while some enthusiasts left their own churches to go sermon-tasting, their more disillusioned neighbours absented themselves altogether or put in only token appearances. The vexed question of communion table versus altar was 'solved' by a decree that it was to be placed against the east end of the church 'where the altar stood' but brought back into the chancel for the sacramental service, 'whereby the minister may be more conveniently heard of the communicants . . . and the communicants also more conveniently and in more number communicate with the said minister'. In effect this enabled those who wanted to go on thinking of the holy table as an altar to do so. Many were the clergy who 'forgot' to move it before the celebration. The popularity of congregational singing was acknowledged:

> for the comforting of such that delight in music, it may be permitted, that in the beginning, or in the end of common prayers, either at morning or evening, there may be sung an hymn, or suchlike song to the praise of Almighty God, in the best sort of melody and music that may be conveniently devised, having respect that the sentence [i.e. 'sense'] of the hymn may be understood and perceived.[25]

The visitation which followed these injunctions was carried out with zest by the appointed commissioners. A new round of iconoclasm was launched as churches were purged of the images and furnishings reinstated by the last regime. Once again there were prominent bonfires of roods, crucifixes and painted panels as the queen's agents went about the final purification of church interiors with a will. Or were they the queen's agents? Elizabeth demonstrated that ability to decree policy and then distance herself from it that would become the bane of her councillors' lives. The tasks of the commissioners were quite clear and included removal of offending features from churches and seeking out of any items that had been hidden away in people's houses. Yet Edwin Sandys, Bishop of London, found himself in trouble for ensuring that royal instructions were carried out to the letter:

> The queen's majesty considered it not contrary to the word of God . . . that the image of Christ crucified with [those of] Mary and [Saint] John, should be placed as heretofore, in some conspicuous part of the church, where they might more readily be seen by all the people. Some of us [bishops] thought far otherwise, and more especially as all images of every kind were at our last visitation, not only taken down, but also burnt, and that too by public authority . . . As to myself, because I was rather vehement in this matter, and could by no means consent that an occasion of stumbling should be afforded to the church of Christ, I was very near being deposed from my office, and incurring the displeasure of the queen. But God, in whose hands are the hearts of kings, gave us tranquillity instead of a tempest, and delivered the church of England from stumblingblocks of this kind.[26]

Elizabeth was, clearly, very nervous about being associated with such dramatic expressions of Protestant backlash, particularly in her capital. She was always conscious of the impression she was giving to foreign diplomats and her own powerful nobles. This goes some of the way towards explaining her adherence to modest decoration in her own chapel. She might hope that such survivals of the old religion would send a signal to foreign courts that Catholic custom had not been totally abandoned. The queen's Janus-like attitude was a constant irritant to her new bishops and her more radical clergy. It was

in 1586 that a petition to Parliament grumbled about the halting nature of reform:

> in the beginning of her Majesty's reign, a number of worthy
> men . . . desired such a book and such order for discipline in
> the church, as they had seen in the best reformed churches
> abroad. But any change from [what] was used concerning
> religion in Queen Mary's days being then thought by such as
> rule the state so dangerous . . . that [what] was then used
> must be retained still, or the former order of King Edward
> [i.e. the 1549 prayer book], a number were wrought diversely
> to yield thereunto, as bearing with it and tolerating it for a
> time, which yet some of the sounder and sincerer could never
> be brought unto.[27]

In the country at large the pace of reform inevitably varied
from parish to parish. The churchwardens of St Michael's,
Gloucester, hastened, in 1559, to acquire copies of the new
prayer book. The following year they disposed of unwanted
church goods and used the proceeds to pay for men to whitewash the church interior. They had to buy extra communion
bread and wine because many of the congregation were eager to
receive the sacrament as presented in the reformed liturgy. And
they paid a bellringer to summon people to hear sermons on
special occasions. But St Michael's was far from being typical;
most neighbouring parishes were much more conservative.[28]

The majority of the queen's subjects were still uncomfortable
about abandoning the ways of their forefathers but much turbulent water had passed under the bridge since the Pilgrimage of
Grace and the number of people prepared to 'stand up and be
counted' as subjects of the pope was small. And the government
denied them goads against which to kick. The Acts of Supremacy
and Uniformity certainly drew a line in the sand but, in practice,
that line tended to be wavy and windblown. Offenders were not
harried from the land or threatened with dire persecution. They
were given every encouragement to make at least an outward

conformity. Proceedings against parishioners who absented themselves from divine service were sporadic. Particularly throughout rural England, away from the hotspots of ideological conflict, loyalty to and affection for the parish churches were strong. Many priests did their best to make the new worship sound and look as much as possible like the old. Some of them visited private houses to say mass in secret. The Catholic leaders, the Marian bishops, were denied crowns of martyrdom, such as Cranmer and his colleagues had received. They were held in relatively comfortable house arrest and carefully watched. Because the messages going out from Westminster were fuzzy the reaction from Rome tended to be equally indistinct. Catholic observers had reason to hope that the last Tudor might edge quietly towards the old faith. Failing that, a royal marriage or a royal death might change the situation overnight. In October 1563 many prayers appeared to be answered when Elizabeth was smitten with smallpox. Catholics saw this as divine judgement but were obliged to listen to the rejoicing of their opponents when her majesty made a complete recovery. The pope sent no clear directions instructing his people to resist the new regime, and this was, in part, thanks to the influence of Philip of Spain, who long hoped to see Elizabeth brought within the Habsburg ambit by marriage to himself or some other suitable prince. It was not until 1566 that an unequivocal and well-publicised order went out from the Vatican constraining Catholics to absent themselves from Protestant worship. For the first decade of the reign it seemed that Elizabeth's softly-softly approach was bearing fruit. There was no tidal wave of faith emigrants eager to shake the dust off their shoes against heretic England. It may well have been only after Elizabeth's dramatic deliverance from her illness that real alarm bells began to sound in Rome and its satellite centres. It became gradually apparent that time might be on the enemy's side. As committed priests and lay Catholics died off, official Protestantism would inevitably strengthen its hold. Certainly it was in the mid-1560s that organised opposition to Elizabeth's rule began.

A trickle of individuals who declined to swear allegiance to the heretic queen had already begun to make their way across the Channel in search of more congenial habitation. As with the earlier evangelical exodus, it tended to be the wealthier individuals and families who were in a position to pull up their roots. Such emigrants were not as numerous as the Marian Protestants who voted with their feet but they were destined to be even more troublesome. There were several Catholic communities on the continent ready to welcome them and just as refugee evangelicals encountered more extreme views in Geneva or Zurich, so Catholic fugitives discovered a more stringent and aggressive brand of their religion in Rome or Louvain (sometimes called the 'Catholic Geneva'). Several of the exiles occupied themselves, as their Protestant predecessors had done, in polemical writings directed against the status quo in their native land. John Gibbons headed the Jesuit college at Trèves but was better known for his three-volume catalogue, *Concertatio Ecclesiae Catholicae in Anglia adversus Calvinopapistas et Puritanos sub Elizabetha...* This was a counterblast to Foxe's *Actes and Monuments*, describing the sufferings endured by English Catholics for their faith. Thomas Stapleton, another Oxford man, was the most prodigious – and was widely recognised as the most effective – controversialist of his day. Between 1565 and 1567 he published no fewer than seven well-researched and well-argued works asserting the continuity of Catholic faith in England from early times. Thomas Harding, one-time Professor of Hebrew at Oxford, engaged John Jewel in a long-running written controversy during the 1560s. Nicholas Sanders, yet another Oxford scholar, wrote an influential account of the persecutions of his co-religionists, *De visibili Monarchiae Ecclesiae*, and died in 1581, after being involved in an abortive invasion of Ireland.

Some of the early exiles eventually joined the Society of Jesus (the Jesuits), the organisation destined to play a major part in the story of Elizabethan England. Founded in Rome in 1540, this band of priests and lay brothers was committed to missionary work and education. It became the spearhead of the

Counter-Reformation after 1580, when it amalgamated its activities with those of other evangelistic agencies pledged to the extirpation of English Protestantism. Englishmen joining the society were sent to work in various centres throughout Europe. Thomas Darbishire, a nephew of Bishop Bonner, spent much of his life after 1563 teaching in Paris. William Good, an Oxford-trained cleric, worked for several years in Ireland and subsequently Flanders. Such enthusiasts were similar to their evangelical counterparts in their devotion to scholarship and their emphasis on preaching and teaching. They became skilled disputants ever ready to engage the enemies of their faith in argument, confronting the crystalline, Bible-based logic of the Calvinists with their own, equally rigid version of Christianity, culled from wide study of the Fathers. They were also inclined to use less exalted methods where they found themselves in power, such as inciting Polish mobs to break up Protestant services and drive out the worshippers. The most significant of the Catholic exiles was William Allen. He settled at Douai, in the Spanish Netherlands, and, in 1568, founded there a college for the training of priests to be sent across the Channel to succour hard-pressed Catholic households. The sober fact was dawning on the Catholic hierarchy that England would be lost if the dwindling ranks of the Catholic priesthood were not reinforced by younger men. So was born the mission to England.

The political realities at the centre of English life took on a distinctly odd appearance. Professor Collinson has called it a 'monarchical republic': 'there were two governments uneasily coexisting in Elizabethan England: the queen and her council.'[29] The leading royal advisers were William Cecil, Robert Dudley, Earl of Leicester (with whom the queen was, for many years, in love) and Sir Francis Walsingham, who, thanks to Cecil's patronage, had rapidly advanced in the queen's service and had, by late 1573, succeeded him as the queen's secretary (Cecil having been appointed Lord Treasurer). These three men, supported by the majority of the Council, were moderate Puritans who used their position to promote evangelicals to leading positions in church and state and who also strove to implement Protestant policies in national and international affairs. They shared two convictions: that they had a duty to both queen and country and that England was in dire peril of falling prey to a Catholic crusade launched from Rome. Try as they might, they could not bring their royal mistress to accept this viewpoint.

It was plain to Elizabeth's ministers, as it is now plain to historians, that they were living in an age of terror. England's position in relation to the Catholic superpowers was not dissimilar to the modern western world's confrontation with militant Islam. Holy men shrieked hatred. Zealots went on suicide missions. State-sponsored terrorism was responsible for plots and massacres. Hired assassins were employed to remove prominent 'enemies of the church'. Wherever the Privy Council looked they saw religious turmoil and they knew it could easily descend on their own country. Early in 1569 Cecil pointed out to his mistress that so far she had been lucky: Spain was preoccupied with war against the Turk; France was convulsed with internal religious strife; and Scotland was riven by noble factions which had forced the queen, Mary Stuart, to abdicate and flee into England where she was now a guest/prisoner at Tutbury Castle, Staffordshire. This state of affairs could not be expected to last. It was time to form a strong political bloc with the Protestant rulers of Denmark, Sweden and the German principalities. It would also be of inestimable benefit to the nation if her majesty would consent to marry while there was still the possibility of her bearing an heir to the throne. To all this reasoning Elizabeth turned a deaf ear.

As if on cue, real threats appeared within months. In January 1570 James Stuart, Earl of Moray, the pro-English regent in Scotland, was shot from an upstairs window in Linlithgow as he rode past. The assassin, a supporter of Mary, fled to the French court. In the following month Pope Pius V, a previous grand inquisitor and ruthless scourge of all who wandered from the path of doctrinal and moral purity, issued a bull, *Regnans in Excelsis*, against Elizabeth. Having catalogued the queen's offences against the 'true religion', Pius declared her to be 'deprived of her pretended title' and assured all who had sworn an oath to her that they were 'absolved from such an oath and any duty arising from lordship, fealty and obedience'. Anyone who 'dare to obey her orders, mandates and laws' would, like Elizabeth, henceforth be excommunicate.[30] In the autumn a long-smouldering plot burst into flames. At the centre of it was the Duke of Norfolk, who entertained the ambition of marrying Scottish Mary and helping her to claim the English throne. He was swiftly dealt with and was soon safely in the Tower. But his allies in the far North, the Earls of Westmorland and Northumberland, resorted to arms. With about 5,500 men they seized Durham and there drew support from Catholic sympathisers who still formed the majority in the remoter parts of the country. The rebels were not slow to demonstrate their religious allegiance.

> they not only threw down the communion tables, tore in pieces the holy bible and godly books, and trod under foot the printed homilies, but also again set up the blasphemous mass as a sacrifice for the living and the dead. And as a farther cloak for their pretended piety, they caused [to be set up] some crosses and some banners of certain saints, whom they believed to be their patrons and defenders.[31]

When a priest was found to conduct a mass in Durham Cathedral, crowds flocked to attend. However, this was no rerun of the Pilgrimage of Grace. Few of the leaders of northern society had any stomach for a challenge to the regime. Whatever their religious allegiance, they were more committed to their legitimate queen. Or, perhaps, they were just tired of sectarian strife. Elizabeth's instinct to keep the religious temperature as low as possible seemed to be paying off. The earls headed for Tutbury to rescue Mary but, with their support dwindling, they had no alternative but to head northwards to the border and, in any case, Mary had already been moved to Coventry. Elizabeth had been frightened and angry. Like her father in 1537, she demanded severe retribution. Her generals interpreted their instructions rather loosely but, even so, it appears that some five hundred of the 'meaner sort' met a traitor's death. Northumberland was handed over by the Scots two years later and executed. Westmorland eked out a dreary existence for several years in the Netherlands as a pensioner of Spain.

The collapse of the rebellion was not the end of the matter. In sniffing out the plot Cecil had discovered a network of Catholic activists. The truth of what came to be called the 'Ridolfi Plot' is still wrapped in layers of mystery. Cecil (who became Baron Burghley in February 1571) presented his findings as an international conspiracy whose tentacles spread from London to the English shires, Scotland, Flanders, Spain and Rome. At its centre was Roberto Ridolfi, a Florentine banker who travelled widely and who, when the story begins, was resident in London. What remains unclear is whether Ridolfi was an arch-conspirator, an agent provocateur in Cecil's employ, a dupe or a self-deluding adventurer with exaggerated ideas of his own importance. Cecil knew from his counter-espionage activities that the web of Catholic activists was wide, that it embraced the Spanish ambassador, Guerau de Spes, the Duke of Norfolk and Mary Stuart's envoy, John Lesley, Bishop of Ross, and that their main objective was placing the Queen of Scots on the English throne. Because the northern rising had failed, the only way to achieve this was by foreign invasion. An army was to be brought over from the Netherlands, whereupon the bulk of the English people would welcome their deliverers with open arms. Somewhere along the line it would probably be necessary to assassinate Elizabeth. This scheme of Byzantine complexity could never have worked – certainly not without plunging the nation into a period of civil war – but in the prevailing atmosphere of religious strife convulsing large areas of Europe it seemed credible. The one person Cecil needed to convince was Elizabeth. He was sure that the Queen of Scots was a constant and very real threat to English security. As long as she lived and maintained (as she did) her claim to the English crown, Elizabeth and the Protestant succession were in danger. But Elizabeth could not be brought to entertain the thought of having Mary, a fellow sovereign, killed.

Throughout 1571 Cecil's agents were busily at work, intercepting correspondence and interrogating suspects. The Duke of Norfolk, having been released from the Tower on giving assurances of his undying loyalty to the queen, was soon drawn back into Ridolfi's intrigues. In September a plan to rescue Mary was foiled. Norfolk was re-arrested. De Spes was sent back to Spain. The security surrounding Mary was redoubled but Elizabeth still refused to go any further. She contented herself with making Norfolk pay the price for the conspiracy; he was beheaded in June 1572. As for Ridolfi, he was out of the country at the time and took good care never to return. The importance for the government of this involved story of plots and suspicions was its propaganda value. It raised the fear of a Catholic enterprise to overthrow the existing regime. It was one more step in connecting Protestantism with nationalism. It revealed to the English people the dangerous intensity of religious feeling which, otherwise, only those with foreign diplomatic or commercial contacts were aware of.

In 1567, from his gaunt palace-monastery of the Escorial, Philip II had despatched the Duke of Alva to stamp out the Calvinist menace in the Netherlands. Alva, a man with a pathological hatred of heresy and a xenophobic contempt for all things not Spanish, inaugurated a reign of terror. In a short space of time he had arrested 9,000 people and had them tried by special tribunals. More than a thousand were executed for heresy or treason. By the end of the decade 100,000 Protestant refugees had fled his tyranny, many of them settling in England. The ensuing revolt merged religious and nationalist sentiment against Spanish rule. By 1572 Alva had overcome most centres of resistance by displaying unalloyed brutality. At Naarden, for example, every single inhabitant was slaughtered. Elsewhere the conquered people were given the opportunity to save themselves – by converting to Catholicism. By the time Philip removed this angel of vengeance from his command the northern Netherlands was in a state of social and economic disintegration. Among the sufferers were English merchants unfortunate enough to be caught up in the turmoil. They had their property seized and several spent weeks in prison.

In 1572, Walsingham saw at first hand the effects of religious bloodlust whipped up by government. He was at that time Elizabeth's ambassador in Paris. For some years Calvinism had been spreading in France. Adherents of the new faith challenged the old church not only with sermons, pamphlets and placards but with attacks on clergy and orgies of iconoclastic destruction. The French Protestants (Huguenots) were led by Henry of Navarre, a distant cousin of the ruling family but the next in line to the throne in the event of all the sons of the queen mother, Catherine de' Medici, dying childless. The Huguenots were a powerful faction among the nobility, the Duke of Condé and Gaspard de Coligny, the Admiral of France, being its leading lights. In August 1572 all the nation's social elite were in Paris to attend the wedding of Navarre with Catherine's daughter, Margaret. On the night of 23–4 August royal troops sealed off all exits from the city. At first light Catherine's guards broke into Coligny's lodging, hacked him to death and threw his body into the street. That was the signal for a hysterical mob purge of Huguenots throughout Paris and, subsequently, throughout France. Thousands of men, women and children became victims of the worst upsurge of bloodletting before the terror of 1793. Walsingham, an unwilling witness of the atrocity, did all he could to protect English nationals but was forced to yield up Huguenots who had sought asylum in the embassy.

1574 was an important date in the planned Catholic reconquest of England. In that year the first priest was ordained at Douai in the Spanish Netherlands and sent clandestinely over the water to cater for the needs of the recusant community (i.e. those who refused to attend Anglican worship). Douai had become the principal launch pad for the English mission. The college established there in 1568 by William Allen was training a new generation of priests ready for the inevitable day when papal religion triumphed once more. From this centre (moved to Rheims in 1578 and taken over by the Society of Jesus in 1586) a steady stream of missionaries entered England. The priests were welcomed by the Catholic faithful and sheltered in the homes of gentry families. There they celebrated mass, heard confessions, conducted baptisms, preached encouraging sermons. They also sowed sedition, for the nature of the mission inevitably changed the longer the Protestant regime proved impossible to dislodge. Many of the incoming clergy claimed that their work was purely spiritual but they were either dissembling or naïve to suppose, when their co-religionists were slaughtering thousands in the name of religion and engaging in plots to impose Catholicism at swordpoint, that issues of faith and politics could be kept separate. In 1572 a new pope, Gregory XIII, had somewhat moderated *Regnans in Excelsis* by indicating that Elizabeth's subjects should only regard themselves as released from their allegiance when it was feasible to do so. But that could only mean when a political challenge was mounted, for example by a foreign invasion. It was this pope's secretary who, in his master's name, declared, 'the guilty woman of England . . . is the cause of so much injury to the catholic faith, and loss of so many million souls, [that] there is no doubt that whosoever sends her out of the world with the pious intention of doing service, not only does not sin but gains merit'.[32] Just as Lollards and early evangelicals had been persecuted minorities, so English Catholic communities now lived as strangers and pilgrims in their own land, looking for the 'day of the Lord' when 'truth' would be enthroned. Like the proto-Protestants, they drew encouragement from events on the continent and hoped that Catholic monarchs might come to their aid, if necessary with prancing steeds and bare steel. Many observers predicted that the northern rebellion would not be the last attempt at a Catholic comeback and that any new insurrection would have foreign support.

'The towns in which we live are abounding in danger, and the dispositions of the men with whom we have to contend are not without their infinite recesses and deep concealments.'[33] So wrote Walsingham to a friend in 1577. Europe in the 1570s and 80s was in a state of cold war driven by rival ideologies. In every nation governments suppressed dissident communities and the Catholic superpowers, no less than the Soviet and Chinese regimes four hundred years later, sought to consolidate their blocs. England's queen was now in her forties and the hope of a Protestant heir had faded. Mary Stuart, next in line to the throne, was utterly unacceptable to the Council. Yet still Elizabeth could not be brought to remove this figurehead of Catholic aspirations. Over this and related issues queen and Council were constantly at loggerheads. Walsingham, now in charge of foreign affairs and beginning to assume that role of spymaster with which history has indelibly stamped him, on more than one occasion had given vent to the impassioned plea that God would 'open her majesty's eyes'. Between him and the queen there existed a state of mutual respect and frustration. The secretary found it hard to suppress his criticism of royal policy and Elizabeth sometimes riposted by accusing him of supporting heretics.

By 'heretics' she meant Puritans and all radicals who displayed what she regarded as secessionist tendencies. Walsingham was no non-conformist but he certainly supported, patronised and spoke up for radical evangelicals as opportunity arose. The style of religion he favoured and the problems it could cause were indicated by events in the London church where he worshipped. The vicar of St Giles Cripplegate in the early 1560s was Robert Crowley, a firebrand preacher and an extremist who objected to the use of vestments. In 1566 he made an unpleasant scene at a funeral because the lay clerks were wearing surplices. This protest got him sacked by the bishop. The St Giles congregation now elected an independent, non-stipendiary preacher, John Bartlett, to be their pastor. The bishop tried, unsuccessfully, to remove him and eventually resorted to placing him under house arrest. The parishioners were indignant at this high-handed attempt to 'muzzle the Gospel' and sixty women of St Giles laid siege to the bishop's palace. Having failed to get Bartlett released, the people elected a parson who was, if anything, even more outspoken than his predecessor. John Field was a close associate of John Foxe and he was soon in hot water over a pamphlet criticising the Elizabethan Settlement and castigating the prayer book as something 'called out of that popish dunghill, the mass book'. For this impertinence Field did a spell in Newgate jail.

The queen, her councillors, her bishops and the parish clergy were all in the business of establishing a godly commonwealth and of nipping in the bud any Romish revival but they did not all see eye to eye on how to go about this. Progressive Protestants took it as read that the people needed a consistent and well-developed programme of Bible-based education. The basic element of such a programme would be preaching. That, in turn, required clergy to be helped and encouraged in their understanding of Scripture. The general standard of parish clergy had improved since the beginning of the reign but levels of scholarship still left much to be desired. One of the earliest impulses of the Reformation had been to improve the educational standards of parish priests and this remained a priority for bishops – or, at least, for the more progressive among them.

Reformist leaders in church and state were agreed that the two most effective ways of achieving the desired ends were setting up 'lectureships' and 'exercises'. Lectureships were posts established for godly preachers to present sermons and sermon courses. They provided paid employment for many Puritan scholars who could not in good conscience apply for parish livings which would have involved them in using the prayer book. Several bishops, municipal corporations, major landowners and churches set up lectureships and it became customary for wealthy benefactors to leave bequests in their wills for the same purpose. By 1585 thirty London churches had appointed lecturers to their clerical staff and there was no diocese totally lacking in what was emerging as a distinct order of ministry. At Cambridge two new colleges (Emmanuel and Sidney Sussex) were founded for the specific purpose of training godly preachers (a simple extension into the Protestant age of what had always been a major function of such establishments).

Exercises or 'prophesyings' took on various forms but were, essentially, Bible study groups. Parties of local clergy would meet together to listen to and discuss an exposition of Scripture. In several places laymen were admitted to such gatherings and they became evangelical hot spots. The Northampton exercise, for example, convened twice a week in the parish church and, on Thursdays, after listening to the exposition, 'the mayor and his brethren [i.e. corporation] assisted by the preacher, minister, and other gentlemen appointed by the bishop' convened for a general discussion of the moral and spiritual welfare of the town.[34]

These assemblies were gatherings of people united by 'sound' doctrine rather than by adherence to the Elizabethan church 'by law established'. They were a nuisance to their traditionalist ecclesiastical superiors in at least two ways. They set up a rival to diocesan organisation – an evangelical network. When like-minded groups of local clergy and laity discussed and administered discipline, the authority of bishops was compromised. A vicar in the Dedham Vale area of Essex, a particularly strong centre of prophesying activity, was advised to refuse baptism to a child unless its parents were brought to repentance. A group of his colleagues attempted to suppress a traditional Whitsun morality play. The ministers did a scissors and paste job on the prayer book and exhorted their brethren to omit sections which offended them. Moreover, these networks paid no attention to diocesan boundaries. The exercises were, in effect, semi-independent evangelical enclaves after the Genevan model. The other nuisance factor arose when prophesyings got out of hand. Some of them attracted crowds of enthusiastic devotees who took it upon themselves to demonstrate against the establishment. They did not go to the lengths of their iconoclastic forebears but they became distinct thorns in the flesh to the more conservative elements in church and state. And no one was more conservative than Queen Elizabeth. She summarised her views on the current divisions in the nation's religious life in a speech to bishops and councillors in 1585:

> I have heard that some of them [Puritans] of late have said that I was of no religion, neither hot [nor] cold, but such a one as one day would give God the vomit. I pray you look unto such men. I doubt not that you will look unto the papists, for that they not only have spite at me, and that very nearly, but at the whole realm and the state of religion. There is an Italian proverb which sayeth, 'From mine enemy let me defend myself, but from a pretensed friend, good Lord deliver me'. Both these join together in one opinion against me for neither would have me to be queen of England . . . [35]

This is a revealing citation. Catholics at home and abroad contemplating or, at least, longing for the 'enterprise of England' were the 'enemy' but they remained at a distance. Elizabeth seldom encountered personally people who maintained allegiance to the pope and she certainly met none who challenged her authority to her face. But puritanical 'pretensed friends' were all around her – in her court, in her Council, in her Parliament, among her bishops and on the list of preachers permitted to perform before her. She also received letters from Protestant leaders abroad who responded to what they believed to be divine inspiration to offer her advice. Protestant radicals seldom minced their words when they spoke about the queen or even directly to her. Elizabeth occasionally had furious arguments with the likes of Dudley, Cecil and Walsingham, the very men on whom she relied most closely. It was a frustrating situation for all concerned and it is not surprising that the queen should have been more *emotionally* affected by the Puritans than by her Catholic critics. Puritan spokesmen did not always give her the respect she felt to be her due. In their ideal polity crowned princes submitted to the guidance, and even to the judgement, of God's ministers in matters spiritual and ethical. In their opinion the royal headship of the church had practical limitations. Elizabeth was convinced that the 'fantastical spirits' who held sway in the exercises were disruptive of good order. She told the bishops,

> you suffer many ministers to preach what they list, and to minister the sacraments according to their own fancies – some one way, some another – to the breach of unity . . . I have heard . . . there be six preachers in one diocese the which do preach six sundry ways. I wish such men to be brought to conformity and unity, that they minister the sacraments according to the order of this realm and preach all one truth; and that such as be found not worthy to preach, to be compelled to read homilies . . . For there is more of learning in one of those than in twenty of one of their sermons.[36]

'Unity', 'one truth' – like every member of her family who had occupied the English throne, Elizabeth believed that religious cohesion was essential to the security of the state. To her it was axiomatic that 'English nation' and 'English church' represented the same phenomenon viewed from different angles. The truth had been established by her father when he claimed, 'this realm of England is an empire . . . governed by one supreme head . . . unto whom a body politic, compact of all sorts and degrees of people, divided in terms and by names of spiritualty and temporalty, be bounden and owe to bear next unto God a natural and humble obedience'. What was clear – and intolerable – was the fact that there now existed within the realm rival religious networks – Catholic and evangelical – with links to foreign supporters and looking to either Rome or Geneva for their authentication. That was why Elizabeth was determined to put a stop to the exercises. In the second decade of the reign she attacked them sporadically via her bishops but her instructions not infrequently put the recipient in an awkward situation because he found himself caught between his royal mistress and local Puritan gentry or even members of the Council. The result was confusion: some exercises were closed; some remained open; some were modified; some changed their location; some lecturers moved to places where they enjoyed more protection from local magnates. This was the situation until 1576, when matters came to a head in a highly dramatic manner.

In the spring of the previous year Archbishop Parker of Canterbury had died. The replacement favoured by Cecil and his friends was Edmund Grindal of York. Elizabeth did not share their enthusiasm and it was seven months before she confirmed his appointment. The appearance of a strong-minded primate in whom she had less than complete confidence coincided with other events which touched Elizabeth on the raw and made conflict inevitable. In February she had to contend with an outspoken parliamentarian who had used Commons privilege to mount a forthright personal attack upon the queen for attempting to manipulate or overawe the representative body and, in particular, to suppress a motion calling for ecclesiastical reform. Peter Wentworth (Walsingham's brother-in-law) pronounced it to be 'a dangerous thing in a prince to oppose or bend herself against her nobility and people'.[37] Wentworth paid for his insolence with a month in the Tower. Grindal lost no time in backing progressive measures. These included attempts to strengthen the anti-recusancy laws, support for clergy who flouted liturgical dress codes and printing new editions of the Geneva Bible. This text, the preferred version of Puritans, with its pointed doctrinal glosses had aroused misgivings among moderate churchmen. Archbishop Parker had tried to counter its influence by sponsoring the Bishops' Bible, a revision of the Great Bible, which was less partisan in tone. Grindal now counter-attacked (with financial backing from Walsingham) by sponsoring four new editions of the Geneva Bible, one in folio format for church use and others designed for private study. He also set Laurence Tomson, a scholar-protégé of Walsingham, to produce an improved translation of the New Testament which contained glosses of a distinctly presbyterian nature. (An edition published in 1578 incorporated a 'puritanised' version of the Prayer Book.) Grindal's appointment had encouraged the exercise movement which now flourished in several areas.

It was particularly strong in the Midlands where the leader of society was Elizabeth's friend Robert Dudley, Earl of Leicester. He made a point of attending the meetings when he was staying at Kenilworth or Warwick. The queen and her more conservative bishops were now faced with the alarming prospect of religious radicalism gaining the upper hand. The epicentre of extremism was the exercise at Southam, Warwickshire. It was led by two celebrities of the Puritan world, John Oxenbridge, the rector of the parish, and Eusebius Paget, a much-lauded roving preacher who had been deprived of his last living. Both men had attracted the attention of the authorities for their outspoken Presbyterianism. Their boldness became a matter of serious concern to Leicester and his friends. As he explained to one of the Puritan ministers, he regarded the exercises as

> profitable both for people and ministers . . . especially where
> they are used with quietness for the conversation and unity of
> the doctrine established already and to the increase of the
> learned ministry . . . [but] I fear that the over busy dealing of
> some hath done so much hurt in striving to make better . . .
> that which is . . . good enough already . . .[38]

Dudley knew only too well how agitated Elizabeth was getting. She had ordered him to bring the offenders to heel and he had already warned the Midland clergy not to rock the boat. Grindal also took action to ward off the queen's anger. In a fresh set of instructions he ordained that exercises were only to be held with episcopal licence and under the presidency of an archdeacon or some other 'grave learned graduate'. These attempts to preserve the exercises came too late; in June Elizabeth ordered Grindal to close down every single one in his province. Furthermore, she insisted that three or four licensed preachers per diocese were quite sufficient; all other clergy should restrict themselves to reading the homilies.

It was not only progressives who regarded this as a giant step backwards, which would undermine one of the principal

objectives of the Reformation – educating the people in biblical truth. Grindal agonised for weeks over his response. The
very long letter he wrote to the queen (doubtless after many
drafts) indicates a clash between church and state scarcely less
poignant than that between Henry II and Becket or Hildebrand
and the Emperor Henry IV.

> because I am very well assured, both by reasons and argu-
> ments taken out of the holy Scriptures and by experience . . .
> that the said exercises for the interpretation and exposition of
> the Scriptures and for exhortations and comfort drawn out of
> the same are both profitable to increase knowledge among
> the ministers and tendeth to the edifying of the hearers: I am
> forced, with all humility, and yet plainly, to profess that I
> cannot with safe conscience and without the offence of the
> majesty of God give my assent to the suppressing of the said
> exercises; much less can I send out any injunctions for the
> utter and universal subversion of the same. I say, with St
> Paul . . . 'I can do nothing against the truth, but for the truth'.
> If it be your Majesty's pleasure, for this or any other cause, to
> remove me out of this place, I will with all humility yield
> thereunto and render again to your Majesty that I received of
> the same . . . Bear with me, I beseech you, Madam, if I choose
> rather to offend your earthly Majesty than to offend the heav-
> enly majesty of God.[39]

This was not the manner in which Elizabeth Tudor was accustomed to being addressed. Doubtless Grindal's response
confirmed the queen's opinion of the arrogance and disloyalty
of the archbishop and 'his kind'. She would have taken Grindal
at his word and sacked him had not wiser counsels prevailed.
Instead, she did the next best thing; she sequestered him from
performing his judicial and administrative functions. He was
allowed to retain his title and to continue his spiritual duties but,
beyond that, Elizabeth resumed into her own hands major
ecclesiastical decisions and, where appropriate, delegated

archiepiscopal functions to others. She, who was very good at nursing grudges, never forgave Grindal. Now she set in hand the task Grindal had refused to undertake; she ordered the bishops to suppress all exercises. Several of them quietly ignored the instruction. The crisis had achieved nothing. Elizabeth would find it impossible to bring into being a church to her taste until the first generation of leaders who had experienced life under the Marian regime had begun to die. Even then, as the upheavals of the seventeenth century were to prove, ardent Catholics, evangelicals, sacramentalists and sacramentaries would find no easy lodgement within the official church of the nation. Speaking of the fashionable radical preachers, the Bishop of London complained, 'the people resort to them as in popery they were wont to run on pilgrimages.' It was a perceptive comment and one that went to the heart of the government's problem. The state could never completely contain religious enthusiasm.

In the wider world religion was seldom far below the surface of important events. Take, for example, the year 1580. In the space of a few late summer weeks the politically informed classes were abuzz with three items of news. The Catholic adventurer James Fitzmaurice Fitzgerald had landed in Ireland at the head of a small army financed by the pope and slaughtered 800 men sent against him by the English lord deputy. The King of Portugal had died and Philip II had sent troops across the border to annexe his realm. At a stroke, not only more European territory but also an extensive overseas empire had fallen into his hands. The King of Spain was now master of the wealth of the Asian trade as well as the treasure of the Americas. He now had the resources to undertake the enterprise of England. However, within weeks, sensational news arrived which stirred English blood and challenged the assumption that the world's great oceans had become a Catholic lake. Francis Drake arrived at Plymouth having accomplished the first circumnavigation to be completed by a single commander. More than that, he disgorged from the *Golden Hind* chestfuls of precious metal looted from one of Philip's silver fleets.

Elizabeth's share was more than enough to cover her government's expenditure for a whole year. Anglo-Spanish tension was growing, fuelled by mercantile rivalry, nationalism and religious zeal. To observers like Cecil and Walsingham the lesson to be learned from the trend of international affairs was obvious: England's queen must assume the role of leader and saviour of Protestant Europe, succouring co-religionists in the Netherlands, forming anti-Catholic alliances and girding her loins for the Armageddon which was certainly coming. This was a part Elizabeth had no intention of playing; she embraced no policy vision beyond the maintenance of peace and was reactive rather than proactive in foreign affairs. But 1580 was also the year in which Roman Catholicism's most charismatic envoys, Edmund Campion and Robert Parsons, were smuggled into England (see below, p. 379f).

In contrast with her sporadic pursuit of Puritans, Elizabeth showed herself remarkably tolerant of stubborn Catholics. She refused to endorse a witch hunt of recusants. In 1579 Walsingham was obliged to circulate some of his contacts among the gentry with a confidential message concerning recently apprehended offenders which must have galled him greatly:

> I cannot but advise you and such others of the best affected gentlemen in that shire to forbear to persecute by way of indictment such as lately were presented, whose names you certified us; for that if you shall proceed therein, you shall not prevail to do that good you desire, but shall rather fail through some commandment from hence, prohibiting you to surcease in proceeding in that behalf, which would breed no less discredit unto you than encouragement to the papists.[40]

The government were in a quandary. Persecution would create martyrs and encourage resistance but lax enforcement of the recusancy laws was having the same effect. 'Papists were never in that jollity than they be at this present time,' Leicester reported from the Midlands[41] and the Bishop of London confirmed this from his own nationwide enquiries: 'the Papists marvellously increase both in numbers and in obstinate withdrawing of themselves from the church and service of God.'[42] The restocking of the Catholic priesthood from Douai and Rheims was working and, in 1579, another English college was established in Rome. Walsingham's spies were able to infiltrate this school and brought back alarming reports of detailed invasion plans being discussed by the students. The arrest and execution of priests for spreading sedition had begun in 1577 but the authorities were loath to apply capital punishment for fear of a popular-opinion backlash but also because they did not want to be tarred with the same brush as the Inquisition.

Protestant regimes lacked the theological justification claimed by their opposite numbers for killing men and women for their faith. Belief in purgatory enabled Catholics to regard ritual murder as simply hastening the offender's soul to that intermediary realm where it could make expiation for its sins. Thus they could remove the heretic from circulation without denying him/her the possibility of ultimate salvation. For Protestants the sombre truth was contained in the Epistle to the Hebrews: 'it is appointed unto men that they shall once die, and then cometh the judgement' (Hebrews, Chapter 9, in Tyndale's 1534 New Testament). Thus, in Protestant thinking, it was monstrous to talk of 'destroying the body to save the soul'; judgement belonged to God and the church had no licence to kill. Where Protestant and Catholic thinkers were in agreement was over the God-given power of life and death allotted to temporal rulers. By this legal stratagem, heretics in Catholic countries could be handed over to the secular arm for despatch. Such an escape hatch did not exist for Elizabeth's councillors and churchmen. Draconian action taken against immigrant priests, recusants and foreign agents had to be justified by *raison d'état*. Europe was in a state of ideological cold war and across the narrow water which separated England from the mainland its Protestant allies were being ruthlessly exterminated. Clashing ambitions and insecurities fostered the culture of espionage. Walsingham, no less than foreign ambassadors, had his spies working both at home and abroad. He strove feverishly to unmask the activities of those who regarded themselves as subjects of the pope and, as such, were committed to the overthrow of England's queen and government. Prisons were filling with captured Catholic missionaries and those suspected of harbouring them. Yet, for all that the air was alive with plots and rumours of plots, Elizabeth's councillors and justices were nervous about appearing to execute men for what could be – and were – construed as religious motives.

By early 1581 it was obvious that firmer measures would have to be taken. There were now more than a hundred foreign-trained priests active in England (it has been estimated that, over the whole reign, about 500 seminarists entered the country), and an increasing number of them were rigorous Jesuits. However, when new measures to deal with the growing crisis were introduced into Parliament it proved difficult to secure a consensus on how harsh penalties against Catholic activists should be. The major objective of the Act to Retain the Queen's Majesty's Subjects in their due Obedience was to force Catholics to attend their parish churches, where, it was hoped, the drip, drip of Bible-based liturgy and preaching would wear down their resistance. Accordingly, recusancy fines were increased from one shilling per week to a swingeing £20 a month. This was a direct response to the hard line taken by the Council of Trent, whose decrees Gregory XIII was energetically putting into practice:

> To be present at heretical conventicles, and to frequent their churches indiscriminately like one of themselves, is not only to obscure our true faith and religion, but also to profess the worship of a false sect through a certain exterior cult designed to that end. This is forbidden by the divine law and cannot be made lawful by any dispensation.[43]

Unlike earlier English separatists – Henrician Lollards and Marian evangelicals – who had been able to hide their identity by outward conformity, Catholics were, thus, urged to nail their colours to the mast. Many, of course, chose not to do so and the hefty fines now decreed obliged more covert Catholics to put in at least an occasional appearance at their parish churches. The activities of priests in converting people to their faith was not made an offence *per se* by the same Act but such proselytising was declared illegal if its objective was to subvert people's allegiance to the Crown. However, since Elizabeth was still excommunicate, it was open to any court to interpret commitment to Rome as treason. Such decisions were left to the local magistrates – and with good reason. Puritans in the House of Commons might, and, indeed, did, demand legislation with sharper teeth but the government had to have workable laws and there were parts of the country where any attempt to impose widespread persecution would have been resisted. What the 1581 Act provided was the opportunity for the regime to take action against selected individuals, when necessary.

The most celebrated case of anti-Catholic persecution was the torture and execution of Edmund Campion. This brilliant Oxford scholar had studied at Douai and Rome and joined the Society of Jesus in 1573. In 1580 he was selected with Robert Parsons to spearhead the Jesuit mission to England. This marked a new phase in Rome's assault on Protestant England. The Jesuits were spiritually strong and idealistically focused. Whereas the earlier seminarists had been primarily concerned with pastoring recusants, the newcomers had a programme for the reconversion of England by setting up secret networks. Campion and his colleagues looked not to the past and the restoration of all the medieval paraphernalia swept away by Henry VIII and Edward VI, but to a revitalised Counter-Reformation Catholicism, working outside the Elizabethan church. The distinction mirrored that of the different strands within evangelicalism; while Puritans tried to reclaim the English church from within, Presbyterians and other sectarians just beginning to emerge tended towards separation.

While living, Campion had little time to make much impression but after his death his impact was considerable.

He was tracked down by Walsingham's increasingly efficient counter-terrorism operation in July 1581, taken to the Tower, tortured, interrogated on numerous occasions, tried (under the Treason Act of 1351 rather than the recent legislation, which, the government feared, might not prove robust enough to achieve the desired objective) and, inevitably, found guilty. Interestingly, the prosecutor was the Attorney-General, Edmund Anderson, who had made a name for himself in proceedings against Protestant extremists. In December, Campion was hanged, drawn and quartered. His defence throughout had been that his role was purely spiritual and that he had never dabbled in political matters. However sincere his protests were, he was far too intelligent not to realise that religion and politics were tightly interwoven and could not be teased apart and rewound at will. Like the sufferings of Marian martyrs at Smithfield, the deaths of Campion and others at Tyburn drew large crowds, among whom were many sympathisers. The executions certainly strengthened the faith of many wavering Catholics. During the whole reign, 124 priests and 59 lay Catholics suffered the prescribed fate of traitors. Printed accounts of their courage and fortitude were not slow in being circulated. The Catholic community at last had something to set alongside the long-running bestseller, Foxe's *Acts and Monuments*.

The total number of executions for reasons connected with religion during Elizabeth's reign was, as far as can be calculated, similar to that of her father's (approximately 183 and 174 respectively, excluding offenders punished for implication in plots and rebellions). The attitudes of the two sovereigns were also comparable. The law against dissidents was meant to be a deterrent. Just as the Act of Six Articles was applied sparingly, so anti-recusancy legislation was not rigidly enforced. Had the fines enumerated in the 1581 Act been mercilessly exacted they would have made a considerable contribution to Elizabeth's cash-strapped treasury. In fact, the amount of money raised in this way was not significant. The government made examples of a handful of high-profile and truculent leading Catholic laymen, such as William, Lord Vaux, who was heavily implicated in harbouring Campion. (Vaux managed to make his peace with the queen but later excused himself from attending Parliament on the grounds that he had been impoverished by the payment of fines.) Out in the shires, where local loyalties and friendships counted for more than religious affiliation, justices were loath to seek out recusants. The majority of priests arrested were imprisoned or deported, rather than being sent to Tyburn. And Walsingham was always on the lookout for Catholic activists who could be 'turned' and used to entrap their erstwhile co-religionists. Just as Henry VIII had protected court favourites suspected of being evangelicals, so Elizabeth shielded Catholics in her entourage whose services she valued. Thus, William Byrd of the Chapel Royal for many years produced religious and secular music for her majesty's delectation.

Queen and Council would have been delighted if comparatively gentle pressure had kept the Catholic 'menace' within bounds. Similarly, the majority of Catholics remained loyal to the Crown and deplored the prospect of foreign invasion or home-grown insurrection. However, the machinations of the Rome–Madrid axis, the activities of headstrong idealists, the existence of the 'auld alliance' of Scotland and France and the presence in the wings of the Queen of Scots as a potential rival for the throne meant that cold war might, at any time, suddenly erupt into hot war. A series of events in the mid-1580s brought that prospect frighteningly close.

In the autumn of 1583 a Warwickshire gentleman by the name of John Somerville or Somerfield was arrested for announcing publicly that he was on his way to London to murder the queen. Walsingham interrogated the deranged zealot and, had times been different, he would probably have had the poor fellow consigned to Bedlam. As it was, the propaganda opportunity could not be missed. Somerville and his associates were put on trial and condemned as traitors. Somerville hanged himself in Newgate. Meanwhile, the queen's close circle was experiencing a severe case of jitters, as the Spanish ambassador, Bernardino de Mendoza, reported:

A soldier returned from Terceira ... came to the Court to
give a letter to the Earl of Bedford ... he found his way to the
place where the Queen was with two other ladies. She ...
cried out angrily for him to be seized and carried to the
chamber of the Earl of Leicester, where he was asked whether
I had sent him to kill the Queen and if he bore arms, though
he having nothing but a blunt knife. [Other councillors] questioned him anew with caresses and promises, whether I had
sent him thither and how many times he had spoken with me
about the [Queen], who replied that he had never seen me ...
Afterwards examining him about the Pope [they urged him
to say] that it was by my intervention that the lunatic desired
to kill the Queen. [She] said publicly to the ambassador of
France that there are three hundred Catholics who have
sworn to kill her.[44]

The background to this was what has been called the
'Throckmorton Plot'. Francis Throckmorton, member of a
family with court and diplomatic connections, had consorted
overseas with Catholic activists up to their ears in plans for the
enterprise of England. Subsequently, he had intrigued with
Mendoza, members of the queen's court and messengers from
Mary Stuart. When Walsingham had him racked in the Tower
the details of a lurid and extravagant plot came out involving the
pope, Philip II and the Duke of Guise who would furnish an
invasion force while the Earls of Northumberland and Arundel
and Lord Paget would undertake a court coup. Whether such a
plot could ever have been successfully carried out is a matter for
conjecture but what mattered was its impact on Elizabeth and
on the public at large. Amid a plethora of rumour and conjecture Throckmorton was executed, Mendoza was dismissed,
Arundel and Northumberland were imprisoned and the latter
shot himself in his cell (or, if the inevitable conspiracy theory is
to be believed, his death was arranged to look like suicide). In
the midst of all this activity news came from the Netherlands, in
July 1584, that William, Prince of Orange, leader of the Dutch

Protestants, had been assassinated. Within days a message from Elizabeth's ambassador in Paris claimed that plans were afoot to deal in the same way with the English queen. 'Seeing there were men cunning enough to enchant a man, and to encourage one to kill the Prince of Orange in the midst of Holland, and a knave found desperate enough to do it, we must think that hereafter anything may be done.'[45]

It was not just the queen's life that was in danger; what was at stake was the Protestant succession. Burghley and his colleagues were determined to secure this at all costs. If Elizabeth were to die suddenly, whether at the hands of an assassin or not, the crown would pass to the Queen of Scots – a triumph for the Counter-Reformation. The obvious way to dispose of this threat was to remove Mary. Elizabeth's closest advisers frequently urged this course of action upon her but she would have none of it. Burghley was forced to come up with a plan 'B'. It had to be made abundantly clear to the enemies of the regime that if anything happened to Elizabeth the Catholics would gain nothing from it. In October 1584 he produced the Bond of Association. This document was both impressive and of dubious legality. It was signed by the members of the Privy Council and it was envisaged that all leaders of society would subscribe to it. Signatories pledged themselves,

> if any such wicked attempt against her most royal person shall be taken in hand, or procured, whereby any that have, may or shall pretend title to come to this crown by the untimely death of Her Majesty so wickedly procured (which God of his mercy forbid!) that the same may be avenged, we do not only bind our selves both jointly and severally never to allow, accept or favour any such pretended successor, by whom or for whom any such detestable act shall be attempted or committed, as unworthy of all government in any Christian realm or civil state:
>
> But do also further vow and protest, as we are most bound, and that in the Presence of the eternal and

everlasting God, to prosecute such person or persons to death, with our joint and several forces, and to act the utmost revenge upon them, that by any means we or any of us can devise and do, or cause to be devised and done for their utter overthrow and extirpation.[46]

This remarkable document stated the attitude of the Protestant executive towards two queens. It served notice that if Mary persisted in her ambitions she would have to wade through blood to achieve them. It also implied that if Elizabeth would take no thought for the future of her country (by identifying a Protestant successor) there were those in the realm who would do so. Within weeks these principles were enshrined in statute law when Parliament passed the Act for the Security of the Queen's Most Royal Person. Burghley would have gone further: he prepared a bill which would have enabled Parliament to offer the crown to a chosen successor in the event of the queen's dying without making such provision. However, Elizabeth firmly quashed this trespass upon her prerogative. The same session also produced the Act against Jesuits and Seminarists. The screw against Catholic activists now received several more turns. Any suggestion that immigrant priests were present for pastoral reasons was firmly rejected. They had been sent, the preamble declared, 'to stir up and move sedition, rebellion, and open hostility'. They were given forty days to quit the realm, after which they risked arrest and execution for treason. All Englishmen currently training in foreign seminaries were ordered to return within six months, after which they would be treated as traitors if they entered the queen's realm. Laypeople aiding priests were to be regarded as felons.[47]

The crisis of the 1580s opened up the cracks in the constitution produced by religious differences between queen, Council and Parliament. Elizabeth's distaste of all sorts of religious enthusiasm increased with age as did her determination to shape her church. She became wary about the role of Parliament in religious matters. There were altogether too many Puritans in that troublesome body. Her contretemps with Wentworth was systematic of her determination to keep the affairs of the church within the exclusive sphere of the royal prerogative. Issues of doctrine, liturgy and spiritual discipline, she frequently warned her Lords and Commons, would be decided by herself and her bishops. After her run-in with Grindal she was careful to water down the radicalism of the episcopal bench by appointing 'sound and sensible' men to vacancies as they occurred. When Grindal died, in 1583, she replaced him with John Whitgift, a narrow disciplinarian with the reputation of being a scourge of Puritans. One of his first acts was to impose on all the clergy of his province subscription to articles of Anglican 'orthodoxy'. The result of this purge was the loss of almost four hundred parish priests who could not accept all the requirements laid down in the prayer book. The Commons were outraged, denounced Whitgift's high-handed action and petitioned the queen for redress of various religious grievances. Elizabeth dug her heels in. She would not, she told the house, accept any 'manner of innovation, nor alter, or change any law whereby the religion of the Church of England standeth established at this day'.[48] It was the Council who came to the rescue of at least some of the stricken clergy by obliging Whitgift to water down his demands. But, with Elizabeth's backing, the archbishop continued his assault on extremists. His chief weapon was the Court of High Commission, set up at the beginning of the reign to administer the Uniformity oath, but now become a judicial body with the power to deprive clergy of their livings for a variety of offences. Over the ensuing decade Whitgift's campaign successfully weeded out all ministers with presbyterian tendencies.

The Privy Council had other ways of influencing the religious life of the nation. The very assumptions of the Bond, if taken to logical conclusions (which they never were), were not far removed from the concept that power was vested in the people. Councils and parliaments were, by definition, servants of the Crown and had no separate existence apart from the sovereign. What the Bond established was that the Council and Parliament *did* continue to exist after the sovereign's death and had authority to choose the next holder of the supreme office. But it was not just in the realm of constitutional theory that Elizabeth's councillors were asserting a measure of independence. They were responsible for most of the routine appointments of JPs and other local officials and did not hesitate to select 'reliable' men as leaders of provincial society. By this they, of course, meant sound Protestants. Throughout many parts of the country networks of approved landowners were setting the tone of life in church and state. And every well-publicised Catholic plot created greater cohesion among their members. By the late 1580s, 'if the Elizabethan "puritan movement" was dead, the evangelical impulse which had given Reformation from below its momentum since Lollard, Edwardian, and Marian-exile days was flourishing.'[49]

The sad history of Robert Browne, the 'first congregationalist', though an extreme case, indicates the tensions within church life at this time, the problems facing those seeking to hold together a nation-church, and those whose consciences would not permit them to settle happily within it. Browne came from one of the leading families of Lincolnshire. He was related to and a friend of William Cecil. At the beginning of the 1580s he was in his early thirties, a Cambridge graduate who had undergone a profound spiritual experience and felt impelled to preach the word wherever he could find an audience. He saw no need to obtain episcopal permission for following what he believed to be his divine vocation. More than that, he believed that the organisation of the church into parishes and dioceses was an encumbrance to the Gospel. It was but a short step to his gathering around him a group of like-minded enthusiasts in Norfolk, soon to be known as 'Brownists'. Like numerous charismatic Christian leaders before and since, he attracted a sizeable following. And, like numerous charismatic Christian leaders before and since, he soon found himself in trouble with the authorities. He seems to have courted opposition by publishing books advocating his own brand of independent, gathered church and two of his followers were actually hanged for disseminating his writings. Between 1581 and 1584 he spent spells in prison, fled for asylum to Middleburg and then to Scotland. Every time he got himself into trouble he turned to Cecil for help, and he did not appeal in vain. It may seem surprising that the queen's first minister should have openly associated himself with such a troublesome maverick but not only did he arrange Browne's release from prison, he even stood surety for this unstable man's behaviour. Burghley's patience was eventually rewarded when, in 1586, his troublesome protégé settled down as master of Stamford Grammar School and, subsequently, as rector of Achurch, a living in Cecil's gift. Unfortunately, cantankerousness returned with age; after a long and peaceful ministry, Browne, when in his eighties, once more allowed his tongue to get him into trouble, and he died in Northampton jail. His old protector was, by then, long dead.

By 1586, England was accelerating down a steepening slope to open war with Spain. Walsingham's agents unearthed more plots. Thousands of prominent subjects had flocked to sign the Bond of Association. The provocative acts of Drake and his fellow mariners were trying Philip's patience to the uttermost. His rebellious Dutch subjects had long pestered Elizabeth for military aid and she eventually, with great reluctance, despatched troops under the command of the Earl of Leicester at the end of 1585. The expedition gobbled up cash but, over the ensuing months, that was not Elizabeth's most pressing problem. She was being almost deafened by the clamour of her Council and Parliament for Mary's head. Walsingham had, by the summer, penetrated to the centre of another web of Catholic intrigue and by cunning stratagems of his own he had, this time, been able to trap Mary Stuart into complicity. Elizabeth was in an agony of indecision and it was October before the captive queen's trial could be held at Fotheringhay Castle. The inevitable verdict threw Elizabeth into an even greater turmoil, as she came face to face with the decision which had haunted her for years. It was the Council who once again took the initiative, organising a parliamentary deputation which begged the queen to act and, at last, wringing the death warrant from her reluctant hands. Then Cecil made the greatest possible haste to get the deed done, while his royal mistress tried to wash her hands of it. On 8 February 1587 Mary Queen of Scots was beheaded, claiming for herself the role of martyr: 'I am quite ready and very happy to die, and to shed my blood for Almighty God, my Saviour and my Creator, and for the Catholic Church, and to maintain its rights in this country.'[50]

Queen and nation steeled themselves to face the inevitable fury of the Catholic world. 1588 brought violent reaction and would for ever be known as 'Armada Year'. The Spanish threat, England's providential deliverance and Elizabeth's rising to the occasion in a moment of high theatre at Tilbury created a mood of national solidarity – Protestant solidarity or, at least, anti-Catholic solidarity. The invasion plan was the first serious attempt to challenge what Henry VIII had claimed fifty-five years before; that 'this realm of England is an empire', with the right to determine its own laws and customs – including its religious identity. Yet, ironically, 1588 was also the year that Puritanism went into self-destruct mode. In the aftermath of the Armada's destruction, and, perhaps, hoping to ride the bandwagon of Protestant triumphalism, an anonymous writer issued a scurrilous pamphlet attacking surviving Romish tendencies within the Anglican establishment. *The Epistle to the Terrible Priests* was the first of what came to be known as the 'Marprelate Tracts'.

There had been an intermittent literary warfare between orthodox and radical churchmen for several years but now the controversy took a highly entertaining turn, as 'Martin Marprelate' aimed at a wider audience. He made personal attacks on some of the bishops and sought by mockery to undermine the concept of episcopacy. One typical passage denounced bishops as 'that swinish rabble, of petty antichrists, petty popes, proud prelates, intolerable withstanders of reformation, enemies of the gospel, and most covetous wretched priests'.[51] The overblown invective and vulgar wit of his diatribes delighted the sort of people who enjoyed the newly fashionable professional acting companies operating on inn-yard stages, the precursors of the Elizabethan and Jacobean theatres. Indeed, when the defenders of the church status quo sought writers who could reply in kind to the Puritan attacks they turned to dramatists such as John Lyly and Thomas Nashe. But the establishment did not confine themselves to entering into unseemly tit-for-tat; they sought out the printing presses and the 'lewd fellows' who fed them. The full weight of the High Commission and its agents was brought to bear in hunting down and punishing the offenders. Yet again in the Reformation story we encounter an underground network of religious activists – preachers, ministers, parliamentarians, students and tradesmen – who devoted themselves to distributing forbidden writings and hiding their authors. Just who those authors were has never been finally decided. The organising geniuses appear to have been John Penry, a Welsh zealot, and Job Throckmorton, a Warwickshire MP and close colleague of Peter Wentworth, and it is likely that they originated some of the satirical material. Other contenders could be the original printer, Robert Waldegrave, or Midlands JP Sir Richard Knightley. The hunted populists moved their headquarters more than once in their attempts to avoid their pursuers but within months some had been arrested and their presses silenced.

The bizarre sequence of events lasted less than a year but its consequences were serious for the Puritan movement. Leading members of the party hastened to dissociate themselves from the unseemly activities of their irresponsible co-religionists, realising how the contretemps played into Whitgift's hands. They were right to be anxious. The archbishop used the Marprelate affair to launch a witch hunt against all extremists and he had the queen's backing. In February 1589, Sir Christopher Hatton, speaking on her behalf, told Parliament that Puritans were more obnoxious than papists, who were, at least, open in their intention to subvert the cause of true religion and sow dissension among her majesty's subjects. Penry, after a brief sojourn in Scotland, was arrested and hanged in 1593, as were two other leading lights of the Marprelate affair. By now the glory days of Elizabethan Puritanism were past. Several of the first-generation leaders had died, including Dudley (1588) and Walsingham (1590). Elizabeth had filled the episcopal bench with men more to her liking. And Whitgift had filled the prisons with extremists.

By the time the queen's reign entered its last decade the Elizabethan Settlement had settled. The vast majority of English men and women conformed to that distinct 'Anglican' pattern of worship and belief that had emerged as a result of seventy turbulent years of religious conflict. Few of them missed the polychromatic splendours of their parish churches which had disappeared under layers of whitewash or hankered after the old jewel-bedecked altars and shrines. There were dissenters, of course. There always had been and there always would be. Many families, including important aristocratic ones, maintained their allegiance to the church of Rome, and Protestant non-conformists, whether or not they outwardly acquiesced in the queen's religion, still managed to meet for fellowship and mutual comfort with their brethren. And we must, once again, acknowledge that those terms we use for convenience sake – 'Catholic', 'Protestant', 'Puritan', 'Anglican' – are woefully inadequate. The spectrum of English religious life was no less broad in 1600 than it had been in 1500. It embraced zealots and doubters, aesthetes and philistines, born-again Christians and those who still understood religion in terms of performing good works. Not all English Catholics appreciated the rigours of Jesuit teaching; one secular priest actually dubbed the missionaries 'puritans, precisions and Genevans'. Protestants of Marprelate's persuasion, as we have seen, were ready to denounce other members of the same church as crypto-papists.

One experience, however, in the life of Elizabeth's subjects was very different indeed from anything their grandparents and great-grandparents had known. In Shakespeare's *Henry IV*, Act IV, Scene 2, Falstaff likens his rag-tag military contingent to 'a hundred and fifty tattered prodigals lately come from swine-keeping, from eating draff and husks'. The reference is to the Geneva Bible's rendering of Luke's Gospel, Chapter 15, verses 15–16: 'he went and clave to a citizen of that country, and he sent him to his farm to feed swine. And he would fain have filled his belly with the husks that the swine ate . . .' That is just one of well over a thousand biblical references in Shakespeare's plays. It goes without saying that he would not have made such allusions if they had been too esoteric for the theatregoers in the pit to understand. This demonstrates just how familiar Scripture was becoming by the end of the century. Elizabeth's subjects were growing accustomed to the Bible, through hearing it read in English Sunday by Sunday and through absorbing its language as they recited it in the liturgy. Several thousands of them owned their own Bibles and it was the only book to be found in many households. Here is an influence more profound than the stripping of altars, the disappearance of monasteries, the squabbling over theological niceties or the grim scenes at Tyburn and Smithfield. As Professor Marshall has observed, 'The text which best equips us for "reading the Reformation" as an agent of cultural transformation may . . . be the Bible itself.'[52]

For that reason it may not be considered inappropriate to close this account of the English Reformation with an event that happened elsewhere. In 1582, the English college at Rheims published a translation of the New Testament for use by Catholics. (It was followed by the Old Testament in 1609–10.) In the preface to this volte-face the editors found it necessary to issue a disclaimer:

> We do not publish upon erroneous opinion of necessity, that the holy Scriptures should always be in our mother tongue, or that they ought, or were ordained by God, to be read indifferently of all . . . but upon special consideration of the present

time, state and condition of our country, unto which divers things are either necessary, or profitable and medicinal now, that otherwise in the peace of the church were neither much requisite, nor perchance wholly tolerable.

If those words reached across the portals of eternity to the likes of Tyndale, Cranmer and Latimer we may well imagine that there was much laughter in Paradise.

Epilogue

To end the story at the conclusion of the sixteenth century might seem to require justification. Some argue that the religious conflict between Charles I and his Parliament belongs to the same narrative. Others insist that the modern pattern of English church life did not emerge until after the Carolean Settlement of 1662, when the rift between the state church and the Nonconformist chapels became final. Such complaints are perfectly reasonable, for, in very truth, the Reformation story has no definable 'end'.

'Change is the only constant.' If that truism holds good, it must also be the case that beneath the surface of every major change continuities lurk. That certainly is the case with the revolution we call the Reformation. The England Elizabeth I left in 1603 was a vastly different country from the one her father had assumed control of in 1509. Yet, if we focus our attention solely on change we miss a vital element in the history of the 'Tudor century'. We can easily find ourselves obliged to identify and account for what happened to effect the transition from one fixed point, 'medieval Catholic England', to another fixed point, 'modern Protestant England'. We may seek to explain that evolution by phenomena unique to the period such as the rise of capitalism, the emergence of nation states, the growth of individualism or the impact of the printing press. If, however, we look behind the social, political and economic developments and concentrate on what the Reformation essentially was – a

religious revival – we soon discover its continuities with what
went before and what came after.

> ... when a deep consideration had, from the very bottom of
> my soul drawn together and heaped up all my misery in the
> sight of my heart, there arose a mighty storm, bringing a
> mighty shower of tears ... I cast myself down, I know not
> how, under a certain fig tree, giving full vent to my tears ...
> and ... spake I much unto Thee: 'And Thou, O Lord, how
> long? How long, Lord? Wilt Thou be angry for ever?
> Remember not our former iniquities.' For I felt that I was
> held by them ... 'Why not now? Why not is there this hour an
> end to my uncleanness?' ... When, lo! I heard from a neigh-
> bouring house a voice, as of a boy or girl – I know not
> – chanting and oft repeating, 'Take up and read. Take up and
> read' ... So, checking the torrent of my tears, I arose, inter-
> preting it to be no other than a command from God to open
> the book [the Bible] and read the first chapter I should find ...
> and in silence read that section on which my eyes first fell:
> 'Not in rioting and drunkenness, nor in strife and envying,
> but put ye on the Lord Jesus Christ.' [Romans 13: 13–14] ...
> No further would I read, nor needed I, for instantly at the end
> of this sentence, by a light as it were of serenity infused into
> my heart, all the darkness of doubt vanished away.[1]

> I used to think that I had penetrated to the depths of Your
> Truth with the citizens of Your Heaven, until You, the Solid
> Truth, shone upon me in your Scriptures, scattering the
> cloud of my error, and showing me how I was croaking in the
> marshes with the toads and frogs.[2]

> In the evening I went very unwillingly to a society in
> Aldersgate Street, where one was reading Luther's preface to
> the Epistle to the Romans. About a quarter before nine, while
> he was describing the change which God works in the heart
> through faith in Christ, I felt my heart strangely warmed. I

felt I did trust in Christ, Christ alone, for salvation; and an assurance was given to me that he had taken away my sins, even mine, and saved me from the law of sin and death.[3]

I, like that thief on the cross, have believed Christ's teaching and been saved. And this is no far-fetched comparison but the closest expression of the condition of spiritual despair and horror at the problem of life and death in which I lived formerly, and of the condition of peace and happiness in which I am now . . . In all this I was exactly like the thief, but the difference was that the thief was already dying, while I was still living. The thief might believe that his salvation lay there beyond the grave, but I could not be satisfied with that, because beside a life beyond the grave life still awaited me here. But I did not understand that life. It seemed to me terrible. And suddenly I heard the words of Christ and understood them, and life and death ceased to seem to me evil, and instead of despair I experienced happiness and the joy of life undisturbed by death.[4]

Augustine, a fourteenth-century Archbishop of Armagh, John Wesley, Leo Tolstoy – all told the same story; all shared the same experience, as did millions of others throughout the intervening centuries and in the years before and since. I have no hesitation in calling it an *evangelical* experience, not in any partisan or doctrinaire sense, but simply because it meets the three basic criteria of what we generally understand as evangelicalism. That is, it was Bible-based, Cross-centred and personal. It was the resort of men and women whose deepest needs were not met by the dogmas and rituals of established church life. They yearned for an affective religion that answered the fundamental problems of human existence, a religion that provided assurance of salvation. When they found it, everything changed for them, including their attitude towards those in whom they had previously invested authority. They realised that they could no longer be comfortably at home under a Christian hierarchy that rested on a different threefold foundation: one that was tradition-based, Incarnation-centred and collective. The old way offered the possibility of salvation through membership of the church and unquestioning obedience to its leaders, even if those leaders presented an image of corruption and spiritual bankruptcy. More importantly, it could not give the anguished soul that certainty it craved concerning life after death. And when it responded to the challenge of unorthodoxy by using threats and violence, that simply confirmed radical believers in their convictions, for did not Christ himself promise 'If they persecute me they will persecute you also' [John 15: 20]. When dissenters were confronted with ridicule, ostracism, imprisonment, torture and death, the majority – such is the frailty of human nature – buckled but in any age there were usually several prepared to 'suffer for truth's sake'. These were the ones who changed history. Some brought a new rigour to monastic life. Some opened up new areas to missionary endeavour. Some challenged their own societies to ethical purity with incandescent oratory. Some walked the lonely path to martyrdom, leaving it to posterity to recognise their virtues by making them saints or venerating them as the founders of new religious groupings.

The congregations of 'holy fools' were always minorities, marching to a different drum. Their neighbours, unless they became converts, were bewildered by them or resentful of them. Bewildered because they could not understand what these breast-beating idealists were talking about. Bewildered because the zealots tended to form exclusivist cliques. Bewildered because, while most folk had quite enough to do eking out a living in a hard world and were content to leave religion to the experts, the oddballs in their midst worried their heads with matters of arcane spirituality which were none of their business. They were resentful because outspoken dissidents challenged the rituals their forefathers had treasured from time immemorial. Resentful because they endangered neighbourhood unity. Resentful because the enthusiasts laid claim to a certainty ordinary people did not dare to grasp for themselves. There had scarcely been any time throughout the medieval centuries when western Christendom had been without 'back-to-the-Bible' sects, precisionist monks and wild-eyed apocalyptic preachers. The church had usually been able to deal with them by incarcerating them within the cloister or branding them as heretics and subjecting them to sporadic persecution.

It was when outside circumstances played into the hands of radical thinkers and religious activists that individual fervour led to local, regional, national or even international tergiversation. Then, for a time at least, the 'awkward squad' attracted their contemporaries and inspired revival. When Urban II launched the First Crusade in 1095, he had no hesitation in pointing to economic pressure as one reason for urging Christian princes to conquer eastern lands:

> The land which you inhabit is closed in on all sides by the sea and the chains of mountains and is crowded by your large numbers, so that it does not suffice for the supply of riches and scarcely provides food for its cultivators. That is why you quarrel among yourselves, wage war and often wound and kill each other.[5]

The second half of the eleventh century was a time of considerable population growth in Europe, with such attendant problems as the pope referred to. Social dislocation was one factor in creating an intense mood for personal holiness and religious reform. There was a prodigious growth in recruitment to monastic orders. It is no coincidence that, to take an example at random, Gloucester Abbey experienced a tenfold increase in membership during the last quarter of the century when the Norman conquerors were brutally imposing their regime on the English. Within a generation, Bernard of Clairvaux had launched his reform movement. His demands for gospel simplicity and the austere application of the rule of St Benedict packed the houses of his order and propelled missionaries into many parts of the continent. The contemporary career of Arnold of Brescia, an Austin canon, took on a more political aspect when he force-fully challenged the corruption and luxury of the Roman curia, an effrontery for which he was executed, his body burned and his ashes scattered in the Tiber to prevent his followers making a pilgrimage centre of his grave.

The late eighteenth century was another time of social disruption. In England industrial revolution was depopulating the countryside and overpopulating the towns. Rapid urbanisation was distancing people from the cycle of agricultural life, which was closely linked to the church's liturgical cycle. Men put down new roots and felt freer to think new thoughts, some of them bearing dangerous similarities to those which caused political upheaval in France and the American colonies. Crime and violence were rife. Among the lower orders despair was a constant and to many it seemed that the established church had little to offer. This was the background to the preaching campaigns of John Wesley and George Whitfield, who took religion outside the church buildings and sparked the first 'evangelical revival' to which that name has been given.

When we consider the English Reformation in the light of such earlier and later 'explosions of faith' the similarities are striking. It, too, occurred at a time of (and was itself an expression of) social dislocation. The fact that there was a revolt against the government in almost every decade between 1520 and 1580 (1525, 1536–7, 1549, 1554, 1569–70), not to mention other conspiracies that were nipped in the bud, is proof enough that there were serious faults in the political fabric of the nation. They were periodically exacerbated by war. English troops gave their blood and English civilians their money in repeated foreign conflicts: 1512–18, 1521–4, 1544–50, 1585–1604. Such interruptions to the nation's commercial life added to the traumas created by price inflation and agricultural change. Vagabondage and crime were problems that would not go away whatever remedies the politicians devised. It was not just philosophers and theologians who were theorising about and trying to realise a fair and just 'commonwealth'. People clamoured for change. And that made the ruling class nervous. Just as comfortable aristocratic society watched anxiously France's drift into bloody revolution in the 1790s, so their ancestors in the 1520s felt the tremors of the Peasants' War and those of the 1570s the reverberations of civil war in France and the Netherlands. State-sponsored change, when it came, turned out to be not what the majority of malcontents had been longing for. The severance of England from Latin Christendom was an immense shock and dismay deepened as liturgical and theological innovation followed in the wake of the breach with Rome. The loss of festivals and holy days, the paring down of Christian ritual, the stripping of the altars (at parishioners' expense), the participation of the laity in regular worship – none of these was the sort of change the Tudors' subjects had been looking for. They could discover little evidence that the protestantising of English church life had changed their own existence for the better. But, then, the brief reactionary interlude of Mary's reign brought no relief either.

It was within this milieu of a disturbed and bewildered society that the upholders of an old gospel – which, to many, seemed new – brought their persuasive oratory, their total conviction and their message of hope. And the result was evangelical conversion which, as Professor Marshall has defined, was 'the result of a powerful synthesis: a profound yearning for personal renewal with a plausible theological explanation of how that yearning could be made effectual'.[6] For many, perhaps most, of the converts the process was a dynamic experience that effected a change of beliefs, personality and social relationships. They spoke of having their 'eyes opened' and having been 'born again'.

Most of the agents of such transformations were preachers. This was an age of heroic religious rhetoric. Hugh Latimer's sermons sometimes lasted three hours and, towards the end of the century, the Puritan veteran Laurence Chaderton, when offering after two hours to bring his address to a close, was greeted with cries of 'No, Sir, no! In God's name, go on!' These were educated men who had learned their theology at university, particularly at Cambridge where, by the end of the century, the new colleges of Emmanuel and Sidney Sussex had been founded for the specific purpose of training Puritan preachers. Reformed faith had its roots in logic. At his famous confrontation with the Emperor Charles at Worms, Luther had declined to recant unless his opinions could be disproved 'by Scripture and pure reason'. Evangelical religion was about the Bible, stripped of the schoolmen's glosses and the fanciful allegorical interpretations of medieval preachers. Once this text had been taken as the sole authority for formulating doctrine and for setting the ethical agenda, it only needed to be expounded – in straightforward, rational terms. It was as simple as that.

And because it was as simple as that the way lay open for men and women, armed with an English Bible and the gift of the gab, to appoint themselves as proclaimers of the word. It was eminently logical that, since all truth was contained in the Bible, there was no need for God's people to undergo extensive theology courses. So 'gospellers' emerged and gathered around them, servants, neighbours, any who would listen. And here is another continuity. These simple evangelical gospellers, unencumbered with a university education, were the heirs of the Lollard cell leaders and of crypto-evangelical preachers who had, over the centuries, appeared, eager to impress on their friends and neighbours the message of salvation they had found in the holy text. They also had links with those alehouse rhetoricians who had always been around and had used a smattering of Bible motifs to support their anti-clerical or anti-government ravings.

> When Adam delved and Eve span
> Who was then the gentleman?

So the 'mad priest of Kent', John Ball, had demanded to know when stirring the peasants to egalitarian revolt in 1381, and he was only one of a number of pseudo-religious celebs of whom medieval churchmen were rightly wary.

But agitators, gospellers and university-reared radicals all had one thing in common: they believed that the Bible was a book to change society. Not only could it, by converting individuals, build up a holy population; by bringing governments to accept God's ordinances for the conduct of human affairs it really could create 'heaven on earth'. This seemed, for a time at least, to have been realised in Reformed municipal centres such as Geneva and Zurich. In England the 'commonwealth men' never formed a 'party' with an agreed agenda for social and political change, but they held many principles in common. They advocated free access to the Bible for all. This underlined the importance of education and the channelling of funds liberated from the superstitious misuses of the old faith into schools and university colleges. They stressed the importance of care for the poor and works of charity, not as means to gain salvation but as responses to a loving God who exhorted his followers to love their neighbours. Private enterprise was encouraged and there was a significant increase in bequests for the establishment of almshouses and hospitals. But preachers also looked to state intervention in such initiatives and they were not slow to condemn royal advisers, and even rulers, who used the spoliation of the church to enrich themselves rather than improve the lot of the poor. Another imperative shared by reformers of all stamps was national moral regeneration. One impetus for the evangelical revival had been the corruption and loose living of the clergy. It followed that ministers of the Gospel ought to set an example in godly living and most preachers also took it as axiomatic that in this area of life, as in all others, governments should take a lead by producing legislation which encouraged virtue and punished vice. The more obvious offences such as prostitution had, of course, always been condemned as sins, but the moral earnestness engendered by the Reformation led to action against 'such dissolute and miserable persons as have been suffered to dwell in common open places called the stews'. The words are from a royal proclamation of 1546 closing down brothels (which, like all such legislation, was doomed to failure).

Crime and immorality are as old as man and so is the condemnation of human failings. The desire to change society for the better was not new in the 1530s. It was, however, given an impetus of unprecedented vigour. And England was changed – profoundly. It *looked* different, thanks to the disappearance of the monasteries and the creating of large and modest estates by the new men. It *sounded* different, as anyone attending divine service in English rather than Latin knew only too well. It *felt* different; being separate from Latin Catholicism made England distinct (perhaps in a manner not dissimilar from modern Britain's aloofness from the Eurozone).

Gradually the evangelical revival faded, as all such revivals always do, but it left its marks, as all revivals do. By the end of the century the 'exciting' years were passed when disciples of the new learning had to keep their beliefs secret. Moderate, non-Catholic liturgy and doctrine formed the established religion into which the bulk of the population settled with comparative ease. Among the leaders of society there were many men and women (and, more importantly, families) of a reformist bent. One of the intriguing features of sixteenth-century political life is the emergence of an evangelical caucus within the royal entourage. By the end of Henry VIII's reign his inner chamber was dominated by followers of intellectually fashionable evangelicalism. A radical caucus ruled the roost during Edward's reign. Elizabeth had a Privy Council dominated by men of Puritan sympathies. The monarch was certainly not always in full accord with his/her closest advisers but their influence was crucial. And not only at the centre of national life. There were several communities throughout the length and breadth of England where evangelicalism set the pattern and the tone of common living. To take just one example, the corporation of Northampton remained for decades in the hands of a Puritan oligarchy which sustained godly preachers in town churches and resisted attempts by the ecclesiastical hierarchy to wrest control from their hands. After March 1603, Stuart kings set up a style of court life which was insulated from earnest, radical religion, but by then such religion had become firmly lodged in Parliament and among the burghers and country squires who sat in the Commons.

The story was not the same at all levels of society. Religious revival, particularly revival which depends on people who, whether literate or not, have their minds attuned to argument based on the written word, often struggles to make an impact among the hewers and toilers.

> At the beginning of the seventeenth century the rector of a parish in Kent found that of four hundred communicants, 'scarcely 40' had any knowledge about sin, Christ, death and the afterlife. It was said of men in south Yorkshire and Northumberland that they were totally ignorant of the Bible and did not know the Lord's Prayer. A Yorkshire boy, when quizzed by the minister, could not say 'how many gods there be, nor persons in the godhead, nor who made the world, nor anything about Jesus Christ, nor heaven or hell'. Otherwise he was 'a witty boy and could talk of any worldly things skilfully enough'. A Lancashire woman when asked about the Jesus Christ mentioned in the Creed, replied 'she could not tell, but by our dear Lady it is sure some good thing or it should never have been put in the Creed, but what it is I cannot tell you'. An old man from Cartmel ... a regular church attender ... when Christ was mentioned ... said, 'I think I heard of that man you spoke of, once in a play at Kendall, called Corpus Christi play, where there was a man on a tree, and blood ran down'.[7]

After the sixteenth-century Reformation, there was the same range of belief and disbelief among English people as there had been before it. The majority were still content to attend their parish churches – and were, indeed, strongly attached to those buildings. The intricacies of the faith they were, by and large, content to leave to their ministers. But there was still a minority who wanted something more and some would, within a generation, be shaking the dust of England from their shoes because religion in the country of their birth was not pure enough. Still, too, there were oddballs who held to a variety of pseudo-Christian beliefs. Men said that the Quakers, Diggers, Fifth Monarchists and other mid-seventeenth-century sects were turning the world upside-down. Of course, it is impossible to evolve a statistical survey of how many people were serious about their religion and how many were simply conformist, but we can say that the numbers of activists were much larger than they had been two generations earlier.

That is one reason for affirming that England was a more religious country in 1603 than it had been a century before. Many activists, whether Catholic or Protestant, were men and women who had had to count the cost of their faith. Those who had not, knew relatives, neighbours and friends who had. Convictions had been affirmed and commitment toughened by decades of conflict. And the devout were better educated. As late as 1551, an episcopal visitation in Gloucester diocese had revealed that 55% of parish clergy could not identify the author of the Lord's Prayer and did not know the Ten Commandments and Gloucester was not atypical. The Puritan exercises and greater episcopal vigilance had begun to overcome this scandal. Though the exercises were eventually closed down, their very existence had broadcast the idea (clearly novel to many incumbents) that a little learning was very far from being a dangerous thing. On the Catholic side this was a lesson also taken on board by those who devised the curricula for the foreign seminaries training priests for the mission to England. The social composition of activist groups had also changed. In the early years of the century religious 'enthusiasm' was mainly to be found among the advocates of Lollardy and the devotees of monastic-style personal devotion. By Elizabeth's reign many men and women of all ranks knew the basics of their faith and were ardent in embracing them.

One change above all had not only shaped England but ensured that it could never revert to an authoritarian polity dominated by kings and priests. This monumental transformation of the national psyche was brought about by a book. The English Bible potentially enabled every man and woman to find faith for him/herself. And as they discovered truths within its pages, so they would apply those truths to every aspect of social, political and economic life. The Reformation did not invent individualism, but it did provide individualism with a textual basis. The Reformation did not inaugurate an age of faith. What it did establish was a national Christianity that could define its own doctrines, invent its own liturgy and regulate its own public morality without dependence on a foreign spiritual superpower. Since church and state were inextricably entwined, this freedom found expression in the government's internal and external relations. England assumed a leadership role in Protestant Europe. In the fullness of time, thanks to its commercial and colonial expansion, it would take its culture and its reformed heritage to the ends of the earth.

Notes

Abbreviations:

BL   British Library.

Ca. S.P. Dom *Calendar of State Papers Domestic of the Reign of Queen Elizabeth*, ed. R. Lemon and M.A.E. Green, 1856–71.

Cal. S.P. Edward VI: *Calendar of State Papers Domestic of the Reign of Edward VI*, ed. K.S. Knighton, 1992.

Cal. S.P. For. *Calendar of State Papers Foreign of the Reign of Queen Elizabeth*, ed. W.B. Turnbull, 1863–.

Cal. S.P. Spain *Calendar of State Papers Spanish*, ed. G.A. Bergenroth and P. de Gayangos, 1862–.

Cal. S.P. Ven: *Calendar of State Papers Venetian*, ed. R. Brown, C. Bentinck and H. Brown, 1864–98.

DNB: *Dictionary of National Biography*, Oxford, 1961 edition.

Ellis: *Original Letters Illustrative of English History*, ed. H. Ellis, 1824–46.

Foxe: *Acts and Monuments of the Christian Religion . . .* ed. J. Townsend & S.R. Cattley, 1838.

L and P. *Letters and Papers, Foreign and Domestic of the Reign of Henry VIII*, ed. J. Gairdner, 1861–3.

ODNB: *Oxford Dictionary of National Biography*, Oxford, 2003.

Prologue:

1   D. MacCulloch, *Reformation: Europe's House Divided, 1490–1700*, 2003, 110.

Chapter 1: Circumference and Centre

1   Cf. P. Clark, *English Provincial Society from the Reformation to the Revolution: Religion, Politics and Society in Kent 1500–1640*, 1977, 14–15.

2   G. Elton, *The Tudor Constitution*, Cambridge, 1960, 176–7.

3   *Complete Works of Thomas More*, III, *Latin Works*, New Haven, 1963–, III, 101–3.

4   J. Scattergood (ed.), *John Skelton, The Complete English Poems*, New Haven, Conn., 1983, 111–12.

5   E. Dudley, *The Tree of Commonwealth*, ed. D. M. Brodie, Cambridge, 1948, 43.

6   *The Complete Works of St Thomas More*, New Haven, 1963–, IV, 281.

7   F. J. Furnivall (ed.), *Ballad Society, 1868–72*, I, 96.

8   *The Complete Works of St Thomas More*, New Haven, 1963–, IV, 56, 61.

9   Ibid., IV, 121–3.

10 *Stow's Survey of London*, ed. C. L. Kingsford, 1908, I, 139.

11 E. Hall, *The Triumphant Reign of King Henry VIII*, ed. C. Whibley, 1904, I, 197.

12 See G. Unwin, *The Guilds and Companies of London*, 1963, 248.

13 L and P, XIII, 749.

14 E. H. Zeydal (ed.), *The Ship of Fools*, 1944, Prologue.

15 P. Vilari, *Life and Times of Girolamo Savonarola*, 1888, 518.

16 Cf. J. Huizinga, *Erasmus of Rotterdam*, 1952, 200.

Chapter 2: Earth, Purgatory, Heaven and Hell

1   *Leland's Itinerary in England and Wales*, ed. L. Toulmin Smith, 1964, II, 27.

2   *The Statutes of the Realm*, Historical Record Commission, 1810–28, 328.

3   Complete Works of St Thomas More, New Haven, 1963—, VIII, 1033–4.

4   E. Duffy, *The Stripping of the Altars*, New Haven, 1992, 24–5.

5 J. P. Dolan (ed.), *Enchiridion Militis Christiani, The Essential Erasmus*, New York, 1966, 66.

6 J. de Varagine, *The Golden Legend: Readings on the Saints*, trs. W. G. Ryan, 1995, II, 50.

7 Ibid., I, 364.

8 Ibid., I, 152.

9 J. Huizinga, *The Waning of the Middle Ages*, 1924, 185–6.

10 A. G. Dickens, *Lollards and Protestants in the Diocese of York, 1509–1558*, Oxford, 1959, 58.

11 P. Heath, *English Parish Churches on the Eve of the Reformation*, 1969, 51.

12 G. Chaucer, *The Canterbury Tales*, Prologue, ll. 479ff.

13 Cf. D. B. Foss, 'John Mirk's *Instructions for Parish Priests*', in W. J. Sheils and D. Wood (eds), *The Ministry Clerical and Lay*, Ecclesiastical History Society, Oxford, 1989, 135.

14 Cf. J. A. F. Thomas, *The Later Lollards 1414–1520*, Oxford, 1965, 186.

15 L. and P., VIII, i, 963.

16 J. H. Lupton, *Life of John Colet*, 1887, 299.

17 D. MacCulloch, *Reformation: Europe's House Divided 1490–1700*, 2003, 88.

18 Cf. R. Whiting, *The Blind Devotion of the People*, Cambridge, 1989, 54.

19 P. Stubbs, *The Anatomie of Abuses: containing a Discovery or Briefe Summarie of such Notable Vices and Imperfections as now raigne . . .*, 1583, 95.

20 D. Knowles, *The Religious Orders in England*, Cambridge, 1959, III, 7.

21 *Leland's Itinerary*, op. cit., I, 152.

22 *The Imitation of Christ*, book 1, ch. 3.

23 A. W. Pollard, *Records of the English Bible*, Oxford, 1911, 79.

24 *Anecdotes Historiques d'Étienne de Bourbon*, ed. A. Lecoy de la Marche for the Société de l'Histoire de France, 1877, 307.

25 M. Lambert, *Medieval Heresy: Popular Movements from the Gregorian Reform to the Reformation*, 1992, 371.

26 Ibid.
27 R. Pecock, *The Repression of Over Much Blaming of the Clergy*, ed. C. Babington, Rolls Series 19, I–II, 1860, I, 33–4.
28 Matthew 18: 20. Cf. also P. Collinson, 'Night schools, conventicles and churches', in P. Marshall and A. Ryrie, *The Beginnings of English Protestantism*, Cambridge, 2002, 231.
29 *A proper dyaloge between a Gentillman and a husbandman*, E. Arber, English Reprints (1926), XXVIII, 165.
30 Foxe.
31 P. Collinson, op. cit., 220.

Chapter 3: Keeping an Eye on the Neighbours

1   *Complete Works of St Thomas More*, New Haven, 1965, IV, 100–1.
2   J. Burckhardt, *The Civilization of the Renaissance in Italy*. ed. L. Goldscheider, 1944, 105.
3   Niccolò Machiavelli, *The Prince*, trs. W. K. Marriott, 1992, 3.
4   L. W. Forster, *Selections from Conrad Celtis*, Cambridge, 1948, 46–7.
5   Cf. G. Strauss, *Manifestations of Discontent in Germany on the Eve of the Reformation*, Bloomington, Ind., 1972, 45.
6   H. T. Lehmann and J. Pelikan (eds), *Luther's Works*, St Louis, Mo., and Philadelphia, Penn., 1955–86, vol. 54, 85.
7   E. G. Rupp, *The Righteousness of God*, 1953, 122.
8   D. MacCulloch, *Reformation: Europe's House Divided, 1490–1700*, 2003, 153.
9   Cf. R. Marius, *Martin Luther: The Christian Between God and Death*, Cambridge, Mass., 1999, 292.
10 Cf. P. A. Russell, *Lay Theology in the Reformation*, Cambridge, 1986, 190.

Chapter 4: Divorce and Divorce

1   Cf. A. G. Dickens, *The English Reformation*, 1989, 99.
2   Foxe, IV, 618.
3   D. Daniel (ed.), *Tyndale's New Testament*, New Haven, Conn., 1989, 9–10; G. E. Duffield (ed.), *The Works of William Tyndale*, 1964, 4.
4   T. More, *Works*, ed. W. Rastell, 1557, 344.
5   L and P, Add. I (i), 752.
6   L and P, IV, 3200.
7   Ibid., 3644.
8   H. Walter (ed.), *Doctrinal Treatises and Introductions to Different Portions of the Holy Scriptures by William Tyndale*, Cambridge, 1848, 131–2.
9   Ibid., 206–7.
10 ODNB.
11 J. Barlowe and W. Roye, *Rede Me and Be Not Wrothe*, ed. D. H. Parker, Toronto, 1992, 103.
12 S. Fish, *A Supplication for the Beggars*, ed. F. J. Furnivall and J. M. Cowper, 1871.
13 L and P, IV, 5416.
14 Cf. M. Dowling, 'Anne Boleyn and Reform', in *Journal of Ecclesiastical History*, vol. 35, no. 1, January 1984, 33.
15 J. Strype, *Ecclesiastical Memorials . . .*, 1820–40, vol. 1, 171–3.
16 Cal. S.P. Span., IV (1), 634.
17 E. Hall, *The Union of the Two Noble and Illustre Families of Lancaster and Yorke*, facsimile edn, Menston, 1970, fol. clxxxix.
18 Matthew 28: 19; I Corinthians 9: 16, Tyndales's New Testament, 1534 edn.
19 T. Stapleton (ed.), *Plumpton Correspondence*, Camden Society, Ist series, iv, 1839, 233.
20 *Complete Works of St Thomas More*, New Haven, Conn., 1963–9, VIII, 590.
21 P. S. Allen et al., (eds), *Opus Epistolarum Des. Erasmi Roterodami*, Oxford, 1906–58, x, 2831, 2659.

22 J. Foxe, op. cit., V. 18f.
23 Ibid, V, 31.
24 Ibid, IV, 219.
25 Ibid., IV, 688.
26 Ibid., V, 32; C. L. Kingsford (ed.), *Stow's Survey of London*, Oxford, 1908, I, 209.
27 S. E. Lehmberg, *The Reformation Parliament 1529–1536*, Cambridge, 1970, 140.
28 E. Hall, op. cit., fol. ccv.
29 Ibid.
30 Cf. D. MacCulloch, *Thomas Cranmer*, 1996, 90.
31 Cf. S. E. Lehmberg, 'The religious beliefs of Thomas Cromwell', in R. L. DeMolen (ed.), *Leaders of the Reformation*, Susquehanna, Penn., 1984; S. Brigden, 'Thomas Cromwell and the "brethren" ', in C. Cross, D. Loades and J. J. Scarisbrick (eds), *Law and Government under the Tudors*, Cambridge, 1988.
32 Cf. J. F. Mozley, *Coverdale and His Bibles*, 1953, 4.
33 Cf. S. Brigden, op. cit., 42.
34 Ibid., 41; G. R. Elton, *Reform and Renewal:Thomas Cromwell and the Common Weal*, Cambridge, 1973, 26–7.
35 ODNB.
36 G. R. Elton (ed.), *The Tudor Constitution*, Cambridge, 1960, 344.

Chapter 5: Heary's Church

1 G. R. Elton (ed.), *The Tudor Constitution*, Cambridge, 1960, 354.
2 J. Stow, *Annales, or, a general chronicle of England*, 1631, 562.
3 L and P, VI, 923.
4 Ellis Ser. I, vol. ii, 1969, 43–5.
5 L and P, VIII, 776, XII (ii), 505, X, 365.
6 G. R. Elton, *Policy and Police*, Cambridge, 1972, 89.
7 L and P, VII, 754.
8 BL, Harleian MS. 419, f. 112–14.
9 Ellis, op. cit., Ser. III, vol. ii, 1969, 285.

10 DNB.

11 G. Burnet, *History of the Reformation*, 1681, II, 442.

12 Ellis, Ser. III, vol. lii, 3–6.

13 ODNB.

14 II Chronicles 9: 8.

15 G. Walker, *Writing Under Tyranny: English Literature and the Henrician Reformation*, Oxford, 2005, 20.

16 T. Cranmer, *Miscellaneous Writings*, ed. J. E. Cox, 1846, 460–1.

17 E. Hall, *The Union of the Two Noble and Illustre Families of Lancaster and Yorke*, fascimile edn, Menston, 1970, fol. ccxviii.

18 T. Stapleton (ed.), *Plumpton Correspondence*, Camden Society, Ist Series, iv, 1839, 223.

19 C. Wriothesley, *A Chronicle of England during the Reigns of the Tudors*, ed. W. D. Hamilton, Camden Society, New Series I, 1875, 82–3.

20 R. W. Dixon, *History of the Church of England 1078–1902*, 1872–1902, I, 413–4.

21 W. Fulke, *A Defense of the sincere and true Translations of the holie Scriptures into the English tong*, Cambridge, Parker Society, 1843, 98.

22 *The Lisle Letters*, ed. M. St C. Byrne, Chicago, 1981, III, 283.

23 L and P, X, 613.

24 L and P, X, 254.

25 L and P, XI, 65.

26 C. Wriothesley, op. cit., I, 55.

27 Cf. W. L. Warren, *Henry II*, 1973, 430–1.

28 W. Tyndale, *Obedience of a Christian Man*, in *Doctrinal Treatises . . .*, ed. H. Walter, Cambridge, Parker Society, 1848, 178.

Chapter 6: England Disunited

1 *A Copy of the Letters wherein the Most Redouted Mighty Prince . . . Kyng Henry the Eight . . . Made Answer unto a*

Certayne Letter of Martyn Luther . . ., Short Titles Catalogue (STC) 13086, 1527, Bii.

2   L and P, XII, I, 1301.

3   L and P, XI, 972.

4   L and P, XI, 970.

5   E. Hall, *The Union of the Two Noble and Illustre Families of Lancaster and Yorke*, facsimile edn, Menston, 1970, fol. ccxxxi.

6   *State Papers*, 1830–52, I, 468–70.

7   Ibid., I, 518–19.

8   The two sets of articles are printed in full in R. W. Hoyle, *The Pilgrimage of Grace and the Politics of the 1530s*, Oxford, 2001, 460–4.

9   Cf. M. H. Dodds and R. Dodds, *The Pilgrimage of Grace, 1536–1537* . . ., 1971, II, 28–30.

10 E. Hall, op. cit., ccxxxi.

11 Cf. S. Foister, 2006, 94.

12 Ellis, I Ser asp 410., vol. iii, 85–6.

13 Ibid., Ser. III, vol. iii, 139.

14 Ibid., 235.

15 Ibid., Ser. II, vol. ii, 612.

16 C. Wriothesley, *A Chronicle of England during the Reigns of the Tudors*, ed. W. D. Hamilton, Camden Society, New Series, 1875, 83.

17 Cf. R. Demaus, *Hugh Latimer*, 1869, 287.

18 Ellis, Ser. III, vol. iii, 100.

19 W. H. Frere and W. M. Kennedy (eds), *Visitation Articles and Injunctions*, 1910, II, 38.

20 C. Wriothesley, op. cit., 86–7.

21 Ibid., 90.

22 Ibid., 81.

23 H. Jenkyns, *The Remains of Thomas Cranmer D.D., Archbishop of Canterbury*, 1833, 346.

24 W. H. Frere and W. M. Kennedy, op. cit., II, 38.

25 A. W. Pollard, *Records of the English Bible*, Oxford, 1911, 271.

26 L and P, XIV, 897.
27 Thomas Becon, *Works*, ed. J. Ayre, Cambridge, Parker Society, 1843–4, I, 38.
28 R. Demaus, op. cit., 261–2.
29 C. Wriothesley, op. cit., 72.
30 Ibid., 80.
31 L and P, XII, ii, 295.
32 *Miscellaneous Writings and Letters of Thomas Cranmer*, ed. J. E. Cox, Cambridge, Parker Society, 1846, II, 351.
33 C. Lloyd, *Formularies of Faith*, Oxford, 1856, 176.

Chapter 7: Building a Christian Commonwealth

1   L and P, XVI, 101.
2   G. E. Duffield (ed.), *The Work of Thomas Cranmer*, Appleford, 1964, 124.
3   Cf. W. G. Hoskins, *The Age of Plunder: The England of Henry VIII*, 1976, 218.
4   Cf. A. Ryrie, *The Gospel and Henry VIII: Evangelicals in the Early English Reformation*, Cambridge, 2003, 148.
5   Richard Hilles to Henry Bullinger, in H. Robinson (ed.), *Original Letters relative to the English Reformation*, Cambridge, Paster Society, 1846, I, 200–1.
6   Ibid., 153.
7   F. J. Furnivall (ed.), *Ballads from Manuscripts*, 1868–72, I, 131–2.
8   Cf. D. MacCulloch, *Thomas Cranmer*, New Haven, 1996, 306.
9   C. Lloyd, *Formularies of Faith*, Oxford, 1856, 217.
10 W. Turner, *The hunting and fyndyng out of the Romish fox*, 1543, 3–4.
11 Foxe, V, 495.
12 J. Strype, *Memorials of ... Archbishop Cranmer*, 1853, I, xxviii, 123.
13 L. M. Higgs, *Godliness and Governance*, Michigan, 1998, 143–4.
14 J. G. Nichols (ed.), *Narratives of the Days of the Reformation*, Camden Society, 1859, 256.

15 J. Stow, *Annals of the Reformation*, 1601, 590.
16 John Hooper to Henry Bullinger, in H. Robinson (ed.), op. cit., I, 36.
17 Cal. S.P. Span., XXI, 1, No. 289.
18 Quoted in J. Childs, *Henry VIII's Last Victim*, 2007, 218.
19 L and Pi, XXI, I, 984.
20 J. Strype, *Ecclesiastical Memorials relating chiefly to Religion . . .*, Oxford, 1820–40, I, I, 595.
21 J. Bale, *Selected Works*, ed. H. Christmas, Cambridge, Parker Society, 1849, 220.
22 L and P, XXI, i, 1491.
23 John Hooper to Henry Bullinger, in H. Robinson (ed.), op. cit., I, 41–2.
24 Foxe, V, 692.
25 D. MacCulloch, *Tudor Church Militant: Edward VI and the Protestant Reformation*, 1999, 104.
26 Bartholomew Traheron to Henry Bullinger, in H. Robinson, op. cit., I, 321.
27 Thomas Cranmer to John à Lasco, ibid., I, 17 (ed.).
28 W. H. Frere and W. M. Kennedy (eds), *Visitation Articles and Injunctions of the Period of the Reformation*, 1910, II, 126, no. 28.
29 Ibid.
30 J. G. Nichols (ed.), *Grey Friars' Chronicle*, 1852, 54.
31 P. Marshall, *Beliefs and the Dead in Reformation England*, Oxford, 2002, 100.
32 J. R. Tanner (ed.), *Tudor Constitutional Documents*, Cambridge, 1948, 115.
33 J. G. Nichols (ed.), op. cit., 54.
34 Foxe, 517.
35 J. E. Cox (ed.), *The Works of Thomas Cranmer*, Cambridge, 1844–6, II, 121.
36 Bartholomew Traheron to Henry Bullinger, in H. Robinson (ed.), I, p. 266 op. cit., I, 323.
37 Ibid.
38 Cf. J. Cornwall, *Revolt of the Peasantry, 1549*, 1977, 115.

39 C. S. Knighton (ed.), *Calendar of State Papers Domestic of the Reign of Edward VI 1547–1553*, 1992, 302.
40 Ibid., 149.
41 Ibid., 301.
42 Calvin to Cranmer, in H. Robinson (ed.), op. cit., II, 713.
43 Foxe, VI, 6.
44 A. F. Leach, *English Schools at the Reformation, 1546–8*, 1896, II, vii.
45 Cal. S. P. Edward VI, 555.

Chapter 8: Sealed in Blood

1 H. Robinson (ed.), *Original Letters relative to the English Reformation*, 1846, I, 141, and II, 593.
2 J. G. Nichols (ed.), *Literary Remains of Edward the Sixth*, 1857, ccxxxiv.
3 D. MacCulloch, *Tudor Church Militant: Edward VI and the Protestant Reformation*, 1999, 116.
4 I. Lancashire (ed.), *Short-Title Catalogue, 13675*, Renaissance Electronic Texts 1.2. 1997.
5 Cf. E. Duffy, *The Stripping of the Altars*, New Haven, Conn., 1992, 533.
6 H. Robinson (ed.), op. cit., I, 110–11.
7 Ibid., I, 105.
8 J. Guy, *Tudor England*, Oxford, 1988, 227.
9 Cal. S.P. Span., XI, 395.
10 Ibid., XI, 217.
11 J. G. Nichols (ed.), *The Chronicle of Queen Jane and two years of Queen Mary . . .*, 1850, 159.
12 Cal. S.P. Span., XIII, 33.
13 Foxe, VI, 658.
14 Ibid., VI, 532.
15 D. MacCulloch, *Thomas Cranmer: A Life*, New Haven, Conn., 1996, 568.
16 H. Robinson (ed.), op. cit., I, 143.
17 Foxe, VII, 550.
18 Cal. S.P. Span., XIII, 147.

19 J. Strype, *Ecclesiastical Memorials relating chiefly to Religion . . .*, Oxford, 1820–40, III, ii, 125.
20 Foxe, VIII, 302.
21 Ibid., VIII, 88.
22 Cal. S.P. Ven., 1555–56, 434.
23 Cal. S.P. Ven., 1555–56, 1549.
24 Cal. S.P. Span., XIII, 366.
25 Cal. S.P. Span., XIII, 148.

Chapter 9: Commitment, Compromise and Conflict

1 L. S. Marcus, J. Mueller and M. B. Rose (eds), *Elizabeth I Collected Works*, Chicago., 2000, 12.
2 W. MacCaffrey, *The Shaping of the Elizabethan Regime*, 1969, 38.
3 S. Alford, *The Early Elizabethan Polity*, Cambridge, 1998, 26.
4 H. Gee and W. J. Hardy (eds), *Documents Illustrative of the History of the English Church*, 1896, 374.
5 Ibid., 417.
6 Ibid.
7 H. Robinson (ed.), *The Zurich Letters, 1558–1579*, Cambridge, 1842, I, 10.
8 Ibid., II 1845, 36.
9 T. E. Hartley (ed.), *Proceedings in the Parliaments of Elizabeth I*, Leicester, 1981, 34–5.
10 Cal. S.P. Ven., 1558–80, 27.
11 D. Laing (ed.), *Works of John Knox*, Edinburgh, 1848, IV, 273.
12 H. Robinson, (ed.), *Zurich Letters*, 21.
13 H. Robinson (ed.), *Original Letters Relative to the English Reformation*, Cambridge, 1847, 754.
14 H. Robinson (ed.), *Zurich Letters*, 61.
15 J. Bruce and T. T. Perowne (eds), *Correspondence of Matthew Parker, D.D*, Cambridge, 1853, 125.
16 H. Robinson (ed.), *Zurich Letters*, 71.
17 Cal. S.P. Ven., 1558–80, 58.

18 H. Robinson (ed.), *Zurich Letters*, 1st series, 16.
19 J.H. Pollen (ed.), *Queen Mary's Letter to the Duke of Guise*, Edinburgh, 1904, 39.
20 Ibid., 17–18.
21 L. S. Marcus, J. Mueller and M. B. Rose (eds), op. cit., 55.
22 H. Robinson (ed.), *Zurich Letters*, 55.
23 Ibid.
24 L.S. Marcus, J. Mueller and M.B. Rose (eds), op. cit., 139.
25 H. Gee and W. J. Hardy (eds), op.cit., 417–42.
26 H. Robinson (ed.), *Zurich Letters*, 73–4 (eds).
27 A. Peel (ed.), *The second parte of a register, being a calendar of manuscripts under that title intended for publication by the Puritans . . .*, Cambridge, 1915, II, 84.
28 C. Litzenberger, 'St, Michael's, Gloucester, 1540–80: the cost of conformity in sixteenth-century England, in K. L. French, G. G. Gibbs and B. A. Kümin (eds), *The Parish in English Life 1400–1600*, Manchester, 1997, 245–6.
29 P. Collinson, 'The Monarchical Republic of Queen Elizabeth I', in *Elizabethans*, 2003, 42.
30 www.papalencyclicals.net/Pius 05/p5.htm
31 H. Robinson (ed.), *Zurich Letters*, 214–15.
32 Cf. A. Hogg, *God's Secret Agents*, 2006, 71.
33 H. Robinson (ed.), *Zurich Letters*, 2nd series, 286–7.
34 J. Strype, *Annals of the Reformation*, 1824, II, 92.
35 L. S. Marcus, J. Mueller and M. B. Rose (eds), op. cit., 179.
36 Ibid., 178.
37 P.W. Hasler, *The House of Commons 1558–1603*, 1981, 599.
38 P. Collinson (ed.), *Letters of Thomas Wood, Puritan, 1566–1577*, 1960, 15.
39 Cf. P. Collinson, *Archbishop Grindal, 1519–1583*, 1979, 242.
40 Cal. S.P. Dom., XIV, 217.
41 T. Wright (ed.), *Queen Elizabeth and Her Times*, 1838, 102.
42 Cal. S.P. Dom., XIV, 22.
43 Clarification of the Tridentine decree later offered by Francis Toletus, an intimate papal adviser and the first

Jesuit to be made cardinal. Cf. F. Edwards (ed.), *Historia Missionis Anglicanae Societatis Jesu of Henry More (1660)*, 1981, 83.

44   Cal. S.P. For., 1583–4, 652–3.

45   BL, Hatfield MSS., III, 45.

46   National Archive, State Papers 12/174.

47   H. Gee and W. J. Hardy (eds), op. cit., 485ff.

48   J. E. Neale, *Elizabeth I and Her Parliaments*, 1953, II, 74–5.

49   J. Guy, *Tudor England*, Oxford, 1988, 307.

50   Cf. J. Guy, *My Heart is My Own: The Life of Mary Queen of Scots*, 2004, 499.

51   J. L. Black, *The Marprelate Tracts*, Cambridge, 2008, 10.

52   P. Marshall, *Reformation England, 1480–1642*, 2003, 165.

Epilogue

1   E. B. Pusey (ed.), *The Confessions of Saint Augustine*, 1921, ch. VIII.

2   W. A. Pantin, *The English Church in the Fourteenth Century*, 1962, 132–3.

3   John Wesley, *Journal*, 1790, I, 103.

4   Leo Tolstoy, *A Confession and What I Believe*, trs. A. Maude, Oxford, 1921, 104–5.

5   Cf. C. Morris, *The Papal Monarchy: The Western Church from 1050 to 1250*, Oxford, 1991, 37.

6   P. Marshall, *Religious Identities in Henry VIII's England*, Aldershot, 2006, 42.

7   B. Reay, 'Popular Religion', in B. Reay (ed.), *Popular Culture in Seventeenth Century England*, 1988, 94–5.

Bibliography

The place of publication is London unless otherwise indicated.

Printed and Early Sources

A Copy of the Letters wherein the Most Redouted Mighty Prince . . . Kyng Henry the Eight . . . Made Answer unto a Certayne Letter of Martyn Luther . . ., Short Titles Catalogue (STC) 13086, 1527, Bii.

A proper dyaloge between a Gentillman and a husbandman, E. Arber, English Reprints (1926).

Allen, P. S., et al (eds), *Opus Epistolarum Des. Erasmi Roterodami*, Oxford, 1906–58.

Anecdotes Historiques d'Étienne de Bourbon, ed. A. Lecoy de la Marche for the Société de l'Histoire de France, 1877.

Ayre, J. (ed.), *Works of Thomas Becon*, Cambridge, Parker Society, 1843–4.

Bain, J., et al., (eds), *Calendar of State Papers relating to Scotland and Mary, Queen of Scots*, Edinburgh, 1898–1952.

Barlowe, J., and W. Roye, *Rede Me and Be Not Wrothe*, ed. D. H. Parker, Toronto, 1992.

Bale, J. *Select Works*, ed. H. Christmas, Cambridge, Parker Society, 1849.

Bergenroth, G. A., and P. de Gayangos (eds), *Calendar of State Papers, Spanish*, 1862–6.

Brown, R., C. Bentinck and H. Brown (eds), *Calendar of State Papers, Venetian*, 1864–98.

Bruce, J., (ed.), *Correspondence of Robert Dudley, Earl of Leycester during his government of the Low Countries*, Camden Society, I series, 27, 1844.

Bruce, J., and T. T. Perowne (eds), *Correspondence of Matthew Parker, DD*, Cambridge, 1853.

Byrne, M. St C. (ed.), *The Lisle Letters*, Chicago, 1980.

Camden, W., *The History of the Most Renowned and Victorious Princess Elizabeth, Late Queen of England*, ed. W. T. MacCattrey, Chicago, 1970.

Caraman, P. (ed.), *William Weston – The Autobiography of an Elizabethan*, 1955.

Cavendish, G., 'The Life and Death of Cardinal Wolsey', in R. S. Sylvester and D. P. Harding (eds), *Two Early Tudor Lives*, New Haven, 1962.

Collinson, P. (ed.), *Letters of Thomas Wood, Puritan, 1566–1577*, 1960.

Corrie, G. E. (ed.), *Sermons and Remains of Hugh Latimer . . .*, Cambridge, 1844, 1845.

Cox, J. E. (ed.), *Miscellaneous Writings and Letters of Thomas Cranmer*, Cambridge, Parker Society, 1846.

Wyatt, T., *Collected Poems*, ed. J. Daalder, Oxford, 1975.

Daniel, D. (ed.), *Tyndale's New Testament*, New Haven, Conn., 1989.

Dasent, J. R. (ed.), *Acts of the Privy Council of England*, 1890–1907.

Digges, D. (ed.), *The complete ambassador*, or, *Two treatises of the intended marriage of Queen Elizabeth, comprised in letters of negotiation of Sir F. Walsingham . . .*, 1655.

Dolan, J. P. (ed.), *Enchiridion Militis Christiani, The Essential Erasmus*, New York, 1966.

Dowling, M. (ed.), 'William Latymer's chronickille of Anne Bulleyne', *Camden Miscellany 30*, 4th series, no. XXXIX, 1990.

Duque de Berwick y de Alba (ed.), *Correspondencia de Cutierre Gómez de Fuensalida*, Madrid, 1907.

Edgeworth, R. (ed.), *Sermons Very Fruitful, Godly and Learned:*

Preaching in the Reformation, c. 1535–c. 1553, ed. J. Wilson, Cambridge, 1993.

Ellis, H. (ed.), *Original Letters Illustrative of English History*, 1824–46.

Elton, G. R. (ed.), *The Tudor Constitution, Documents and Commentary*, Cambridge, 1960.

Erasmus, D., *The Praise of Folly*, trs. C. H. Miller, New Haven, 1979.

The First and Second Prayer Books of Edward VI, Everyman edn, 1951.

Fish, S. *A Supplication for the Beggars*, ed. F. J. Furnivall and J. M. Cowper, 1871.

Frere, W. H., and W. M. Kennedy (eds.), *Visitation Articles and Injunctions of the Period of the Reformation*, 1910.

Fulke, W., *A Defense of the sincere and true Translations of the holie Scriptures into the English tong*, Cambridge, Parker Society, 1843.

Gairdner, J. (ed.), *Letters and Papers, Foreign and domestic of the Reign of Henry VIII*, 1861–3.

—— (ed.), *Paston Letters, AD 1422–1509*, 1904.

Gee, H., and W. J. Hardy (eds), *Documents Illustrative of the History of the English Church*, 1896.

Gough Nichols, J. (ed.), *Documents of the English Reformation*, Cambridge, 1994.

Giustiniani, S., *Four Years at the Court of Henry VIII ... January 12th 1515 to July 26th 1519*, R. Brown, 1854.

Hall, E., *The Triumphant Reign of King Henry VIII*, ed. C. Whibley, 1904.

Hall, E., *The Union of the Two Noble and Illustre Families of Lancaster and Yorke*, facsimile edn, Menston, 1970.

Hall, E., *The Union of the Two Noble and Illustre Families of Lancastre and Yorke*, ed. H. Ellis, 1809.

Hamilton, H. C., et al. (eds), *Calendar of State Papers relating to Ireland*, 1860–1905.

Historical Manuscript Commission (HMC), Calendar of Manuscripts of Marquis of Bath at Longleat, 1904–80.

HM Calendar of Manuscripts of Marquis of Salisbury at Hatfield House, 1883–1923.

Hume, M.R.C., (ed.) Calendar of Letters of State Papers . . . in the Archives of Simancas, 1847.

Kervyn de Lettenhove, J. M. B. C., and I. Galliodts-van Severen (eds), *Relations politiques des Pays-Bas et de l'Angleterre sous la regne de Philippe II*, 1882–1900.

Kingsford, C. L. (ed.), *Stow's Survey of London*, 1908.

Knighton, K. S. (ed.), *Calendar of State Papers Domestic of the Reign of Edward VI*, 1992.

Laing, D. (ed.), *Works of John Knox*, Edinburgh, 1848.

Lehmann, H. T., and J. Pelikan (eds), *Luther's Works*, St Louis, Missouri, and Philadelphia, Pennsylvania, 1955–86

Lemon, R., and M.A.E. Green (eds), *Calendar of State Papers Domestic of the Reign of Queen Elizabeth*, 1856–72.

MacCulloch, D. (ed.), 'The Vita Mariae Angliae Regina of Robert Wingfield of Brantham', in Camden Miscellany XXVIII, 1984.

Martin, C. T. (ed.), *Journal of Sir Francis Walsingham*, Camden Miscellany VI, 1870.

Miller, C. H. (ed.), *The Complete Works of Thomas More*, New Haven, 1963–

Murdin, W. (ed.), Collection of State Papers, relating to affairs in the reign of Queen Elizabeth . . ., 1759.

Nichols, J. G. (ed.), *The Chronicle of Queen Jane and two years of Queen Mary* . . ., 1850.

—— (ed.), *Grey Friars' Chronicle*, 1852.

—— (ed.), *Literary Remains of Edward the Sixth*, 1857.

—— (ed.), *Narratives of the Days of the Reformation*, Camden Society, 1859.

Pecock, R, *The Repression of Over Much Blaming of the Clergy*, ed. C. Babington, Rolls Series 19, I–II, 1860.

Peel, A. (ed.), *The second parte of a register, being a calendar of manuscripts under that title intended for publication by the Puritans* . . ., Cambridge, 1915.

Pollen, J. H. (ed.), *Queen Mary's Letter to the Duke of Guise*, Edinburgh, 1904.

Robinson, H. (ed.), *Original Letters relative to the English Reformation*, Cambridge, Parker Society, 1846.

—— (ed.), *The Zurich Letters, 1558–1579*, Cambridge, Parker Society, 1842.

Scattergood, J. (ed.), *John Skelton, The Complete English Poems*, New Haven, 1983.

Stapleton, T. (ed.), *Plumpton Correspondence*, Camden Society, Ist series, iv, 1839.

The Statutes of the Realm, Historical Record Commission, 1810–28.

Stow, J., *Annales, or, a general chronicle of England*, ed. E. Howes, 1631.

Strype, J., *Annals of the Reformation*, 1824.

——, *Ecclesiastical Memorials relating chiefly to Religion . . .*, Oxford, 1820–40.

——, *Memorials of the Most Reverend Father in God, Thomas Cranmer*, 1853.

Stubbs, Philip, *The Anatomie of Abuses: containing a Discovery or Briefe Summarie of such Notable Vices and Imperfections as now raigne . . .*, 1583.

Tawney, R. H., and E. Power, *Tudor Economic Documents*, 1924.

Turnbull, W. B. (ed.), *Calendar of State Papers Foreign of the Reign of Queen Elizabeth*, 1863.

Turner, W., *The hunting and fyndyng out of the Romish fox*, 1543.

Tyndale, W., *Obedience of a Christian Man*, in *Doctrinal Treatises . . .*, ed. H. Walter, Parker Society, 1848.

Walter, H. (ed.), *Doctrinal Treatises and Introductions to Different Portions of the Holy Scriptures by William Tyndale*, Cambridge, 1848.

Wright, T. (ed.), *Three Chapters of Letters Relating to the Suppression of the Monasteries*, Camden Society, no. XXVI, 1843.

Wriothesley, C. *A Chronicle of England During the Reigns of the Tudors*, ed. W. D. Hamilton, Camden Society, new series, nos XI, XX, 1875–7.

Secondary Works – Books and Articles

Ackroyd, P., *The Life of Thomas More*, 1998.

Adams, S. L., 'Eliza Enthroned? The Court and its Politics', in C. Haigh (ed.), *Reign of Elizabeth I*, 1989, 55–7.

Alford, S., *Burghley: William Cecil at the Court of Elizabeth I*, New Haven, 2008.

——, *The Early Elizabethan Polity*, Cambridge, 1998.

——, *Kingship and Politics in the Reign of Edward VI*, Cambridge, 2002.

Allen, J. W., *A History of Political Thought in the Sixteenth Century*, 1960 edn.

Alvarez, M. F., *Charles V: Elected Emperor and Hereditary Ruler*, trs. J. A. Lalaguna, 1975.

Andrews, K. R., *Elizabethan Privateering: English Privateering during the Spanish War, 1585–1603*, Cambridge, 1964.

Anglo, S., *Spectacle, Pageantry and Early Tudor Policy*, Oxford, 1969.

Archer, J. M., *Sovereignty and Intelligence: Spying and Court Culture in the English Renaissance*, Stanford, California.

Aston, M., *England's Iconoclasts, I, Laws Against Images*, Oxford, 1988.

——, *The King's Bedpost: Reformation and Iconography . . .*, Cambridge, 1993.

Aveling, J. C. H., *The Handle and the Axe: The Catholic Recusants in England from Reformation to Emancipation*, 1976.

Axton, M., *The Queens' Two Bodies: Drama and the Elizabethan Succession*, 1977.

Bagchi, D., ' "Eyn Mercklich Underscheyd": Catholic reactions to Luther's doctrine of the priesthood of all believers', in W. J. Sheils and D. Wood (eds), *The Ministry: Clerical and Lay Studies in Church History*, no. XXVI, Oxford, 1989.

Bartlett, K. R., 'The English Exile Community in Italy and the Political Opposition to Queen Mary I', *Albion*, 13, 1981.

——, 'The Role of the Marian Exiles', in P. W. Hasler (ed.), *The House of Commons, 1558–1603*, I, app. xi, p. 12, 1981.

Basing, P., 'Robert Beale and the Queen of Scots', *British Library Journal*, 20, 1994.

Baumann, U. (ed.), *Henry VIII in History, Historiography and Literature*, Frankfurt, 1993.

Baumgartner, F. J., *Radical Reactionaries: The Political Thought of the French Catholic League*, Geneva, 1975.

Beckingsale, B. W., *Thomas Cromwell: Tudor Minister*, 1978.

Beer, B. L., *Northumberland: The Political Career of John Dudley, Earl of Warwick and Duke of Northumberland*, Kent, Ohio, 1973.

Bellamy, J., *The Tudor Law of Treason*, Toronto, 1979.

Bernard, G. W., *Anne Boleyn – Fatal Attractions*, New Haven, 2010.

——, 'Anne Boleyn's religion', *Historical Journal*, no. XXXVI, 1993.

——, 'The fall of Anne Boleyn', *English Historical Review*, no. CVI, 1990.

——, *The King's Reformation: Henry VIII and the Remaking of the English Church*, New Haven, 2005.

Black, J. L., *The Marprelate Tracts*, Cambridge, 2008.

Block, J., *Factional Politics in the English Reformation, RHS Studies in History*, no. LXVI, 1993.

Bossy, J., *Giordano Bruno and the Embassy Affair*, 1991.

Bowker, M., *The Henrician Reformation: The Diocese of Lincoln under John Longland 1521–1547*, Cambridge, 1981

Bradshaw, B., and E. Duffy (eds), *Humanism, Reform and the Reformation: The Career of Bishop John Fisher*, Cambridge, 1989.

Brenan, G., and E. P. Statham, *The House of Howard*, 1907.

Brigden, S., *London and the Reformation*, Oxford, 1989.

——, *New Worlds, Lost Worlds: The Rule of the Tudors*, 2000.

—— 'Thomas Cromwell and the "brethren" ', in C. Cross, D. Loades and J. J. Scarisbrick (eds), *Law and Government under the Tudors*, Cambridge, 1988.

Bromiley, G. W., *Thomas Cranmer, Theologian*, 1956.

Burnet, G., *History of the Reformation of the Church of England*, Oxford, 1865.

Cameron, E., *The European Reformation*, Oxford, 1991.

Caraman, P., *The Other Face: Catholic Life under Elizabeth I*, 1960.

Carroll, S., *Martyrs and Murderers: The Guise Family and the Making of Europe*, Oxford, 2009.

Chambers, R. W., *Thomas More*, 1976 edn.

Chapman, H. W., *The Sisters of Henry VIII*, 1969.

Chibi, A. A., *Henry VIII's Bishops*, Cambridge, 2003.

Childs, J., *Henry VIII's Last Victim: The Life and Times of Henry Howard Earl of Surrey*, 2006.

Clarification of the Tridentine decree later offered by Francis Toletus, an intimate papal adviser and the first Jesuit to be made cardinal. Cf. Edwards, F. (ed.), *Historia Missionis Anglicanae Societatis Jesu of Henry More (1660)*, 1981.

Clark, P., *English Provincial Society from the Reformation to the Revolution: Religion, Politics and Society in Kent 1500–1640*, 1977.

Clegg, C. B., *Press Censorship in Elizabethan England*, 1997.

Cliffe, J. T., *The Puritan Gentry*, 1984.

Cole, M. H., *The Portable Queen: Elizabeth I and the Politics of Ceremony*, Amherst, Mass., 1999.

Coleman, C., and D. Starkey, *Revolution Reassessed*, 1986.

Collinson, P., *Archbishop Grindal, 1519–1583: The Struggle for a Reformed Church*, 1980.

——, 'De republica Anglorum, or, History with the politics put back', in P. Collinson (ed.), *Elizabethan Essays*, 1994.

——, 'The Elizabethan Church and the New Religion', in Haigh (ed.), *Reign of Elizabeth I*, 1984.

——, *Elizabethan Essays*, 1994.

——, *The Elizabethan Puritan Movement*, 1967.

——, *Elizabethans*, 2003.

——, *The English Captivity of Mary, Queen of Scots*, Sheffield, 1987.

——, *Godly People*, 1983.

——, *Godly Rule: Essays on English Protestantism and Puritanism*, 1983.

——, 'The monarchical republic of Queen Elizabeth I', in J. A. Guy (ed.), *The Tudor Monarchy*, 1997.

——, 'Night schools, conventicles and churches', in P. Marshall and A. Ryrie, *The Beginnings of English Protestantism*, Cambridge, 2002.

——, *The Religion of Protestants: The Church in English Society, 1559–1625*, Oxford, 1982.

Condon, M., 'Ruling elites in the reign of Henry VII', in C. Ross (ed.), *Patronage, Pedigree and Power in Late Medieval England*, Gloucester, 1979.

Cornwall, J., *Revolt of the Peasantry, 1549*, 1977.

Cross, C., *Church and People, 1450–1600: The Triumph of the Laity . . .*, Hassocks, 1976

——, D. Loades and J. J. Scarisbrick, 'Law and government under the Tudors', essays presented to Sir Geoffrey Elton, Cambridge, 1988.

Davies, C. S. L., *Peace, Print and Protestantism: 1450–1558*, 1977.

De Molen, R. I. (ed.), *Leaders of the Reformation*, Selinsgrove, 1984.

Demaus, R., *Hugh Latimer: A Biography*, 1869.

Dickens, A. G., *The English Reformation*, 1989.

——, *Later Monasticism and the Reformation*, 1994.

——, *Lollards and Protestants in the Diocese of York 1509–1558*, 1982, rev. edn.

——, *Thomas Cromwell and the English Reformation*, 1959.

——, and W. R. D. Jones, *Erasmus the Reformer*, 1994.

—— and J. M. Tonkin, with K. Powell, *The Reformation in Historical Thought*, Oxford, 1985.

Dixon, R. W., *History of the Church of England 1078–1902*.

Dodds, M. H., and R. Dodds, *The Pilgrimage of Grace and the Exeter Conspiracy 1872–1902*, Cambridge, 1971.

Doran, S., 'Revenge her Foul and Most Unnatural Murder? The Impact of Mary Stewart's Execution on Anglo-Scottish Relations', *Historical Association*, 85, 2000.

Dowling, M., 'Anne Boleyn and Reform', *Journal of Ecclesiastical History*, vol. XXV, no. 1, January 1984.

Duffield, G. E. (ed.), *The Works of William Tyndale*, 1964.

Duffy, E., *The Stripping of the Altars: Traditional Religion in England 1400–1580*, New Haven, 1992.

Edwards, E., *Robert Persons: The Biography of an Elizabethan Jesuit*, St Louis, 1995.

Elton, G. R., *England Under the Tudors*, 1955.

——, 'King or minister? The man behind the English reformation', *History*, no. XXXIX, 1954.

——, *Policy and Police: The Enforcement of the Reformation in the Age of Thomas Cromwell*, Cambridge, 1972.

——, *Reform and Reformation*, 1977.

——, *Reform and Renewal: Thomas Cromwell and the Common Weal*, Cambridge, 1973.

——, 'Sir Thomas More and the opposition to Henry VIII', *Studies in Tudor Politics and Government*, 1974.

——, (ed.) *Studies in Tudor and Stuart Politics*, 1974–84.

——, 'Thomas More, councillor', in *Studies in Tudor and Stuart Politics and Government*, 1974.

——, 'Tudor government: the points of contact', *Royal Historical Society*, 1976.

——, *The Tudor Constitution*, Cambridge, 1960, 2nd edn, 1982.

——, *The Tudor Revolution in Government: Administration Changes in the Reign of Henry VIII*, Cambridge, 1953.

Erickson, C., *Bloody Mary*, 1978.

Fleisher, M., *Radical Reform and Political Persuasion in the Life and Writings of Thomas More*, 1973.

Forster, S., *Holbein in England*, New Haven, 2004.

Forster, L. W., *Selections from Conrad Celtis*, Cambridge, 1948.

Foss, D. B., 'John Mirk's *Instructions for Parish Priests*', in W. J. Sheils and D. Wood (eds), *The Ministry Clerical and Lay*, Ecclesiastical History Society, Oxford, 1989.

Fox, A., and J. Guy (eds), *Reassessing the Henrician Age: Humanism, Politics and Reform, 1500–1550*, Oxford, 1986.

Fox, A., *Thomas More: History and Providence*, Oxford, 1982.

Foxe, J., *Acts and Monuments of the Christian Religion*, ed. G. Townsend and S. R. Cattley, 1838.

French, K. L., et al., *The Parish in English Life, 1400–1600*, Manchester, 1997.

Furnivall, F. J. (ed.), *Ballads from Manuscripts*, 1868–72.

Garrett, C. H., *The Marian Exiles: A Study in the Origins of Elizabethan Puritanism*, 1938.

Gikes, R. K., *The Tudor Parliament*, 1969.

Graves, M., *Thomas Norton, The Parliament Man*, Oxford, 1994.

Grell, O., *Calvinist Exiles in Tudor and Stuart England*, Aldershot, 1996.

Gunn, S. J., *Charles Brandon, Duke of Suffolk c. 1484–1545*, Oxford, 1988.

——, *Early Tudor Government, 1485–1556*, 1995.

——, and P. G. Lindley (eds), *Cardinal Wolsey: Church, State and Art*, Cambridge, 1991.

Guy, J. M., *My Heart is My Own: The Life of Mary Queen of Scots*, 2004.

——, *Tudor England*, Oxford, 1988.

——, *The Cardinal's Court: The Impact of Thomas Wolsey in Star Chamber*, 1977.

——, *The Public Career of Sir Thomas More*, Brighton, 1980.

Haigh, C., *English Reformation: Religion, Politics and Society under the Tudors*, Oxford, 1993.

—— (ed.), *The English Reformation Revisited*, Cambridge, 1987.

——, *Reformation and Resistance in Tudor Lancashire*, Cambridge, 1975.

—— (ed.), *The Reign of Elizabeth I*, 1984.

Haller, W. (ed.), *Foxe's Book of Martyrs and the Elect Nation*, 1963.

Harrison, S. M., *The Pilgrimage of Grace in the Lake Counties*, 1981.

Hartley, T. E. (ed.), *Proceedings in the Parliaments of Elizabeth I*, Leicester, 1981.

Hasler, P. W., *The House of Commons 1558–1603*, 1981.

Hassell Smith, A., *County and Court – Government and Politics in Norfolk 1558–1603*, Oxford, 1974.

——, *Elizabeth and the English Reformation: The Struggle for a Stable Settlement of Religion*, Cambridge, 1970.

Haugaard, W. P., 'Katherine Parr: the religious convictions of a Renaissance queen', *Renaissance Quarterly*, no. XXII, 1969.

Haynes, A., *The Elizabethan Secret Services*, Stroud, 2000.

——, *Walsingham, Elizabethan Spymaster and Statesman*, 2004.

Head, D.M., *The Ebbs and Flows of Fortune: The Life of Thomas Howard, Third Duke of Norfolk*, Athens, Georgia, 1995.

Heal, F., and R. O'Day, *Church and Society in England, Henry VIII to James I*, 1977.

Heath, H., *English Parish Churches on the Eve of the Reformation*, 1969.

Higgs, L. M., *Godliness and Governance in Tudor Colchester*, Michigan, 1998.

Hoak, D. (ed.), *Tudor Political Culture*, Cambridge, 1995.

Hoak, D.E., *The King's Council in the Reign of Edward VI*, Cambridge, 1976.

Hogg, A., *God's Secret Agents*, 2006.

Holmes, P. J., *Resistance and Compromise: The Political Thought of the Elizabethan Catholics*, Cambridge, 1982.

Holt, M., *The Duke of Anjou and the Politique Struggle During the Wars of Religion*, 1986.

Holt, M. P., *The French Wars of Religion, 1562–1629*, Cambridge, 1995.

Hoskins, W. G., *The Age of Plunder: King Henry's England, 1500–1547*, 1976.

Howarth, D., *Images of Rule: Art and Politics in the English Renaissance, 1485–1649*, 1997.

Hoyle, R.W., *The Pilgrimage of Grace and the Politics of the 1530s*, Oxford, 2001.

Huizinga, J., *Erasmus of Rotterdam*, 1952.

——, *The Waning of the Middle Ages*, 1924.

Hunt, E. W., *Dean Colet and His Theology*, 1956.

Hutton, R., *The Rise and Fall of Merry England*, Oxford, 1994.

Israel, J. I., *The Dutch Republic: Its Rise, Greatness and Fall, 1477–1806*, Oxford, 1995.

Ives, E. W., *Anne Boleyn*, Oxford, 1986.

——, 'Anne Boleyn and the early Reformation in England: the

contemporary evidence', *Historical Journal,* no. XXXVII, 1994.

——, 'Faction at the court of Henry VIII', *History,* no. LVII, 1972.

——, *Faction in Tudor England, Historical Association Appreciations, VI,* 1979.

——, *The Life and Death of Anne Boleyn,* Oxford, 2004.

J. de Varagine, *The Golden Legend: Readings on the Saints,* trs. W. G. Ryan, 1995.

James, M. (ed.), 'Obedience and dissent in Henrician England: the Lincolnshire rebellion, 1536, in *Past and Present,* no. XLVIII, 1970.

—— (ed.), *Society, Politics and Culture, Studies in Early Modern England,* Cambridge, 1986.

Jenkyns, H., *The Remains of Thomas Cranmer D.D., Archbishop of Canterbury,* 1833.

Jensen, D., *Diplomacy and Dogmatism: Bernardino de Mendoza and the French Catholic League,* 1964.

Johnson, P., *Elizabeth I: A Study in Power and Intellect,* 1974.

Jordan, W. K., *Edward VI – The Threshold of Power,* 1970.

——, *Edward VI – The Young King,* 1968.

Kingdon, R., *Myths About the St Bartholomew's Day Massacres 1572–76,* Cambridge, Mass., 1988.

Knowles, D. E., *The Religious Orders in England,* Cambridge, 1948–59.

Lake, P., and Dowling, M. (eds), *Protestantism and the National Church in Sixteenth-Century England,* 1987.

Lake, P. G., 'Calvinism and the English Church, 1570–1635', *Past and Present,* no. 114, 1987.

——, *Moderate Puritans and the Elizabethan Church,* Cambridge, 1982.

Lambert, M., *Medieval Heresy: Popular Movements from the Gregorian Reform to the Reformation,* 1992.

Leach, A. F., *English Schools at the Reformation, 1546–8,* 1896.

Lehmberg, S. E., *The Later Parliaments of Henry VIII, 1536–1547,* Cambridge, 1977.

——, *The Reformation Parliament, 1529–1536*, Cambridge, 1970.

——, 'The religious beliefs of Thomas Cromwell', in R. L. DeMolen (ed.), *Leaders of the Reformation*, Susquehanna, 1984.

Leimon, M., and Parker, G., 'Treason and Plot in Elizabethan diplomacy: the "Fame of Sir Edward Stafford" Reconsidered', *English Historical Review*, 1996.

Lipscomb, S., *1536 – TheYear that Changed HenryVIII*, 2009.

Litzenberger, C., 'St Michael's, Gloucester, 1540–80: the cost of conformity in sixteenth-century England,' in K. L. French, G. G. Gibbs and B. A. Kümin (eds), *The Parish in English Life 1400–1600*, Manchester, 1997.

Lloyd, C., *Formularies of Faith*, Oxford, 1856.

Loach, J. and R. Tittler, *The Mid-Tudor Polity, c. 1540–1560*, 1980.

Loades, D.M., *John Dudley, Duke of Northumberland, 1504–1553*, Oxford, 1996.

——, *The Tudor Court*, 1987.

——, *England's Maritime Empire – Seapower, Commerce and Policy, 1490–1690*, 2000.

——, *Politics and the Nation, England, 1450–1660*, Oxford, 1974.

——, *The Reign of Mary Tudor: Politics, Government, and Religion in England, 1553–1558*, 1979.

Lodge, E., *Illustrations of British History*, 1971.

Lupton, J. H., *Life of John Colet*, 1887.

MacCaffrey, W. T., *Elizabeth I: War and Politics, 1588–1603*, 1992.

——, *Queen Elizabeth and the Making of Policy, 1572–1588*, Princeton, NJ, 1981.

——, *The Shaping of the Elizabethan Regime: Elizabethan Politics, 1558–1572*, 1968.

MacCulloch, D., *Reformation: Europe's House Divided, 1490–1700*, 2003.

—— (ed.), *The Reign of Henry VIII, Politics, Policy and Piety*, 1995.

——, *Suffolk and the Tudors*, Oxford, 1986.

——, *Thomas Cranmer, A Life*, New Haven, 1996.

——, *Tudor Church Militant – Edward VI and the Protestant Reformation*, 1999.

——, 'Two dons in politics: Thomas Cranmer and Stephen Gardiner, 1503–1533, *Historical Journal*, no. XXXVII, 1994.

Machiavelli, Niccolò, *The Prince*, trs. W. K. Marriott, 1992.

McConica, J. K., *English Humanists and Reformation Politics Under Henry VIII and Edward VI*, Oxford, 1965.

McCullough, P. E., *Sermons at Court: Politics and Religion in Elizabethan and Jacobean Preaching*, Cambridge, 1998.

McDermott, J., *England and the Spanish Armada: The Necessary Quarrel*, New Haven, 2005.

McGrath, P., *Papists and Puritans under Elizabeth I*, 1967.

Manning, R. B., 'The Crisis of Episcopal Authority during the Reign of Elizabeth I', *Journal of British Studies*, 11, 1971.

Marcus, L. S., J. Mueller and M. B. Rose (eds), *Elizabeth I Collected Works*, Chicago, 2000.

Marius, R., *Martin Luther: The Christian Between God and Death*, Cambridge, Mass., 1999.

——, *Thomas More*, 1984.

Marshall, P., *Beliefs and the Dead in Reformation England*, Oxford, 2002.

——, *Reformation England, 1480–1642*, 2003.

——, *Religious Identities in Henry VIII's England*, Aldershot, 2006.

Marshall, P., and A. Ryrie, *The Beginnings of English Protestantism*, Cambridge, 2002.

Martienssen, A., *Queen Katherine Parr*, 1973.

Martin, J. W., *Religious Radicals in Tudor England*, 1989.

Mattingley, G., *Catherine of Aragon*, 1942.

——, *Renaissance Diplomacy*, 1955.

Miller, H., *Henry VIII and the English Nobility*, Oxford, 1986.

Moat, D. (ed.), *Tudor Political Culture*, Cambridge, 1995.

Mozley, J. F., *Coverdale and His Bibles*, 1953.

——, *William Tyndale*, 1937.

Neale, J. E., *Elizabeth I and Her Parliaments*, 2 vols, 1969.
——, *The Elizabethan House of Commons*, 1963.
Neame, A., *The Holy Maid of Kent: The Life of Elizabeth Barton, 1506–1534*, 1971.
Nolan, J. S., *Sir John Norreys and the Elizabethan Military World*, Exeter, 1997.
Oberman, H. A., *Masters of the Reformation: The Emergence of a New Intellectual Climate in Europe*, Cambridge, 1981.
Ogle, A., *The Tragedy of the Lollards, Tower*, 1949.
Parker, G., *The Dutch Revolt*, 1977.
——, *The Grand Strategy of Philip II*, New Haven, 1998.
——, 'The Place of Tudor England in the Messianic Vision of Philip II of Spain', *Transactions of the Royal Historical Society*, 2002.
——, *Spain and the Netherlands, 1559–1659*, 1979.
Parmalee, L. F., *Good Newes from Fraunce: French Anti-League Propaganda in late Elizabethan England*, Rochester, 1996.
Parry, J. H., *The Spanish Seaborne Empire*, 1966.
Pettegree, A., *Foreign Protestant Communities in Sixteenth-Century London*, Oxford, 1986.
Pollard, A. F., *Thomas Cranmer and the English Reformation, 1489–1556*, 1905.
Pollard, A. W., *Records of the English Bible*, Oxford, 1911.
Porter, H. C., and D. F. S. Thomson, *Erasmus and Cambridge*, Toronto, 1963.
——, *Reformation and Reaction in Tudor Cambridge*, Cambridge, 1958.
Price, D., and C. C. Ryrie, *Let it Go Among Our People – An Illustrated History of the English Bible*, Cambridge, 2004.
Pulman, M. B., *The Elizabethan Privy Council in the 1570s*, Berkeley, Ca., 1971.
Raymond, J., *Henry VIII's Military Revolution*, 2007.
Read, C., *Lord Burghley and Queen Elizabeth*, 1960.
Read, C., *Mr Secretary Cecil and Queen Elizabeth*, 1955.
Redworth, G., *In Defence of the Church Catholic: The Life of Stephen Gardiner*, Oxford, 1990.

Regnans in excelcis, www.papalencyclicals.net/Pius 05/p5.htm

Richardson, W. C., *Stephen Vaughan, Financial Agent of Henry VIII*, Baton Rouge, Louisiana, 1953.

Ridley, J. G., *Henry VIII*, 1984.

——, *The Statesman and the Fanatic: Thomas Wolsey and Thomas More*, 1982.

——, *Thomas Cranmer*, Oxford, 1962.

Rupp, E. G., *The Righteousness of God*, 1953.

——, *Studies in the Making of the English Protestant Tradition*, Cambridge, 1947.

Russell, P. A., *Lay Theology in the Reformation*, Cambridge, 1986.

Ryrie, A., *The Gospel and Henry VIII – Evangelicals in the Early English Reformation*, Cambridge, 2003.

Scarisbrick, J. J., *Henry VIII*, New Haven, 2nd edition, 1997.

——, *The Reformation and the English People*, Oxford, 1984.

Seaver, P. S., *The Puritan Lectureships: The Politics of Religious Dissent, 1560–1662*, Stanford, 1970.

Simon, J., *Education and Society in Tudor England*, Cambridge, 1966.

Slavin, A. J., *Politics and Profit: A Study of Sir Ralph Sadler, 1509–1547*, Cambridge, 1966.

Smith, A. G. R., *The Government of Elizabethan England*, 1967.

Smith, L.B., *Treason in Tudor England: Politics and Paranoia*, 1986.

——, *Tudor Prelates and Politics*, 1953.

Soman, A. (ed.), *The Massacre of St Bartholomew's: Reappraisals and Documents*, The Hague, 1974.

Somerset, A., *Elizabeth I*, 1991.

Starkey, D., 'Court, council and the nobility in Tudor England', in R. G. Asch and A. M. Birkie (eds), *Princes, Patronage and the Nobility: The Court at the Beginning of the Modern Age c. 1450–1650*, Oxford, 1991.

——, *Henry, Virtuous Prince*, 2008.

—— (ed.), *Henry VIII: A European Court in England*, 1991.

——, *Six Wives: The Queens of Henry VIII*, 2003.

Stewart, A., *Philip Sidney: A Double Life*, 2000.

Strauss, G., *Manifestations of Discontent in Germany on the Eve of the Reformation*, Bloomington, Indiana, 1972.

Sutherland, N. M., 'The Marian Exiles and the Establishment of the Elizabethan Regime', *Archiv für Reformationgeschichte*, 78, 1987.

Thomas, H., *The Golden Age – The Spanish Empire of Charles V*, 2010.

Thomas, J. A. F., *The Later Lollards 1414–1520*, Oxford, 1965.

Thomas, K., *Religion and the Decline of Magic*, 1971.

Tiernagle, N. S., *Henry VIII and the Lutherans: A Study in Anglo-Lutheran Relations from 1521 to 1547*, St Louis, 1965.

Tracy, J. C., 'Ad Fontes: the humanist understanding of Scripture as nourishment for the soul', in J. Raitt (ed.), *Christian Spirituality – High Middle Ages and Reformation*, New York, 1988.

Trimble, W. R., *The Catholic Laity in Elizabethan England*, 1964.

Tyacke, N., *Aspects of English Protestantism, c. 1530–1700*, Manchester, 2001.

Unwin, G., *The Guilds and Companies of London*, 1963.

Walker, G., *John Skelton and the Politics of the 1520s*, Cambridge, 1988.

——, *Writing Under Tyranny: English Literature and the Henrician Reformation*, Oxford, 2005.

Warnicke, R. M., *The Marrying of Anne of Cleves: Royal Protocol in Tudor England*, Cambridge, 2000.

——, *The Rise and Fall of Anne Boleyn*, Cambridge, 1989.

Wegg, J., *Richard Pace, Tudor Diplomat*, 1937.

Wernham, R. B., *Before the Armada: The Emergence of the English Nation, 1485–1558*, 1966.

——, *The Making of English Foreign Policy, 1558–1603*, Berkeley, 1980.

Whiting, R., *The Blind Devotion of the People: Popular Religion and the English Reformation*, Cambridge, 1989

Wilson, C., *Queen Elizabeth I and the Revolt of the Netherlands*, 1970.

Wilson, D., *England in the Age of Thomas More*, 1978.

——, *Henry VIII – Reformer and Tyrant*, 2009.

——, *In the Lion's Court: Power, Ambition and Sudden Death in the Reign of Henry VIII*, 2001.

——, *Out of the Storm: The Life and Legacy of Martin Luther*, 2007.

——, *Sir Francis Walsingham: A Courtier in an Age of Terror*, 2007.

——, *Sweet Robin: A Biography of Robert Dudley, Earl of Leicester, 1553–1588*, 1997.

——, *A Tudor Tapestry: Men, Women and Society in Reformation England*, 1972.

——, *Uncrowned Kings of England: The Black Legend of the Dudleys*, 2003.

Wood, A., *The 1549 Rebellion and the Making of Modern England*, Cambridge, 2007.

Worden, B., *The Sound of Virtue: Philip Sidney's Arcadia and Elizabethan Politics*, 1996.

Wright, T. (ed.), *Queen Elizabeth and Her Times*, 1838.

Yates, F., *Astraea: The Imperial Theme in the Sixteenth Century*, 1975.

——, *The Occult Philosophy in the Elizabethan Age*, 1979.

Zeydal, E. H. (ed.), *The Ship of Fools*, 1944.

Index

442

Index